THE

EPISTLE GENERAL OF JAMES.

BY

J. P. LANGE, D.D.,

PROFESSOR OF THEOLOGY IN THE UNIVERSITY OF BONN,

AND

J. J. VAN OOSTERZEE, D.D.,

PROFESSOR OF THEOLOGY IN THE UNIVERSITY OF UTRECHT.

TRANSLATED FROM THE SECOND REVISED GERMAN EDITION, WITH ADDITIONS ORIGINAL AND SELECTED,

BY

J. ISIDOR MOMBERT, D.D.,

RECTOR OF ST. JAMES'S CHURCH, LANCASTER, PA.

FIFTH EDITION.

Wipf & Stock
PUBLISHERS
Eugene, Oregon

Wipf and Stock Publishers
199 W 8th Ave, Suite 3
Eugene, OR 97401

The Epistle General of James
an Exegetical and Doctrinal Commentary
By Lange, John Peter
ISBN 13: 978-1-55635-399-4
ISBN 10: 1-55635-399-5
Publication date 4/4/2007
Previously published by Charles Scribner, 1870

TRANSLATOR'S PREFACE.

In the preparation of this Commentary on the Catholic Epistles no pains have been spared to make it useful to Anglo-American readers. More than three years of labour have been bestowed upon it; and the translation of several Epistles, originally made from the *earlier* German editions, has been carefully revised by the *latest.* The *addenda* are numerous, and have entailed a vast amount of work. They will speak for themselves. It is hoped that the readings of the *Codex Siniaticus,* uniformly embodied in this Commentary, the constant reference to the best English and other divines, ancient and modern, and the extracts from their comments on this section of the New Testament, will place the reader in possession of every element necessary to the understanding of these Epistles.

I have endeavoured faithfully to comply with the general principles regulating the translation; and if the reproduction of the style of four different writers presented peculiar difficulties, it is gratifying to me that none of the Catholic Epistles in Lange's Commentary have ever before been translated into English. The diversity of style, to which I have just referred, will be especially apparent in the Introduction and the Critical and Exegetical portions of the Epistles of St. James, from the pen of Dr. Lange. He has an extraordinary genius for word-coining, and some of his combinations are so graphic, telling and original, that I have deemed it proper to reproduce them in English for the reason that these somewhat grotesque and strange-looking words have often the effect of stimulating the mental activity of the reader. The context is generally their commentary; where this was not the case in the original, due recourse has been had to periphrastic explanations.

On many questions I differ from the authors, and the addenda are mostly made to remove onesidedness of statement. In numerous instances, however, I hesitated to express my dissent, because I did not think it fair to carry on a controversy with them in the pages of their own works. I am only responsible for the matter in brackets, [ ], marked M.

May the Divine blessing rest upon my humble endeavours to aid in the elucidation of this important and interesting section of the Inspired Volume!

To the reader I would say: "*Errores pauci fuerint si forte libello,—errores paucos tollat amica manus!*"

J. Isidor Mombert.

Lancaster, Pa., April 1, 1867.

DR. LANGE'S

PREFACE TO THE FIRST EDITION OF JAMES.

THIS Commentary on the Epistle of James is the joint work of my respected friend, Dr. van Oosterzee and myself. The Introduction, the translation and the Critical and Exegetical notes, are my work; the Doctrinal and Homiletical sections have been supplied by Dr. van Oosterzee. I heartily thank my friend and collaborator for the cheerful and valuable help he has thus far bestowed upon this Commentary.

With respect to the sections undertaken by me, there were especially two reasons which made the work one of peculiar interest to me. In the first place, I was anxious to improve this opportunity to testify against the old Ebionito-apocryphal fiction of non-apostolic brothers of the Lord, who were, at the same time, held in high Apostolic repute. In the second place I desired to express my conviction that the Epistle of James (like the First Epistle of Peter and the Epistle to the Hebrews) cannot be sufficiently appreciated unless the history of the world, at the time when it was written, be constantly referred to, viz., the beginnings of that great Jewish revolution against the Romans, which, with its national sympathies, was, to the Jews in general, a great temptation to become hardened, and to the Jewish Christians an equal temptation to apostasy. This historical reference, hitherto neglected, in my opinion, can only prove advantageous to the exposition of this Epistle. In this sense I have been working; may the fundamental thought of my work be attested by blessed results.

I only add that I did not expect that my honoured collaborator would forthwith apply in the Doctrinal and Homiletical sections the aforesaid points of view, which have still to fight for recognition among theologians. On the contrary I thought it most desirable that the universal side of the Epistle should be fully developed in the Doctrinal and Homiletical sections without special reference to its historical points; and, indeed, the independence of my friend, led me to expect an execution of his work carried out in this sense. The Commentary, as a whole, has doubtless gained in allsidedness by this recognition of the universal by the side of the historical point of view.

DR. LANGE'S

PREFACE TO THE SECOND EDITION OF JAMES.

MY respected friend and coöperator, Dr. van Oosterzee, has charged me to represent him also in this Preface to the second edition. The first thing to be said imports the assurance that each has carefully, revised, and here and there rectified or improved his respective part, without subjecting the original shape of the work to unnecessary changes.

Since the publication of the first edition Dr. van Oosterzee has been called and translated to Utrecht in the capacity of *Professor ordinarius* of Theology; he himself has thus occasioned the first and very gratifying change on the title-page. Another call, namely, the removal of our friend, the Rev. Chantepie de la Saussaye, from Leyden to Rotterdam, had, alas, the consequence that the note on page 5 of the first edition [not inserted in the translation for this very reason—M.] could not be fulfilled, according to which he had undertaken the preparing of the Johannean Epistles, but found himself for an indefinite period prevented to carry his task into effect. But, by the help of God, said section of this Commentary passed from one competent hand to another. Our whole work, moreover, has lately made considerable progress; the publishers, as well as the authors, may look back upon the road already traversed, with cheerful gratitude, and forward to the goal with increasing hope.

With reference to exegesis there have appeared since the publication of the first edition in 1862, four theological novelties in our field of labour, which deserve to be noticed: The second edition of the *Commentary on James*, from the pen of Dr. Huther, appeared in 1863; last year the third edition of the respective section of de Wette's *Handbook*, prepared by Dr. Brückner; in the same year also a new commentary, of considerable extent, on this Epistle, from the pen of the lately deceased venerable Professor Bouman of Utrecht, published after his death by his sons under the title of "*Hermanni Bouman, Theol. Dr. et in Acad. Rhenotraject. Prof. Ord. Commentarius perpetuus in Jacobi Epistolam post. mortem auctoris editus. Trajecti ad Rhenum apud Kemink et Filium,* 1865." To these Commentaries must be added the publication of the *Codex Sinaiticus.*

The second edition of Huther's *Commentary on the Epistle of James*, having been concluded as early as October, 1862, has not led to reciprocal discussions between it and our exegetical work. Interesting is Huther's discussion with his reviewer, Professor Frank of Erlangen, introduced into the preface owing to the circumstance that his reviewer misconstrued the statement that Paul also teaches a consideration of works in the final judgment. Dr. Brückner has referred to our work both in the Introduction and in his exposition. The circumstance, that we could not move that highly-esteemed theologian to pronounce in favour of the radical modifications of the exegesis of this Epistle, in consequence of the definite historical construction which we have put on it, does not disturb us or fill us with doubt; it must also be borne in mind that he had to deal with the revision of a book which, as the preparation of a mandatary work, imposed upon him the most rigid self-constraint. In opposition to our statement that the author designed to fortify the Jewish Christians against the already roused revolutionary spirit of the Jews, without incautiously drawing the impending revolution in over-distinct colours, Brückner simply contends that then the "political fanaticism" ought at least to have been touched in the Epistle. In reply we have to observe, that it is characteristic of the apostolical wisdom of the author to oppose political fanaticism only in its religious motives and roots. These motives and roots, however, appear plain enough by replies to the following questions: 1. Which was the greatest *common cause* of all the twelve tribes of the Jews in part believing, in part still receptive of belief, during the sixth decade after the birth of Christ? 2. Which could be the manifold common temptations which through patience and steadfastness they were to change into all joy? Or, to be still briefer, which was at that time the common great trial of faith of the twelve tribes? And wherein had, consequently, the common proof to consist? 3. Why does the Apostle, after the general warning against representing the general temptation as a temptation from God, *i. e.* as a provocation, pass at once to the condemnation of wrath? 4. And what, in particular, is the import of the warning in chapter iii. 13 sqq., which even progresses to the naming of ἀκαταστασία as the result of ζῆλος and ἐριθεία? Similar questions arise from each separate section of our Epistle in opposition to the *non-historical* construction of our Epistle as being merely a collection of edifying exhortations to good moral conduct, but where it is anything but edifying that the author straightway assumes that the poor were disregarded at worship and otherwise neglected in all the twelve tribes of the dispersion, and that the rich Christians were guilty of conduct that he felt justified or rather constrained to utter a woe on them. We reiterate the expression of our conviction, that the non-appreciation of the historical motives and prophetico-symbolical phraseology of the Epistle leaves its great one fundamental thought well-nigh unopened, and this is proved by the extraordinary misconstructions which have been put upon it.

Bouman, the venerable veteran of Dutch theology, who left his Commentary in manuscript, like a testament, to the care of his sons, has first of all gladdened us by the decisiveness and scientific force with which he represents in the Introduction the view that the author of our Epistle could have been none other than the Apostle Jacobus Alphäei. May this example be a sign that theological science begins to turn away from the all-confounding and self-confused prejudice, that a non-apostolical James had risen to the highest apostolical repute in the apostolical Church, because he was a brother of the Lord according to the flesh, who at a late period became converted to the faith. We discover also a welcome agreement of the author with this Commentary in the assumption that the Epistle, though primarily addressed to Jewish Christians, had also the secondary design of converting the receptive Jews to the faith; and that this circumstance accounts also for the prophetical colouring of the Epistle. His attaching particular importance to the parallelism between the Apostle as the head of the Church at Jerusalem and the High priest with reference to the Jewish dispersion, appears to us as not unfounded; but the hypothesis that the Epistle dates from the earliest time of the propagation of Christianity, does not induce us to change the view expressed by us in this respect in this Commentary, or to fortify it by the production of new arguments. The exposition itself resembles variously the Scholia-form, and moves in the track of the customary general and abstract construction of the Epistle, takes, however, in a learned and independent manner, cognizance of modern exegetes, and manifests also with reference to the *Codex Sinaiticus* a free critical judgment.

The readings of the *Sinaiticus*, wherever they appeared to be important, have mostly been added to the critical notes.

May the joint preparation of this Epistle continue to be blessed in promoting the vital appreciation of the glorious totality of the Scripture as the Word of God, which appreciation must be consummated in the belief that all the writings of Paul and of James are in perfect agreement with one another, and with the whole Scripture.

THE EDITOR.

BONN, *January* 6, 1866.

THE

EPISTLE GENERAL OF JAMES.

INTRODUCTION.

THE EPISTLE OF JAMES BEING THE FIRST AMONG THE SO-CALLED CATHOLIC EPISTLES, IT IS NECESSARY TO FOUND THE PARTICULAR INTRODUCTION TO THE EPISTLE OF JAMES ON A MORE GENERAL INTRODUCTION TO THE CATHOLIC EPISTLES.

I. THE CATHOLIC EPISTLES IN GENERAL.

1. THE TERM "CATHOLIC EPISTLES" AND THEIR STATUS (GERM. *Bestand*).

The term "Catholic Epistles" embraces the seven Apostolic Epistles, which, besides the Pauline Epistles and the Epistle to the Hebrews added to them, are found in the Canon of the New Testament; namely the Epistle of James, the two Epistles of Peter, the three Epistles of John and the Epistle of Jude.

According to the primary and original meaning of *ἐπιστολὴ καθολική*, it denotes an encyclical writing, which as such was primarily addressed not to individual Churches or persons, but to a larger ecclesiastical sphere, to a number of Churches. In this sense Clement of Alexandria (*Stromat.* iv.) calls the Epistle of the Apostles and of the Church at Jerusalem addressed to Christian congregations according to Acts xv. 22-29 an *ἐπιστολὴ καθολική*. So Origen (*contra Celsum* i. 63) calls the Epistle of Barnabas, the contents of which characterize it an encyclical writing, *καθολική*. Eusebius (*Hist. Eccl.* v. 18) reports that Apollonius reproached Themison, the Montanist, with having written in imitation of the Apostle (probably John) an *ἐπιστολὴ καθολική*. This shows that the universal character of the First Epistle of John was designated by the term 'Catholic' as early as the time of Apollonius, that is: in the beginning of the third century. Even Origen applies this designation in this sense to the First Epistle of John (*in the Commentary of John*), to the First Epistle of Peter (according to Euseb. vi. 25), and to the Epistle of Jude, but in passages which are found only in a Latin translation (*Comment. in epist. ad Roman.*). In the time of Eusebius, the term 'Catholic' was already applied to the whole group of Epistles, which we call Catholic. "James," he says "is said to have written the first of the Catholic Epistles;" and then adverts to "the seven Epistles called Catholic." (*Hist. Eccl.* ii. 23). The meaning "Epistles more general as to their contents and object," which Guerike considers to be primary, could only be secondary, because it generally resulted from the nature of the encyclical writing; for the very first Catholic Epistle (Acts xv.) was not general as to its object and contents. There was but one step from changing the originally somewhat general character of these circular letters which assigned to them a more enlarged sphere of the Church, into one altogether general. Thus the Apostolical Epistle (Acts xv.) was already destined to apply to the whole Gentile-Christian Church, while the Epistle of James and probably that to the Hebrews were designed for the whole Jewish-Christian Church. In this sense, Oecumenius (*Prolegom. in Epist. Jacob.*) declared that they had been called 'Catholic,' inasmuch as they had not been addressed to a particular people or city, like the Epistles of Paul, but to believers in general (as a whole, *καθόλου*), whether to Jewish Christians of the dispersion or even to all Christians, as members of the same faith.

In the Western Church the term *epistolæ canonicæ* instead of *catholicæ* obtained great currency from the time of Junilius and Cassiodorus (see Credner, *Introd.* p. 570). That this could not have been the original sense follows decisively from the fact that Eusebius (*Hist. Eccl.* ii. 23) applies the term 'Catholic' also to the Epistles of Dionysius of Corinth to the Churches at Lacedæmon, Athens, etc. But Eusebius probably combined also here with the idea of the encyclical character the idea of the universal, for he remarked concerning said Dionysius and his Epistle, "that he was most useful to all (*ἅπασιν* absolutely) in the Catholic Epistles which he addressed to the Churches." Yet Eusebius gave already occasion that the idea of general reception or canonicity was combined with the idea of partial or entire universality by saying of the First Epistle of Peter: "The First Epistle of Peter is universally acknowledged, but the Acts of Peter, the Gospel according to Peter, the Preaching and the Revelation of Peter are not among the Catholic writings." [*Hist. Eccl.* iii. 3—M.].—It is evident that neither the idea of universality nor that of canonicity could be applied absolutely to the Catholic Epistles as contrasted with those of Paul. If they were called universal, the reference was to their more general tenor, if they were called canonical, the reference was at once to their more general contents and to their direct general authority, without any intention of seeking thereby to weaken the less direct universality and canonicity of the Pauline Epistles.

Besides this definition of the term 'Catholic Epistles,' another has arisen in modern times, Hug in his *Introduction to the Writings of the New Testament* ii. p. 429 observes as follows: "After the Gospels and the Acts had been referred to one division and the writings of St. Paul to another, there were still remaining the writings of different authors which might again be collected under one head and had to be distinguished by a name of their own. They might most aptly be called *καθολικὸν σύνταγμα* of the Apostles and the writings contained in it *κοιναί* and *καθολικαί*, these two words being frequently used as synonymes by Greek writers." In proof of this statement, Hug brings forward the declaration of Clement of Alexandria concerning the Apostolical Epistle, Acts xv. 23, namely, the Catholic Epistle in which all the Apostles took part. But *τῶν ἀποστόλων πάντων* has not the meaning which Hug discovers in it. He then cites the judgment of Eusebius that the "First Epistle of Peter is universally acknowledged, but the Acts of Peter, the Gospel according to Peter, the Preaching and Revelation of Peter are not among the Catholic writings." This, according to Hug, denotes the class to which the Apostolical writings in general were then referred. But the citation from Eusebius established rather the contrast between writings acknowled and writings not acknowledged. The circumstance, finally, that the Epistle of Barnabas is called Catholic, he tries to account for by the assertion that Barnabas also was sometimes called an Apostle. But the true explanation must be sought in its contents, for in the time of Origen, the Epistle of Barnabas was neither acknowledged as Apostolical nor as Canonical. In the sense of Hug, it has also been attempted to draw a parallel between the origin of the Canon of the Old Testament and that of the Canon of the New. For it is maintained that as in the formation of the Canon of the Old Testament, after the Thorah and the Prophets had been collected under their respective heads, the remaining sacred writings, in general, were collected under the head of Hagiographa, so, in the formation of the Canon of the New Testament, after the Gospels and the Pauline Epistles (*εὐαγγέλιον* and *ἀπόστολος*) had been collected, the remaining sacred writings of the New Testament were collected under the head "Catholic Epistles," *i. e.* writings of the New Testament in general (*καθόλου*).—Apart from possible objections to that view of the Old Testament, it is self-evident that in that case the reference ought to have been to Catholic *writings* and not to Catholic *Epistles*, and that then both the Revelation and the Epistle to the Hebrews ought to have been included in the last-named class.

Credner gives the following natural account of the old arrangement of the Canon of the New Testament: "First historical notices of Jesus (the Gospels); then such notices of the Apostles; then general (catholic) Epistles of the Apostles; then Epistles to separate congregations and to individuals (the Epistles of Paul). This primary arrangement originated in a clear perception of what was collected and why it was collected."

But the ideal principle of division has evidently been modified by historical relations. A division purely made with reference to subject-matter, would require the Epistle to the Ephesians and that to the Hebrews to be included among the Catholic Epistles, the second and third Epistles of John to be excluded from them. The latter, however, were considered as supplemental to the first Epistle of John, and the former retained by the great mass of the Pauline Epistles, as it were, by attraction.

2. THE IMPORT OF THE CATHOLIC EPISTLES IN THE CANON OF THE NEW TESTAMENT.

The Catholic Epistles, comprehending only a small part of the New Testament Canon, are of the utmost importance on account of the completeness and fulness of that part. As the four Gospels are designed mutually to complement each other, so here the types of the doctrine of James, Peter and John, complement the type of the doctrine of Paul. By this complementing they preserve the Christian consciousness from a one-sided culture of the Pauline expression; by the variety and fulness of their modes of treatment and expression, they guarantee the fulness of Christian cognition and the full vitality and motion of the churchly spirit. Paul has been called the Apostle of faith; John the Apostle of love, Peter the Apostle of hope. This is a very imperfect mode of distinction, because, to name only one reason, it is exclusively Pauline; it denotes, nevertheless, the riches of the Apostolical complements furnished by the Catholic Epistles. These Epistles, moreover, are highly important as mirroring the condition of the Church during the latter period of the Apostolic age. In this respect they constitute an indispensable connecting-link between the Acts and the Pauline Epistles (excepting the Pastoral Epistles to which they are intimately related) on the one hand, and the Apocalypse and the Apostolical Fathers on the other.—While in the Book of Acts and the Pauline Epistles, we have the exhibition of the external diversity of the Churches which were springing up every where, as yet predominating over the certainly existing internal unity, the encyclical character of most of these Epistles (as also of that to the Hebrews) gives already greater prominence to the consciousness of a full, and moreover, of an external unity of the Church. This holds also good of the Epistle of James, for he addresses Christendom of Jewish origin not as an Ebionite Jewish-Christian but as an Apostle. These Epistles moreover acquaint us with the further developments of Church-life in the Apostolic age; with the springing up of the Ebionite and Gnostic weeds among the wheat of pure doctrine, and on the other hand, with the development of the more distinct, the dogmatically more conscious Apostolic and church-testimony. Ebionitism is perfectly drawn in symbolical characters not sufficiently appreciated—in the Epistle of James (ch. ii. 2, etc.), in the first Epistle of John (ch. ii. 22, etc.), and probably also in the third of John (v. 9); Gnostic libertinism, on the other hand, is condemned in the Epistle of Jude, in the second of Peter (ch. ii.), and in 1 Jno. iv. 1, etc. With respect to ecclesiastical constitution, our Epistles confirm the identity of the Presbyterate and the Episcopate; but the dignity of the presbyter-bishop becomes more distinct in the position taken by Jude, James, John (2 Jno. 1) and Peter. That is, we have to deal with Apostolical men who, as leading presbyters, had even then entered upon close relations with specific ecclesiastical circles; this applies at least to James and John. We also obtain hints of the form of worship (Jude 12; 2 Pet. ii. 13), and of a certain method and gradation in the presentation of Christian doctrine (1 Jno. ii. 12, etc.).

With respect to the relation of the different New Testament types of doctrine, so richly represented in the Catholic Epistles, we take for granted that in this field a conflict of doctrine is impossible but that differences of doctrine, various types, *i. e.* individual views, conceptions and modes of statement are necessary. All the Apostles are agreed in that they see in Christianity the New Testament, that is: 1, the fulfilment and therein the harmonious contrast of the Old Testament, the completed religion of revelation; 2, the fulfilment and contrast of all incomplete religions in general, the perfect religion absolutely; 3, consequently they see in the New Testament the primeval, even the everlasting Testament, the everlasting religion which, while it must branch out into the two æons of struggling development and of glorious consummation, car nevermore be followed by another religion. In these respects James is not by a hair's breadth less evangelical (German: *neutestamentlich*) than Paul and John.

The New Testament, according to all the New Testament types of doctrine, is the fulfilment, the real form, therefore, of the religion which the Old Testament had traced in the symbolical shadow.

Christianity is the fulfilment of the law of the Old Testament, hence the royal law of love, the law of liberty, of spiritual life, of unity; such is the teaching of James.

Christianity is the fulfilment of the theocracy of the Old Testament, hence the real kingdom of God, the real royal priesthood, which, first a kingdom of suffering, finds its consummation in a kingdom of glory; such is the teaching of Peter.

Christianity is the fulfilment of the old Covenant, of the sacraments of the Old Testament, hence the real circumcision and regeneration, hence the real passover, the real redemption and the real new human life as the principle of a real new world of the resurrection, the New Covenant of faith and the new covenant-jubilee of the communion of faith; such is the teaching of Paul.

Christianity is the fulfilment of the worship of the Old Testament, hence the real eternal Divine worship of the completed word, of the completed Sabbath, of completed sacrifice and of the completed festive-church (Germ: *Fest-Gemeinde.*); such is—closely following Paul—the teaching of the Epistle to the Hebrews.

Christianity is the fulfilment of all the symbolism of the Old Testament, and of all the symbolism of primitive monotheism (Germ.- *Urmonotheismus*) in general, on which the Old Testament is founded, hence the real new world in the development of its glorification (Germ. *Verklärung*) by the Personal Word in the threefold lustre of real light, real love and real life; such is the teaching of John.

The Epistles of Peter (on the character of Peter see my *Apostol. Age*, I., p. 354, and the Article "*Petrus*," in Herzog's *Real-Encyclopædia*,) are connected with the speeches of Peter in Acts, and the Petrine Gospel of Mark. They form a connecting link between the doctrine of James and that of Paul.

The fundamental idea of the First Epistle of Peter is ch. i. 3, 4, the regeneration of Christians out of suffering unto an incorruptible inheritance (*Land of inheritance and kingdom of inheritance*). The division is as follows:

Introduction: The new hope of the spiritual Israel flowing from the resurrection of Christ from the dead, ch. i. 1–3. The theme already specified, ch. i. 4.

I. Believers destined for this blessedness of the inheritance, ch. i. 5–9.

II. The Old Testament pointing to this inheritance, v. 10–12.

III. The pilgrimage of the spiritual Israel to this goal. Their sanctification. Their redemption. Their brotherly love on the ground of their common heavenly descent by means of regeneration, ch. i. 13–25.

IV. The New Covenant. The preparation of the New Testament. Christ the living stone, antitype of Sinai. Christians, the new theocracy ch. ii. 1–10.

V. The wilderness-pilgrims (v. 11) and their behaviour towards pagans; *a.* according to the relations of the pagans, v. 12–17; *b.* according to the relations of the Christians. The behaviour of enslaved men (*males*); that of wives, especially in mixed marriages, ch. ii. 18—iii. 2.

VI. The behaviour of Christians among themselves, ch. iii. 3–8.

VII. Their behaviour towards persecutors, ch. iii. 9–22.

VIII. Readiness and blessedness of suffering, ch. iv.

IX. The proper relation of the leaders of the flock of God and those who are led, especially as the proper preparation against the adversary, ch. v. 1–9. Conclusion, Benediction and Salutation, v. 10–14.

But compare the First Epistle of Peter in this commentary. As to its literature, we have still to mention *Schott's* commentary, which has recently appeared. Erlangen 1861.

With respect to the Second Epistle of Peter, we refer to our work, "The Apostolical Age" (*Das Apostolische Zeitalter*, Vol. I., p. 156). We continue to maintain the hypothesis there advanced, that the Epistle of Jude according to its contents was at a later period inserted in the original Epistle of Peter.[1] The fundamental idea of the Second Epistle of Peter is this: Christians are promised to become partakers of the Divine nature by the knowledge of Christ's glory and virtue; hence they are charged *to make their godliness* [εὐσέβεια—M.] *sure by perseverance*, ch. i. 3, 4. Conformably thereto is the Introduction, which serves the purpose of wishing and recommending them to grow in the knowledge of God and in Christ, ch. i. 1–3. Why this is necessary is shown by the argument.—The above mentioned theme, ch. i. 3, 4.

DEVELOPMENT: I. They are to grow therein practically by the development of their Christian life, ch. i. 5–9.

II. Their growth in knowledge is necessary, because otherwise they would fall through stumbling, v. 10–12.

III. Such a stumbling might be occasioned to them by his impending departure (his martyr-death) and lead to their doubting the promise of Christ's advent, v. 13–19. (But prophecy is established as the word of the true prophets of God contrasted with the false prophets who shall arise, ch. i. 20—iii. 2).

IV. The coming of those who deny the advent of Christ, ch. iii. 3, 4.

V. Refutation of their denial, v. 5–13. Conclusion, with a reference to misinterpreted sayings of Paul, concerning the advent of Christ, v. 14–18.

THE EPISTLE OF JUDE (on the character of Jude, see my *Life of Jesus*, II., 149, 699; *Apostolical Age*, I., p. 364.—Compare the Epistle of Jude in this work) may be regarded as the forerunner of the apocalyptic descriptions of Gnostic Antinomianism (2 Pet. ii.; Rev. ii. 6; vv. 14 15). The type of its doctrine and the symbolical mode of its expression connect it with the Epistle of James. Its more definite analogies in the Old Testament as revelations of the judgment are the books of Obadiah, Nahum, Habakkuk and Zephaniah. On the Apostolicity of its Author compare our special introduction to James.

The fundamental idea of the Epistle of Jude: contending for the true faith against the false belief or unbelief of the (Gnostic) Anomists, v. 3. The introduction pursuant to this theme: a word addressed to *those who continue preserved in Christ* vv. 1, 2. The theme, v. 3. Division of the short Epistle.

I. The real character of the Anomists: turning the grace of God into wantonness, v. 4.

II. The ancient types of these Anomists and of their judgment; *a*, the people of Israel in the wilderness; *b*, the rebel-angels; *c*, the Sodomites, vv. 5–7.

III. More definite characteristics. Fanaticism unfolding on the one hand into voluptuousness, on the other, into contempt of authority, vv. 8–10. The development of their ruin, v. 11. Their pseudo-Christian and anti-Christian character, vv. 12, 13.

IV. Their coming foretold as to the fundamental trait of their character, viz., murmuring against revelation; *a*, by Enoch, the most ancient prophet (according to Jewish tradition, to which the book of Enoch also must be supposed to have been indebted); *b*, by the Apostles of Christ, v. 14–20.

V. Exhortation to proper behaviour towards them; *a*, defensive, vv. 20, 21; *b*, polemical, v. 22, 23. Conclusion. Benediction for the preservation of the readers and doxology, vv. 24, 25.

THE EPISTLES OF JOHN join with the Epistle to the Hebrews, as the last type of the developments of Pauline doctrine. They form in conjunction with his Gospel and Apocalypse the last and most completed type of New Testament doctrine. On the unity of this grand trilogy, compare my *History of the Apostolic Age*, II., p. 571.

The much misunderstood unity of the three Epistles of John, flows from the relation of the second and third Epistles to the theme and division of the first. For the theme of the first Epistle is not, as is commonly supposed, communion with God through Christ, but the mutual communion of Christians based upon that communion. The true communion of the Church based upon walking in the light, ch. i. 7. The Introduction leads to this. The end of all Apostolical preaching is to bring about Apostolic communion as a medium of communion with the Father and the Son. For historically the communion with God is made to depend on communion with

[1] I did not know at the first advancing of my hypothesis, that Bertholdt had already considered the second chapter as an interpolation.

the Apostles; but then the communion of Christians among themselves as a communion of perfect joy (the κοινωνία=ἐκκλησία) is made to depend on communion with the Lord. Hence:

I. The communion of God and Christ on which the communion of Christians is made to depend: *a*, permanent reconciliation; *b*, confession of sins; *c*, faith in the Advocate; *d*, the keeping of His commandments; *e*, that is, of His word; *f*, *i. e.* of the commandment of brotherly love; *g*, formation of this behaviour in fathers, young men and children; *h*, the rooting of this behaviour in the love of God, as contrasted with the love of the world, ch. i. 7—ii. 17.

II. The communion of Christians as contrasted with the Ebionito-Antichristian denial of Christ and hatred of the brethren, evidenced by *the abandonment of communion*, ch. ii. 18—iii. 24. The Antichristians; *a*, seceded; *b*, denial that Jesus is the Christ, the Son; *c*, exhortation to perseverance in faith; *d*, the protection of the anointing (with the Holy Ghost); *e*, the dignity of adoption [*Kindschaft*=state of being the children of God—M.]; *f*, the demonstration of adoption: righteousness, brotherly love.

III. Maintenance of purity of communion as contrasted with Gnostic spirits who deny Christ having come in the flesh, ch. iv. 1–6.

IV. The vitalizing of the communion of Christians among each other, ch. iv. 7—v. 12; *a*. The source of brotherly love: God is Love; *b*, Maintenance of this love by brotherly love, by the Holy Ghost, by the confession of Christ; *c*, the perfecting of this love in joyfulness before God; in rejoicing in the brethren as God-born; *d*, Test of true brotherly love by the love of God as evidenced by faith in the Son of God. Conclusion. Exhortation to faith; to prayer; to intercession for erring brethren; to confidence; to watchfulness against deifying the world, ch v. 12–21.

Now since the First Epistle of John manifestly sets forth the law of the life of Christian communion, his two lesser Epistles are clearly corollaries of the first, the second (to the κυρίᾳ) warning against a lax loosing of the limits of communion, and the third (to Gaius) contending on the other hand against a fanatical narrowing of its large-hearted and wide-reaching sphere.

The Epistle to the Hebrews, being so variously connected with the Catholic Epistles and more particularly with the Epistle of James, we also add a brief notice on its construction. Its fundamental idea is: Christ, the fulfiller of the revelation of the Old Testament as the Son of God, is as such *the eternal Mediator of the real atonement-religion* [Germ. *Versöhnungskultus*, the real worship of the religion of atonement—M.], and therefore the eternal and heavenly *Centre* thereof, ch. i. 2, 3.

I. As such He is superior to the mediators of the Old Testament economy; *a*, to angels, even as God-Man, ch. i. 4—ii. 18; *b*, to Moses, the servant of the house, as the Son preparing the house, ch. iii. 1–19; *c*, to Joshua, the mediator of Sabbath-rest in Canaan, ch. iv. 1–13; *d*, to Aaron, the Highpriest, as a Priest forever, who has offered obedience, ch. iv. 14—v. 14; *e*, to Mosaism in its entireness, *to which the readers of the Epistle cannot return without falling away*, ch. vi.; *f*, to Abraham even, as the real Priest of God, typified by Melchizedek, ch. vii. 1–11.

II. As the priesthood of Christ is superior to the status of the Old Covenant, so is also the New Covenant with its services superior to the Old Covenant. *a*, The superiority of the new law and covenant, ch. vii. 12–22; *b*, the superiority of the new priesthood, vv. 23–28; *c*, the superiority of the new sanctuary and its services, ch. viii. 1—x. 39. (1, The new tabernacle, 2, the New Testament, 3, the new entrance of the new High-priest into the holiest of holies. The new covenant-blood and sacrifice. 4. *Warning against the new or the New Testament apostasy*).

III. Hence the New Testament faith is also the sublime completion and fulfilment of the old faith, ch. xi. 1–40. *Warning against apostasy from this faith*, ch. xii. 1–17.

IV. Hence also the new congregation on the spiritual Mount Zion, is superior to the old congregation at Mount Sinai, ch. xii. 18–24. *Warning against disobedience*. Exhortation to thank-offering; to the manifestation of this living service in brotherly love, ch. xii. 25—xiii. 7. Conclusion. The application, ch. xiii. 9. Caution against false teachers. Exhortation to bearing the reproach of Christ, to the life of prayer, to churchly disposition [*i. e.* with reference to ch. xiii. 17—M.]. Appropriate benediction and salutation, ch. xiii. 10–24.

3. LITERATURE ON THE CATHOLIC EPISTLES.

See the GENERAL COMMENTARIES. Those on the New Testament HEUBNER, (Vol. IV., has since been published), HEIDEGGER, *Enchiridion*, p. 617. DANZ, *Universal Dictionary*, p. 513; Supplement, p. 60. WINER, *Manual of Theol. Literature*, 1, p. 270; Supplement, p. 42. LILIENTHAL, *Bibl. Archivarius*, p. 734. REUSS, *Introduction*, p. 132. WIESINGER, *The Epistle of James* (Olshausen's Commentary, Vol. VI., part 1., p. 45).

On the CATHOLIC EPISTLES IN GENERAL OR IN PART: CLEMENT OF ALEX., DIDYMUS, Ven. BEDE, GRYNÆUS, ARETIUS, JUSTINIANUS, HORNEJUS, HERDER, *Epistles of two brothers of Jesus in our Canon, Lemgo*, 1775.

ON SEPARATE EPISTLES: SCHRÖDER, SEEMILLER, SEMLER. ROOS, MORUS, HOTTINGER, ZACHARIÆ, *Paraphrase Exposition.* Göttingen, 1776. BENGEL, *Explanatory Paraphrase of the Catholic Epistles and the Revelation of John*, Tübingen, 1781. Commentary by G. SCHLEGEL, 1783.—CARPZOV, *Epist. Cathol.*, Halle, 1790. J. L. W. SCHERER, the *Catholic Epistles* Vol. I., James, Marburg, 1799. AUGUSTI, the *Catholic Epistles*, Lemgo, 1801–1808. POTT, *Epist. Cathol.*, 2 vols., 1786–1810. GÖPFERT, the *so-called Catholic Epistles*, Lemgo, 1801–1808, GRASHOF, the *Epistles of the Holy Apostles James, Peter, John and Jude, translated and explained*, Essen, 1830. JACHMANN, *Commentary on James*, Leipzig, 1838. SCHARLING, *Jacobi et Judæ Epistolæ*, etc., Copenhagen, 1841.

TREATISES ON THE CATHOLIC EPISTLES:—STÄUDLIN, *Comment. de fontibus Epistol. Cathol.* Göttingen, 1790. STORR, *de Cathol. Epist. occasione et consilo, Tübingen*, 1789. J. D. SCHULZE, *on the Sources of the Epistles of Peter*, etc. *The literary character and value of Peter, Jude and James*, Weissenfels, 1802. F. LÜCKE ἐπιστολαὶ καθολικαί, and *Epistolæ Canonicæ* in *Theol. Studien und Kritiken*, 1836, p. 643–650. MEYER'S Commentary (Parts XII. XIV., XV., Commentary by HUTHER); DE WETTE, *Exeget. Handbuch*, I Vol. 3; III. Vol. 1.

[Besides the *General Commentaries* of MATTHEW HENRY, SCOTT, GILL, CLARKE, WHITBY, D'OYLY AND MANT, BARNES and the *Greek Testaments* of BLOOMFIELD, ALFORD and WORDSWORTH, there are also the following: APOSTOLICAL EPISTLES: CAJETANUS, Folio, Venet., 1531. TITELMAN, F., *Elucidatio in omnes epistolas apostol.*, 8vo., Anto., 1532.—GUALTHERUS, R. *Homilæ in omnes epist. apostol.*, Folio., Tiguri, 1599.—HEMMINGIUS, *N. Comment in Omnes Epist. Apostol.*, Foiio, Lips., 1572.—ESTIUS, GUILELMUS, *In omnes Epist., item in Cathol. Comment.* Moguntiæ, 1841–45. DICKSON, D., *Expos. analyt. omnium Apostol. Epistol.*, Glasg., 1645.—PYLE, THOMAS, *A paraphrase, with notes upon the Acts, and all the Epistles*, 2 vols. 8vo., London, 1737.—MACKNIGHT, JAMES, *A new literal translation from the orig. Greek of all the Apostolical Epistles*, etc., London, 1816.

ON THE CATHOLIC EPISTLES: THEOPHYLACT, OECUMENIUS, AQUINAS, HUS, FABER, CALVIN, COCCEIUS, CRIT. SACR., CORNELIUS A LAPIDE, RICLOT, DOM LOUIS, *Paraphrase des Epîtres Canoniques*, 12vo., Metz 1727. (Much commended by CALMET). COLLET, SAMUEL, *Pract Paraphr. on the seven Catholic Epistles*, etc., Lond., 1834. BENSON, G., *The seven Catholic Epistles.* SUMNER, ABP., *Pract. Expos. of the general Epistles of James, Peter, John, and Jude* 8vo., Lond. 1840.—M.].

II. THE EPISTLE OF JAMES.

1. THE AUTHOR.

James, who describes himself as Author of this Epistle, must be either the Apostle James the Less (Mark xv. 40), or the son of Alphæus, Jacobus Alphæi (Matth. x. 3; Mark. iii. 18; Luke vi. 15; Acts i. 13), or also "the Lord's brother" (Gal. i. 19; ch. ii. 9), who is altogether identical with Jacobus Alphæi (Acts i. 13; xii. 17; xv. 13; xxi. 18).

This definite hypothesis does not follow solely from the Introduction of this Epistle, in which he calls himself "a servant of God and of the Lord Jesus Christ." But it does follow from it, that James claimed to possess a prominent position in the Church, and felt conscious of being known to the whole Jewish-Christian Church as James, the servant of God and of Jesus Christ in an exclusive sense, which rendered it impossible to confound him with any other James.

But that the tradition of the Church ascribed to him (with a preponderance of testimony) Apostolical authority follows from the reception of his Epistle into the Canon, although it was enumerated among the Antilegomena; indeed it is matter of inquiry, whether during the third century it was not by confounding data and opinions first included for awhile among the Antilegomena.

It is settled, however, that James the Elder, the son of Zebedee, cannot have been the author of this Epistle, because he suffered martyrdom as early as A. D. 44 (Acts xii. 1, 2), while the internal allusions and statements of this Epistle belong to a much later period. The subscription in the Peschito and that in an old Latin translation ascribe without any reason the authorship to him, and Luther took him for the pretended author.

The question of the authorship of our Epistle would thus be settled, had not an old error diffused the opinion current in ancient tradition and modern theology, that it is necessary to distinguish the Apostle Jacobus Alphæi from the Lord's brothers. *It is the old Ebionite apocryphal legend of the Lord's brothers.*

Adhering to the simple statements of the New Testament all doubt concerning the identity of James with "the Lord's brother" must vanish; although we do not at once see why James the son of Alphæus should be called the Lord's brother.

For James, the son of Alphæus, passes at once from the lists of the Apostles, given in the Gospels (Matth. x. 2; Mark iii. 16; Luke vi. 14), into the list of the Apostles given in Acts (ch. i. 13). Here he appears as yet as James the son of Alphæus, by the side of his prominent name-sake, the son of Zebedee, who is therefore called simply James. But immediately after the death of this prominent James (Acts xii. 2) there is mentioned another James, who bears that name without all further qualification (Acts xii. 47); and the assumption is highly improbable that James, the son of Alphæus, should in so short a time, have vanished from the stage past all tracing, without being thought worthy of having even his death noticed by Luke, the historian, and that there should suddenly have sprung up some non-apostolical James, who actually occupied a prominent position among the Apostles. We are thus forced to maintain that if after the death of James the son of Zebedee, who was simply called James, there arose forthwith another James who went simply by that name, that James must have been the son of Alphæus. And thus he is mentioned all through Acts, ever the same and ever in the same position of a mediator of the new Christian faith and the historical national consciousness of his people (ch. xv. 13; xxi. 18). But while the last meeting of Paul the Apostle, and this James of the Acts, who is called James without any further addition to his name, occurred about 59–60, A. D., it is to be noticed, that Paul made mention of James, as the Lord's brother (Gal. i. 19; ii. 9) several years before that time (about A. D. 56–57); so also the appellation "the Lord's brother," simply, or "James" simply (1 Cor. ix. 5; ch. xv. 7 about A. D. 58). Here, again we have to call attention to the circumstance that Paul, in the first chapter of Galatians, conjoins the same James, whom in the second chapter he describes as one of the pillars among the Apostles, with the rest of the Apostles, as the Lord's brother.

In the first place, then, we must hold fast the hypothesis that James the son of Alphæus, and the Lord's brother, are identical. The question now comes up, what is the relation of this supposition to the most ancient tradition of the Church? The oldest tradition is represented by Hegesippus and Clement of Alexandria. Hegesippus, according to Eusebius, iv. 23, reports as follows: "James, the brother of the Lord received the government of the Church conjointly with the Apostles, who from the time of the Lord until our own was surnamed the Just by all; for many were called James, but this one was consecrated from his mother's womb." Then follows an account of his holiness, the character of a pious Nazarite and a faithful Christian martyr. He undertook the government of the Church with the Apostles, that is, he was not the exclusive bishop, but the coöperation (in the office) was reserved to the Apostles as such. As bishop in the Apostolical sense, according to which every overseer of the Church was subject to the joint Apostolate of the Church, he was distinguished from the Apostles although he was at the same time an Apostle,[1] just as Peter was distinguished as spokesman from the other Apostles, although

[1] Huther (p. 4, Note 3) thinks that the prominent position of James at Jerusalem could not have been owing to his

he belonged to their number, Acts v. 29 (ὁ Πέτρος καὶ οἱ ἀπόστολοι). If we here press the letter in the sense of a distinction of the son of Alphæus from the brother of the Lord, Hegesippus in another passage (Euseb, III., 22) on the descent of James declares himself in favour of the identity. He says that Simeon the son of Cleophas succeeded James the Just as bishop, this one again being a descendant of the same uncle of the Lord (θείου αὐτοῦ referred to the next following ὁ κύριος), and that all gave him this preference, as being the second relative of the Lord (ἀνεψιός).[1] Cleophas, or what amounts to the same thing, Alphæus (cf. Bretchneider's Lexicon) was consequently our Lord's uncle, James and Simeon (the same as Simon) his sons, James and Simon brothers, both the sons of Alphæus, both cousins of the Lord, but the former, as appears from what has gone before, revered by the surname "the brother of the Lord." Still more important is the testimony of Clement of Alexandria (*Euseb.* II., 1): "The Lord imparted the gift of knowledge (the gnosis) to James the Just, to John and Peter after His resurrection. These delivered it to the rest of the Apostles." He then adds expressly, "there were, however, two Jameses; one called the Just, who was thrown from a battlement of the temple and beaten to death with a fuller's club, and another, who was beheaded." To this must be added the testimony of Origen in his *Commentary on Matthew*, ch. xvii. But the testimony of the Gospel according to the Hebrews that Christ, after His resurrection, had appeared to James the Just, the brother of the Lord must be taken in conjunction with the testimony of Paul (1 Cor. xv. 7), that "Christ was seen of James, then of *all* the Apostles." The same appearing therefore is called once an appearing to James the Apostle, and again an appearing to the brother of the Lord.

The list of the brothers of Jesus, given in the Gospels, specifies James, Simon and Judas (Matth. xiii. 55). The list in Acts also specifies James, Simon and Judas, but it distinguishes the James there introduced as the son of Alphæus, from James the son of Zebedee, the Peter there introduced, as Zelotes or the Canaanite from Simon Peter, and the Jude there introduced, as Lebbæus or Thaddæus from Judas Iscariot.[2] In the Apostolical Epistles we find after the death of the elder James, the name of a James who is an Apostle and also a brother of the Lord (Gal. ii.; Gal. 1)[3], who is also a brother of Jude, and to whom we are indebted for an Apostolical Epistle.

The most ancient tradition (that of Hegesippus) informs us therefore that James the brother of the Lord, was the brother of Simon, and that both were the sons of Cleophas=Alphæus. But from Clement we actually learn that there existed no other James of any importance than James the Elder and James the Just, who was one of the most distinguished Apostles (so distinguished that Clement, indeed, erroneously confounds him with James the Elder). Lastly concerning Jude, Hegesippus reports likewise a Jude who was *called* the brother of our Lord, according to the flesh (Euseb. III., 19, 20). Eusebius after his uncritical manner, or as an erring exegete, turns the phrase "*he was called* a brother of the Lord" into, "he *was* a brother of the Lord." For in like manner he makes Simeon the son of Cleophas, whose death is reported by Hegesippus (Euseb. III., 32), the grandson of Cleophas, because he understood the phrase "Maria Cleophas" to denote "Mary the daughter of Cleophas."

This identity, which is everywhere transparent, follows also from the most striking particular evidences. Mary, the mother of James the Less or of James the son of Alphæus, is also the mother of Joses (Matth. xxvii. 56; Mark xv. 40; v. 47, ch. xvi. 1). This proves that four brothers of the Lord bore the same names as the four sons of Alphæus, viz.: James, Simon, Jude

Apostleship "which pointed rather to missionary activity than to the episcopal government of a congregation." But where was *the* Apostle of the Jews to reside, if not at Jerusalem? If Christ did charge the Apostles "Go ye into all the world," He surely did not mean to exclude the centre of Judaism.

[1] On the view of Neander, who makes Ἰάκωβον the subject of αὐτοῦ, cf. my article "*Jacobus*" in Herzog's *R. E.* p. 407, and my *Apostolical Age*, I. p. 194. Nor does the note of Huther (p. 5) affect our explanation, especially as it proposes to *leave undecided* the account of Hegesippus, that Simeon the son of Clopas was ἀνεψιός of the Lord.

[2] Huther will not admit that this Jude is a son of Alphæus, but the son of a James, because he is called Ἰούδας Ἰακώβου in Luke vi. 16 and Acts i. 13. But Jude 1 proves that a Jude might be thus designated with reference to his honoured and universally known brother. Lebbæus also is placed in juxtaposition with James in Matth. x. 3 and we must not press the circumstance that he is not expressly called his brother. In the case of this Jude it was contemplated to distinguish him as much as possible from Judas Iscariot (see Jno. xiv. 22), and this was accomplished by designating him as the brother of the well-known James.

[3] Stier's and Wieseler's proposed distinction between the James of Gal. 1 and Gal. 2 is so forced as to render all refutation unnecessary.

and Joses. On the numerous complications of both lines, see this commentary on Matth. xiii 53–58.[1]

The opposite view, that the brothers of the Lord constitute a line of the same name to be distinguished from said Apostles is a development which through different stages must be traced back to the Jewish-Christian consciousness; treated with respect to the real point of observation, we may designate it as a view of *Ebionite-apocryphal* origin. Its first stage is the New Testament emphasis on the sons of Alphæus as being the brothers of the Lord. The Jewish-Christians gave peculiar prominence to the respective Apostles of the Jews, especially to James, particularly as contrasted with the authority of Paul. Paul admits this emphasis as to its historic value and recognizes as a climax of authority in which we have first the Apostles in general, then the Apostolical brothers of the Lord and then Peter, the Apostle (1 Cor. ix. 5). But his language in Gal. 2 shows how far he is from according to this historical authority any thing like Apostolical priority. The continuance and growth of this Jewish-Christian emphasizing follows especially from the report of Hegesippus. But he still insists upon the identity of the brothers of the Lord with the sons of Alphæus, he still designates their brotherhood as an original cousinship, he still holds fast to the coördination of the Apostles.—All this was changed with the full development of Ebionitism. The first Ebionite fanatics, who brought about a decided schism, denounced the aged bishop Symon, doubtless because he opposed their heresy, as a descendant of David, consequently as a relative of Jesus, doubtless after immoderate veneration had changed into immoderate hatred (Euseb. III. 32). But the later Ebionites (according to the *Clementines*) highly exalted James as the Lord's brother even above Peter. Now since Peter was unmistakably the most distinguished member of the whole Apostolical College, the distinction of the brothers of the Lord from the like-named Apostles became inevitable. In the case of the common Ebionites was superadded the natural interest that this facilitated the view which made Jesus the actual son of Joseph, and Mary the mother of a number of children.—This spurious, apocryphal tradition imposed upon and misled the uncritical Eusebius, who was wont to huddle every thing together, who was consequently either greatly at variance with himself or uncertain in himself. As by misunderstanding Papias, in the interest of Theology against the Apocalypse (see *Apostol. Age* I., p. 215) he conjured up the phantom of a presbyter John, and made Judas Lebbæus Thadæus one of the seventy disciples (i. 12, 13), so he made also James, the brother of the Lord one of the seventy, that is: distinguished from James the Apostle (i. 12), although in every instance he takes refuge behind tradition.

This laid the foundation of the vacillations of the later fathers concerning the brother of the Lord, among whom Gregory of Nyssa and Chrysostom favoured the distinction, Epiphanius and Augustine the identity, while Jerome is undecided (see Article *Jacobus* in Herzog, p. 408). Since all these fathers depend on Eusebius, their opinion, as opposed to the original tradition in this matter, is devoid of all independent weight. In modern and most modern times the majority of theologians beginning with Luther (that the author of the Epistle "was some good, pious man") have decided for the distinction; but they are opposed by a great number of eminent theologians (see Winer, Art. *Jacobus;* Wiesinger, *The Epistle of James*, Introd. p. 4 and others).

The only question, however, relates to the merit of the arguments advanced in support of the two opposing views. But first of all must be settled the question how it was possible that the sons of Alphæus and of a Mary different from the mother of Jesus, could be or become the brothers of the Lord. According to Hegesippus (Euseb. III., 11) Alphæus or Clopas the father of Symeon the second bishop of Jerusalem, was the brother of Joseph and consequently Symeon the cousin of Jesus, by origin. But Mary the wife of this Alphæus is commonly and erroneously considered to have been the sister of Mary, the mother of Jesus. For Wieseler (in *Studien und Kritiken* 1840, Vol. III., p. 648) has shown that Jno. xix. 25 ought to be rendered: "But there stood by the cross of Jesus His mother, and the sister of His mother (Salome; after the manner

[1] Huther who characterized this presentation of the remarkable complications of said names as exaggerated (p. 4) supports his statement mainly by the assertion that it is erroneous to maintain the identity of James the Just and James the son of Alphæus. But this is just what follows from the report of Hegesippus (Euseb. IV., 22). δεύτερον evidently belongs to the immediately preceding ἀνεψιόν and sustains the exposition that "Simeon the son of Cleophas our Lord's uncle, next was appointed bishop."

of John only to indicate personal relations without specifying names), Mary the wife of Clopas and Mary Magdalene." Hence the sons of Alphæus were at the most cousins of the Lord in the legal sense through their father Alphæus and Joseph the foster-father of Jesus, while the sons of Zebedee were at all events His cousins in a stricter sense, as the sons of Salome, the sister of Mary the mother of Jesus. Hence the reference to a *wider* sense of the term *brother* as denoting a relative or cousin (ἀνεψιός) is altogether insufficient to account for the constant appellation of James as the brother of the Lord. "But in this place arises the most simple hythosesis, supported by the custom of the Jews everywhere (see John xix. 26, 27). Cleophas was dead, Joseph the foster-father of Jesus was his brother, (Hegesippus in *Euseb.* xi. 3); he now became also the foster-father of the sons of his brother Cleophas and thenceforth the family of Joseph and the family of Alphæus-Cleophas, the other Mary, therefore, and her sons James and Joses, Simon and Jude, with several daughters formed one household (Matth. xiii. 55; Mark vi. 3). Now after the decease of Joseph also, the oldest brothers of Jesus, who most probably were older than Jesus, especially James, gradually became the heads of this household and this circumstance would account for the disposition of these brothers even at a later period, to assume some kind of guardianship over Jesus (Mark iii. 31; Jno. vii. 3.—See my article *Jacobus* in *Herzog's* Lexicon)."—The sons of Alphæus were then according to Jewish law the brothers of Jesus.[1] Schneckenburger on the false hypothesis of Mary Cleophas having been the sister of the mother of Jesus conceived that upon the early decease of Joseph, Mary the mother of Jesus went to live with her sister the wife of Alphæus.—

We now purpose giving (with reference to the Article *Jacobus* in Herzog's *Real-Encyclopædia* already quoted repeatedly) a brief account of the reasons and counter-reasons of the distinction between James the son of Alphæus and James the brother of the Lord.

Reasons: 1. James the son of Alphæus, being only the cousin of Jesus, could not be called the brother of the Lord. This difficulty is set aside by the above discussion of the subject.

2. The most ancient tradition of the Church does not make mention of James, the brother of the Lord, as of an Apostle. We have seen that the most ancient tradition affirms the opposite.

3. In the title of the Epistle of James the author simply calls himself the servant of Christ. But Paul also describes himself by the same title in the Epistle to the Philippians, John in the two lesser Epistles calls himself presbyter, and James had reasons of humility, wisdom and faith for calling himself the servant of Christ especially as he might well notice the abuse to which the appellation "brother of the Lord" had given rise.

4. Jno. vii. 5, we read that "the brethren of Jesus did not believe in Him," at a time when James the son of Alphæus had been received already among the Apostles. But John doubtless refers to the same unbelief or want of resigned obedience of faith[2] according to which his mother also did not believe in him, Mark iii. 31, or Peter, Matth. xvi. 23 and Thomas, Jno. xx. 25.

5. The passage Acts i. 13, 14, besides enumerating the Apostles, mentions the brothers of Jesus. The primary reference may be to Joses and his sisters; but just as Mary, who certainly belonged to the women, is introduced besides the women by the special designation of Mary the mother of Jesus, so also the Apostolical brothers of Jesus, besides having been included in the list of the Apostles, may be introduced by the special designation of the brothers of Jesus.

6. 1 Cor. ix. 5, introduces the brothers of the Lord alongside of the Apostles. To be sure; but Peter also is mentioned in particular according to the climax: a, Apostles in general, b, the brothers of the Lord as distinguished Apostles in the estimate of the Jewish-Christian opponents of Paul, c, Peter as the most distinguished Apostle.

---

[1] Huther says p. 7 that this hypothesis is devoid of all solid reason but he substantiates his assertion only by the statement that tradition is ignorant of the early death of Clopas and the adoption of his children by Joseph. *History* knows that the sons of Alphæus and Mary the mother of Jesus formed one household in which the former wielded some authority. Huther (p. 8) thinks it more probable that Mary and the brothers of Jesus believed (according to Mark iii. 21, 31), Jesus to be beside Himself, than to have had recourse to a pretext in order to extricate Him from supposed imminent danger. Mary is to have believed the report that Jesus was out of His mind!! We use here for once two marks of attention against the one of Huther, who, after the manner of Meyer expects it to produce a sensation and for the rest remind our readers of Luther's well-known flight to the Wartburg.

[2] "Altogether arbitrary," says Huther, although the matter may be elucidated by the analogous cases in the conduct of Mary, of Peter, of the sons of Zebedee and of Thomas.

Counter-reasons. 1. It is hardly conceivable that Luke (Acts xii. 2) should suffer James the son of Alphæus to vanish from the stage without all further mention and to let some other James, until then not an Apostle, forthwith (Acts xii. 17) enter the circle of the Apostles and enjoy peculiar distinction, without offering any explanation of the fact.

2. It is purely inconceivable, considering the importance attached by the Apostles to a duly authenticated call to the Apostleship (Acts i. 21, etc.), that they should have agreed to acknowledge as a man of Apostolical vocation, James a recently converted non-apostle, although he was a brother of the Lord; and especially that Paul, who was obliged so emphatically to defend his apostolicity against Judaizing Christians, should have accorded so prominent a position among the Apostles (Gal. ii.) to a non-apostle.

3. If any thing, it is still more inconceivable that the names of three real Apostles should have been extinguished without all trace by the names of three non-apostles who had acquired Apostolical authority, viz.: James, Simon, Jude.

4. Equally inconceivable is this threefold dualism of three names of equal dignity, equal descent and relationship, and of equal fraternity, that is,

a. James, Simon and Jude were Apostles. Another James, another Simon and another Jude acquired Apostolical distinction in their stead.

b. James the Apostle was the son of an Alphæus, the non-apostle James and his brothers were also the sons of an Alphæus.

c. In like manner James the Apostle and Joses were brothers, being the sons of Maria Alphæi. The non-apostles James, Simon, Jude and Joses being the sons of Alphæus probably would be also the sons of the same Mary.

5. In the passage 1 Cor. xv. 7, a distinction is drawn between the appearing of Christ to James and His appearing to all the apostles indicating that he had been mentioned before as a single Apostle.

6. The passage Gal. i. 19: "But another of the Apostles saw I not save James the Lord's brother," can only by finesse be construed to mean that James was not counted among the Apostles, as has been done by Hess and Neander, but each in a way of his own. To this must be added:

7. Moreover the coördinate authority of the same James with Peter and John Gal. ii. to which Paul offers not the least objection although he had taken the watchword "to know nobody after the flesh." We have still to superadd:

8. The above-mentioned most ancient church-tradition with its decisive testimony.

9. The demonstrability of the obscure Ebionite-apocryphal origin of the legend of the Lord's brothers taken in conjunction with the insecurity of Eusebius and the false security of the fathers who sustain their opinion by his.

10. The agreement of the characteristic traits of the brothers of the Lord according to the Gospels with the characteristic traits of the like-named Apostles with reference to the *caution* of James (Mark iii; Acts xv. xxi. 18; the Epistle of James), to the *fiery vivacity* of Judas Lebbæus Thaddæus (Jno. vii. 3; Jno. xiv. 22; the Epistle of Jude), which may also have been the characteristic trait of *Simon Zelotes* at an earlier period of his life; cf my *Life of Jesus*, p. 148; *Apost. Age* 1, p. 364. We have elsewhere repeatedly affirmed the identity of James and the brothers of the Lord with great decisiveness (*Life of Jesus; Apost. Age*, Article *Jacobus* in Herzog's *Encyclopœdia*, in this Commentary on Matthew); but here it was impossible to avoid repeating a short resumé of the process and it is necessary to use every effort towards the removal of the groundless and unreasonable *Apocryphon* of false learning from the field of theology.

After what has been said we may briefly sketch the life-portrait of James. It follows from the foregoing statement that James also must have been among the brothers of Jesus, who after His first appearance at Cana in Galilee accompanied Him to Capernaum. The Evangelist designates these companions of Jesus to have consisted of His mother, His brothers and His disciples. We have seen that there was good reason for the continuance of the two categories, *His brothers and His disciples*, at a later period, because the two lines did not fully cover each other, that is, because Joses and the sisters never belonged to the circle of the Apostles. But while we assume that the sons of Alphæus at that time were not yet disciples, their inclination to believe seems to follow from their having joined the company of Jesus.[1] Soon after, after the first festive journey, Jesus appeared at Nazareth (Luke iv. 22; Matth. xiii. 55), and on that occasion His brothers are mentioned as follows, James, Joses, Simon, Judas. Matthew according to his arrangement has assigned the respective event to a later period, probably because he connects it with a subsequent appearance of Jesus at Nazareth. Even then only the sisters, probably married, appear to reside at Nazareth (Math. xiii. 56; Mark vi. 3). Again at a somewhat later period took place the first sending of the twelve disciple-Apostles and among them we find the name of James the son of Alphæus and the names of his brothers Lebbæus Thaddæus or Judas and Simon Zelotes or the Cananite. But the surname the son of Alphæus distinguishes our James from James the son of Zebedee. The separation of the Apostles had occurred some time before the visit of Jesus to the feast of Purim in the second year of His official life. At that feast Jesus had incurred the hatred and persecution of the Jewish hierarchy by the performance of a cure on the Sabbath day; hence He soon after was put to great straits in Galilee and His mother and brothers (Mark iii. 21–35), conceived it their duty to restrain Him from His bold attitude towards His enemies and to save Him from their hand by stratagem. There is as little difficulty in supposing James the son of Alphæus to have participated in this rashness as there is difficulty in admitting the rashness of the sons of Zebedee (Luke ix. 54), of Peter (Matth. xvi. 22), and in the unbelief of Thomas. Indeed we may go even so far as to suppose that James was the chief prompter in this matter, which exhibits a sinful caution, whose purified and spiritualized counterpart we meet again in his later conduct (cf. Acts 15, and ch. xxi.). For the same reason we may suppose that in the second exhibition of rashness in the opposite direction, on the part of the brothers of Jesus, which took place in the autumn of the same year before the feast of Tabernacles (Jno. vii. 3, 4), it was not James who was prominent but his brothers, especially Judas, who although silenced did at a later period revert once more to the idea of inciting Jesus to manifest Himself to the world (ch. xiv. 22), although it is to be noticed that Jesus had again greatly raised the courage of the disciples on the mountain of transfiguration and at the foot of the same. The degree to which the family of Alphæus emulated the sons of Zebedee (Matth. xx. 20), in their sympathy with our Lord in His end at Jerusalem, is apparent from the fact that Mary the mother of James the Less and Joses was among the women that were spectators of the crucifixion. Yes, it was she only, who on the evening of the burial of Jesus in company with Mary Magdalene, sat over against His tomb (Matth. xxvii. 61); in the same manner, she and Mary Magdalene were among the first of those women who on Easter-morning hastened forth to the tomb of Jesus (Matth. xxviii. 1). Meanwhile James quietly matured into one of the much distinguished Apostles. After the martyrdom of the elder James, who seems already to have stood in a nearer relation to the government of the Church at Jerusalem, because Herod Agrippa laid hands on him first, James the Less, according to a tacit presupposition, seems to step into his place; for Peter charges those, to whom he showed himself after his deliverance from prison, to tell James and the brethren. At the Apostolic Convention at Jerusalem (Acts xv.) James is one of the most distinguished speakers; and here we perceive clearly that he deemed it his task to be the mediator of the religious liberty of the Gentile Christians and the national customs of the Jewish Christians. He stands on precisely the same platform of faith as that of Peter and Paul; what he proposes in order to pacify the Jewish Christians is not a religious but an *ethical* dogma; a measure of missionary wisdom, which accordingly meets the approbation of all the Apostles. That he did not Judaize, and indeed as an Apostle he could not judaize, is evident from the decided ground he took against judaizing demands, which was also fully accorded to him by Paul (Gal. ii.). On the other hand, in his cautious consideration for the Jews, whom in their national totatility he would gladly have saved for the Christian faith, he went to the utmost limit, as is evident from the counsel which he and his immediate associates gave to Paul on his last visit to Jerusalem (Acts xxi.). Paul was to give proof to the Jews that he did not despise the customs of the fathers by accom-

1 According to *Huther* they went with Him from Cana to Capernaum, not because they were inclined to believe, but because they belonged to their mother. He seems to conceive them to have been young children, but Mark iii. clearly shows that such was surely not the case.

plishing the vow of a Nazarite in the temple at Jerusalem. We cannot consider this counsel in the light of an inspiration; it miscarried and actually produced the very opposite effect that had been contemplated. But Paul, who also before this entertained a high esteem for James (Gal. i. ii.), saw nothing to object to it, although he could offer the most decided resistance to every judaizing tendency, even when Peter was guilty of it. But this cautious position of James, this keeping sacred the national custom of his people enables us to understand how the judaizers might make such manifold abuse of his name (as is apparent from Gal. ii. 4, 12, and similar indications). James, then, is above all things an Apostle, a witness of Christ, everyways the equal of the other Apostles; Christianity is to him the fulfilment of the Old Testament, a new, absolute, eternal principle of religion and in this respect he, Paul and John occupy the same platform. But, in the next place, he is also the Apostle of the Jews '*par excellence;*' that is, he conceives of Christianity in its close connection with the Old Testament, as the new perfect law of spiritual life and of liberty, because on the other hand he apprehends Judaism as passing into Christianity [Germ. *werdendes Christenthum*] and feels conscious of a special call for his people. As to the form of James's ideas, it is to be noticed that he addresses Jewish Christians (for it is settled already that our Epistle can belong to only one James) to whom the mediating dialectical form would be a heterogeneous element. The purity of his Greek style indeed has been to some an enigmatical phenomenon. But it characterizes also the Apostle of holy carefulness.

Baumgarten (Acts iv. 127) has treated at large of the grandness of the ecclesiastical position of James. The following sentence however requires to be examined. "James refuses to acknowledge any other liberty than that formed within the measure of the law and in this sense he calls the law, the law of liberty."—In that sense the law has always been a law of liberty; but here the reference is rather to a liberty, developing and manifesting itself as a new law of life, and which preserves holy Jewish custom *in* Jewish-Christianity but patriarchal custom *with* (alongside of) Jewish-Christianity. "James represents the Christian dogma in the form of the Jewish Ethos [ἔθος=custom—M.]. He has removed the Old Testament law, as such, from the sphere of religion into the sphere of *national custom*. And this was the very task assigned to him, because he had to put forth the best effort of love with a view to gain the Jewish *nation* to Christianity. This effort is recorded by historical tradition." (See Herzog's *Real-Lexicon*, Art. *Jacobus*). Three reports are in perfect agreement on the characteristics of James and also with the sketch of his character found in Holy Writ. The Gospel according to the Hebrews narrates of him, that James after the death of Jesus took the vow, that from the time he had shared the last meal with Jesus he would not eat any thing until he saw Him risen from the dead; that the risen Saviour soon afterwards appeared to him and told him, "Go eat thy bread, for the Son of Man is risen from the dead." This report sounds rather apocryphal; but its subject-matter, although not its very words, are confirmed by the statements of Hegesippus, that James was a Nazarite, and by the fact that he also recommended Paul to fulfil the vow of a Nazarite (Acts xxi). This Nazarite vow on the part of James surely does not denote a wavering faith, as Neander thinks, but rather an over-bold form of his assurance of faith. In a general way, however, the account in the Gospel of the Hebrews concerning a special appearing of Christ to James agrees with the statement of Paul 1 Cor. xv. 7. The second particular, for which we are indebted to Josephus (*Antiq.* XX. 9, 1) consists of a general notice of the martyrdom of James. He reports "that the high-priest Ananus, a Sadducee, in the interval between the departure of Festus from Palestine, A. D. 62 [Josephus speaks of his death—M.], and the arrival of Albinus, the new Procurator, caused *the brother of Jesus, who was called Christ, whose name was James and some others,*[1] whom he had accused as breakers of the law, to be stoned to the great dislike of the more moderate citizens, who therefore informed against him before Albinus." Eusebius (II. 23), superadds the words of Josephus that all the calamities of the destruction of Jerusalem did happen to the Jews to avenge James the Just who was brother of Him that is called Christ and whom the Jews had slain, notwithstanding his preëminent justice. To this we must add in the third place the detailed account of Hegesippus in Eusebius (II. 23). "With the Apostles James, the brother

[1] On the doubt concerning the genuineness of the words in Italics expressed by Clericus and others, see Huther p. 2 Note. But the several notices of Eusebius seem to sustain Josephus.

of the Lord, succeeds to the charge of the Church—that James who has been called the Just and from the time of our Lord to our own day, for there were many of the name of James. He was holy from his mother's womb (a Nazarite, one consecrated), he drank not wine or strong drink, nor did he eat animal food; a razor came not upon his head; he did not anoint himself with oil; he did not use the bath. He alone might go into the holy place (εἰς τὰ ἅγια)."—This expression is falsely interpreted as designating the holiest of holies. The expression may admit of such an interpretation, but the Jewish law forbids it. The acknowledged Nazarite might probably go with the priests into the temple proper (Acts xxi. 26).—"For he wore no woollen clothes but linen. And alone he used to go into the temple and there he was commonly found upon his knees, praying for forgiveness for the people, so that his knees grew hard-skinned like a camel's, from his constantly bending them in prayer and entreating forgiveness for the people." On account therefore of his exceeding righteousness he was called "Just" and "Oblias" (according to Stroth עֹפֶל עָם), which means in Greek "the bulwark (pillar) of the people" and "righteousness," as the prophets declare of him (in the opinion of the Jewish people). Some of the seven sects of the Hebrews inquired of him, "What is the door (doctrine) of Jesus?" And he said that this man was the Saviour, wherefore some believed that Jesus is the Christ. Now the forementioned sects did not believe in the Resurrection, nor in the coming of one (Christ, Messiah) who shall recompense every man according to his works; but all who became believers believed through James. When many therefore of the rulers believed etc. At last, reports Hegesippus, there arose a general conflict of opinions among the people and at the Passover they placed him on the gable of the Temple and bade him solemnly declare in the audience of all the people what he believed concerning Jesus, because he was the Just and would speak in conformity with his convictions. From that lofty place he then cried with a loud voice: "Why ask ye me about Jesus, the Son of Man? He sits in heaven on the right hand of great power and will come in the clouds of heaven." And many were convinced and gave glory on the testimony of James, crying, Hosannah to the Son of David. But the Scribes and Pharisees cried "Oh! oh! even the Just is gone astray," rushed up and threw him down. Below they then stoned him (symbolically, therefore, the whole act was of course a zealotical stoning and so Josephus, from his centre of observation, correctly reports the event) and slew him with a fuller's club."—This narrative affords also a full illustration of the forementioned statement of Josephus superadded by Eusebius that the wisest among the Jews agree with him in regarding the destruction of Jerusalem as the punishment of this crime. Josephus and the Jews who were of his mind seem to have had an obscure foreboding that James was the last preacher of repentance sent to the Jewish people as a nation, and that the murder of this witness of the truth was the decisive stubbornness of the people as a people, upon which the judgment had inevitably to follow. Neander and Schaff have discovered without reason much legendary matter and an Ebionite mode of thinking in the report of Hegesippus. Hegesippus was certainly a Jewish Christian but not an Ebionite. It must not be overlooked that his opinion of James momentarily commingles in his report with his opinion of the Jewish people. But this narrative is strongly authenticated in all its main features. That James was a Nazarite is supported by Acts xxi. 23 etc., and by the citation from the Gospel according to the Hebrews. The zeal of James in interceding for the Jewish people is reflected in every thing we know of him. Josephus also testifies to the veneration James enjoyed among the Jewish people. But most important, in the last place, is the account of that public crisis which was to determine the decision of the Jewish nation for or against faith in Christ; and the antecedents of similar analogous crises, particularly in Acts v. 13; vi. 7; xxii. 22, as well as its internal truthfulness, give decided support to this the main feature of the account of Hegesippus. The Nazarite character of James would also explain the reason why, to judge from later indications, the Essenes in particular became converts to Christianity and were more especially attached to the person of James not only as Jewish Christians but also in the direction of the Gnostic Ebionitism. The veneration with which Jewish Christians were wont to regard "the brother of the Lord," which had already before that period become extremely one-sided, would be heightened in their case and the Clementines in particular supply evidence that this veneration had actually been thus heightened, for they exalt James above Peter and all the Apostles and make him the supreme Bishop of all Christendom. James has here been made the symbol of *judaistico-chiliastic* claims to the government of Church and the world. According to Epiphan *hæres.* XXX. § 16 there were among the glorifications of James actually ἀναβαθμοὶ Ἰακώβου, descriptions of his pretended ascension. Epiphanius also notwithstanding his antagonism to the Ebionites, holds similar exaggerations (*Hæres.* XXIX. 4 and LXXVIII. 13). Probably it is only owing to Epiphanius misunderstanding Hegesippus that he states, "that James was like the highpriest permitted to enter once a year the holiest of holies because he was a Nazarite and wore the highpriest's mitre (τὸ πέταλον). This myth is not on a level with the account of Polycrates respecting John (Euseb. V. 24). Polycrates doubtless accorded the highpriest's mitre to John in a symbolico-ideal sense; which is hardly so in the case of Epiphanius. (See Herzog, Art. *Jacobus*). An ambiguous notice in Eusebius (VII. 19) states that the Church at Jerusalem in token of their veneration of James had preserved as a holy relic, his official seat.

Owing to the mythical difference between James the Just and James the Apostle the myth took further occasion to decorate particularly the end of the latter, considered separately. Nicephorus, II. 40, reports him to have first appeared as a messenger of faith in South-Western Palestine, then in Egypt; and that he was crucified at Ostracina in Lower Egypt. (For particulars see Natalis *Alex. Sæc.* I. p. 59.) On the Church legends of the supposed two Jameses cf. Stichart, *Ecclesiastical legend of the holy Apostles*, Leipzig, 1861, p. 79 etc. The chronology of Eusebius fixes the death of the real and one James in the year A. D. 63. Eusebius judiciously connects his death with Paul's appeal to Rome (II. 23). Until then the hatred of the Jews had been directed mainly against Paul whom they tried to kill by all means. But by his appeal to Rome he escaped further persecution on their part. But since James had consorted with him at Jerusalem, it was natural that the hatred of many Jews should now be turned against him, the most distinguished representative of Christianity among them. But from this it does not follow that Eusebius intended to say that James was killed as early as the time when the appeal took place; nor does it follow from Eusebius. III. 11 that the death of James took place immediately before the destruction of Jerusalem. The notice of Josephus that James was killed after the departure of Festus and before the arrival of Albinus leads to about the time given in the chronology of Eusebius, for Festus was called away in A. D. 62.

"Among the Apostles James is, *par excellence*, the representative of Christian wisdom, gentleness, mediation and union; as apostolical presbyter-bishop of Jerusalem he is the representative of Jewish nationality and custom in its Christian transformation and transfiguration. As the son of Alphæus he presents a contrast to the fiery, impetuous Judas Lebbæus Thaddæus and exhibits the character of a sage and a sufferer matured, according to his charisma, in caution by constant spiritual discipline. Thus he was the last and most engaging expression of the Gospel to the Jewish people; and after the stoning of this messenger of faith, the city and people were sealed unto judgment, which was acknowledged not only by Eusebius, but even resented by Josephus. Jerusalem rejected Christianity especially because it hated in it the union with Gentile Christians." (From the article "*Jacobus*"). On the literature of treatises on the supposed two Jameses see Winer's *Real Wörterbuch*, Art. *Jacobus*, p. 525. Also Wiesinger's *Commentary* p. 21 and the *Introduction* of Theile.

[Excurses on the Brothers of the Lord.

[The family relations of Joseph and Mary demand more than a passing or one-sided notice. This interesting, but very difficult and complicated subject involves the question: *Was Jesus the only child in the Holy Family, or were there other children, and if so, who were they?*

The New Testament answers the first part of the question in the negative, and says concerning the second that Jesus had brothers and sisters. They are mentioned with or without their names twelve times in the Gospels (Matth. xii. 46, 47; xiii. 55, 56 (ἀδελφοί and ἀδελφαί); Mark iii. 31, 32; vi. 3 (sisters also); Luke viii. 19, 20; Jno. vii. 3, 5, 10, once in Acts (i. 14), once in 1 Cor. (ix. 5) and once in Gal. (i. 19), where James of Jerusalem is called the Lord's brother.

St. Matthew (xiii. 55) gives the names of the four brothers, viz. James, Joses or *Joseph*, Simon and Judas.—St. Mark (vi. 3) calls them James, Joses or *Josetus*, Simon and Juda.

Neither the names nor the number of sisters are mentioned, but they cannot have been less than two.

It is to be noticed that in all the passages referred to they are also called *His* brothers and sisters, *i. e.* the brothers and sisters of Jesus, never His cousins (ἀνεψιοί) or kinsmen (συγγενεῖς), and that these brothers and sisters are always mentioned in connection with Mary.

These are the simple facts of the case, and in any other case, the terms used would have been received in their natural sense, the brothers and sisters would have been regarded as brothers and sisters, nothing more or less. But dogmatical prejudices and ascetic extravagances concerning the sanctity of celibacy began at a very early period to apply a non-natural interpretation to the terms brothers and sisters with reference to our Lord. At least *three* leading theories have been advanced towards the solution of this question.

I. The theory which makes the brothers and sisters of Jesus the children of Joseph by a former marriage, or the adopted children of Joseph.

II. The theory which makes them the children of Mary, the sister of Mary the mother of Jesus, or the cousins-german of Jesus. As a variation of this theory, there is another which makes them His cousins both on the side of Joseph and Mary.

III. The theory according to which they were the children of Joseph and Mary, or the actual brothers and sisters of Jesus.

A condensed survey of these theories will enable us to form an idea of the difficulties connected with our subject.—

I. The hypothesis that the brothers and sisters of Jesus were the children of Joseph by a former marriage or his adopted children is founded on traditional notices drawn from the apocryphal gospels, which represent Joseph as a man of 80 years when he married Mary, the father of four sons and two daughters by his former wife Escha. The names of the children are variously given. This is the earliest tradition concerning the parentage of the brothers and sisters of the Lord, but need not detain us long, because even Jerome, the strenuous advocate of the *cousin*-theory, denounced it as "*deliramenta apocryphorum*," as "apocryphal nonsense." But notwithstanding this strong censure of Jerome, and ample margin being left to the reputed *age* of Joseph at the time of his marriage, it contains nothing intrinsically improbable. It is indeed, and we think justly, pronounced by Stier and Greswell a mere fiction devised to save the ἀειπαρθενία of Mary, and advocated on grounds of *expediency* by modern authors, but although the children of Joseph might and would be called the brothers and sisters of Jesus, the hypothesis is open to very grave objections, because it makes them the seniors of our Lord, which conflicts with their constant attendance on Mary and our Lord's being the legal heir to the throne of David, a prerogative that could only have been enjoyed by the first-born, not by the last-born; for the people clearly knew nothing of His supernatural origin and here we have to deal altogether with popular impressions.

A modification of this hypothesis is Lange's *adoption-theory*. He supposes Joseph to have had a brother Clopas or Alphæus, who married a certain Mary, not the sister of Mary the mother of Jesus. He died early and Joseph adopted his children who thus became the legal brothers and sisters of our Lord. Their mother also became an inmate of Joseph's family. It is hard to realize such a state of things, if we consider that Joseph was a poor carpenter, and that Mary the supposed mother of those children should have relinquished her maternal rights over them. The hypothesis, although very ingenious, is purely speculative, countenanced neither by exegesis nor tradition, and evidently the result of dogmatic and critical perplexity.

Lichtenstein makes Joseph and Clopas, two brothers, marry two sisters both named Mary. At the death of Clopas, Joseph took Mary, the widow of Clopas, into his family, and thus the children were doubly related to our Lord, legally on their father's side and naturally on their mother's side—and might therefore after their adoption be styled the brothers and sisters of the Lord.

The *Levirate* hypothesis, according to which Joseph on the death of his brother Clopas, married his widow, and that the brothers and sisters of Jesus were the fruit of this marriage, belongs under this head, but needs neither discussion nor refutation.

II. We come now to the *cousin*-theory, which makes the brothers and sisters of our Lord the children of Clopas and Mary, the sister of Mary the mother of our Lord, and alleges that these children by a lax use of the words brother and sister were regarded to sustain the fraternal relation to our Lord.

This theory rests upon the following assumptions, 1. That Alphæus and Clopas are identical; 2. that Mary the mother of James, Joseph, Simon and Jude was his wife and the sister of Mary the mother of Jesus; 3. that the lax use of the term "brother" is a fact. These assumptions are open to weighty objections.

a. The identity of Alphæus and Clopas rests on the slender foundation that James the Less, one of the twelve is called the *son of* Alphæus ('Ιάκωβος ὁ τοῦ 'Αλφαίου Matth. x. 3; Mark ii. 14; iii. 18; Luke vi. 15; Acts i. 13) and that one of the spectators of the crucifixion, called Mary (Clopa=Μαρία ἡ τοῦ Κλωπᾶ) was the mother of James the Less, because a Mary, the mother of two sons James and Joses is mentioned in Mark xv. 40; and that the Hebrew חַלְפַּי and the Greek 'Αλφαῖος are supposed to be different forms of the same name. This is probable but not certain. Matthew or Levi, moreover was also a son of Alphæus, and if the ellipsis in 'Ιούδας 'Ιακώβου (Luke vi. 15; Acts i. 13) is to be filled up, as is commonly done, by inserting ἀδελφός, the Apostle Jude also was a son of Alphæus. Furthermore, if this Mary was also the mother of Simeon, another Apostle, we have the extraordinary fact that *four Apostles*, claimed by the advocates of this theory as the brothers of Christ, did not believe in Him, for John expressly informs us that His brethren did not believe in Him. (John vii. 3 sqq.).

b. The assumption that Mary the mother of Jesus, and Mary the mother of James and Joses were *sisters* is founded on a solitary passage in John, which admits however of a very different and far more probable solution. It is Jno. xix. 25, which as punctuated and read by the advocates of the *cousin*-theory, enumerates the three Marys as spectators of the crucifixion. "Now there stood by the cross of Jesus His mother, and His mother's sister Mary the wife of Clopas, and Mary Magdalene," but the more correct reading is "Now there stood by the cross of Jesus His mother and His mother's sister (Salome, the mother of John the Evangelist), Mary the wife of Clopas and Mary Magdalene."—We know from Matthew that Salome, the mother of Zebedee's children was present at the crucifixion, and this indirect reference to his mother, accords with the usual delicacy of John.

Instances of two sisters having the same name are indeed occasionally met with, but they are far from common; considered as a question of probability, it must be decided in the negative, and this decision will be corroborated by the other arbitrary and illogical elements of this hypothesis.

Let us look at it from another point of view. The Evangelists enumerate James, Joseph (for that is the *true* reading in Matthew) Simon and Jude as the four brothers of our Lord. The advocates of the cousin-theory allege that they were his *cousins*, but were *called* his brothers. We read also of another Mary the mother of James and Joses, who is nowhere called the mother of Simon and Jude. Now because she had one son, or if you will, two sons, whose names were identical with those of the brothers of the Lord, it is inferred that she was the mother of the brothers and sisters of the Lord. But the most authentic codices and the most reliable critics pronounce *Joseph* to be the correct reading in Matthew, and this develops the extraordinary logic that because here is a mother of *two* sons one of whom has the same name as that of a son of a mother of *four* sons, THEREFORE she is the mother of the four. The acumen of Aristotle, surely, is not needed, to detect this fallacy.—Add to this that the brothers of Jesus appear uniformly in the company of Mary, the mother of Jesus, that the Hebrew אָח, the representative of the Greek ἀδελφός, is used only twice in a lax sense, and then only in the case of *nephews*, that the words ἀνεψιός, *consobrinus*, or cousin (Col. iv. 10 applied to Mark the cousin of Barnabas), υἱὸς τῆς ἀδελφῆς, sister's son (Acts xxiii. 26), and συγγενής, *kinsman* or *relative* form part of the New Testament vocabulary, that neverthless the Evangelists use the word ἀδελφοί and not any of the new terms, that the *brothers* did not believe in Christ before His resurrection, that therefore they could not have been *Apostles*, and that after His resurrection, even as *believers* they are expressly distinguished from the Apostles, and the inference is all but irresistible that this whole theory, from beginning to end, is involved in chaotic confusion and endless contradiction.

Much stress is laid by the advocates of this theory on the celebrated passage Gal. i. 19: "But other of the Apostles saw I none, save James, the Lord's brother." Read and construed as the verse stands in E.V. it is argued that Paul here declares to have seen at Jerusalem James, a brother of the Lord, who was an Apostle, that this must have been James of Alphæus or James the Less, because James the son of Zebedee was dead at that time, that here is a clear case of the word brother being used in the sense of cousin, and that consequently the Lord's brethren are His cousins, the children of Alphæus and Mary. The passage bears however the very opposite interpretation and some of the best Greek scholars have shown, and we think conclusively, that we ought to render "I saw none other of the Apostles (besides Peter to whom he had referred in the preceding verse) but I saw James, the Lord's brother." In other words Paul distinguishes James the Lord's brother from the twelve. Still it is only fair to add that although James was not an Apostle, yet both on account of his exemplary piety and wisdom and on account of his relation to our Lord, and as first bishop of Jerusalem, he enjoyed apostolic dignity and authority. "That such was the case is evident from various passages in Acts, in the Epistle to the Galatians, from Josephus, Hegesippus and the tradition of the Eastern Church."

III. The only remaining theory is that the brothers of Jesus were His actual brothers, that is: the children of Joseph and Mary. This view is the most natural, but beset by dogmatical difficulties. We will first state the arguments in its favour and then consider the dogmatical difficulties.

1. The language used by the Evangelists is such as to intimate that Joseph and Mary were man and wife.
2. The term 'first-born' although of technical value and importing certain privileges, may fairly be construed as implying the existence of children born subsequently, especially if it is considered that the Evangelists record events as historians after those events had become history, and that if they had intended to say that Jesus was Mary's *only-born*, it was as easy for them to select that term, which forms part of the N. T. vocabulary as the ambiguous 'first-born,' which although susceptible of a non-natural interpretation, imports generally the existence of later-born children.
3. The Evangelists mention brothers and sisters of Jesus.
4. These brothers could not have been Apostles, for they continued to disbelieve in Jesus during His life-time.
5. The hypothesis that the brothers and sisters of Jesus were the children of Joseph and Mary simplifies the domestic relations of the holy family.
6. The objection which is sometimes brought against this hypothesis that Jesus would not have commended his mother to *John*, if she had other sons to take care of her (Jno. xix. 26). "But why," asks *Andrews* if James and Judas were *Apostles* and *His* cousins, sons of her sister and long inmates of her family, and it was a question of kinship, did He not commend her to *their* care? The force of the objection remains then unbroken on the *cousin*-theory. The true reasons why our Lord confided His mother to John and not to His brothers, seem to have been the following:

a. The brothers did not believe in Him, and consequently could not sympathize with Mary in her great sorrow.

b. Between John, the most intimate friend of Jesus, who understood and appreciated Him better than all the disciples, and Mary there was the strongest bond of sympathy in their love of Jesus, and *John* was therefore most likely to uphold and comfort her with filial tenderness in her sad trials.

John, moreover, was the *cousin* of Jesus, being the son of Salome, the sister of Mary, and the *brothers of Jesus* were probably married, as the notice of Paul in 1 Cor. ix. 5, seems to imply.

The last two points we do not urge as reasons, but merely state as matters of interest.

These plain facts, drawn solely from Scripture, conflict however with the old and wide-spread view of the perpetual virginity of Mary and the feeling that it was lowering the dignity of the Saviour and that of Mary to admit the probability or even possibility of further descendants. To preclude the possibility of such an hypothesis was doubtless the ruling motive of those who gave currency to the apocryphal fiction that Joseph was eighty years old when he married Mary.

The cousin-theory which may be traced back to Papias, although made current in the Church by Jerome, clearly originated in the desire to establish the superiority of the unmarried to the married state. Gnostic principles began early to prevail in the Church and to induce the desire to separate Christ as widely as possible from other men. To obliterate, if possible, any and everything He might be supposed to have in common with other men, was believed to add to His exaltation. This exaltation would naturally pass from Him to Mary, and with the development of Mariology and Mariolatry become an article of faith. Due allowance must also be made for the feeling "that the selection of a woman and that of a virgin to be the mother of the Lord, carries with it as a necessary implication that no others could sustain the same relations with her." (J. A. Alexander). It is of course very difficult to account for the extent of this feeling, but there can be no doubt that it is not altogether free from an undervaluation of the honour and dignity conferred by our Lord on our common humanity by His Incarnation. The inspired writers of the New Testament seem to emulate each other in portraying the true humanity of Christ and in showing how He ennobled, glorified, and with reverence be it uttered, deified that nature which at the first came pure and holy from His creative Mind. It is surely an ineffably touching and consoling thought that the holy Jesus passed through every relation of human childhood and from having been a pattern of humility, modesty and forbearance to His brothers and sisters, from having borne with their impatience and want of sympathy, to evidence Himself in this respect also as our true Highpriest that He might be touched with a feeling of our infirmity." And then as to Mary, her memory will not be less dear and sacred to us, as the mother of the brothers and sisters of Jesus, than as the ever-virgin. Marriage is a divine institution and has been made doubly divine by the human mother of our Lord.—

The question has from the earliest times been variously answered; the view that Jesus had actual brothers and sisters is as old as any of the other theories and we believe, with Neander, Winer, Meyer, Stier, Alford and Farrar that it accords best with the evangelical record, and barring dogmatical prejudice or feeling, is at once the simplest, most natural and logical solution of this otherwise hopelessly confused question, which fortunately is an open one in *our* Church and most of the Reformed bodies.

Those who desire to *study* this question are referred to ANDREWS, *Life of Christ* pp. 104–116. ALFORD *Greek Testament*, Introduction to Epistle St. James, DR. SCHAFF's excellent Essay: "*Das Verhältniss des Jakobus, Bruders des Herrn, zu Jakobus Alphæi*, Berlin 1843, his annotation to Lange's *Matthew* pp. 256–266, and to my Article in the *Princeton Review* for January 1865: "*Are James the Son of Alphæus and James the Brother of the Lord identical?*"—M.].

2. GENUINENESS OF THE EPISTLE.

A. *Notices which presuppose the early existence and reception of the Epistles* in Clemens Romanus Ep. 1. ch. x.; in Pastor Hermas, *Similit.* viii. 6; in Irenæus, *adv. Hæeres*, iv. 16. *Abraham amicus Dei* (Jacob. ii. 23). Tertullian *adv. Judæos* Cap. ii.: *Abraham amicus Dei.* See on it Guerike, *Isagogik*, p. 441, and Huther p. 24.

B. *Testimonies.* The ancient Syriac Peschito contains this Epistle. Clemens Alex. knew it according to Euseb. *Hist. Eccl.* VI. 14. He also alludes to James ii. 8 in *Stromat* VI.—Origen mentions the Epistle of James in Tom. 19 on John and occasionally calls it *divina Jacobi Apostoli Epistola.* Homil. 13 in Gen. etc.—Dionysius of Alexandria appeals to it in several places and Didymus of Alexandria wrote a commentary on it.—Cyril of Jerusalem and Jerome, *Cat.* 3 considered it to be genuine (Guerike p. 442).

C. *Ancient doubts of its genuineness.*—These were the natural outgrowth of the apocryphal Jewish Christian account of distinguishing James the son of Alphæus from James the brother of the Lord. It is certainly not surprising (Kern supposes it *is*) that the testimony of Hegesippus is wanting for the Epistle in Euseb. ii. 23, where he is only cited as the chronicler of the life and martyrdom of James. But Eusebius takes occasion to mention the Epistle itself in order to add the observation that it was accounted spurious, as many of the ancients had neither mentioned it nor the Epistle of Jude; but that they were publicly read in most of the Churches. The reason adduced is clearly of little weight against the genuineness of the Epistle. Origen may at first have intended to give a faint intimation of existing doubt; but this is rather doubtful (see Guerike 443, note 4). Eusebius placing the Epistle among the Antilegomena simply proves that in his time its genuineness was not universally acknowledged; he himself appears to have essentially shared those doubts, owing to his indecision in his historical view of the person in question. The doubts stated by Jerome are now only regarded as historical references; the alleged contradiction of Theodore of Mopsuestia cannot be authenticated, but even if it could, it would only be the statement of a critical view belonging to a later period.

D. *Doubts at the time of the Reformation.* Luther, in the preface to the Epistle of James A. D. 1522 says: "This Epistle of James, although rejected by the ancients (which is false) I praise and esteem good withal, because it setteth forth not any doctrine of man and drives hard the law of God (which is incorrect). But to give my opinion, yet without the prejudice of any one, I count it to be no Apostle's writing, and this is my reason. First, because contrary to St. Paul's writings and all other Scripture it puts righteousness in works (a misunderstanding; and if it were so, how could he praise it and esteem it good withal?). "Lastly he thought that the Author was some good, pious man." Yes, "some good pious man" who understood better how to warn Jewish-Christians of the insurrection of the Jews than Luther knew to warn the Evangelicals of the insurrection of the peasants.—His opinion is couched in stronger terms in the preface to the Edition of the N. T. of 1524: "On that account the Epistle of James, compared with them (the Epistles of Paul and the remaining Epistles of the N. T.) is a veritable straw-Epistle. For it lacks all evangelical character." It is striking enough that Luther held also to the opinion that the early-deceased James, the son of Zebedee was the author of this Epistle. Similar opinions rejecting the Epistle found in the Table talk (*Tisch-Reden*) proves that Luther retained this view to a later period although the respective passages were omitted in later editions of the New Testament. (See Huther p. 25). The opinion of Luther was followed by the *Magdeburg Centuriators*, Hunnius, Althammer and others; among the Reformed by Wetstein. It is known that Luther's view could not do justice to the book of Revelation and other books of Holy Writ; it was the enthusiastic prominence he gave to the doctrine of justification (the work to which he had been especially called), connected with his misapprehension of the general tendency of the Epistle and with the new born deep consciousness of evangelical liberty of thought as contrasted with exegetical tradition, that made him pronounce so embarrassed an opinion of our Epistle. In the *Dorpat Magazine for Theology and the Church* Vol. I. pt. 1. 1859, p. 152, von Oettingen reviewing Huther's Commentary on the Epistle of James says concerning the fore-mentioned opinion of Luther: "This opinion of Luther not only has been recently adopted by the Tübingen school *utiliter* for its tendencies but it has also been repeated by the Gnesio-Lutherans, as is proved by the following hasty statement of Ströbel (in a review of Wiesinger's Commentary in *Guerike and Rudelbach's Magazine for Lutheran Theology*, 1857, II. p. 356. "No matter in what sense we take the Epistle of James, it is always in conflict with the remaining parts of Holy Writ." Very justly von Oettingen expresses his censure of that opinion in the name of the *Biblia Stroebeliana* (see in Huther p. 28). In the Roman Catholic Church doubts were uttered by Erasmus and Cajetanus.

E. *Modern doubts.* Forerunners: Faber, Bolten, Bertholdt: James wrote in Aramean, the Greek translation the work of another hand.

De Wette, *Introduction to the New Testament.* It is difficult to see why James should have written an Epistle to all the Jewish Christians in the world. Its contents are ambiguous. It lacks personality. The missed contradiction of Paul is undignified. Ch. ii. 25 seems to refer to

Hebrews xi. 31 and consequently to betray a later author. How could James write such good Greek? For counter-statements see Guerike, *Contributions*, p. 160 etc.

Schleiermacher:—*Introduction to the New Testament*, edited by Walde. He finds the opinion of Luther confirmed, the style in part ornate, in part clumsy and as to the contents of the Epistle, he finds much bombast.—

Kern:—*The character and origin of the Epistle of James*, Tübingen Magazine 1835, II. Why Hegesippus did not mention the Epistle?

Baur:—"*Paulus*," p. 677; "*Christianity of the first three centuries*, p. 96."—On the ground of the well-known Ebionite hypothesis and of the assumption that the Epistle teaches a righteousness of good works against Paul. Schwegler in the train of Baur: "*The Post-apostolic Age*, vol. I. p. 413 etc. Reasons for the alleged spuriousness: 1, The want of individuality; 2, Christian antiquity unacquainted with the Epistle and its later recognition as canonical; 3, the mild form of Ebionitism it sets forth; 4, the internal church-relations assumed in it; 5, its acquaintance with the Pauline Epistles, the Epistle to the Hebrews and the Gospel according to the Hebrews.—Quite new, but also quite untenable is here especially the discovery of Ebionitism. The very name of James, the address to the twelve tribes, the word synagogue for Church are adduced in proof of the Ebionitism of the Epistle; the rich πλούσιοι—are to denote the Gentile Christians. But in that case, ch. ii. 2 would make the congregations addressed by the author non-Ebionite, Notwithstanding the strong language used against the rich (=Gentile Christians) the Epistle is alleged to be ironical, and said to aim at effecting a compromise between Jewish and Gentile Christians. For further counter-remarks see Huther p. 301 and Reuss § 146, Note. Huther p. 31 treats also Ritschl's view of the Epistle of James (which has however been modified in the 2d edition) and mentions Rauch's attack on the integrity of the passage ch. v. 10–12, which has been repelled by Hagenbach and Schneckenburger (see Guerike p. 448).

Credner considers the Epistle genuine as the production of the brother of the Lord and denies the authorship of James the Apostle. But this point is decided by the right apprehension of the Author's person (§ 1). Moreover it is to be noticed that Schott has revived the view of Bolten etc., that the Epistle is a free translation of the Aramean original; an assumption, devoid of all foundation.

The circumstance of the Epistle not being generally known to the ancient Church at an early date may be accounted for by the following considerations:

1, It was addressed to Jewish Christians (hence it occurs already in the Peschito, because in Syria in particular there were many Jewish Christians; this circumstance is rendered prominent by Ritschl);

2, The Epistle, in its tendency, presented only few dogmatical points, whereas the ancient Church reverted especially to dogmatical points;

3, The absence of the apostolic designation in the title and similar matter. See Guerike p. 444. The chief reason lay probably in the circumstance that the consciousness of the concrete relation of the Epistle, which made it appear in its whole weight, became gradually less prominent.

[Alford: " On the whole, on any intelligible principles of canonical reception of early writings, we cannot refuse this Epistle a place in the Canon. That that place was given it from the first in some part of the Church; that in spite of many adverse circumstances, it gradually won that place in other parts; that when thoroughly considered, it is so consistent with and worthy of his character and standing whose name it bears; that it is marked off by so strong a line of distinction from the writings and Epistles which have not attained a place in the Canon; all these are considerations which, though they do not in this, any more than in other cases, amount to demonstration, yet furnish when combined a proof hardly to be resisted, that the place where we now find it in the N. T. Canon is that which it ought to have, and which God in His Providence has guided His Church to assign to it."—M.].

3. OCCASION, DESTINATION AND OBJECT OF THE EPISTLE, ITS THEOLOGICAL AND STYLISTICAL CHARACTER.

We should be obliged to treat twice of the contents of this Epistle, were we to omit to consider first the question stated at the head of this section. For in order to gain a thorough appreciation of the full import and apostolical value of this Epistle our exposition should be duly influenced by the character of James, by his relation to the Jews and to Jewish Christians, by Jewish affairs belonging to its date and by the Christian-prophetical stylistic which demanded an address to his people. To the circumstance, that the Epistle of James, in most instances, has been dissociated from all these vital considerations, is mainly to be ascribed the manifold misunderstanding of the same. The consideration of the contents according to the leading thoughts and the total impression of the Epistle, to be sure, ought to precede the investigation relating to occasion, object etc., but the exposition of its historic genesis will enable us to understand it with reference to the whole of its glorious contents, that is, then also to set forth its contents in detail.

The title v. 1 shows that the Epistle of James was addressed to Jewish Christians in the widest sense of the term, for the whole people was only one *diaspora* (dispersion) viewed as a huge whole. The same remark applies to the First Epistle of Peter with reference to the Jewish Christians of Asia Minor and also to the Epistle to the Hebrews with reference to the Jewish Christians of Palestine.—The date of the Epistle of James falls most probably (as we conclude from the developed condition of the Jewish Christian Churches) into the latest period of his life, about A. D. 62. The date of the composition of the first Epistle of Peter we fix with Thiersch (63–64) at about A. D. 64 (see my *History of the Apost. Age*, I. p. 148 and II. p. 574) not with Weiss and Fronmüller A. D. 54 or 55, because at the latter period the prolonged activity of Peter at Babylon and the multiplication of Jewish Christian Churches in Pontius are entirely out of the question. To the same period, to A. D. 62–64, belongs the Epistle to the Hebrews (see my *Apostolic Age*, I. 75; cf. this Commentary on the Epistle to the Hebrews, where for good reasons the date given is the interval between the death of James in A. D. 61 or 63, and the beginning of the Jewish war in A. D. 67).

Said three Epistles addressed to Jewish Christians originated therefore in a period when the Jewish revolution against the supremacy of the Romans had already begun to germ and ferment in the minds of the Jewish people. The proper foundation of this revolution had already been laid by the crucifixion of Christ, but especially by the rejection of Christianity sealed with the execution of James (see my *Apost. Age*, Vol. II. p. 427). Thereby the preserving and saving element had been separated from the Jewish nationality, which henceforth, developed into perfect pharisaism, stood arrayed in deadly enmity both against the pagans and the Christians. The pagan instinct, however, returned this antagonism also in its representatives, the Roman governors and thus provocation and persecution increased on the part of the pagans, and fanatical commotions and tumults on that of the Jews. So already Felix, the proconsul, treated the Jews worse than his predecessors and the Jews in their turn resented his maltreatment by several insurrections, especially under the leadership of an Egyptian who took 30,000 men to the Mount of Olives. Similar jarrings and revolts were repeated under Festus. The Jews on the whole, restrained themselves as yet under the proconsulate of Albinus (A. D. 63–65). But the war broke out in A. D. 66 under Gessius Florus. The rupture among the Jews and Gentiles turned into open revolution first at Cæsarea; immediately afterwards at Jerusalem and the flames of the most atrocious religious war spread on all sides, to Scythopolis, Damascus, Askalon, Ptolemais, Hippo and Alexandria; everywhere the Jews were slaughtered by thousands.

It must be assumed, that the same excited, enthusiastic and fanatical disposition flashed from Jerusalem through the entire Jewish diaspora and that the hope of miraculous deliverance and the impulse of revolutionary self-help and revenge conspired every where with their animosity against the Gentiles, who in their turn were filled with equal deadly hatred.

Such was the situation. But now must be taken into account the powerful effect of such national sympathy and antipathy on the Jewish Christians. Nationally they were still Jews and Jewish blood stirred and boiled in their veins. They were in common with the Jews attacked and tempted on the one hand, by the hatred, contempt and oppression of the pagans; and on the other by Jewish-national sympathy, by their yearning for deliverance and by their chiliastic, enthusiastic hopes. The national movements of modern and quite recent times offer appropriate illustrations of the powerful influence of such a national revolutionary current on the individual members of the respective people. That movement was consequently the great seductive alternative that lay before the Jewish Christians of that period. Standing aloof from the revolutionary movement, they were cursed and persecuted as apostates by their national brethren. We know from history how much the Christians had to suffer in this respect during the later insurrection of the Jews under Bar Cochba in the time of Hadrian. Bare sympathy on the other hand with the chimerical enthusiasm of the Jews, was entering the road to apostasy (for they exchanged the faith in Christ for the hope of a pseudo-messianic deliverance), falling into unbelief of the justice of God in the judgment that was coming on their people and severing the bond of church-fellowship with the Gentile-Christians, while they were restoring religious fellowship with Christ-murdering fanaticism.

Hence the Spirit of Christ on all sides warned them and confirmed their faith in this their situation; and the above-mentioned three Epistles are the documents of this guardian Spirit, and in this light alone can they be rightly understood. They are therefore the most appropriate sequel to the prophetical warnings, cautions and exhortations of the eschatological speech of Christ in Matth. xxiv. 16 etc.

Even if the revolutionary spirit had been less developed during the last days of James, his prophetical forebodings would sufficiently account for his hortatory Epistle (v. ch. v. 1); as in a similar manner a prophetical presentiment of the Church anticipated a dearth (Acts xi. 27); and foretold the imprisonment of Paul (Acts xxi. 10).

James had the immediate and wide-reaching vocation to confirm the Jewish Christians, without incautiously delineating the impending revolution in colours too positive. Hence he issued a circular letter to the twelve tribes in the dispersion.

This address has been variously interpreted: it is maintained that the Epistle addresses converted and unconverted Jews (Grotius, Wolf, Credner etc.), Jewish Christians and Gentile Christians as divided parties (Kern), as a closed society (de Wette and others), Jewish Christians (Neander, Guerike, Wiesinger etc.). See Wiesinger's Introduction. (The views, which assign to the Epistle a wholly particular destination, *e. g.* Noesselt: to the Christians at Antioch, see in Hertwig's Tables p. 51). Huther (p. 12) lays stress on the consideration that the Author saw only in Jewish *Christians* true Jews and that there did not then exist so sharp a separation of Judaism and Christianity.

We rather think it necessary to lay stress on the circumstance that James, according to the relations he bore to his people, and as long as that people had not set the seal to their obstinacy in the last symptoms of their apostasy (viz.: the execution of their bishops and their chiliastic revolution against the pagan authorities which involved their renunciation of Christian salvation), not only saw in the Jews catechumens of Christianity by birth, but he also saw in the Jewish Christians the true Jews. Addressing therefore the twelve tribes, he did not address the Jews in a dogmatical sense as associates of the old religious communion, but he did address the Jews as his theocratico-national brethren, the noblest part of whom had already become his brethren in the faith and all of whom were *called* to become his brethren in the faith. His primary object of course was to warn the Jewish Christians against taking part in the fanatical revolutionary spirit of the Jews, but surely his secondary purpose was to warn the Jews against being carried away by the hostility and oppression of the tyranny into revolt and the final falling away from the patience of Christ. We admit therefore the correctness of the following remark of Guerike (p. 435) "Strictly speaking the twelve tribes in the diaspora certainly denote only those living out of Palestine, but in a more general sense the term does not exclude the Jews living in Palestine and the contents of the Epistle show that the term is here used in the latter sense."

The point, therefore, on which James felt constrained to speak to all his brethren was to advert to the fact that they were exposed to a great and manifold temptation and that they needed great perseverance in the spirit of Christ's patience. Especially he felt called upon to encourage believers (ch. i.); solemnly to threaten those who had thus far persevered in unbelief and self-righteousness (ch. v. 1); variously to instruct, warn and admonish the tempted and manifold-wavering brethren (ch. ii. etc.]. On the other hand he had to couch his warning against the chiliastico-political fanaticism of his time in terms sufficiently general and cautious in order to avoid the suspicion of being mixed up with the political issues of the question, that is, he had to treat it on purely religious grounds.

The further destination of his pastoral Epistle for all Jewish Christians, relatively including the Jews, accounts also for the careful Greek diction which is characteristic of the Epistle. It also explains the Hebrew-symbolical character of the Epistle whereby it is related to the prophetical style of the O. T. This character surely is wholly misunderstood, if the Epistle is made to yield the result that in the Churches, whom James addresses, the poor on account of their faith were oppressed by the rich, that the rich were flattered in their religious assemblies etc. As in ch. i. the twelve tribes represent the people of God in its present state of development of actual and future Christliness,* as the ἀνὴρ δίψυχος denotes the man who doubtingly wavers between faith and apostasy, so the poor represent the humble and those who believe through humility, but the rich denote the self-righteous and those who are unbelieving through self-righteousness. And again as in ch. ii. the synagogue describes the assembly of the congregation, and the rich man with a gold ring and a splendid garment denotes the proud, Ebionitising Jewish Christian parading his ring of the Jewish Covenant, while the poor man with a vile garment describes the Gentile Christian, so faith denotes here in the theocratic sense the Jewish theocratic rightness-of-belief (Thiersch, too strong: *Jewish orthodoxy*), while the work of faith on the other hand signifies the energy and consistency of life exhibited in faith-work, which is the evidence of living faith; the New Testament faith, consistency of life, the work *in grandi*, which is the evidence of the vitality of the O. T. faith, but especially the N. T. faith as brotherly love towards Gentile Christians (the poor brother, the poor sister). And as in ch. iii. the becoming teachers of many (πολλοὶ διδάσκαλοι γίνεσθε) denotes the doctrinal, propagandistic nature of the Jewish Christians and the Jews (v. Rom. ii. 17 etc.), so the fiery spark which grows into a great conflagration describes Jewish fanaticism. In ch. iv. the wars and disruptions (E. V. *fightings*) probably denote not only disputes and sectarism, but the adulterers and adulteresses describe not such persons in a literal but in the O. T. religious sense, viz.: apostates or such as are inclined that way. As ch. iv. 13, 14 contains a prophetical allusion to the sad transformation of the gain-seeking Jewish diaspora, so ch. v. foretells the great judgment impending on the rich, on self-righteous Judaism. These hints may suffice to show that the character of the Epistle answers to its end and aim. For this very reason its specifically Christian character comes out only in general outlines. The wide-reaching destination of the Epistle would hardly admit of a too definite dogmatical treatment.

That the receivers proper of the Epistle were really Christians is manifest from its fundamental Christian tone: "Servant of the Lord Jesus Christ—brethren, beloved brethren,—he begat us with the word of truth—the good (E. V. worthy) name—the killing of the Just—the nearness of the Lord—" etc. see Huther, p. 12. That on the other hand these Christians were Jewish Christians is evident from "the synagogue" ii. 2; the prominence given to monotheism ii. 19; the enumeration of Jewish formulæ of oaths v. 12 etc.; and still more from the characteristic features of Jewish improprieties which are denounced; such as pride of faith, fanaticism, conceit and such like (Wiesinger, Schaff, Thiersch, Huther).

As regards the place of writing, the Authorship of James determines also the place where he wrote the Epistle, viz. Jerusalem: "The conjecture of Schwegler that the real place of writing was not Jerusalem but Rome, is nothing but a fiction invented in favour of his hypothesis." Huther.

*** The German has "in seinem jetzigen Entwicklungsstande *gewordener* und *werdender* Christlichkeit"—the literal meaning of *geworden* is "that to which it already has attained," of *werdender* "that to which it is attaining, or which it is in process of *becoming*;" actual and future seemed the best equivalents we could find without a lengthy circumlocution. Christliness is a word of my coining—I had to coin it, because the German Christlichkeit has no English equivalent or representative.—M.].**

[Jerusalem was the centre of attraction to the Jews of the Diaspora; many of the Jewish Christians were doubtless in the habit of attending the feasts and thus centrally located, James had every facility of information as to the religious condition of those Jewish Christians and of oral or written intercourse with them.—The physical notices found in the Epistle support the supposition that the Epistle was written at Jerusalem. The author wrote not far from the sea, ch. i. 6; iii. 4; he lived in a land blessed with oil, wine and figs, iii. 12; he was familiar with salt and bitter springs, iii. 11, 12; the land was exposed to drought, rain was a matter of great importance to the inhabitants, vv. 17, 18; the land was burnt up quickly by a hot wind (ch. i. 11, καύσων, a name especially known in Palestine); the author names the former and the latter rain, πρώϊμος and ὄψιμος, as they were called in Palestine, ch. v. 7. See Hug. Einleitung, ed. 4, p. 438 etc. and Alford, Prol. to James III., 2, 3.—M.].

On the *date* of the Epistle opinions are much divided. Pfeiffer (*Studien und Kritiken*, 1852, Ch. I., p. 95), Schneckenburger, Theile, Neander, Thiersch, Hofmann, Schaff (and in less decided language also Huther) say that it was written before the Apostolic Council at Jerusalem, but Schmidt, Guerike and Wiesinger maintain that it was written after it. Huther gives the ollowing reason: "After that time the Pauline doctrine that man is justified not ἐξ ἐργων but ἐκ πίστεως not only had become generally known but also had so profoundly moved the mind of Christendom, that it is inconceivable that James in view of this circumstance could utter his ἐξ ἐργων etc. in perfect ignorance of it." This reason may also be reversed thus: If James wrote this Epistle earlier in an anti-Pauline sense, he would not have declared at the Apostolic Council that he was in agreement with Paul. We ought rather to distinguish between the historico-theocratic sense (Monotheism) and the specifically-Christian sense of the word faith. The chief reasons for the later date of the Epistles, namely, shortly before the death of James, are these. The spread of Christianity through the entire Jewish diaspora, and the general recognition of the authority of James by the entire Jewish Diaspora in relation to the death of James (A. D 62–63) required to be fixed at the latest possible date.—Then we have the important consideration that a general temptation of all Jewish-Christendom to falling away from the faith arose for the first time with the first germinating beginnings of the Jewish revolution or with the more positive opposition of the hatred of the pagans to the fanaticism of the Jews. To this must be added the highly important consonancy in which our Epistle in this respect stands to the first Epistle of Peter and the Epistle to the Hebrews.*

4. THE RELATION OF OUR EPISTLE TO THE PAULINE EPISTLES, THE CATHOLIC EPISTLES, TO THE MOST HOMOGENEOUS EPISTLES VIZ. THE FIRST OF PETER AND THAT TO THE HEBREWS. ITS NEW TESTAMENT PECULIARITY.

A. JAMES AND PAUL.

The apparent contradiction between the doctrine of James (ch. ii. 24) and the doctrine of Paul (Rom. iii. 28; iv. 2) concerning justification and the question connected with it as to the relation of faith and works, did already cause Luther to be greatly staggered, and because he considered the contradiction as founded on fact, to induce him to pass the above-mentioned unfavourable opinion on the Epistle of James. In modern times theology has been much engaged with the discussion of the question whether or not James and Paul contradict each other.

The answer of this question has occasioned a group of different questions:

1. In favour of a real contradiction are Luther and his immediate followers, and recently Strœbel, Cyrillos Lucaris (see Neander's *History of the Planting* etc., *Bohn's edition*, Vol. I., p. 357), de Wette, Kern, Lutz (*Bibl. Dogmatik*, p. 170), Baur, Schwegler.

2. For a contradiction against the misinterpretation and the abuse of the Pauline doctrine on the ground of an essential agreement between Paul and James, are several ancient expositors. Augustine, Grotius (see his *Annotationes ad N. T.* II. p. 973), Gebser, p. 214, and others.

3. There is no contradiction either of Paul himself, or of the abuse of his doctrine; this view starts on the supposition that the dogmatical tropus of James, which differs from that of Paul,

* Only for the sake of noticing it, we have to add that Schwegler has removed the origin of the Epistle to a late period of the second century.

took shape sooner than the latter—so Schneckenburger, Theile, Neander, Schaff, Thiersch, Hofmann, Huther (p. 35).

4. There is no contradiction, but an antithesis and difference of dogmatical tropus. Although according to its internal relations it is the first and earliest of the N. T., it does not follow that it must also have preceded the doctrine of Paul chronologically. Schmid, Wiesinger and others.

Ad. 1. It has been supposed that the illustration of Abraham ch. ii. 21 was chosen intentionally in opposition to the application of the same illustration in Rom. iv. 1 etc.; and the illustration of Rahab, the harlot ch. ii. 25 in opposition to the application of the same illustration in Heb. xi. 31. The following circumstances, apart from the otherwise perceptible unity of spirit in the two Epistles, militate against the supposed contradiction.

a. The historically-proven assent of James to the doctrine of Paul, see Acts xv. and Gal. ii.

b. The manifest and demonstrable difference of James and Paul in the definition of the terms πίστις, ἔργα, δικαιοῦσθαι.

c. The actual agreement of doctrine which follows from an unprejudiced conception of the differing points of view and from the exposition of the respective passages. For while with James πίστις does not denote orthodoxism, because this faith may be animated by energy of life or the evidence of works (ch. i. 25), it does denote the historico-theocratical orthodoxy, which is to evidence its efficient power in consistency of life, indefatigable activity (ἐντέλεχεια) and energy of Christian deportment. And it is this very energy, which St. Paul calls faith, the evidence of which is its working by love.

ἔργα with James are not the dead works of the law (ch. ii. 10) but the living evidence of faith in works (ch. ii. 8). If it is alleged that James had developed a defective idea of faith, it may be alleged with equal force that Paul has developed a defective idea of works. But both would be false. With Paul living faith as the work of works excludes dead works: with James the living work-of-faith as the evidence of faith excludes dead faith. Faith without works is dogma-righteousness, *orthodoxism.* Works without the foundation of faith are work-righteousness, *ergism.*

But James as well as Paul acknowledges the δικαιοῦν ἐκ πίστεως; only he calls it λογίζεσθαι εἰς δικαιοσύνην (see ch. ii. 23) while he understands by δικαιοῦσθαι Paul's δοκιμάζεσθαι, σφραγίζεσθαι. See Calvin *ad loc.* Huther, p. 127, and others; my *Apost. Age,* I., p. 171; the Article *Jacobus* in Herzog, p. 417.

But his point of view is not the work-righteousnes of the Jews, but the dogma-righteousness of the Jewish-Christians and Jews, a tendency which Paul also has distinguished from the tendency of ergism, as one at once Jewish-Christian and Jewish. See Neander, *Plant.*, Vol. I., p. 358., Brückner on de Wette, p. 199.

Ad. 2. It is not probable, that an abuse of the Pauline doctrine should have spread just among the Jewish-Christians, to whom James wrote. Neander, *Plant.* Vol. I. p. 359; Brückner, p. 189; Huther, p. 32.

Ad. 3. The supposition that James' dogma-tropus as related to Paul's must be taken as being undeveloped as to its forms (Neander, Schaff and others), cannot be proved.

a. Because the circular Epistle of James cannot be regarded as a complete development of his system of Christian dogma.

b. Because the use of gnomical and tropical forms in James alongside of the dialectical forms in Paul does not constitute an inferior degree of completeness, but rather the coordination of a Jewish Christian mode of teaching with the Gentile Christian mode of teaching of Paul. In like manner the historical conception of this view which assigns a very early date to the Epistle of James, has not been proved (see section 3).

Ad. 4. The view advanced under this head, as to its most important features, is sufficiently conclusive from the foregoing explanations.

On the other relations of Paul and James, relations of affinity and contrariety, which have been explained as relations of dependence and polemics, cf. Brückner on de Wette's Commentary, p. 188. [The treatise of Bp. Bull, *Harmonia Apostolica,* discusses this whole question very fully and learnedly, and the eminent author reaches the conclusion that our Epistle is not contradictory, but rather supplementary to the Epistles of St. Paul to the Romans and Galatians. Compare also on the same side Barrow's Sermon on Justifying Faith, Works, Vol. IV., Serm. 5, p. 123.—M.].

B. THE EPISTLE OF JAMES AND THE CATHOLIC EPISTLES IN GENERAL.

Besides its evangelical destination, which this Epistle has in common with most of the Catholic Epistles, it shares with all of them the Jewish-Christian type of doctrine which puts dialectics in the background and gnomical and symbolico-figurative forms in the foreground (see Huther, p. 21). Its gnomical mode of statement establishes its chief affinity to the Epistles of John, its symbolical expression establishes its affinity to the Epistle of Jude, the second of Peter (ch. ii.), and besidés, to the Epistle to the Hebrews which is closely connected with the Catholic Epistles.

C. THE EPISTLE OF JAMES, THE FIRST EPISTLE OF PETER AND THE EPISTLE TO THE HEBREWS, A TRILOGY.

Above we have already pointed out the sole significance of this trilogy. They have in common the tendency of earnestly preparing the Jewish Christians in the impending outbreak of the Jewish war for the great temptation to apostasy, to which they were exposed by the hostility and oppression of the pagans and the fanaticism and revolutionary spirit of the Jews. They all aim at strengthening the Jewish-Christian people for that great temptation and at warning them of the great apostasy (see above). Here James the Apostle [?] starts with the harmony of the Jewish law itself as necessarily leading to its perfection in the Christian law of liberty, the first Epistle of Peter starts with the fulfilment of the promise of the Old Testament-kingdom in the New Testament-kingdom of inheritance, while the Epistle to the Hebrews starts with the superiority of the cultus of the New Testament to the covenant-cultus of the Old Testament. The warning of James describes the principal danger of his brethren as a *double-mindedness gravitating at once towards God and the world and the breaking out in impatience* the warning of Peter delineates it as *indecision and visionary enthusiasm* (ch. i. 13), while the warning of the Epistle to the Hebrews characterizes it as *unbelief, apostasy and rebellion.* But the spheres of their operation also are different. The first Epistle of Peter is addressed to the Jewish-Christians in Asia Minor written at Babylon, the Epistle to the Hebrews is probably addressed chiefly to the Jewish-Christians in Palestine written at Rome or in Italy, the Epistle of James is addressed to the Jewish-Christians throughout the world, written at Jerusalem.

D. THE NEW TESTAMENT PECULIARITY OF JAMES.

Besides the references of our Epistle to the Old Testament, to the book of Jesus the Son of Sirach and to the Gospels in general (ch. i. 17 to Matth. vii. 11; i. 20 to Matth. v. 22; i. 22 to Matth. vii. 21; i. 25 to Jno. xiii. 17 etc.), its references to the Sermon on the Mount also have been particularly noticed. See Brückner on de Wette, p. 187; Huther, p. 18.—James, to be sure, exhibits the glorification of the Old Testament law into the New Testament law of the Spirit, of the inner life (see Messner) in perfect analogy to the manner of Christ in the Sermon on the Mount. And this then is also his peculiar dogma-tropus. It bears as much the character of the New Testament as does the dogma-tropus of Paul and that of John, but in respect of the development of the doctrine of Christ, it occupies the first place among the dogma-tropes of the New Testament, without ignoring however the specific features of the later dogma-tropes (see my *Apost. Age,* II. p. 577). And this is the peculiarity of James. The wisdom which had been personified individually in the Logos of Truth, is also to be personified in the life of believers by *believing heart-decision* and thereby to conduct them through the fearful ruin of apostasy into which the fanatical disciples of the *double-hearted* earthly wisdom plunge headlong (ch. iii. 15) it is to evidence itself in them as steadfast patience in the joyous expectation of the advent of Christ. To this mode of teaching answers the gnomical, New-Testament-Solomonic-calm radiance of his language, the festively sententious form of which exhibits an affinity to the language of John, although unlike the latter it is not the expression of a contemplative intuition, but that of a practical energy.

5. THE CONTENTS OF OUR EPISTLE.

The theme of the Epistle is evidently contained in the macarism ch. i. 12. "Blessed is the man that *endureth* temptation etc." Here it is noteworthy that the reference is not to man in general but to man in a sexual sense and that we read immediately afterwards "The wrath of man (ἀνδρός) worketh not the righteousness of God." We confidently assume that the reference is to a temptation to which Jewish-Christian *men* were peculiarly exposed; viz.: the thought cherished by the Jewish *men* that the righteous judgment of God on the pagans would have to be executed by an armed insurrection against them. This fundamental theme is resumed in the final theme, ch. v. 7: "Be patient (persevering in long-suffering) therefore, brethren, unto the coming of the Lord."

The Salutation and Introduction, in the first place, correspond to the leading thought. In the Salutation the Apostle introduces himself as a *bondman* of God and of the Lord Jesus Christ, intimating thereby that in virtue of this servile relation he was freed from the *bondage* under which the Jews were groaning (Jno. viii. 36). He addresses the Epistle to the twelve tribes of the dispersion because he wants to include in one category the Jews as yet unbelieving and the believing Jews, the category, that is, of theocratico-historical catechumens of Christianity, inasmuch as the final historical hardening of Israel had not yet taken place. His Salutation is couched in the Greek form χαίρειν, and apart from the example of toleration indicated by the selection of this expression, this word serves also the purpose of introducing his first idea. They should not yield to the gloomy and desponding disposition which was animating the rebellious spirits, but rejoice conformably to their Christian faith (v. 2).

The Introduction states that they should also rejoice in their *versicoloured* temptation (ποικίλοις probably more than divers, manifold), use them for their proof [δοκίμον—M.] and not to run to ruin by wavering. The means he recommends is prayer, but prayer in faith without doubting; consequently a firm and undivided heart. Along with this the brother, who is crushed by his humble lot (surely with particular reference to his national position), is to glory in his Christian exaltation; but the Jewish-Christian, conscious of his theocratico-national riches, is to glory in his lowness. This can hardly mean his poverty in spirit or his humility before God but his historical lowness, the bondage-form of his Jewish and Christian life of faith. For the time of glory has already gone by, the grass is withered and the flower has fallen. The confident rich man (the Jew in the pride of his theocratic riches) will fade away in his occupation or schemes. Ch. i. 1–11.

The Apostle now expatiates on the theme of the Epistle viz. the exhortation to perseverance in temptation from ch. i. 13—v. 6.

I. The most important admonition, then, the Apostle names first. *Let them not in the enthusiasm of self-delusion pervert their temptation into the cause of God,* which was really done by the Jewish fanatics. Here James delineates first the contrast between the false, hypocritically decorated phantom of temptation and temptation in its true, hideous and deadly form; secondly the actual providential rule of God in its most universal character, who had made them, as Christians, the first-fruits of His creatures. Ch. i. 13–18.

II. The second admonition warns them *against fanatical zeal itself.* The wrath of *man* [sexually=ἀνδρός—M.] does not accomplish the decree of the righteousness of God. Its development must be traced to the rashness and recklessness of self-complacency. Do they wish to avoid it, let them not think that they are pure and rich but laying aside their uncleanness and overflowing riches of malice let them meekly yield themselves to the efficient operation of the implanted word. As doers of this word they will effectually guard themselves against self-deception. But they must steadily contemplate this word and enter into it, as into the perfect law of liberty. The Jew considers himself to be religious [θρῆσκος=observant of God's outward service—M.] in that his zeal of wrath gives the reins to his tongue; but their Christian true service [θρησκεία=outward service—M.] should be evidenced in their care of the orphan and widow (especially of the crushed people in its orphanage and widowhood) and their self-preservation from the pollution of the world. Ch. i. 19–27.

III. The third admonition opposes *their contempt of the pagans, especially also their contempt of Gentile-Christians.* On this account James starts with faith in Jesus Christ, the Lord of glory which admits of no respect of persons. Hence we see in the man with a gold ring on his finger, in a splendid garment, the portrait of the Jewish-Christian or the Jewish convert according to Jewish notions, in the poor man, on the other hand, in a vile garment the portrait of the Gentile-Christian or of the Gentile convert. [Lange understands by the Jewish convert and the Gentile convert those whose conversion is going on, in process of being, but not yet completed.—M.]. They ought to consider both as equals in their synagogue (assembly); yea, they should remember that those poor of this world are rich in faith, while those really rich are the proud Jews, their persecutors and the defamers of their Christian name. They are therefore to observe the royal law "Thou shalt love thy neighbour (co-religionists in a higher sense) as thyself" and to have no respect of persons. The law is a unit. Now in supposing that as true Israelites they avoid the adultery of apostasy, while with their unmerciful fanaticism they kill their Christian Gentile brother (cf. 1 Jno. iii. 15), they are transgressing the whole law. In this form the law itself becomes a law of liberty; its living totality delivers from the bondage of its single letters. In connection with this thought,—faith contrasted with works—denotes further the theocratic, Jewish-Christian orthodoxy, while the works denote the living, energetic proof of faith. The monotheism of the Jew, says James, is altogether insufficient, for the devils also participate in it. True faith must prove its vitality in the work of love, especially in brotherly love. The examples chosen in illustration are most telling. Abraham, sacrificing Isaac his son is a type of the Jewish-Christian who sacrifices his national claims; Rahab, the harlot is a type of the Gentile Christian, who came by the work-of-faith into communion with the people of God. Ch. ii.

IV. The Apostle, in the fourth place, considers it matter of great moment, to *dissuade the Jews from their fondness for fanatical teaching*, which was their characteristic both in their intercourse with the pagans in particular and with those of a different turn of mind in general (cf. Matth. xxiii. 15; Rom. ii. 19). They transgressed particularly with their irrepressibly-busy, didactic tongue, inclined to condemn and curse. The consequence of such a tendency the Apostle shows to be an earthly, sensual and devilish wisdom, born of envying and strife; with this he contrasts heavenly wisdom with the beautiful attributes of love and the blessing of peace. Ch. iii.

V. The Apostle, in the fifth place, now indicates to the Judaistically prejudiced Jewish Christians and with them to the Jews the infallible mark whereby they may perceive that their stand-point is not true; *fanatics*, he says, *live in strife and war among themselves as well as with others.* The *root* of this quarrelsomeness, he says, are lusts and worldly desires, which in their sensual life are at war with one another; its *fruit*, disappointment and the failure of all their striving, contention and even of their prayer. Ch. iv. 1–3.

VI. James now proceeds in the sixth place, to disclose the ground of those egotistical, pleasurable lusts. It is *the apostasy of the (spiritual adulterers and) adulteresses from the living God* by their worldly-mindedness; their friendship with the world (in a spiritual garb) is enmity with God. Here the portrait of Judaism appears in the foreground with increasing distinctness. It lacks the spirit which is opposed to hatred, the spirit of humility to which grace is accorded. Pursuant thereto are the exhortations which follow: Be *true* Israelites in relation to God; *true* subjects of God, *truly* praying and sacrificing to God (v. 8), *truly* purified and God-affianced (v. 8), *truly* poor and humble in the sense of the Old Testament (vv. 9, 10). Be *true* Israelites in relation to the brethren; avoid slandering, condemning and cursing! Be *true* Israelites in your dispersion-life (Diaspora-life, so *German.*—M.]! Do not yield yourselves in blind confidence to your planning, to go from city to city with a view to traffic and gain, but realize your transitoriness and dependence on God! Otherwise all your knowledge of good will turn to sin and judgment (vv. 11–17). Ch. iv. 4–17.

VII. These admonitions, the Apostle concludes, in the seventh place, by *a powerful denunciation of woe on the rich, doubtless on the Judaizing Jewish-Christians and Jews* who called themselves poor but thought themselves rich in their Jewish privileges, and here the affinity of his mode of statement with that of the prophets, becomes quite prophetical. It contains the prophecy of judgment, of a judgment which, with the destruction of Jerusalem, soon afterwards came upon

Judaism. Let them weep, *i. e.* be penitent. Their riches are corrupted etc., *i. e.* all their self-righteousness has turned to sin and disgrace. They confide in and boast of this treasure before the near day of judgment. But that which brings judgment rapidly near is the crying of the hire withheld from their labourers and reapers, the ingratitude to and the rejection of Apostles and believers, who had undertaken the harvest of Israel. The day of slaughter, which shall come on their pleasure-life, is nigh at hand, and has opened with the condemnation and murder of the Just, who now no longer arrests their running into destruction (ch. v. 1–6).

Then follows the final theme and the conclusion. Once more he addresses the brethren. Let them in long-suffering patience persevere unto the coming of the Lord (v. 7).

1. Encouragement thereto: the example of the husbandman waiting for the harvest (vv. 7, 8).
2. Conditions of that patience.
   a. They must not murmur against one another in disaffection, *i. e.* they must not nourish in their hearts the spirit of fanatical hardness and alienation. Examples: the prophets; the patience of Job; the end of the Lord (vv. 9–11).
   b. The excitement of swearing and complications by oaths they must avoid, and hallow their minds (v. 12).
   c. They must cheer their minds by prayer, praise, the help of the presiding officers of the Church, and the confession of sins (vv. 13–16).
3. Elias the type of wonder-working [effective—M.] prayer, whose first prayer effected the miracle of chastisement and his second the miracle of mercy (vv. 17, 18).
4. Conclusion. Exhortation containing a promise of blessing on the effort of reclaiming an erring brother. Every one should engage in this work, and whoever succeeds, does thereby save a soul from death and prevent the multitudinous evil of sin (vv. 19, 20). Ch. v. 9–20.

The existing tables of contents do not exhibit a perfect, organical structure of the Epistle, because the idea which animates all its separate parts, has not been laid down as the foundation of the Epistle. The construction of the Epistle has been treated *in extenso* by Pfeiffer, *On the connection of the Epistle of James*, Stud. and Krit., 1850, Part 1; in Wiesinger's division in his Commentary, p. 46; in Huther's division in his Commentary, p. 15; de Wette and Schleiermacher see neither plan nor order in the Epistle. See Brückner, p. 182 (his own exposition, p. 184); Schleiermacher, p. 421.

6. LITERATURE.

See HEIDEGGER, *Enchiridion*, I., p. 617. LILIENTHAL, *Bibl. Archivarius*, p. 784. WINER'S *Handbuch der Theol. Literatur*, I., pp. 268 and 271. *Supplement*, p. 42. DANZ, *Universal-Wœrterbuch*, p. 421. *Supplement*, p. 51. DE WETTE, *Introd.* 6th ed. p. 362. *Wiesinger's* Commentary, p. 45.—See General Works on the Bible. (Among the most recent works on the Bible is the Critical and Practical Commentary on the New Testament, by C. W. NAST, Cincinnati and Bremen, 1860);—also Commentaries on the *Catholic Epistles*.

Particular exegetical works.

ROMAN CATHOLIC: LORINUS, 1622; PRICÆUS, 1646.

LUTHERAN: WINKELMANN, ALTHAMER, BROCHMANN, LAURENTIUS etc

REFORMED: ZWINGLI, CALVIN, COCCEIUS and others.

MODERN: BENSON, SEMLER, BAUMGARTEN, HERDER, (*Briefe Zweener Briefe Jesu in unserm Kanon*), STORR, MORUS, HENSLER, HOTTINGER, POTT, SCHULTHESS, GEBSER (Berlin, 1828), SCHNECKENBURGER (1832), THEILE (1833), KERN (1838), J. J. CELLERIER (*Etude et commentaire sur l'Epitre de St. Jaques*, Genève, 1850), A. NEANDER, *Pract. Exposition, edited by Schneider* (1850), WIESINGER (Vol. VI. Sect. 1 of Olshausen's Commentary), HUTHER (Sect. 15 of MEYER'S Comment., 2d ed., 1863), BRÜCKNER'S edition of DE WETTE'S Commentary, Vol. III., Part. 1, 3d ed., 1865.

DUTCH WORKS: *De Brief van Jac., bearbeid door J.* CLARISSE, Amsterdam, 1802; M. STUART, *Amsterdam*, 1806; *Proeve eener Verklaring etc. door* G. VAN KOSTEN, Amsterdam 1821; JACOBUS etc. VAN FRIESEMA, Utr., 1842; G. VAN LEEUWEN, 1855; VINKE, 1861; *Dis-*

sertatio de Jacobi Epistolæ cum Syracidæ libro etc. convenientia, Gröningen, 1860; Recently appeared: H. BOUMANN, *Comm. perpet. in Jacobi Epistolam*, Utrecht, 1865.

FOR THE PARTICULAR TREATMENT OF THE EPISTLE see HEISEN, FLACHS, FABER. WINER, I. p. 272; DANZ, p. 421 etc.; *Supplement*, p. 51. WIESINGER, p. 46. HERTWIG, *Tabellen*, p. 51.—We must also mention, *The Apocryphal Protevangelium of James*, edited by SUCKOW (Breslau, 1841).

FOR DOGMATICAL TREATMENT consult the works on Biblical or New Testament Theology in general. See the list in HAGENBACH'S *Encyclopædia*, 6th ed. p. 201.

ON THE DOCTRINE OF THE APOSTLES: LUTTERBECK, die *Neutestamentlichen Lehrbegriffe*, 1852; MESSNER, die *Lehre der Apostel und Neutestamentlichen Schriftsteller*, 1856; *History of the Apostolic Age*, NEANDER, SCHAFF, LANGE.—RITSCHL, *Origin of the Old-Catholic Church*;—SCHAFF, das *Verhältniss des Jacobus, Bruders des Herrn, zu dem Jacobus Alphœi, Berlin*, 1842.

FOR SPECIAL PRACTICAL TREATMENT see BALTHASAR KERNER, *Jakobsstab oder Erklärung der Epistel Jacobi in* 60 *Predigten*, Ulm, 1639. HARTMANN CREIDIUS, *Jakob's Schatz, oder* 91 *Predigten über die Epistel Jacobi*, Frankfurt, 1694; DANIEL GRIEBNER, *Erklärung etc.* in 79 Predigten, Leipzig, 1720. GOLTZIUS, *de allgemene Sendbrief des Apostels Jacobus verklaart en toegeeygent, Amsterdam*, 1698; Similarly JANSSONIUS, Grœningen, 1742.—K. BRAUNE, *die Sieben Katholischen Briefe.—Die Briefe des Jakobus und Judas*, Grimma, 1847; JAKOBI, *der Brief des Jakobus, ausgelegt in* 19 *Predigten*, Berlin, 1835; STIER, *der Brief des Jakobus in* 32 *Betrachtungen ausgelegt*, Barmen, 1845; DRÆSEKE, *Predigten über den Brief Jakobi*, 1851; VIEDEBANDT, *der Brief Jakobi in Bibelstunden*, Berlin, Schulze, 1859; *Jakobus, der Zeuge vom lebendigen Glauben. Eine Reihenfolge von Predigten über den ganzen Brief Jakobi, von G. Porubszky*, evang. Pfarrer in Wien, Wien, 1861.

[*English Commentaries on James.*

TURNBULL, RICHARD, *Exposition on the Canonical Epistle of St. James* in 28 lectures, 4vo., Lond., 1606; MAYER, JOHN, *Praxis Theologica, or the Epistle of the Apostle James resolved, expounded and preached upon, by way of doctrine and use*, 4vo., Lond., 1629; MANTON, THOM., D. D., *A Practical Commentary: or an Exposition with Notes on the Epistle of James*, 4vo., Lond., 1653. Repr. imp. 8vo., Lond, 1840; 8vo, Lond., 1842.

See also STANLEY, *Essays and Sermons on the Apostolic Age*, Lond., 1852; the *General Commentaries*, those *on the Apostolical and Catholic Epistles.*—M.]

COMMENTARY.

THE EPISTLE GENERAL OF JAMES.[1]

I. INTRODUCTION.

THE SALUTATION OF THE SERVANT OF GOD AND OF THE LORD JESUS CHRIST TO THE TWELVE TRIBES IN THE DISPERSION. REFERENCE TO THE VARIEGATED TEMPTATIONS TO WHICH THEY ARE EXPOSED, AND TO THE JOYFUL DESIGN OF THE SAME: THEIR CONSUMMATION.

CHAPTER I. 1–11.

JAMES, a servant of God and of the Lord Jesus Christ, to the twelve tribes which
2 are scattered abroad,[2] greeting.[3] My brethren, count[4] it all joy when ye fall into
3 divers temptations.[5] Knowing *this*, that the trying[6] of your faith[7] worketh patience.[8]
4 But let patience[9] have *her* perfect work,[10] that ye may be perfect and entire, wanting
5 nothing.[11] If any of you lack wisdom,[12] let him ask of God that giveth to all *men*
6 liberally,[13] and upbraideth[14] not; and it shall be given him.[15] But let him ask in faith,
nothing wavering:[16] for he that wavereth is like a wave of the sea driven with the
7 wind and tossed.[17a] For[17b] let not that man think that he shall receive anything of
8 the Lord. A doubleminded man[18] *is* unstable in all his ways[19]. Let the brother of low
9 degree[20] rejoice[21] in that he is exalted.[22] But the rich,[23] in that he is made low[24]: be-
10 cause as the[25] flower of the grass he shall pass away. For the sun is no sooner risen[26]
11 with a burning heat[27], but it withereth the grass, and the flower thereof falleth, and
the grace of the fashion of it perisheth: so also shall the rich man fade away in his
ways.[28] [29]

[TITLE. [1] Eusebius ends his account of James the Just thus: τοιαῦτα καὶ τὰ κατὰ Ἰάκωβον οὗ ἡ πρώτη τῶν ὀνομαζομένων καθολικῶν ἐπιστολῶν εἶναι λέγεται. *Hist. Eccl.* ii. 23. A. C. Sin. omit the title.—M.]

Verse 1. [[2] ἐν τῇ διασπορᾷ. *In the dispersion.*—M.]

[[3] χαίρειν. Lange "*Freudengruss,*" *Freude zum Gruss*=Salutation of joy, joy the burden of his salutation; the English "greeting" is sometimes used in the same sense; so de Wette, van Ess etc.—M.]

Verse 2. [[4] The Codex Colbertinus has ἡγεῖσθε. ποικίλοις, literally, versicoloured.—M.]

[[5] The whole verse in Lange's version, "Count it all joy, my brethren, when ye fall into divers (variegated) temptations."—M.]

Verse 3. [[6] γινώσκοντες=since ye know. δοκίμιον=proof.—M.]

[7] The omission of τῆς πίστεως according to Cod. B. has been dropped on good grounds by Tischendorf, according to the decided majority of MSS. A. C. G. etc. [It is inserted in A. B. C. K. L. Cod. Colb. Cod. Sin. Vulg. Syr. Copt. Aeth. Arm. etc.—M].

[[8] ὑπομονήν=endurance. Lange's version. "Since ye know that the proof of your faith worketh endurance."—M.]

Verse 4. [[9] ὑπομονή=endurance.—M.]

[[10] ἔργον τέλειον=a perfect work.—M.]

[[11] Lange's version: "But let endurance have a perfect work (*the perfect operation of Christliness*) that ye may be perfect and entire people (*Christians*), in nothing deficient (*verkuemmert*, stunted).—M.]

Verse 5. [[12] λείπεται σοφίας=falls short of wisdom.—M.]

[[13] ἁπλῶς=*a*, liberally, *b*, sincerely.—M.]

[[14] μὴ ὀνειδίζοντος=upbraideth not, *i.e.* who gives without exprobration.—M.]

[[15] Lange's version: "But if any of you is deficient in wisdom, let him ask it from the God who giveth to all men (*also to the pagans*) sincerely (*without reservation and delusion*) and upbraideth not with it (*turns it not into the disgrace of the recipients, according to the notion of work-righteousness*), and it shall be given to him.—M.]

Verse 6. [[16] μηδὲν διακρινόμενος=nothing doubting, not in the least (Lange) doubting.—M.]

[[17a] Lange's version: "But let him ask in faith, not in the least (*faltering*) doubting, for he that doubteth is like a wave of the sea, agitated by the wind and tossed hither and thither."—M.]

Verse 7. [[17b] Lange renders γὰρ=also, but we prefer "*nor* let that man etc."—M.]

Verse 8. [18 19 Lange's version: "A double-minded (*faltering*) man: a seditious (*excited*) disturber of peace in all his ways." But this rendering is too fanciful; we prefer therefore the strictly grammatical rendering: "A two-minded man, unstable in all his ways," taking the verse in apposition with v. 7.—M.]

Verse 9. [20 ὁ ἀδελφὸς ὁ ταπεινὸς=the brother who is low.—M.]

[21 καυχάσθω=glory.—M.]

[22 ἐν τῷ ὕψει αὐτοῦ=in his exaltation. "But let the brother who is low glory in his exaltation."—M.]

Verse 10. [23 ὁ πλούσιος=the rich man.—M.]

[24 *Lange* understands a second "glory," makes the passage ironical, and renders "but the rich in his humiliation."—M.]

[25 ὡς ἄνθος χόρτου=as *a* flower of the grass.—M.]

Verse 11. 26 The Aorist with its narrative force should be retained.—M.]

[27 καύσων may mean the dry parching East wind, *Kadim*, but "*the burning heat*" of E. V. is very felicitous.—M.]

28 πορείαις. A. and several lesser MSS. read πορίαις, an orthographical blunder, according to Schneckenburger, because there is no noun πορία with a fixed meaning. [πορείαις is stronger than *ways*; it denotes the eager pursuit of some business or pleasure.—M.]

[29 Render the whole verse, "For no sooner rose the sun with the burning heat (wind) and dried up the grass and the flower thereof fell away and the beauty of its appearance perished; thus also shall the rich man wither in his ways" (journeyings something like Lange's "*Glücksfahrten*").—M.]

EXEGETICAL AND CRITICAL.

1. Introduction. Analysis. The address and salutation; v. 1.—Reference to temptation as a proof of endurance tending to joy: vv. 2–4.—The means of endurance, wisdom; hence deficiency in wisdom to be met by the prayer of undoubting faith; vv. 5, 6.—Caution against instability; vv. 6, 7.—Particular advice to the lowly and to the rich (in their own opinion); vv. 8–10.—The fate of the rich; v. 11.

VER. 1. *Address and Salutation.* **James,** (on James, see Introduction above) **servant of God,** applied in the widest sense to Christians in general (1 Pet. ii. 16; Eph. vi. 6), denotes in the narrower sense, in the official use of the word, apostolical men (Phil. i. 1); but here the word in its fullest weight signifies not only the head of the church at Jerusalem, but also the Apostle whose special work lay among the Jewish Christian and the Jewish Dispersion (of which Jerusalem was the centre). Rom. i. 1; Tit. i. 1. [Oecumenius: *ὑπὲρ πᾶν δὲ κοσμικὸν ἀξίωμα οἱ τοῦ κυρίου ἀπόστολοι τὸ δοῦλοι εἶναι χριστοῦ καλλωπιζόμενοι, τοῦτο γνώρισμα ἑαυτῶν βούλονται ποιεῖσθαι, καὶ λέγοντες, καὶ ἐπιστέλλοντες καὶ διδάσκοντες.*—M.].

Of God and of the Lord.—*Of God* not the attribute of *Jesus Christ*, as some expositors have rendered, but God the Father and the Lord Jesus Christ represented as wielding *one* dominion (cf. Jno. xvii. 3); thereby James also wisely takes together the Old Testament and the New. The Apostolical and Christian office is *one* service; however not service rendered to man but service rendered to God and Jesus Christ with undivided consciousness, obedience and operation. [*Oec.* "*θεοῦ μὲν, τοῦ πατρός· κυρίου δὲ, τοῦ υἱοῦ.*" Bengel: "*videri potuisset, si Jesum sæpe appellaret, id ex ambitione facere, cum esset frater Domini. Atque eo minus novit Christum secundum carnem.*" It is certainly remarkable that James mentions Christ only here and in ch. ii. 1, while in his speeches (Acts xv. and xxi.) he does not name Him at all.—M.]

To the twelve tribes in the dispersion.—That is, in their Christian calling, and in being called to Christ. To Jewish Christians primarily (so Laurentius, Hottinger, Schneckenburger, Neander and others), but, secondarily also to the Jews, as far as their adoption of Christianity had not yet been given up (*sofern sie noch nicht aufgegeben sind als werdende Christen*). See Introduction. As yet all were treated as the theocratico-ideal unity of the people of Israel called to (the reception of) the faith. Of course they are distinguished from the Gentile Christians (against Huther; see Wiesinger).

The twelve tribes (τὸ δωδεκάφυλον Acts xxvi. 7) Matt. xix. 38; Rev. vii. 4–8, etc. *The dispersion*, see Deut. xxx. 3; Nehem. i. 9; Ps. clxvii. 2; Jno vii. 35, etc.

Greeting.—*χαίρειν*, the Greek form of salutation (*χαίρειν* sc. *λέγει* 1 Macc. x. 18; 2 Macc. ix. 19); used also in the Apostolical decree Acts xv. 23 (to which Huther, following Kern, rightly calls attention). The Hebrew שָׁלוֹם Is. xlviii. 22 etc. Cf. the forms of salutation used by the other Apostles; as here, they always correspond with the fundamental ideas of the several Epistles. James desires to preserve to his brethren the true joy and to become instrumental in their securing it. Hence *χαίρειν* of v. 1 relates to *χαρά* v. 2, which we seek to express in the translation, "Salutation of joy (*Freudegruss*)." [See above in Appar. Crit. v. 1.—M.].

VER. 4. *Reference to the temptation and its design.* **All joy.**—*πᾶσα χαρά*, not as some of the older expositors render "the highest joy," but all joy, joy throughout (*ὅλως* Carpzov., Huther; entire joy) unless indeed the joy, as an all-sided one, is to correspond with the *ποικίλοις πειρασμοῖς* ["all sorts of joy," "all conceivable joy," Alford; "*rem revera omnique ex parte lætam,*" Theile. —M.]. But this *χαρά* is not mere *gaudendi materia* (Huther): rather, they are to convert the objective substance of joy into subjective riches of joy. *ἡγήσασθε* is therefore emphatic. [The repetition at the beginning of a verse or sentence, of the last word in the one preceding, called by grammarians *duadiplosis* is characteristic of the style of James; *e. g.* *χαίρειν, χαράν* v. 1 and following; *ὑπομονήν*, v. 3; *λειπόμενοι*, v. 4; *διακρινόμενος*, v. 6; compare also v. 13, 19, 21, 22, 26.—M.].

My brethren.—Primarily used to denote community of faith, but here also community of theocratic nationality (see ch. i. 16, 19; ii. 5; iv. 11; v. 7, 9, 19). [Wordsworth remarks that "this address is very suitable in an Epistle like the present, characterized by the language of stern rebuke; inspired like the reproof of St. Stephen, by the Spirit of *Love.* James, '*the Lord's brother,*' having the Spirit of the Lord, addresses even them as '*brothers.*'"—M.].

When ye fall into divers temptations.—These *πειρασμοί* are the chief motive of the Epistle. And certainly they are not only in a general sense the *θλίψεις* which an unbelieving world prepares for believers (Luke viii. 13; Matth. xiii. 21 (Huther); nor are they parallel to 1 Pet. i. 6. Still less are they in essential antithesis to πειράζεσθαι v. 13 (as Wiesinger thinks), the antithesis is at the most that of objective incitement and its corresponding subjective irritability. It is a very definite, concrete idea, the elements of which may be gathered in part from the circumstances of the time (see Introduction), and in part from the Epistle itself. The Jewish Christians were then tempted, on the one hand by the hatred of the pagans, on the other by the national fanaticism of the Jews (an alternate *odium generis humani*), and their ever-rising chiliastic desire of rebellion; they were tempted to participate in the antipathy to the pagans and to transfer it to the Gentile-Christians, to sympathize with the visionary Jewish national sentiment and thus to be again surprised by the old legal service. They were tempted to Ebionitism, which was already germinating (ch. ii), and beyond it to zealotry (ch. iii), to insurrection, (ch. iv.), and to apostasy (ch. v.). The temptation came therefore from every side and took the most variegated shapes of alluring and threatening, while their hereditary Judaïstic lust presented a counter-impulse (v. 13.). Thus the one great πειρασμός resolved itself into the πειρασμοὶ ποικίλοι. Now since the adjective ποικίλος denotes not only the diverse, but primarily the variegated, it probably contains an allusion to the manifold-dazzling glitter of colours in which the Jewish-Christian and Jewish temptations presented themselves and whereby they might even appear in the guise of Divine revelations and prophetical warnings urging them to be zealous for the honour of God. Into the midst of such temptations they had fallen; on all hands they were surrounded by them (on περιπίπτειν consult the Lexica and Huther). [περιπίπτειν to fall into the midst of anything, so as to be wholly surrounded by it. Luke x. 30; Acts xxvii. 41. So ὅστις ἂν τοιαύταις ξυμφοραῖς περιπέσῃ Plato, Legg. 9, 877. c; μεγάλοις ἀτυχήμασιν ὑπ' Αἰτωλῶν, καὶ μεγάλαις συμφοραῖς περιπεσόντες Polyb. p. 402, l. 5; πανικῷ περιπεσόντες, *Ib.* p. 670, l. 6; λῃσταῖς περιέπεσε Diog. Laert. 4, 50; κακοῖς, 2 Macc. x. 4, etc.—M.]. The design of every affliction of believers to turn by proof (δοκιμή) into spiritual joy (Acts iv. 23; Rom. v. 3, etc.) was consequently in an eminent degree peculiar to this great temptation. But this temptation did doubtless bring many an inconstant Jewish-Christian to ruin before the Jewish war, as did that under Bar Cochba.

Ver. 3. **Since ye know that the proof of your faith worketh endurance.**—The Participle γινώσκοντες explains ἡγήσασθε and indicates by way of encouragement the manner how they might turn the heart-grief of the proof into joy (hence neither "and know" (Luther), nor "for you know" Pott). Τὸ δοκίμιον (found only here and 1 Pet. i. 7) may mean the medium of proof (the proper signification of δοκιμεῖον, which occurs as a different reading of this passage, also as opposed to δόκιμον), but also *proof* (δοκιμή) as the result of the test. Huther following Oecumenius insists upon the latter sense, Wiesinger with Semler, Theile, and others, the former. And rightly so, although in 1 Pet. i. 7 the word signifies proof; for this δοκίμιον is designed to effect the endurance consequent upon δοκιμή. Wiesinger rightly cites Rom. v. 3, 4, where θλῖψις effects ὑπομονή, etc. Huther says that then we ought to have τοῦτο τὸ δοκίμιον. But the temptation and the proof are not purely identical. The tempting element of the proof emanates from the evil one, while the proving element of the proof comes from God. Temptation is proof under the aggravating coöperation of evil incitement to evil. This settles also the objection that temptations may result in failure (of proof); for temptation as a test ever contemplates proof on condition of good behaviour. It explains also, how in the concrete manner of the Scriptures proof may be described as temptation (but with reference to existing difficulties in the proof, Gen. xxii.), and temptation as proof. On κατεργάζεσθαι, to work, effect, see Rom. v. 3 and other passages; ὑπομονή manifestly denotes here *endurance.*—Baumgarten, Theile, Wiesinger, Huther: The μένειν ὑπό standing one's ground in temptation. Schneckenburger remarks that if ὑπό be emphasized we get the idea of *patientia ac tolerantia malorum*, if μένειν, that of *constantia, firmitas, perseverantia.*

Ver. 4. **But let endurance have a perfect work.**—Wiesinger: The emphasis is on τέλειον. The majority of commentators understand the perfect work as the perfecting of ὑπομονή itself. So Huther, Wiesinger: the proof of ὑπομονή (cf. 1 Thess. i. 3). Huther: ὑπομονή is not only passive but also active. This active ὑπομονή is not only to persevere unto the end (Luther: Let patience abide firm unto the end: similarly Calvin, Jerome and many others); ὑπομονή is to be deficient in nothing, neither in joy (Bengel) nor in any essential point; especially, wisdom, confidence, etc.—But James evidently contemplates not only inward demeanour but also and chiefly the outward exhibition of the same, which he deplored to see manifoldly omitted. Hence that interpretation is right, which distinguishes the perfect work, viz., the accomplishing of endurance, as the proof of endurance from endurance itself. So Erasmus, de Wette and others; but these commentators err in limiting this outward proof of endurance to something general, viz.: the exhibition of morality, etc. (see Huther). But James in his Epistle looks at a definite object. The ἔργον τέλειον by which the Jewish Christians were to verify their endurance consisted according to ch. ii. in the unreserved acknowledgment of their Gentile Christian brethren, and according to ch. iii., iv., v. in their open rupture with judaïstic faith-pride and fanaticism. Yes, James cherished the hope of gaining the Jewish Christians and along with them even the Jews themselves, to a greater or less extent, for this perfect work of submitting to the practical results of the Christian life. But if the more general sense is preferred, we have the meaning that Christian endurance must evidence itself in the full carrying out of the practical consequences of the Christian faith. An ἔργον τέλειον of the ὑπομονή in our day would consist in the thorough acknowledgment of Christian humanism and the thorough renunciation of the spirit of sectarianism and fanaticism. Ἐχέτω is decidedly emphatic. To this endurance must hold, this it must receive, acquire and this it must have to show. It is therefore at once=κρατείτω (Schulthess) and παρεχέτω (Pott).

That ye may be perfect and entire;—ἵνα decidedly expresses the word [used in the telic sense.—M.], and is explained by ch. ii. 22. Τέλειοι and ὁλόκληροι are not altogether synonymous (Huther), although the LXX. use both for תְּמִים. The former expression denotes perfection in the sense of completed development or vitality, the latter perfection in its completed manifestation. [Alford defines ὁλόκληρος as "that in which every part is present in its place," and cites Plato, *Tim.*, p. 44, c. and *Corp. Inscrip.* 353, 26.—M.]. But it denotes here specifically: If you want to become entire Jews and close the entire Jewish development, you must become entire Christians; but if you want to sustain the character of entire Christians you cannot dispense with the mark of perfect fraternization with the Christians, also with Gentile-Christians, and that of being opposed to the world, and also to the judaistic world. For the τέλειος is one who has reached his τέλος, the ὁλόκληρος one, *cui totum est, quod sorte obtigit* (*Wahl=nulla parte mancus*). The Jew was by origin a symbolic κλῆρος; as a Christian he was to become a real κλῆρος and thus ὁλόκληρος. The primary reference here is manifestly neither to moral perfection in general (Huther), nor to perfection hereafter, but to the rudimental [German: *principiell*] perfection of the faith of Christians as Christians; but the expression of James involves also the rule of absolute Christian perfection.

In nothing deficient;—λείπεσθαι means primarily to stay behind, to be inferior to another, but also to be wanting, deficient in a thing (v. 5). The latter sense is advocated by Theile, de Wette, Wiesinger, Huther with reference to v. 5 and 1 Cor. i. 7, the former by Storr, Augusti and others, whose view we consider correct notwithstanding the modified sense of the word in v. 5. For the opposite of having reached the end, or of being τέλειος is just the having stayed behind. The decay consequent upon quiescence and retrogression, the very characteristics of Ebionitism developed at a later period, and of Nazarite-Christianity, is the primary idea which corresponds with the connection of the whole Epistle. The Jewish people itself became most emphatically the λειπόμενοι of the world's history. James with a prophet's eye foresaw all this growing (*werdend*) decay. It springs indeed from a guilty deficiency in spiritual things or at least from a deficiency that might have been avoided, a point to which James refers immediately after. The sequel moreover shows that he sees in a perfect outward proof of life the full expression of character.

VV. 5, 6. *Wisdom a condition of endurance; prayer for wisdom in undoubting faith.*

But if any of you;—εἰ δὲ points hypothetically, and with reference to individuals, to a manifold probable or rather perceptible deficiency in general. Deficiency of wisdom has the form of the Judaistic and Ebionite element.

Deficient in wisdom.—Σοφίας without the Article acknowledges in a forbearing manner this lack of wisdom, supposing the deficiency to exist only in part. Oecumenius defines wisdom as τὸ αἴτιον τοῦ τελείου ἔργου, Huther as the insight of the problem of life as a whole as well as in its particular phases, which incites us to work. The reference here is not only to the Proverbs of Solomon, the Wisdom of Solomon and Jesus the Son of Sirach. The New Testament stadium of theocratical insight was objectively wisdom manifested in person (Matth. xi. 19), and therefore subjectively the right perception of the signs of the time and the christological fulfilment of the theocracy in the Church as well as in the faith of individuals.* The distinct relation of this want of wisdom to the temptations (Calvin) cannot be denied with Huther, although, wisdom, to be sure, must not be identified with endurance. As it is a fundamental condition of the same, so it is also one of the chief modes of its exhibition according to ch. iii. 17.

Let him ask from the God.—See Matth. xx. 20; Acts iii. 2; 1 Jno. v. 15. The further definition shows how important it is that real prayer must be free from the admixture of any conception which obscures the holiness and goodness of God. The Judaizer did also pray, but his conception of the Deity was a Jewish God, partial, legal and measuring His blessings according to merit. The position of the words τοῦ διδόντος θεοῦ (Cod. A. τοῦ θεοῦ τοῦ διδόντος) gives prominence to the idea that God is a giving God (Huther). See v. 17. Wiesinger: "*Who is known to give.*" The sense is: a giving comprehending every thing that is good, hence no object is indicated (Gebser and al).

To all.—Huther with Calvin and others supply τοῖς αἰτοῦσιν; but God's giving in the most general sense may not be measured by man's asking, although He is wont according to the measure of asking and beyond asking to give good gifts and even the Holy Spirit. [Any and every qualification of πᾶσιν reflects on the graciousness of the Giver.—M.].

Sincerely.—ἁπλῶς occurs only here in the New Testament. Huther [and Alford—M.] renders *simply* and sees in it an exclusive reference to the gift (nothing else is added to it with reference to Wisd. of Sol. xvi. 27), but the reference is not to the quality of the gift, but to the mode of giving; on this account the definition *candide, sincere* (Kerne, Theile and others), is preferable. Sincere (*pure*) giving is opposed to calculated giving which according to the view of the law, is at once suspicious and half compulsory. It refers indirectly to the source of *benignitas* (Bede and al.) and also to the liberality of giving (*affluenter*, Erasmus and al.) [Wordsworth explains: "who giveth ἁπλῶς, liberally, that is, *sinu laxo*, expanding the lap of his bounty and pouring forth its contents into your bosom. Cf. 2. Cor. viii. 2; ix. 11, and the use of the word ἁπλοῦν, *dilatare*, by the LXX. in Is. xxxiii. 23; and therefore the word ἁπλῶς is rendered *affluenter* here by the *Vulgate*, and *copiously* by the Syriac version."—M.].

* The Jews indeed had already before that time been deficient in the right comprehension of the *Solomonic* doctrine of wisdom, that is, of the universalism of the Old Testament, and for this very reason they had misunderstood and misinterpreted the *Davidic* Messianism from a particularistic point of view; just as Evangelical theology for the same reason has fallen short of its task in consequence of not sufficiently appreciating Christian humanism.

And upbraideth not with it.—Negative explanation of the preceding or of that which is consequent upon God's sincere giving. Wiesinger also explains μὴ ὀνειδίζοντος with Luther: "and upbraideth none with it" with reference to Sir. xli. 28: μετὰ τὸ δοῦναι μὴ ὀνείδιζε; ch. xx. 15; xviii. 17 (see Huther's note from Cicero). Huther disputes this exposition; Semler and al. interpret ὀνειδίζειν: *qualemcunque reprehensionem.* But then James would utter an untenable sentiment, because God notwithstanding those who ask, in various ways covers men with confusion. The expression also would be too brief in that sense; it is only intelligible if we take it with what goes before as one idea. But the exposition "to put those who ask to shame with a refusal" (Morus, Augusti and al.), is certainly unfounded; although it is less far-fetched than that of Huther; he who afterwards upbraids with his gifts is equally disposed to be hard beforehand and according to circumstances to send away the asker (without claims). "The side-look on the rich, v. 10; ch. v. 9," also, which Huther and Wiesinger detect here, cannot be sustained because it has first of all to be determined whom James means by the rich. The conception of a θεοῦ ὀνειδίζοντος would certainly agree with the religious views of said rich and then also indirectly with their behaviour.

And it (wisdom) **shall be given to him.**—There is not sufficient reason for taking δοθήσεται (with Huther and Wiesinger) impersonally: it will be given to him. See Matth. vii. 7-11; Luke xi. 13; 1 Kings iii. 9-12.

VER. 6. **But let him ask in faith.**—James having objectively defined real prayer as the worship of the true God of revelation, now also defines it subjectively as prayer in faith. See ch. v. 15; Sir. vii. 10; Jno. xvi. 23. It certainly follows (according to Wiesinger) from the appended negative definition that πίστις here designates first of all undivided confiding, full and firm heart-trust. Such trust is only possible as a looking up to the God of free grace according to revelation; Huther therefore rejects without reason the exposition of Calvin: "*fides est quæ, dei promissionibus freta, nos impetrandi, quod petimus, certos reddit,*" as one which lacks sufficient intimations; even the still closer definition of some of the older expositors, "πίστις Ἰησοῦ Χριστοῦ" would seem to be included *implicite.* That is, while Wiesinger rightly observes that πίστις both with James and Paul denotes the mind's moral attitude to God, yet with James this very attitude presupposes a looking up to "the giving God" according to revelation. Hence the μηδὲν διακρινόμενος excludes at once subjective wavering and doubting the certainties of evangelical salvation, because the attempt of fixing the heart outside of the sphere of revelation (in the case of Christians outside of the name of Jesus) would be pure fanaticism. A similar conjoining of "faith and not doubting" also in an objective sense, occurs in Rom. iv. 20; cf. ch. xiv. 23; Matth. xxi. 21; Mark xi. 24. James' conception of faith as given here is consequently his full conception of faith; it is only in such an energy of praying and doing that faith is to him vital, but without it dead. Διακρίνεσθαι=being at discord with oneself, being divided in oneself, and hence doubting must be still further defined as inward false discriminating, judging and deciding, and in this root it is joined with false discriminating and judging, ch. ii. 5. The hard and austere mind on the one hand produces a hard and austere conception of God, and on the other a hard and austere deportment. Huther: "While πίστις is 'yes,' and ἀπιστία 'no,' διακρίνεσθαι is the union of yes and no, yet so that the preponderance lies with 'no.'" That is, where διακρίνεσθαι has become habitual, a governing trait of character; this is the force of the Participles. But Huther (after Calvin) also mentions the possibility of doubting alongside of honest, yet weak faith (see Note p. 48).

Caution against wavering. vv. 6, 7.

VER. 6. **For he that doubteth is like a wave of the sea.**—Ἔοικε occurs only here and v. 24 in the New Testament. Huther sees in the γάρ of v. 7 the repetition of the γάρ in v. 6. That is, he thinks that James gives only one reason, not two and that the figurative description of him that doubteth v. 6, is only intended to bring out a clearer exhibition of the fickle mental constitution of the doubter. But "this apparently helpless disunion" assumes another form if we take v. 6 not only as a colouring but as a declaration that the doubter falls under foreign, anti-divine influences. The sea, according to the Old Testament, is the figure of the constrained (*unfrei*) life of nations, floating hither and thither in pathological sympathies (Ps. xlvi. 93; Dan. vii. 3; Is. lvii. 20; Rev. xiii. 1). James was doubtless conscious of this theocratic influence at a time, when "the waves of the sea" already began to roar. The symbolical figure of the wind (Eph. iv. 14; cf. ch. ii. 2) however, must be put in the background, because it is only expressed in verbs. But even here we can hardly fail to recognize an allusion to a restless spiritual commotion (*Geistesleben*) tossing the sea of nations, especially because ἀνεμίζεσθαι is an ἅπαξ λεγ., not found elsewhere (in classical Greek we have ἀνεμοῦσθαι, to be moved by the wind), and ῥιπίζεσθαι also occurs only here in the New Testament. On the different derivations of the word, see Huther. Note 2, p. 48; viz.: from ῥιπίς, a bellows or fan, or from ῥιπή, rush (of the wind) or storm. The latter derivation seems to lie nearest. These expressions are therefore not altogether synonymous (Huther). Bengel makes the former to denote motion from without and the latter motion from within. But both, the wind and the storm come from without; the inner element is here expressed by the sea-nature of the wave. According to Theile, the former indicates the cause, the latter the effect. But the two denote two different relations of degree: the sea in waves, the sea in billows; the breeze, the storm, the excitement of spirits, the rebellious commotion (*vide bellum Jud.*). From these considerations it seems to follow that the first γάρ has a more limited signification; it pronounces the διακρινόμενος incompetent to pray aright, because he is governed by the evil influences of the world. The second γάρ, on the other hand, bears in a wider sense upon that man's faithless relation to God. We cannot indeed conveniently render γάρ twice by *for* and repeat it therefore *intensiter* by '*also*.' Calvin makes it=ergo, Huther=namely, that is to say (*nämlich*), Pott, a particle of transition. The lively figure is charged with prophetico-symbolical matter.

VER. 7. **Also let not that man think** [or as I should prefer to render "*Nor* let that man think." Μὴ γάρ as an elliptic phrase denotes absolute denial and an Imper. or Optat. verb is then always supplied; here the context, on any interpretation that may be adopted, involves absolute denial and the *nor* has intensive force; the meaning is "let not that man *by any means* think" or "let that man *by no means* think."—M.]. The second γάρ has particular reference to the doubter's deficiency of faith in God, which is involved in his worldly dependence. Sure, he seeks to supply that deficiency of faith by superstitious or fanatical delusions, but he deceives himself with these delusions. He must become conscious of the nothingness of these delusions before matters can mend with him. The severe handling of false praying is a very ancient characteristic of exhortations to repentance according to Is. i. 15; Luke xviii. 11, this passage and the Reformation.

That man, the one who doubts and has fallen into human weakness. [Alford sees in these words a certain slight expression of contempt.—M.].

That he shall receive any thing.—He receives *nothing;* see ch. iv. 3 where another reason is specified why he does not receive any thing. [The reference is to the things for which he prays; there are many things, temporal blessings, which he does receive.—M.].

From the Lord.—The reference is of course to God, as in v. 12; ch. iv. 10, etc., but there is a reason for the use of κύριος instead of θεός; James means Jehovah, the living covenant-God, who has now fully revealed himself in Christ. For details, see Wiesinger. [Alford quotes Hofmann, who remarks that where the Father is not expressly distinguished from the Son by the context, the Godhead in its unity is to be understood by ὁ θεός; and the same may be said of ὁ κύριος.—M.].

VER. 8. **A two-minded man.**—The connection of this sentence with that which precedes it, is variously explained. The expositions of Pott: "*væ homini inconstanti,*" and of Baumgarten who wants to join δίψυχος with λήμψεται may be passed over. Winer, Wiesinger and Huther [also Wordsworth—M.] take it in apposition with the former verse and as explanatory of the figure v. 6, and render "he, a two-minded man." But the explanation of a figure and especially of one so thoroughly self-explanatory would not suit the style of our Epistle. Although the necessity of the Article before ἀνήρ (Schneckenburger), if the latter exposition is given, is unfounded, the exposition itself runs into a feeble tautology. Hence we agree with Luther and many expositors in taking ἀνὴρ δίψυχος as the subject and ἀκατάστατος as the predicate and the omission of the copula (is) as elevating the sententious weight of the proposition. Huther says that this would make the thought too abrupt. But in the masculine gender it is this formal abruptness which elevates the sentence, while in point of matter the connection is perfect. The doubter is delineated first as to how he stands to the world (a wave), then as to how he stands to God (a visionist, a man of conceits), and lastly as to how he stands to and by himself. And here it is noteworthy that James speaks of man in the masculine gender, probably not only on account of his proverbial character, but because the dangers against which James cautions his readers, are more especially dangers which threaten the Jewish male-world. The δίψυχος is not the same as the διακρινόμενος (so Luther and al.). According to Huther this word "characterizes the inward being of the doubter." To be sure, the inward being, not however as the ground of doubting (Huther, Kern, Wiesinger), but as the result of doubting. For two-mindedness is forthwith mentioned as the ground in relation to the manner how the doubter proceeds. Two-mindedness indeed lies already germ-like in doubt itself, but it is doubtfulness which develops wavering and irresoluteness, wherein man has, as it were, two souls, the one touched by God, the other occupied by the world. He is false in both directions, false to God and false to the world by his double reservation, just as he is false to himself by the reservation of his egotism over against his piety and *vice versa.* But this makes him not forthwith a consummate liar and hypocrite; "he has not only, as it were, two souls in conflict with each other" (Huther), but as yet his enthusiasm glows *psychically* now for God and now for the world in two changing forms of the psychical life. The word δίψυχος is admirably formed after the analogy of δίγλωσσος and similar words; it appears to occur nowhere prior to this Epistle (see also ch. iv. 8), but besides the analogies just mentioned, it has its type in the Hebrew בְּלֵב וָלֵב (see also Jesus Sir. I, 28), and has been adopted by Clemens Rom. and other church authors (see Huther p. 51). [Alford proposes to make the whole sentence predicate and all to apply to ὁ ἄνθρωπος ἐκεῖνος. On the whole, however, we give the preference (with Wiesinger, Huther and Wordsworth) to the certainly most grammatical construction of taking ἀνὴρ δίψυχος in opposition with v. 6; not as an explanation but as an *expansion* of the figure in v. 6. This construction is by no means in conflict with the abrupt and predicative style of James, for the transition from the figure of the wave of the sea to the two-minded man is certainly bold, if not abrupt, there is indeed a transition from a physical to a psychical illustration; the word δίψυχος itself, used here for the first time in Greek literature, by its novelty would arrest attention and thus in the language of Lange, "elevate the sententious weight of the proposition."—M.].

An (excited) **seditious disturber of peace.** —The ordinary rendering '*unstable*' [E. V.] or *inconstant* (Luther and al.) does justice neither to the original nor to the connection. For firstly, the expression is already half settled by what precedes it as well as by the words "in all his ways;" for although the latter phrase may bear a good sense, it seems to be used here in a bad sense (Sir. II, 13 ἐπιβαίνει ἐπὶ δύο τρίβους) Secondly, the expression, as the representative of

סער (Is. liv. 11, LXX.), is too feeble in point of degree. And although, lastly, it may passively denote one driven about by the storm as well as actively a storming seditionary, ch. iii. 16 (ἀκαταστασία) recommends here the use of the active signification The wavering man, indeed, is exciting and seditious because he is ruffled and driven by the storm (of public excitement). The wave of the sea, related passively to the winds, strikes actively against "the rock."

Particular advice to the lowly [in station—M.] *and particular advice to the rich*. vv. 9, 10.

VER. 9. **But let the brother, who is low, glory in his exaltation.**—Δὲ indicates a contrast of proper behaviour with what has just been described (Theile), [i. e. with διψυχία—M.]. It directs the brother to turn the particular temptations to wavering into instruments of constancy. Commentators are divided with regard to ἀδελφός. De Wette and Wiesinger apply the term both to the more remote πλούσιος and to the nearer ταπεινός. Then ταπεινός must not be taken spiritually according to Matth. xi. 29, but like πλούσιος with regard to outward circumstances, while the exaltation in which the lowly is to glory, would denote his heavenly dignity. But Huther, representing the opposite view, remarks that that exposition conflicts with the connection, which forbids such a distinction of Christians into poor and rich; that the reference is rather to the πειρασμοί; that a Christian, moreover, as a rich man would hardly have required so urgent a reminder of the transitory nature of things temporal. But three things are here overlooked. 1. That the πειρασμοί affect the rich in a higher degree than they do the poor; 2. That the Apostle, as we have seen in the Introduction, treats both of Jewish Christians (among whom were already rich men) and of Jews. Moreover he addresses, at the very beginning of the Epistle, the twelve tribes as his brethren. 3. The contrast between the *poor* and the rich had as yet not become prominent, but a contrast of those *low in station* [E. V. brethren of low degree—M.], and the rich. But that the *low in station* and the *poor* are, as brethren, nearer to James than the rich, becomes increasingly apparent as the Epistle runs on, especially in ch. v. Primarily, the lowly and the rich are described as brothers, for James indicates also to the rich a means of deliverance. There is still a third view, represented by Morus and Theile, which comprises both ideas: those who are outwardly poor and persecuted for righteousness' sake, Matth. v. 19; 1 Pet. iii. 14. Huther contests this union (p. 52), but afterwards reaches about the same conclusion. We have first to remember, that the brother of low station is not identical with the poor in ch. ii. Glancing at the characteristics of that time, we find that it designates the Jewish Christian and the Jew absolutely in their low, oppressed theocratic condition as contrasted with the heathen world and the secular power; and still more particularly the theocrat, inasmuch as he deeply feels this condition. He is to glory in the dignity of his heavenly and royally-glorious vocation, *i. e.* to derive from it consolation and joy and to strengthen himself with it. But the rich, *i. e.* again the Jew and the Jewish Christian, inasmuch as he sees the hopeless situation of the Jewish people in a very different and brilliant light, inasmuch as he is not only rich in the consciousness of his Jewish prerogatives, but also rich in the chiliastic and visionary expectation of the Messianic or pseudo-Messianic restoration of his Jewish theocracy,—he is exhorted to glory in his humiliation, that is, to become reconciled with Christian or pious humility to all his theocratical humiliation, the full development of which in all its fearful magnitude is as yet impending (v. 11), in order that he may find in this Divine judgment turned into deliverance, the source of rejoicing and exaltation and of real glorying.

And here a general explanation must suffice for our passing on to the general import of the double antithesis: the low-in-station and the rich; the poor and the rich. For we hold the opinion that, after the type of the Old Testament and the Gospels, these expressions are throughout prophetico-symbolical, and that the common literal acceptation of this antithesis has unspeakably flattened the Epistle, weakened its purport and obscured its interpretation. Is it possible to suppose that in the time of James, in all the Jewish Christian congregations among all the twelve tribes the rich were in the habit of slighting the poor and that the unbelieving Jews were everywhere the rich? And that James was so reliably informed on that point, as to feel constrained to call all the twelve tribes to account for it? Such conduct, I should think, could not be generally charged on the Jews proper. The rich among the Jews, as a rule have at all times exhibited much sympathy with and regard for their poor. And this very regard is supposed to have been wanting in such fearful generality in the Apostolic age, at a time where even in Gentile-Christian congregations collections were made for their Jewish Christian brethren! Nor was this the only point on which James felt bound to reprimand, but it is still further supposed that he had to denounce the sexton-rudeness of assigning good seats to the rich and of allowing the poor either to stand or to sit on the bare floor, which rudeness had become prevalent throughout all the twelve tribes! If James, "the good, pious man" had only received a little more credit [for capacity—M.], *i. e.* the Apostolical spirit united with prophetico-symbolical style, doubtless more would have been found in his Epistle.

The brother must therefore be taken in a general sense, like v. 2. The low (in station) is the Jewish Christian or the Jew who as such (not primarily as a private individual) felt his theocratic humiliation; this intimates, of course, that he was the more humble just as a being pinched in private affairs might also further such consciousness; this is quite analogous to the Old Testament and the Gospels. (Ps. lxxiv. 21; 1 Cor. i. 27).

Glory.—The stronger rendering for Peter's (1 Pet. i. 6) ἀγαλλιᾶσθαι, analogous to Paul's expression in 2 Cor. xii. 9. A real glorying or a rendering prominent by glorying, inasmuch as such glorying is in contrast with egotistic self-glorying; or also the condition of Divine grace and assistance.

In his exaltation; ἐν denotes the object in which they shall glory, as a foundation of their well-being. It is the glory, given now already in the form and inwardly, which hereafter however shall also be outwardly manifest (see 1 Pet. 1), the process of its development being diametrically opposite to the rich man's flower. Ὕψος is therefore not=steadfast courage (Augusti), or only future exaltation (de Wette), but=*sublimitas jam præsens, sed etiam adhuc futura* (Theile, Huther).

VER. 10. **But the rich in his humiliation.** Here we must evidently repeat καυχάσθω. As to the irony contained in this clause (Thomas, Beza and al.), it is not much greater than that in the preceding sentence: let the lowly glory in his exaltation; for 1. such glorying emancipates from vain-glorying, 2. the rich also finds a source of comfort and praise in the full knowledge of his humiliation and its blessed import (see Matth. v. 3).

Because as a flower of the grass.—An Old Testament figure applied to man in general, Job. xiv. 2; Ps. ciii. 15, to the ungodly with particular emphasis, Ps. xxxvii. 2 (Ps. xcii. 8). But here it is not to be explained with reference to the ungodly (so Huther), but as a historical figure with reference to the decay of the Old Testament glory, which in a surprising manner exhibits the realization of the law of the universal decay of human glory, even as foretold by Is. xl. 6 etc. to which this passage doubtless has special reference. But in this decay there lay really concealed a consolation (just as in the universal decay of man), at which the thoughtful theocrat might well rejoice. The flower of the Old Testament glory was decaying, but the fruit-time of the Gospel of the New Testament had set in; "Comfort ye, comfort ye my people!" Hottinger has erroneously referred ἄνθος to Is. xi. 1, where the LXX render נֵצֶר by ἄνθος. The words "flower of the field" (Is. xl. 6) are changed into "flower of the grass" with reference to v. 7 "the grass withereth and the flower fadeth." So in the parallel-passage 1 Pet. i. 23, 24.—

The fate of the rich. v. 11.

VER. 11. **For the sun rose** (*already*).—This again is not only the colouring of the preceding, but considering the reference to Is. xl. 6 etc., this passage contains an application to Jewish history perfectly intelligible to an Israelite. What Isaiah had represented as having been done in the Spirit, was now fulfilled in reality; the old theocratic glory of Israel had passed away with the crucifixion of Christ. Hence the Aorists ἀνέτειλε etc., as symbolical expressions, must retain their literal force and neither be construed as used for the Present (Grotius and al.), nor as the mere representation of whatever repeats itself in one past fact (Huther). This historical style serves, of course, the purpose furnishing us with a lively picture in the rapid succession of the separate stages of the process of decay (Winer).

The sun with the burning heat (wind).—Grotius, Pott and al. distinguish ὁ καύσων, the hot, burning wind which accompanies the rising sun (or the arid East wind, קָדִים which coming from the desert of Arabia scorches the plains of Palestine) from the sun itself, referring to Ezek. xvii. 10; xix. 12; Hos. xiii. 15 etc. Huther, however, applies the expression to the scorching heat of the sun and cites Is. xlix. 10, Matth. xx. 12; Luke xii. 55. But in Is. xlix. 10 the heat of the sun is expressly distinguished from the sun, as a higher degree of the ordinary sunshine which oppresses Orientals, and the reference is to the relation of this incumbrance to *men*, so also in Matth. xx. 12, while in Luke xii. 55 the sun is not mentioned at all. The supposition that sunrise and the development of the sun's heat are forthwith imperilling vegetation, would be almost too strong even to an Oriental imagination. To this must be added the presence of the Article before καύσων. But the view, that the sun with the development of its power frequently wakens the hot wind, as a kind of supplemental counterpart of its beneficent operation, is current in Holy Writ. So according to Mal. iv. the day of the Lord comes hot as a burning oven on all the proud, while the Sun of Righteousness rises with healing in His wings on all that fear the Lord. So Matth. xiii. 6, the scorching heat is distinguished from the rising sun; in the interpretation of the parable v. 21 it is called tribulation or persecution because of the word. Now, as we Occidentals make use of the well-known symbolical language, "the rising sun calls up vapor, fog, and thunder gusts," so the Oriental is wont to say, "it wakens the hot wind." Hence the application of this passage to Christ (Laurentius), was not far from its real meaning, but we do not press it; at all events the hot wind of the law, which scorched the glory of Israel, was developing with the sun of the finished revelation. And indirectly it was also the effect of the sun itself ("a stone of stumbling etc.").

And the beauty of its appearance.—Huther connects the second αὐτοῦ not with τὸν χόρτον but with τὸ ἄνθος. But we cannot imagine that a fallen flower is still to lose its beauty; the flower is gone with the falling; the flower itself and not only its beauty. And thereby (by the falling of the flower) the grass or the plant itself lost all its beauty, the dress of its appearance, without, however, having wholly perished. And this was then precisely the case of Israel. Its flower had fallen away in the most significant manner; like grass, low on the ground, it continued vegetating in its cumbersome existence. The word εὐπρέπεια occurs only here in the New Testament; πρόσωπον often denotes outward appearance. Ps. civ. 30; Matth. xvi. 3 etc.

Thus also shall the rich man, that is: the fate of the withered, stunted plant, or the general fate of the Jewish people will also be the fate of each individual Jew or Jewish Christian if he persists in the conceit of his riches, or refuses to learn to glory in his humiliation. οὕτως=so quickly, so thoroughly." Wiesinger. "Μαραίνεσθαι. a ἅπαξ λεγ· in the New Testament occurs in the LXX. as the translation of יָבֵשׁ Job xv. 30, in the same sense, Wisd. of Sol. ii. 8." Huther.

In his journeyings.—Luther has "in his possession," which rendering rests on the false reading πορία (=εὐπορία, good way, favour of fortune, wealth). Herder, following Laurentius and Piscator, "in his journeyings," with reference to ch. iv. 13. Huther, "in his ways" (=ὁδοῖς, v. 8; cf. Prov. ii. 8). Wiesinger, "in his walk," with reference to de Wette, "in his luxurious enjoyment of life." The word denotes in classical language 1, a going, a journey; 2, walking along, course. In LXX, *way*, Nah. ii. 5; Jer. xviii. 15; Jon. iii. 3, 4; but also a *journey*, 2 Macc. iii. 8; cf. Luke xiii. 22. From these passages it is evident, that πορεία is not used as much as ὁδός in a metaphorical sense. We avoid therefore this expression and render: in his journeyings (of fortune). Huther: "The prominent idea is, that the rich man, overtaken by judgment, perishes in the midst of his doings and pursuits as the flower in the midst of its blossoming falleth a victim to the scorching heat of the sun."

DOCTRINAL AND ETHICAL.

1. If the purely evangelical character of the Epistle of James has ever been impugned, its opening words may be referred to as furnishing proof that we are moving not on the ground of the Old Testament, but on that of the New. *Joy as the burden of salutation* is the watchword given to the first readers of the Epistle, who, however, were troubled by manifold temptations. Luke ii. 10. The beginning of the Epistle of James sounds like an echo of Christ's first sermon at Nazareth, which the Author had probably heard, Luke iv. 18, 19. This χαίρειν makes him homogeneous with Paul (Phil. iv. 4) and Peter (1 Pet. i. 6), the beginning of whose Epistle exhibits a remarkable agreement with the beginning of that of James. James, like Elihu, knows a God "who giveth songs in the night." Job. xxxv. 10.

2. The very beginning of the Epistle testifies of the truly Christian as well as of the morally exalted character of its Author. The demand "to count it all joy if one has fallen into manifold temptations," has so lofty and bold a sound as to prompt the question whether such a demand is not beyond the reach of man's ability. Cf. Heb xii. 11. Such a demand must severely strike the natural man as a piece of consummate folly and scandalize him. For counting temptation *all joy* is infinitely more than to be silent in it and to pray, even more than to be grateful for it; it is not sufficient that we readily submit to temptation, but we must glory in it that it is so and not otherwise, and this not only in isolated temptations but in the many temptations which spring from the sufferings of earth. Cf. Rom. v. 3. Such a demand makes the Festuses exclaim "James, thou art beside thyself." Acts xxvi. 24. But the Christian, hearing this first word, feels and is conscious of the spirit of him who addresses him in that word. For how could flesh and blood have been able to reveal what is here so clearly and explicitly put on record, viz. the Christian's deepest grief at once the source of his highest joy? No other religion, beside the Christian, had raised the suffering of earth to a new ground of gratitude. Bacon's saying is well known: "Prosperity is the blessing of the Old Testament, adversity that of the New." Compare the treatise, still worth reading, of F. V. Reinhard, *de præstantia religionis Christianæ in consolandis miseris etc.*, and on the other hand the *Diatribe de consolatione apud Græcos, auctore A. C. van Heusde, Traj. ad Rhen.* 1840.

3. *Since ye know.*—In order to make a joy like that which he had just recommended to them possible to their πίστις, James now points to the fruit of their γνῶσις. Faith also had a science of its own, but a science, different in kind although not inferior in value and reliability to the knowledge whose province is purely natural. On the one hand even Christians are constrained to acknowledge "we are but of yesterday and know nothing," Job viii. 9, but on the other, the things which were hidden from the wise and prudent are revealed to them, Matth. xi. 25, 26. And this science is fully competent to enable him to secure the joy here recommended; he knows from whom the temptation comes, he knows the purpose temptation serves, viz. *the proof of faith.* This view alone is calculated to reconcile him to the sufferings he has to endure. It is not chance if the Christian, more than many others, falls into manifold temptations, as little chance as if the smelter, in order to refine gold or silver, heats the furnace to a certain degree. Still less is it a just punishment but rather a means of purification, improvement and education, without which it is impossible for us to attain any degree of greatness in the kingdom of God. Thus we have here also a confirmation of the words of Seneca: "*Opus est ad notitiam sui experimento. Quod quisque possit, nisi tentando haud didicit.*

4. Christian *endurance* is infinitely diverse from stoical indifference with its motto: "*res mihi, non me rebus subjungere conor.*" It has a more sublime origin, a milder character, a greater duration, a more glorious fruit.

5. It is remarkable that James insists in the very beginning of the Epistle upon Christian perfection, so that in v. 4 the same word is twice used. So also the perfect law, ch. i. 25, the perfect man, ch. iii. 2, etc. Cf. the beautiful essay of Ad. Monod in his *Adieux*, 1856: "*Tout dans l'Ecriture est idéal.*"

6. The exhortation in v. 4 contains the profound hint that where endurance has its perfect work, the Christian, as to principle, is perfect and in nothing deficient. For where Christian endurance holds sway, there the power of sinful selfishness is broken, of selfishness which perchance would love to take a position either independent of God or higher than God, but in no event under God. For the heroism of faith is evinced in two ways, it is suffering or militant. The former is higher than the latter, because it demands the greatest self-denial, and he who really attains to it, by so doing carries also within himself the principle of Christian perfection.

7. The short Epistle of James treats relatively much of prayer, see ch. i. 5; iv. 2, 3, 8; v. 13–18. Herein also the Apostle appears as the true servant of Him who not only did conduct His disciples to the school of prayer, but was to them in this respect also a pure and perfect pattern, Luke xi. 1. The manner in which James speaks

of prayer shows clearly that he recognizes a direct connection between prayer and its answer, not only in the sense of modern unbelief that prayer can only psychologically exert a beneficial influence on the heart of the person praying, but also that prayer is the Divinely appointed means for the direct obtaining of our wants, which also without such prayer we should certainly not receive. If prayer were only psychologically operative on the person praying, it would be altogether inexplicable why James also so earnestly and emphatically enjoins prayer for *others* (intercession, ch. v. 13–18), as in the former case prayer could not possibly be of any use to them. Cf. this commentary on 1 Tim. ii. 1–7.

8. The Christian never needs more wisdom than when in temptation everything depends upon his enduring it in the right manner and according to the will of God. We often speak of the wisdom which men need in prosperity lest they become ungrateful, haughty or arrogant and this assertion is correct. But in adversity also we need the Divine light not less if we would truly understand the lesson God is teaching us thereby and not be driven by our own excited feelings into lamentable error. This was duly understood and appreciated by the sacred bard, Ps. xciv. 12. There never was a sinner converted by the highly praised benefit of tribulation alone, as long as the Lord Himself did not render the wholesome chastisement efficacious with the rod of His Word and the light of His Spirit. In the day of tribulation we probably need Divine wisdom even more than in the days of joy; wisdom in order that we really choose the true way without turning to the right or to the left; wisdom, in order that we may understand what God wants us to do when He denies us the realization of some cherished desire, or when He lays on us a heavy burden, etc.

9. What James says of the indispensable necessity of faith in prayer, is also taken from our Lord's own teaching, Matth. xxi. 21, 22. His charming figure of the waves of the sea originated probably in his own recollection of the lake of Gennesareth. The striking truth of this figure is best understood, if we apply it to our inward experience of life. The soul is like the sea, but doubt blows over it like a tempest which upheaves the waters from their lowest depth; in such a condition, the heart of the *δίψυχος* is not susceptible of the enjoyment of answer to prayer. Cf. 1 Kings xviii. 21, where the expression "to halt between two opinions" [German: "to halt on both sides."—M.], indicates a similar inward breach, with a probable allusion to a bird limping from twig to twig without finding rest anywhere.

10. James seems to present us with a new paradox in the exhortation (v. 9) "*Let the brother, who is low, glory in his exaltation.*" There is however an exaltation seen by God and the Lord, which does not depend upon earthly honour and perishable riches and is mostly to be found where superficiality would last and least look for it. To be humiliated can only be irritating and disagreeable to flesh and blood; but if it happens for the sake of Christ's name, if the humiliation is borne with the eye turned to Christ and united to Christian nobility of soul, then it is not counted a disgrace, but borne as the highest honour. Cf. Matth. v. 11, 12; Acts v. 41, 42. Here we are involuntary reminded of Pascal's beautiful saying concerning man: "*Gloire et rebut de l'univers, s'il se vante, je l'abaisse; s'il s'abaisse, je le vante.*"

11. The number of the rich who were able to glory in their humiliation has always been small. Cf. Matth. xix. 23–26. Still history here and there shows us individuals in the fire of the fiercest assault and temptation. Hear only *e. g.* the splendid language of Chrysostom in his speech after the fall of Eutropius, *Opera*, vol. 3, p. 586, ed. Montf. "Why did we not tremble? Because we do not fear any of the adversities of this life. What could inspire us with terror? Death? We run so much the sooner into the haven of repose. The loss of earthly riches? Naked I came out of my mother's womb and naked I shall return into the mother-womb of the earth. Exile? The earth is the Lord's and what therein is. False accusations? Rejoice and be exceeding glad when men shall say all manner of evil against you falsely, for great shall be your reward in heaven. I saw the swords above me and looked up to heaven. I expected death and thought of the resurrection. I looked at earthly adversities and counted up the blessings at the right hand of God. I looked upon the perils and my eye beheld in spirit the crown of glory. What I am constantly preaching in my sermons, was constantly preached by the deed in the market-place. The wind blows and scatters the leaves, the grass withers and the flower fades." (The last sentence probably contains an indirect allusion to James i. 11.)

12. The crown of life, of which James here speaks, presents not only a contrast to the perishable laurel-crowns for which the Greeks contended in the games, but also to that fading flower to which James referred in the preceding verse (v. 11). In the doctrine of the reward of grace accorded to persevering faith, James is in prefect agreement with our Lord and His other Apostles. Cf. Matth. xix. 28; 1 Cor. ix. 24–27; 1 Pet. v. 4; Rev. ii. 10; iii. 21. His mentioning the crown of life which is ready for all who love the Lord, affords a not indistinct view of "the election of grace."

HOMILETICAL AND PRACTICAL.

V. 2–8. Epistle for 3d Sund. in Lent, v. 9–12 Epistle for 22d Sund. after Trinity in the Grand Duchy of Hesse and elsewhere. [V. 1–12 Epistle for St. Philip and St. James's Day in the Church of England and the Prot. Epis. Church in the U. S.—M.].

How the vocation of being servants of Jesus Christ was especially committed to the authors of the New Testament and how it still is the prerogative of all believers.—The servant of Jesus Christ can do nothing better than to strengthen his brethren.—In Christ is joy for all people.—How Christianity renders possible what seems to be impossible.—The sufferings of this time the Christian's proof of faith. It is this very fire proof [noun, to give the full force of German "Feuerprobe"] which establishes 1, the genuineness 2, the standard and 3, the intrinsic value of this gold of faith. Cf. 1 Pet. i. 7.—Endurance under all temptations the daughter of faith, the mother of all other virtues.—The Christian life a God-consecrated sacrifice which must be without spot or blemish. "Ask, what I shall give thee," 1 Kings iii. 5.—The difference between Divine and human benevolence, cf. Sir. xviii. 18. The great value of believing prayer and its indispensable necessity in times of great temptation. The curse of wavering; the value of Christian decision of character. — Riches and poverty viewed in the light of faith.—Abasement the way to exaltation, want the way to enjoyment, fighting the way to the crown.—The beatitude of the servant of Christ (v. 12) compared with the beatitudes of the Master, Matth. v. 3–12.

On the whole section vv. 1–12.—The Christian's threefold duty in temptation: 1. *Suffering* (v. 2–4), *a.* with grateful joy: *b.* with enduring patience; 2. *Prayer* (v. 5–8), *a.* for a precious gift at the hands of a magnanimous giver; *b.* in simple faith without any doubt; 3. *Glorying* (v. 9–12), *a.* in the present conflict; *b.* in the expectation of the future crown.

THOLUCK (Sermons I. 5, 340) on v. 2. "Why the Christian counts his temptation all joy." 1. He knows whence it comes; 2. He knows whither it leads.

STAAG:—The Christian's behaviour in crosses and temptations: 1. The bliss of the cross; 2. the prayer of the cross; 3. the disposition of the cross; 4. the promise of the cross.

BECK: (v. 5)—The true wisdom.

KLEMM:—The prize in the arena of life.

DRÄSEKE:—Humility the condition of all true moral greatness, for it is, 1. its beginning, 2. its food, 3. its support and 4. its crown.

ARNDT:—Happy is the man who endures temptation.

PORUBSZKY: (vv. 1–4).—The temptations of faith: 1. How they are occasioned. 2. How they effect endurance. 3, How they excite believing activity.—(v. 5). Prayer the first act of faith.—(vv. 6–8). The doubter's torment and deliverance.—(vv. 9–12). Through abasement to exaltation. I. The end: exaltation, 2. the means: abasement.

STARKE:—To be the servant of God is to a believer a precious title of honour, in which he may always glory.

CRAMER:—The Church of the New Testament is not confined to one locality as in the time of the Old Testament, "but in every nation he that feareth Him and worketh righteousness, is accepted with Him" Acts x. 35.

QUESNEL:—One of the chief cares of conscientious teachers is to comfort those who suffer for the Lord's sake, 1 Cor. xiv. 3.

HEDINGER:—Great art! To laugh in weeping, to be glad in sadness. But there is still time to learn it; our strength is nothing, it is altogether God's work and doing, Phil. iv. 11–13.

CRAMER:—Different medicines are required for different maladies, different chastisements for different sins, Tit. iii. 3.

STARKE:—Sincere faith is not dead but alive and works all manner of good, 2 Pet. i. 5, 6.—Crosses and suffering promote patience just as the wind strengthens the roots of the tree, v. 2.—He that has begun well must persevere unto the end or all former labour is lost.—Patience in the first hour is not sufficient. The end brings the crown.—It is great wisdom to bear suffering aright, and that wisdom is of God's supplying.

HEDINGER:—A rich man who is charitable is a rare spectacle; to be giving and never tire of beggars is more than human; but to give above all that we can ask is Divine (Eph. iii. 20).

OSIANDER:—Because God does not angrily upbraid us with His benefits, therefore we should still less reproach our neighbour with the good we show him.

LANGII OP.:—The highest honour which a creature can confer upon God is to trust Him in every thing by faith and to rely in the full assurance upon His promises, which is also the purest worship, Rom. iv. 20, 21.

QUESNEL:—Faith is the fountain of Christian prayer; the stream does not flow, if the fountain is dried up, Rom. x. 14.—True believers are not fickle and changeable, but constant and steadfast, Col. ii. 5.—Would you serve God, then let it be your serious endeavour not to tempt God.—A divided heart longs not for God, Matth. xxii. 37.—A poor believer is as much a brother in Christ as a rich, Philemon v. 16.—Humility and abasement have been made by Christ true exaltation; Job. xxii. 29.

HEDINGER:—Riches are not culpable in themselves, but they may easily make men haughty.

CRAMER:—God willeth that the rich and the poor should dwell together.

LANGII OP.:—The transitoriness of life and instability of outward prosperity are to be well considered.

HEDINGER:—Rich and ungodly—a double hell-rope. Take care that avarice put it not round your neck, 1 Tim. vi. 9, 10.

LANGII OP.:—Believing Christians are not only the subjects but the sharers of Christ's reign, as those who rule and govern with Him, 1 Cor. vi. 2, 3.

CRAMER:—What is marred by the crown of thorns, which we have to wear here on earth, will be amply compensated by the crown of life in heaven, 2 Cor. iv. 17, 18.

STIER:—In order to do justice to the deep, rich meaning of every word and sentence of this Epistle, we have ever to begin with the beginning without ever exhausting its fulness. What a sermon might be preached on the single *joy* (*χαίρειν*) which sounds into our tribulation.—What a lofty saying is the verse connected with it—"Count it all joy if you fall into manifold temptations," etc.

HEUBNER:—Proofs (trials) a Divine blessing.—To have a good beginning and to omit the prosecution is disgraceful.—Wisdom, that is not from God, is no wisdom.—Faith and prayer are mutual conditions.—Where the will is still wavering, there is no trust.—1 Sam. ii. 30 holds good of belief and unbelief.—Christianity exalts a Christian above his station.—It is a touching spectacle, that commands respect, to see a Christian, whose position in the world is commanding, clothed with humility.

[v. 1. It is the duty of the Church to send greetings of joy to the dispersed children of God and to use every means for turning the wilderness of the dispersion into the garden of the Lord. (Missionary Sermon)—v. 2. The true Christian sees in temptation of every kind and of every degree cause for unmingled joy. Cf. Rom. v. 3; 2 Tim. ii. 12.—v. 3. The Christian in the furnace: 1. Experiencing the heat of temptation, 2. Rejoicing in the watchful care of his superintending Master, 3. Jubilant at the result of the fiery process. Mal. iii. 3; 1 Pet. i. 7.—vv. 4, 5. γνῶσις may be acquired in the schools, σοφία is the gift of God. Cf. Lactantius, "*on true and false wisdom.*"—True wisdom the gift of God to prayerful believers.—The characteristic of true wisdom—it makes wise unto salvation.—v. 6. The doubter like a wave. *a*, in his conduct—driven hither and thither, by contrary winds or lashed into a billow by the tempest; *b*, in his end—touching the shores of safety but dissolving into spray and returning to the treacherous sea.—v. 7. Instability the characteristic of schism.—v. 8. The mountain is reached from the valley.—v. 9. The riches of wealth—the riches of learning—the riches of station—the riches of earthly honour no grounds for glorying.—True riches are riches toward God.—vv. 10, 11. The fate of earthly greatness symbolized in the fate of the flower. v. 12. Earthly afflictions and trials destined to become amaranths in the crown of life.—On the whole section James i. 1–12 compare John xiv. 1–14.—M.].

[Bp. Conybeare: v. 4.—Our very joys are broken and interrupted, and our distresses are so frequent and sharp, that we scarce know how to support ourselves under them: and yet borne that must be which cannot be avoided by us. The will of God must be submitted to by His creatures, both in the ordinary dispensations of Providence and in the more eminent exercise of its powers. Patience will then come in as a necessary duty in common life. We need it almost every day on some occasion or other; and therefore should arm ourselves with such principles as may enable us to go through with innocence. —M.].

[*That ye may be perfect and entire.* Probable allusion to the sacrificial victims which must be without blemish. The sacrifice of body, soul and spirit with all we have and hold, as a reasonable service rendered unto God by His faithful servants.—M.].

[v. 5. Dr. Jortin:—The wisdom of resisting any sort of temptation may very well be extended so as to mean pious wisdom in general, or a practical knowledge of our duty and true interest, by which we shall overcome every thing that opposes and endangers our salvation.—M.].

[Bede:—This text contains a warning against the erroneous notion of Pelagianism, that men may obtain wisdom by their own free will, without Divine grace. Cf. v. 16, 17.—M.].

[Wordsworth:—The description of the Divine bounty is like a summary of our Lord's words, exhorting to prayer. Matth. vii. 7–12.—M.].

[Bp. Andrewes:—This text presents the strongest motives to genuine liberality. See Wordsworth.—M.].

[v. 6. Bp. Sanderson:—A large and liberal promise; but yet a promise most certain and full of comfortable assurance, provided it be understood aright, viz., with these two necessary limitations: if God shall see it *expedient*, and if man pray for it *as he ought* . . . . To make all sure then here is our course. Wrestle with God by your fervent *prayers:* and wrestle with Him too by your faithful *endeavours;* and He will not for His goodness' sake, and for His promise' sake He cannot, dismiss you without a blessing. But omit either, and the other is lost labour. Prayer without study is presumption, and study without prayer is Atheism. v. 8. Hermas says of the double-minded man: "Cast away from thyself double-mindedness; be not anywise two-minded in asking of God; say not, how can I *ask* of God and obtain it, when I have sinned so much against Him? Nay, but rather turn with thy *whole heart* to the Lord and ask of Him without hesitation, and thou shalt feel the abundance of His mercy, for He is not like *men*, who *remember injuries;* but if thou doubtest in thy heart, thou wilt receive nothing from Him, for they who doubt concerning God, are the *double-minded* men and receive none of their requests." Hermas, *Pastor, Mandat.* 9, p. 596 ed. Dressel. See also Wordsworth and Whitby, who produce other passages.—M.].

II. THE THEME.

THE BEATITUDE OF ENDURANCE IN TEMPTATION AS A WARNING AGAINST YIELDING TO IT.

Chapter I. 12.

12 Blessed *is* the man[1] that endureth temptation: for when he is tried, he shall receive the crown of life, which the Lord[2] hath promised to them that love him.[3]

Verse 12. [1] The reading ἄνθρωπος in Cod. A. and several minuscule Mss., being a false correction, calls attention to the significant ἀνήρ.

[2] ὁ κύριος is wanting in A. B. Cod. Sin., and rejected by Lachmann, Tischendorf, (Alford—M.) and al. Theile retains it with G. K. (C. without the Article) and al. the Syriac, [Armenian—M.] and other versions. Several minuscule Mss. and versions [Vulg. Syr. Copt. Aeth. and al.—M.], read ὁ θεός. As the insertion is more readily accounted for than the omission, we may presume that the Apostle in λήμψεται reverts to λήμψεταί τι παρὰ τοῦ κυρίου [v. 7—M.]. But summary sentences have generally a summary mode of expression. We follow therefore Bouman. p. 63.

[3] Lange: Blessed (is) the man . . . . for when he has become approved . . . .

EXEGETICAL AND CRITICAL.

That this verse contains the proper theme of the whole Epistle and indicates the dominant fundamental idea of the same follows from the twofold consideration that 1. the same thought comes up already in the Introduction v. 2 and 2. that it is repeated in a corresponding final theme at ch. v. 7. It is a beatitude after the manner of the sermon on the mount and moreover the last of these beatitudes of our Lord, in which all the preceding ones blend (Matth. v. 10, 11), appropriately adapted to the situation of the readers in the time of James.

Blessed (is) **the man.**—ἀνήρ instead of ἄνθρωπος not only with reference to Ps. i. 1, for it occurs repeatedly (see v. 5, here, v. 20 and ch. iii. 2) and we have already intimated that it may be accounted for by the temptations of the time, which James had in view, making the round especially among Jewish *men*. Thomas appears to have noticed, but not to have understood this characteristic, as would seem from his comment: "*beatus vir, non mollis vel effœminatus, sed* vir."

Who endureth temptation.—[Bengel reads with K. L. ὑπομενεῖ, Future; but ὑπομένει is the ordinary reading and, the blessing being absolute, the tense is immaterial.—M.]. Although the proposition is valid and will be valid as a general dogma, the πειρασμός here does not primarily denote the concrete unity of all the πειρασμοί mentioned in v. 2, for the reference to these very πειρασμοί runs through the whole Epistle. Therefore not: ὅταν περιπέσῃ (Wiesinger). Hence ὑπομένει like ὑπομονή in v. 3 and μακροθυμήσατε ch. v. 7, etc.

Because when he has become approved. One who has become approved, not only proved: one who has become approved by the fact of proof. [He has stood the test of the δοκίμιον v. 2 and thereby has become δόκιμος—M.]. The idea is identical with that expressed in ch. ii. 23: Abraham has become the friend of God by δικαιοῦσθαι. And here we see how James and Paul agree in their dogmatical views, for Paul also mentions the δοκιμή as the consequent of ὑπομονή Rom. v. 3. But the subjective and inner side of this proof is σφραγίζεσθαι according to Eph. i. 13. Krebs, Augusti and al., have found here an allusion to the trial preceding the contest of the athletes, but such an allusion is out of place, so is that of Gebser, Theile and al., to the refining of metals by fire, for that figure presupposes the idea of refining, which although involved in the trial or proof, is not identical with it. The same situation presupposes the certainty of success in refining, questions it in the trial and endangers it in temptation. De Wette and Wiesinger reject a figurative reference; but the crown of life, which is here promised, at least reminds us of the idea of the race-course also in Paul, 1 Cor. ix. 24; 2 Tim. ii. 5.

He shall receive the crown of life; στέφανος, garland, chaplet of victory or honour in its fullest significance denotes a crown and in this sense we are warranted to take it here, according to Matth. v. 9 and Rev. v. 10.—Τῆς ζωῆς is explained by Huther as the Genitive of apposition: "The ζωή i. e. eternal, blissful life is the crown of honour wherewith he that endures is adorned." But Jno. iii. 36 says: "he that believeth hath everlasting life"; does "the crown of righteousness" 2 Tim. iv. 8 signify "righteousness is given me as a crown?" If the crown denotes the crown of honour of the finished proof, matured in the life of faith but also objectively awarded and glorified by God, it is the crown of life, *i. e.* the crown granted to a life which has developed itself into coronation, as life, the *Summum* of life as life's prize of honour; our Genitive is consequently the Genitive of possession or dependence. Cf. 1 Pet. v. 4, Rev. ii. 10. If the legal men [*i. e.* sticklers for the Jewish Law. M.] of that time were perhaps wont to say with reference to Ps. i.: Blessed is the man that ever keeps to the law, he is the tree by the rivers of water, his leaves do not fade *i. e.* his life shall retain perpetual freshness, the beatitude of James expressing his continuance and promise of life would receive a peculiar significance. Although we cannot assert with Zwingli, Michaelis, Wiesinger and al., that the foundation of this figure is as in 1 Cor. ix. the idea of the Grecian games, it may be shown that the Jews also regarded the crown or diadem not only as "a symbol of *peculiar* honour" (Huther referring to Ps. xxi. 4; Wisd. of Sol. v. 16, 17), but also of an honour accorded by God to a *well-endured* warfare of life. Both the Jews and the Greeks started with the presumption that persevering wrestling in a higher course of life constituted the condition of the diadem and that presumption repeats itself more or less among all mankind in the most diversified forms. This law of life was recognized in the Old Testament especially in the case of the typical Judah, of David, of the ideal man (Ps. viii.), and of the Messiah (Ps. cx.). The crown of believers is contrasted with the perishable garland of honour in 1 Cor. ix. 25 and it is also alluded to in 1 Pet. i. 4; v. 4. Why is the antithesis here wanting? The Jews and the Jewish Christians of that time might readily remember it; all their visionists wanted to see the day of the kingdom of Zion, of the coronation of their chiliastic Messiah, the crowning of the Jewish rulers of the world. On this account Peter also points the suffering Christian pastors to the crown of glory (1 Pet. v.) and the promise of the Epistle to the Hebrews also is the kingdom which cannot be moved (Heb. xii. 28).—

Which He (the Lord) **has promised.**—See Critical Note. "If ὁ κύριος is the right reading, it signifies not Christ (Baumgarten, Schneckenburger), but God (Gebser, Theile, Wiesinger [and Alford—M.]." Huther.—But that means nevertheless: God revealed in Christ. But might not James by this very omission have designed a supplying which he had prepared in v. 1?—

To them that love Him.—Ch. ii. 5; Ps. xcvii. 10; cxlv. 20; Rom. viii. 28; 2 Tim. iv. 8. The love of the Lord, with James and Paul is consequently the real and eternal nature of faith, its root, its sap and its crown; and it is love which proves itself in endurance and by it attains to completion. Cf. Jno. xv. [*Amor parit patientiam.* Bengel.—M.].

[In *Shemoth Rabba*, sect. 31, p. 129 and in *Rab. Tanchum* p. 29, 4, we read: "Blessed is the man, who stands in his temptation; for there is no man whom God does not *try*. He tries the *rich*, to see if they will open their hands to the poor: He tries the *poor*, to see if they will receive affliction and not murmur. If, therefore, the rich *stand in his temptation*, and give alms to the poor, he shall enjoy his riches in this world, and his horn shall be exalted in the world to come; and the holy blessed God shall deliver him from the punishment of hell. If the poor *stand in his temptation*, and do not repine, he shall have double in the world to come."—M.].

For "DOCTRINAL AND ETHICAL" and "HOMILETICAL AND PRACTICAL" see the preceding section.

III. FIRST ADMONITION WITH REFERENCE TO THE FIRST FORM OF TEMPTATION: VISIONARINESS.

CAUTION AGAINST THE VISIONARINESS WHICH REPRESENTS THE TEMPTATION AS GOD'S CAUSE. THE HIDEOUS FORM OF THE SELF-TEMPTATION OF THE ERRING AND THEIR END, DEATH.—THE OPPOSING IMMUTABILITY OF THE FATHER OF LIGHTS IN HIS BLESSING RULE AND THE EXALTATION OF HIS PRINCELY CHILDREN BORN BY THE WORD OF TRUTH.

CHAPTER I. 13–18.

(VV. 16–21. *Epistle for Fourth Sunday after Easter.*)

13 Let no man say when he is tempted, I am tempted of God:[1] for God cannot be
14 tempted with evil, neither tempteth he any man: But every man is tempted, when
15 he is drawn away of his own lust, and enticed. Then when lust hath conceived, it
16 bringeth forth sin; and sin, when it is finished, bringeth forth death. Do not err,
17 my beloved brethren. Every good gift and every perfect gift is from above, and
cometh down from the Father of lights, with whom is[2] no variableness, neither sha-
18 dow of turning.[3] Of his own will begat he us with the word of truth, that we should
be a kind of firstfruits of his creatures.

Verse 13. [1] Only several minuscules sustain the reading τοῦ θεοῦ. [τοῦ is omitted by A. B. C. K. L.—M.] Cod. Sin. reads ὑπὸ θεοῦ, but in v. 17 erroneously ἀποσκίασματος. Lange: "No one, who is tempted [stands in temptation] shall say: I am tempted from God, for God is not temptable in respect of evil things, but He Himself tempteth [out of Himself] no one.

[Let no man, being tempted, say that (ὅτι *recitantis*) I am being tempted from God; for God is not experienced in respect of evil things, but He Himself tempteth no man.—M.]

Verse 14. Lange: . . . tempted in that he is drawn away [rendered an apostate] by his own lust and allured [by his evil inclination.]

[. . . being drawn away and lured by his own concupiscence.—M].

Verse 15. Lange: . . . conceived [is impregnated] . . . , but sin, when it is completed [has ripened] bringeth forth death.

Verse 16. Lange: M. Be not ye deceived, my beloved brethren.

Verse 17. [2] [Cod. Sin. ἔστιν for ἔνι.—M.]

[3] [Cod. Sin. ἀποσκίασματος.—M.]

Every good giving and every perfect gift [donation] cometh [and cometh] down from above, from the Father of the lights [beings of light], with whom there is not existing a change, nor a shadow-casting of a turning.

[Every good bestowing and . . . coming down from . . . with whom there is [essentially] not a change or shadow of turning.—M.]

Verse 18. Lange: Pursuant to free decree hath He begotten us by the word. [of His own Will [because He willed it, Alford; by the act of His own will, Wordsworth.] etc.—M.].

EXEGETICAL AND CRITICAL.

ANALYSIS:—The first form of temptation—visionariness. The representation of the tempting thought as of God's cause and caution against the deceptiveness of this temptation, v. 13.—The hideous form of the self-temptation of the erring and their end,—death, vv. 14–16.—The opposing image of the true God in His blessing rule and His fixed immutability, v. 17.—The exaltation of His princely children begotten by the word of truth, v. 18.

The first form of the temptation—fanaticism, represented as a glorious cause of God, or a Divine admonition.

VER. 13. **Let no one who is tempted say.**—Caution against the deceptiveness of the temptation. It is incorrect to affirm that James opposes ὃς ὑπομένει πειρασμόν to ὃς πειράζεται, etc.; something like Huther, Pott, Olshausen, Schneckenburger and al. For how could any one abide the temptation, without having first been tempted? James in this dehortation refers indeed to those who really say that they are tempted from God (which is also indicated by the forcible participial form) but even these he desires to reclaim while warning his better readers against their error. According to Calvin (and Wiesinger) James here treats *de alio tentationis genere*. But the matter is simply this; James now explains the *one* great πειρασμός according to the separate ποικίλοις πειρασμοῖς and begins with the first form of the temptation.—[The force of the Participle should be brought out in the translation.—M.].

Shall Say,—λεγέτω according to Schneckenburger and al.=*cogitet or sibi persuadeat*, which is of course implied but not all, as Huther justly observes, [Bengel: *corde aut ore*—M.]. James connects this saying with the uncommonly much-saying of the Judaizing Jewish Christians and Jews, to which he alludes.

I am tempted from God.—Grotius, Hottinger and al. have rightly felt that the word 'tempt' bears a somewhat different sense in the two places, while Huther asserts without sufficient reason that the sense in both cases must be identical, viz.: to be inwardly solicited to sin. Let no one say: I am inwardly solicited to sin of God; but with such an exhortation James could not possibly have warned the twelve tribes. Said expositors miss however the correct distinction by saying that in the one instance it denotes: *adversa pati*, and in the other *malis ad defectionem sollicitari*. It is a sententious oxymoron conveying the idea: Let no one say that the impulse, which to him is really a temptation, and in the end a devilish one (ch. iii. 15), in which he is already entangled (πειραζόμενος), is a monition of God, a cause of God, an incentive to maintain His honour. For this the Jews at a somewhat later period did really say in their uprising against the Romans, this they said even then in their fanatical utterings against the pagans, and the Judaizing Jewish Christians said in a similar manner: It is the will of God that we maintain His law and therefore separate from the Gentile Christians, as far as they do not receive the whole law or only in part. But James doubtless chose this poignant mode of expression in order to reproach those sayers with their making, though unconsciously, God the Author of evil. But it cannot be absolutely assumed that he is here inveighing against an impertinence generally or variously current among Jewish Christians, which made them charge God with temptations to evil, of which they were conscious, for we have no data to warrant such an assumption. This was not the language of the Sadducees, nor of the Pharisees, or Essenes (as has been thought by Bull, Ittig and Schneckenburger with reference to their doctrine of the εἱμαρμένη), still less could he aim at Simon Majus (Calov); on the other hand the reference is not simply to the general bias of the natural man to charge God somehow with the πειράζεσθαι, which the Jews might strengthen by misinterpretations of the Old Testament (Huther; see also the Note p. 59; Prov. xix. 3; Sir. xv. 11, 12); for our Epistle deals throughout not with mere generalities, but with concrete relations.—ὅτι is a much used formula of quotation; ἀπό, as Huther observes, is not as strong as ὑπό. [See Winer, p. 382, ἀπό= through influences proceding from God.—M.].

For God is not temptable.—The reasons for the foregoing in a twofold assertion respecting God. First, He is ἀπείραστος. This ἅπαξ λεγόμενον in the New Testament must not be confounded with the classical ἀπείρατος (in the sense of inexperienced) as denoting: God has no experience of evil (Schulthess, de Wette, Huther). Equally objectionable is the active construction of the word (Luther following the Vulgate '*intentator*'), for its weak grammatical basis, the Genitive κακῶν, its tautology both with respect to what goes before and to what follows forbid the active construction. The passive-adjective construction, however, not tempted, not temptable, which is generally adopted is not only not against grammatical usage as Huther maintains, (see the adjectival ἀκατάστατος v. 8), nor against the connection, as he thinks also. For James wants to strengthen the dehortation, "Let no man say, etc." For this saying, like all fanaticism, was a tempting God, and therefore vain and impious, because God does not suffer Himself to be tempted. Hence we might feel inclined to take κακῶν in the Masculine and to denote evil men; but this would probably be expressed more definitely. To think of evils (Oecumenius) is somewhat far-fetched, but also the evil in the Singular would be too general; the Plural in the present connection points to concrete and intensively *evil things*. [But there is an insuperable objection to Lange's derivation of the word from πειράζω; for ἀπείραστος is=untempted, not temptable: but James argues not concerning God *being tempted*, but concerning God tempting. I therefore prefer the common usage of the word 'inexperienced in'; so Alford, Winer and (in part at least) Wordsworth, who adds, "that James may perhaps refer to the false tenet of some of the heretics of the early Church, who said that it was the duty of men to have *experimental knowledge of all evil*, in order to the attainment of perfection." See Palm and Rost's Lexicon and Weststein for examples in favour of '*inexperienced in*'.—M.]. Secondly: **But He Himself tempteth no one.**—[Lange takes no notice of δὲ which has here adversative force and makes therefore against his rendering 'not temptable,' while it favours the rendering 'inexperienced in;' and δὲ here is="not so, but" Alford.—M.]. Second negation aimed at the substance of the proposition "I am tempted from God" (Huther). Αὐτός is construed differently; Huther takes it as antithesis to what follows in the sense: it is not *He* who tempts, but every man is tempted etc. Theile and Wiesinger take it in contrast with what goes before: He Himself (self-active). And this is probably right; He suffers Himself not to be drawn by God-tempting fanatics into their unholy interests, but He Himself becomes tempter to no man; the solicitation to evil, in the trial which He appoints, is not from Him. Stress must therefore be laid on both—*not He,—tempteth not any one*. [Lange hardly does justice to Huther whose view is very lucid. "Let no one say when he is tempted to evil, from God I am tempted: for God has no part in evil: but as to the temptation, *He* tempts no man etc."—M.].

[Wordsworth here quotes Augustine, *Tractat. in Joann.* 43 and *de consensu Evang.* ii. 30, who raises a question on this passage. If God *tempts no one*, how is it that He is said in Scripture to *tempt Abraham* (Gen. xxii. 1)? To which he replies that St. James is speaking of temptations arising *from* evil *motives* with a view to an *evil end*. *No such* temptations are from *God*. But God is said to have tempted, that is, to have *tried* Abraham, from a good motive and for a good end. He tried him, in love to him and to all men, in order that he might become the Father of the faithful and be an example of obedience to all ages of the world." See also Tertullian *de Orat.* c. 8. "God forbid that we should imagine that He tempts any one, *as if He were ignorant* of any man's faith, or desired to make any one fall. No, such ignorance and malice belong not to God, but to the devil. Abraham was commanded to slay his son, not for his temptation but for *the manifestation of his faith*, as a pattern and proof to all, that no pledges of love, however dear, are to be preferred to God.—Christ, when tempted by the devil, showed *who* it is that is the author of temptation, and *who* it is that is our *Guardian* against it."—M.].

With reference to the seemingly contradictory passages Gen. xxii. 1; Deut. viii. 2 and others, it is first of all necessary to distinguish as much between temptation and obduracy as between Abraham and Pharaoh. According to the concrete expression of the Old Testament God tempts Abraham by subjecting him to a trial to which the popular idea, handed down by tradition, clings as an element of temptation. He tempts Pharaoh by subjecting him to a trial in which the judgment of his self-delusion must reach its consummation. God therefore has no part whatsoever in the temptation itself as a solicitation to evil but throughout concurs in it, in the beginning trying or proving, at the end judging, at the intermediate stages chastising and punishing. It is with reference to the punishing feature in temptation that we pray: lead us not into temptation. God, as Calvin remarks, is never the author of evil.

The hideous form of the self-temptation of the erring by evil concupisence and its fruit—death. vv. 14–16.

VER. 14. **But every one is tempted.**—Wiesinger wrongly insists upon the necessity of distinguishing the being tempted in this verse from the falling into temptation v. 2, as an intrinsical occurrence. The representation of tempting lust under the figure of an unchaste woman rather shows that James thinks of the lust belonging to the person tempted objectively in some folly which he encounters extrinsically, just as in Prov. vii. 5, etc. But he is quite right in opposing the above drawn course of good demeanour in temptation to the now drawn course of misdemeanour. But this point we shall touch further on. The objective folly, therefore, encountered by the person tempted, is, according to the Apostle's idea, really nothing else than his very own (*ἰδία* emphasized) lust; first, because it springs also, as the temptation of Satan and the world, from the same ungodly *ἐπιθυμία*, from the *alter ego* of his own sinfulness, and secondly, because his evil lust which has now become objective can only control him by his subjective evil lust. If, according to a well-founded distinction, we are tempted by the world, the devil and our own flesh and blood, we must further explain this thus: the temptation of the world and the devil also is in its nature uniformly homogeneous worldliness and selfishness and it is only in a man's self-own and subjective evil lust that temptation is able to become to him an ensnaring temptation in a narrower sense. Thus the great temptation of that time was everywhere only *one* temptation both to the Jews and the Jewish-Christians; all those glittering, variegated visionary expectations which seductively met the individual, had sprung from the matter of the chiliastic, world-lusting, spiritual pride. It is on this property in the dazzling object that James lays principal stress, because every one must overcome the world and Satan in his own strength by overcoming himself. In the first place we have now to inquire why he renders the *ἰδία ἐπιθυμία* objective in the figure of the unchaste woman. According to Theile and Wiesinger the words: *Every one*, etc., should be construed thus: *Every one is tempted by his own lust in that he is lured* etc. The pure expression of the antithesis: "tempted from God," "tempted by his own lust," seems to favour it. But this construction wipes out the figure that follows in its very conception. The sense is rather: "*Every one is tempted, in that he*," etc., according to the construing of Luther, de Wette and Huther; viz., his own inward concupiscence meeting him as a soliciting unchaste woman. For this image is immediately indicated by the verbs *ἐξέλκειν* and *δελεάζειν*. Schneckenburger observes on it: *Verba e re venatoria et piscatoria in rem amatoriam et inde in nostrum tropum translata.* *ἐξέλκειν* (in N. T. ἅπαξ λεγ.) and *δελεάζειν* are not synonymous (Pott: *protahere in littus*), in fact it has hardly a specific meaning in the *res venatoria* (Schultess: *elicere bestias ex tuto*); but in the *res amatoria* we may distinguish it from allurement proper in that it draws men from their intrinsicality and independence by dazzling interest (to draw off and to allure—Germ. *ablocken* and *anlocken*); *δελεάζειν* (from *δέλεαρ*=*esca exposita ad capienda animalia*) occurs also 2 Pet. ii. 14, 18, and is used also by the classics metaphorically, always in a bad sense. Now we must not overlook the force of the Participles *ἐξελκόμενος* etc., they denote the process of development (becoming) in the course of which temptation becomes entanglement as far as man continues in it. He is first drawn out from his inward self-control and fortress and then attracted (drawn to) by the unchaste woman's allurings. [This is the reason why I have retained the Participles in my translation.—M.]. But the intrinsical decision proper is further expressed by *εἶτα συλλαβοῦσα.* Ἐπιθυμία however does not denote "innocent sensuousness." "The word occurs here, as it always occurs in the N. T. (except where its specific object is indicated, as in Luke xxii. 15; Phil. i. 23; 1 Thess. ii. 17) also without the addition of *κακή*, *σαρκική*, or some similar adjective, *in sensu malo*." Huther. Ἐπιθυμία is not, indeed, birth-sin *per se* (as Huther rightly observes), but just as little only an evil lusting for the commission of the deed springing from birth-sin, as he argues against Wiesinger, whose almost equivalent exposition he scruples to admit. It is birth-sin itself in its concrete activity ("*prava concupiscentia*") viewed from its positive side as worldliness and selfishness, assuming in different situations innumerable variations. Maintaining with Pott the figurative description of different personifications, we find that the reference is not to four but to three generations. We have in succession the unchaste mother or the *ἐπιθυμία*, the unchaste daughter or *ἁμαρτία* in the narrower sense of deed-sin and the son and grandson of the voluptuous mothers, the murderer-son death. Man yielding with his will to the allurement of evil lust, his moral relations assume a kind of natural sequence and the rest follows of itself. Lust becomes impregnated and brings forth sin, while sin brings forth (as it were out of itself or pursuant to its essential connection with ἐπιθυμία—hastening along with its own maturity the maturing of the hereditary death-germ) death.

VER. 15. **Then, when lust hath conceived.**—This denotes man's proper surrendering to his evil lust in a manner which indicates that it was to be expected because he kept standing (continued,) in the allurement (δελεαζόμενος). The evil lust is fecundated *i. e.* it has obtained the mastery over the will of man.

It bringeth forth sin. (וַתַּהַר וַתֵּלֶד).—De Wette and al. make ἁμαρτία denote the intrinsical act of sin and ἁμαρτία ἀποτελεσθεῖσα the extrinsical deed-sin. But Wiesinger and Huther are right in saying that the intrinsical act is involved in συλλαβοῦσα. On the other hand Calvin, Schneckenburger, Wiesinger and al. take the ἁμαρτία ἀποτελεσθεῖσα to denote the whole sinful life. But Huther says that it denotes the equal deed-sin, yet, in its entire development passing through its different stages until it subjects man to itself so that all reaction is at an end. "For ἀποτελεῖν is neither =*perpetrare* (Pott), nor=*operari* (Laurentius), nor=τίκτειν (τεχθεῖσα, Baumgarten), but=to complete; hence ἡ ἁμαρτία ἀποτελεσθεῖσα = sin advanced to the completeness of its development. Now since sin makes its first appearance as a new-birth the allusion to the now matured unchaste young woman which several commentators have found in the ἀποτελεσθεῖσα, is not outside the cycle of James's thoughts; the expression certainly brings out the idea that she did reach a false τέλος which is the opposite of the τέλος to which the believing Israelite attains in virtue of his well-demeanour. True Judaism has matured into Christianity, Judaizing into antichristian apostasy. In point of meaning the exposition of Wiesinger coincides pretty much with that of Huther, but the latter has the preference of firmly keeping up the image of sin itself in its process of completion.

Bringeth forth death.—"The word ἀποκύει (found in the N. T. only here and in v. 18) differs from τίκτει only in that the former indicates more clearly that the ἁμαρτία is from the outset pregnant with the θάνατος." Huther.—Huther and Wiesinger explain death both of temporal and eternal death, Rom. vi. 23. But between the two lies the historical, indeterminate (*unabsehbar*) death (which being indeterminate must therefore be distinguished from absolute death [*Untergang*]), and as soon as we consider the concrete import of this passage, this feature of death becomes of the utmost importance. And here we have to call attention to the antithesis which Wiesinger has found between vv. 3, 4 and this passage. The first proposition that "the trial of faith by tribulation answers to the incitement of the will by lust" we consider to be false; to fall into temptation and to be tempted are identical. But the consciousness of the πειράζεσθαι and the ἐξελκόμενος and δελεαζόμενος in connection with the antithesis of operative πίστις there and operative ἐπιθυμία here, this is one real antithesis; the second is the ὑπομονή there and ἁμαρτία here. Again the ἔργον τέλειον there and the ἁμαρτία ἀποτελεσθεῖσα here; lastly the τέλειοι there (connected with the στέφανος τῆς ζωῆς v. 12) and the θάνατος here. The last two antitheses Wiesinger has taken together. Applying now the whole passage to the circumstances peculiar to the time of James, the completed sin denotes the completed apostasy of the Jewish people and death their historical judgment (see ch. v. and Rom. x.). This of course does not exclude the more general meaning of our passage which opens the prospect of eternal death as well as the most specific meaning according to which every mortal sin is followed by spiritual death. We have still to notice the different dogma-tropes: sin brings forth death (James), sin is followed by death as its wages or punishment (Paul), sin is death (John).—Likewise we must guard our passage against the [Roman] Catholic inference that sin as such must be distinguished from evil concupiscence (lust) with Calvin: "*Neque enim disputat Jacobus, quando incipiat nasci peccatum, ita ut peccatum sit et reputetur coram deo, sed quando emergat.*" James, to be sure, and all Holy Scripture prompt us to distinguish intrinsical deed-sin or the evil counsel of the heart from the direct and natural motions of sinful desire. Lastly we must avoid the presumption that James by the use of this frightful image simply wanted to didactically prove that temptation does not come from God; he also wanted his readers to understand it as to its real nature, origin and working. Hence the further admonition: "Be ye not deceived." [Alford develops another view of the above image. "The harlot ἐπιθυμία, ἐξέλκει and δελεάζει the man: the guilty union is committed by the will embracing the temptress: the consequence is that she τίκτει ἁμαρτίαν sin, in general, of some kind, of that kind to which the temptation inclines: then ἡ ἁμαρτία that particular sin, when grown up and mature—herself ἀποκύει, '*extrudit*,' as if all along pregnant with it, death, the final result of sin. So that temptation to sin cannot be from God, while trial is from Him."—He also recalls the sublime allegory in Milton's Paradise Lost (Book II) where Satan by his own evil lust brings forth sin ("out of thy head I sprung"), and then by an incestuous union with sin

(——Back they recoil'd afraid
At first and called me sin, and for a sign
Portentous held me; but familiar grown,
I pleased and with attractive graces won
The most averse, thee chiefly, who full oft
Thyself in me thy perfect image viewing
Becam'st enamour'd, and such joy thou took'st
With me in secret, that my womb conceived
A growing burden.—)

causes her to bring forth Death.—M.].

VER. 16. **Be not ye deceived.**—Although this sentence refers also to what follows (Theile) and not solely to what goes before (Gebser) the reference to the latter (Wiesinger) is greater than that to the former. The expression, moreover, has the full pregnancy of a warning against objective images and spirits of temptation, according to de

Wette, "be not ye deceived," and not with Gebser, "err not." The warmth of this caution is heightened by the address:

My beloved brethren, although they were to find the means of strengthening and confirming this exhortation in the subsequent instruction concerning the true God of revelation. Huther: "The same formula is found in 1 Cor. vi. 9; xv. 33; Gal. vi. 7 (a similar one 1 Jno. iii. 7 [*μηδεὶς πλανάτω ὑμᾶς*—M.], in all these passages it follows up a thought peculiar to the Christian consciousness, *by which an antecedent statement receives its confirmation.*" [Wordsworth: The formulas *μὴ πλανῶ* "be not *thou* deceived," and *μὴ πλανᾶσθε* "be not *ye* deceived," are the preambles used in Scripture and by ancient Fathers, in order to introduce cautions against, and *refutations* of some popular error, as here.—M.].

The opposing image of the true God, etc.

VER. 17. **Every good giving** (bestowing).—We ask leave to reproduce the Hexameter (see *Winer*, § 68, 5a, p. 663) because nothing but a close consideration of the text has led us to do so. [The German rendering is as follows: "*Jegliche gute Bescherung und alle vollkommene Gabe*"—the Greek original reads thus: *πᾱσᾰ δῠ|σῑς ᾰγᾰ|θη̄ κᾱι|πᾱν δω̄|ρη̄μᾰ τε̆|λεῑον*, the last syllable in the second foot *σις* being lengthened by the arsis.—M]. Standing by the side of *δώρημα*, *δόσις* can hardly have the same meaning as the former (as Huther maintains); *δόσις* rather denotes primarily the act of giving and secondarily the gift. But alongside of *δώρημα*, which denotes gift, donation, present, it becomes at all events the lesser giving, while *δώρημα* is the more weighty expression. To this must be added the gradation of the adjectives *ἀγαθή*, *τέλειον*. It is certainly unfounded to apply *δόσις* to gifts of nature and *δώρημα* to gifts of grace, but this does not involve an identity (so Huther) which is here very tautologically expressed. *Τέλειον* must be made the starting-point of the exposition. According to the New Testament idea of *τελείωσις*, *τέλειον* corresponds with the *ἔργον τέλειον* and the Christians as *τέλειοι*, and with the *ἁμαρτία ἀποτελεσθεῖσα*, v. 15. And just as the perfect work can only be understood as the consistent practical exhibition of the theocratical faith in Christianity, and as the *τέλειος* describes one who has decided for Christ, while sin completed denotes the sin of Christ-inimical apostasy, so also *δώρημα τέλειον* signifies the gift of God completed in Christianity. Our *δώρημα* reminds us of Christ as *χάρισμα*, Rom. v. 15; but here the reference is probably to the Christian revelation in the fulness of its gifts. This would make *πᾶσα δόσις* to denote everything which served to prepare this completed gift in the olden time, especially in the old covenant, according to the analogy of Heb. i. 1. The readers here and there should know that the one and only God presides over the difference and antithesis between the Old Covenant and the New. It is not to be wondered at that several commentators (Raphelius, Augusti) were tempted to take *πᾶσα* and *πᾶν* in an exclusive sense, for the antithesis lay near: God tempts no man, nothing but good comes from Him. This would be a more distinct statement of the antithesis, but James wanted to present it in a richer form: not only does no evil come from God, nay rather all good comes from Him. It is moreover *ἄνωθεν καταβαῖνον* in uninterrupted permanence, a perpetual rain and sunshine of gifts. The Participle is to be duly considered and we ought really to render: it comes and comes. The word *gift* for *δώρημα* is rather weak and donating would be more weighty than donation. [Bengel renders *δόσις datio* and *δώρημα donum.* On the whole *δόσις*=*datio*=giving, and *δώρημα*=*donum*=gift, is probably the nearest rendering which the Latin and English tongues admit. Bp. Andrews, who has two sermons on this text, vol. iii. p. 36, and vol. v. p. 311 observes p. 313, that *δόσις ἀγαθή*, *donatio bona* or *good giving*, represents rather the act of giving which bestows things of *present use* for this life, whether for our souls or bodies, in our journey to our heavenly country; but *δώρημα τέλειον* or *perfect gift*, designates those unalloyed and enduring treasures, which are laid up for us in eternity. I have retained the *Participle* in my translation.—M.].

From the Father of the lights.—Huther and Wiesinger agree with the majority of modern commentators that the lights here signify the heavenly bodies. But we do not believe that a single passage of Holy Writ can be produced in support of such an abnormal mode of expression. Ps. cxxxvi. the LXX. say concerning the stars *τῷ ποιήσαντι φῶτα μεγάλα*, Jer. iv. 23 *τὰ φῶτα αὐτοῦ*. But Scripture as well as the Nicene Creed uniformly distinguish *make* from *create* and *beget*. Job xxxviii. 28 surely does not mean that God is the father of rain. Setting aside the following explanations of the lights: *knowledge* (Hornejus), *joy* (Michaelis), *wisdom or goodness* (Wolf), it is hardly necessary to think of the *Urim and Thummim* (Heisen) and even the reference to the angels (Kern and Olshausen) cannot be retained. But the reference to the Sermon on the Mount, with which James is so intimately connected, is less remote. In Matth. v. 14, the disciples are called *τὸ φῶς τοῦ κόσμου* and in v. 16, they are actually distinguished from their light as candlesticks or light-bearers. The Messiah is often called a Light in the Old Testament (Is. ix. 2; xlix. 6, etc.) and in the New Testament it is an appellation by which He describes Himself (Jno. viii. 12; cf. ch. i. 4 and other passages). Also John the Baptist He calls a light Jno. v. 35 and Phil. ii. 15 Christians are referred to: *ὡς φωστῆρες ἐν κόσμῳ*. If in favour of the aforesaid exposition it is alleged that God Himself is called *φῶς* 1 Jno. i. 5 (cf. 1 Tim. vi. 15) it is necessary clearly to distinguish that ethical idea from the physical. The subsequent metaphors: *παρ' ᾧ*, are claimed in favour of the disputed exposition; but they constitute an antithesis between God, the Light without shadow and the symbolical bodies of light, which are not without casting their shadows. Besides all this, believers as *God-begotten* children are distinguished in v. 18 as an *ἀπαρχή* from the *κτίσματα*. The *Scholion ap. Matth: ἤτοι τῶν ἀγγελικῶν δυνάμεων, ἢ τῶν πεφωτισμένων ἀνθρώπων*, seems accordingly to be right in the last clause in the sense that the whole line of organs of revelation from Abraham to Christ as the representatives of all good spirits is what is meant here. [Bengel: *Patris appellatio con-*

gruens huic loco; sequitur ἀπεκύησεν. *Ipse Patris, et matris, loco est. Est Pater luminum etiam spiritualium in regno gratiæ et gloriæ. Ergo multo magis Ipse Lux est,* 1 John i. 5. Lucis *mentione statim, ut solet, subjungitur mentio* vitæ, *ex regeneratione.* v. 18. There is no reason why the two interpretations should not be combined. God is the Father of *all* lights, the lights of nature and the lights of grace; the Father not only of the light of reason and conscience, the light of knowledge and goodness but also the Father of the children of Light. To enter in this connection upon hair-splitting distinctions between create, make and beget, seems hardly the thing. Whatever is gross and material is of course eliminated from the meaning of any of said three expressions, and if the spiritual conception of the Divine character as Maker, Creator and Father, has once been reached, metaphysical quibbles may well be dispened with.—M.].

With whom (as peculiar to whom) **there is not existing.**—We give this construction of the passage on account of ἔνι, without discussing the question whether ἔνι is a peculiar form (Buttmann, Winer), or an abbreviation of ἔνεστι (Meyer, Huther).

A change or a shadow-casting.—In the first place it is to be remembered that these words are ἅπαξ λεγ. in the New Testament. Then the first word, being the more general, must be explained by the second and more definite one. The Greek commentators limit the figurative to the ἀποσκίασμα (Oecumenius, Theophylact and al.): with God there is no mutation or a shadow (*i. e.* a trace or appearance of a change, or also of a reservation; they are followed among modern expositors by Morus, Rosenmüller, Hensler, Theile. The Latin commentators, on the other hand (Justinianus, Estius, a Lapide and al.) apply the expression *ad solis vicissitudines et conversiones.* Then also Luther (see the Translation), Grotius, Wetstein, Flatt, Schulthess. For a full treatment of the passage see Gebser, who explains it of the shadows cast by the solstice. Wiesinger suggests changes of the moon, solar and lunar eclipses and regards the shadow as the effect of τροπή; similar is the exposition of Huther: the shadow cast on the heavenly body, effected by its changing position. But solar and lunar eclipses are phenomena too rare and transient in order to give a pregnant expression to the idea in question. And although there may not be used here any *termini technici* of Astronomy (as Huther observes) in their strict sense, the contemplation of the world in every age led probably to a sufficient knowledge of astronomy in order to recognize in the diurnal phenomenal revolution of the sun, the moon and the stars the cause of all nocturnal obscurings of the earth. The sun has not only its annual but its diurnal solstice. In like manner the moon and the stars rise and set and leave us in absolute night. But God is in a very different sense the Light of the world, a Sun that never sets. To this refer Ps. cxxxix. 9, 12; Job. xxxiv. 22; it was also symbolized by the pillar of fire in the camp of the Israelites. Now if the expression τροπῆς ἀποσκίασμα denotes such a *phenomenal* shadow-casting of the revolving heavenly bodies, we can hardly take παραλλαγή in a purely general sense (Huther)=mutation, but as a figurative description of a change of position (standing-place). This alternation is the first thing: the constant progression of the celestial bodies, the turning, follow as the result. Now if the heavenly bodies, as the created symbols of the Divine being of light, possess the property of being not without shadow and night we get the antithesis that God, the Father of the Lights is eternally the same, not only *per se*, but also in the phenomena of these lights: that is to say, He makes no revolution with the Old Testament which could cast a night-shadow on the New (as the Talmud at a later period attempted to make such a revolution), nor does He suffer the New Testament to cast a night-shadow on the Old (according to the later opinion of the Gnostics and of all rationalists). The Father of the lights remains unchanged even in this antithesis. ["God is always in the meridian." Wetstein.—Bengel's note will be found useful: "παραλλαγή *dicit mutationem in intellectu;* (vide LXX. 2 Reg. ix. 20), τροπή *mutationem voluntatis. In utroque vocabulo est metaphora a stellis, huic loco,* ubi luminum *mentio fit, aptissima.* παραλλαγή *et* τροπή *est in natura* (vid. τροπάς Job. xxxviii. 33) *quæ habet quotidianam vicissitudinem diei et noctis, et longiores modo dies modo noctes: in Deo nil tale est. Ipse est Lux mera,* παραλλαγή *et* τροπή, *si qua accidit, penes nos est, non penes Patrem luminum.* ἀποσκίασμα *interdum dicit* ὁμοίωμα. *Sic enim Hesychius interpretatur. unde Gregorius Naz.* τὸ τῆς ἀληθείας ἴνδαλμα καὶ ἀποσκίασμα *tanquam synonyma ponit: et apud Tullium, Budæo observante,* adumbratio rei *opponitur* perfectioni ejus; *sed hoc loco opponitur* luminibus, *adeoque magis proprie sumitur, ut* ἀποσκίασμα τροπῆς *sit* jactus umbræ primulus, revolutionem habens conjunctam. *Idem Hebraismus genitivi mox,* abundantiam malitiæ, *ex quo colligere licet,* τὸ transmutatio *opponi* τῷ datio bona, *quemadmodum* vicissitudinis obumbratio *opponitur* τῷ donum perfectum. παραλλαγή *aliquid majus est. Hinc gradatio in oratione negante:* ne quidem vicissitudinis adumbratio. *Hoc demum efficit* perfectionem; *illud* bonum *est.* Perfectior *est, qui ne quidem vicissitudinis adumbrationem habet.*"—M.].

The exaltation of the children of God begotten by the word of truth.

VER. 18. **Pursuant to free decree hath He begotten us.**—The connection of these words with what goes before is differently construed: 1. as coördination: God the Father of lights is also the Author of our regeneration (Theile); 2. as exemplification: *generatio spiritualis, quasi exemplum aliquod donorum istorum spiritualium* (Laurentius, de Wette); 3. as an inference drawn from the general idea of the former (Huther). But regeneration, as matter of experience, cannot be inferred from a dogma concerning God; 4. as proof or demonstration (Gebser, Kern). Wiesinger's remarks are excellent: "The greatest δώρημα (v. 18) which consists in the Divinely effected regeneration of man by the word of truth, is now mentioned by the author in lieu of everything else as the brightest actual proof that nothing evil, but all good comes from God. This act of His holy love is at once the strongest exhortation to a demeanour well-pleasing to Him. (v. 19 etc.)." The Apostle shows therefore how the heaven-descended δώρημα τέλειον had evidenced itself as such by its effect, viz. the regeneration of believers. Now in thus laying the strongest emphasis on the exalted dignity, the ὕψος of Christians following from their regeneration, he also emasculates thereby the fallacy of that seductive fanaticism, which would fain mislead them to pursue a false phantom of this exaltation on chiliastic and revolutionary paths. At the same he presents to all Jews this true life-picture of their exaltation. Βουληθείς is the emphatic beginning of the sentence. "*Pursuant to his established* (Aorist) *free decree.*" The element of love (Bengel: *voluntate amantissima*) lies primarily not in the word itself but in its connection. The antithesis is (according to Bede, Calvin and al.) the meritoriousness of good works. It lies however nearer to see the primary reference to the Jewish claims to the kingdom (Rom. ix.), especially because the βουληθείς at any rate contains the element of voluntary determination. The verb itself, used here, shows plainly that reference is made not to natural birth, but to regeneration, for ἀποκύειν is the synonyme of γεννᾶν etc. (1 Jno. iii. 9; 1 Pet. i. 23; 2 Pet. i. 4)." So Huther rightly answers Pott, who wants to explain ἀποκύειν by *facere, efficere.*

Us, i. e., the Christians. But the objective regeneration of humanity in Christ was primarily also designed for the Jews as the regeneration of the nation and the theocracy, and to this teleological element the sequel constrains us to give a proper share of our consideration. Besides this objective element, subjectively realized by believers, we must also take cognizance of the emphasis: begotten by the Father of lights and thus destined to the enjoyment of the most exalted dignity. [Bengel, as usual, gives us the pith of the whole riches of thought in a nutshell and supplies commentators with mental food. Much of Lange's view may be traced back to Bengel, and some of the beautiful reflections of Wordsworth, which we shall produce under *Doctrinal and Ethical*, seem to flow from the same source. He says: βουληθεὶς, volens, *voluntate amantissima, liberrima, purissima, fœcundissima.* Hebr. אָב ab אבה voluit; cf. Jno. i. 13. *Congruit* ἔλεος, misericordia, 1 Pet. i. 3. *Antitheton*, concupiscentia cum conceperit.—ἀπεκύησεν. *Antitheton*, ἀποκύει, v. 15 (cf. also what he says on v. 17, *Ipse* (*Deus*) *Patris et matris loco est.*—M.].

By the word of truth.—*The Gospel as the completion of the whole word of revelation.* The word of truth regarded not only as opposed to the law as such, or even to the tradition of the law, but especially also as opposed to the lies and frauds of fanaticism which promised to make the readers of the Epistle sons of the kingdom. This also chimes in with the antithesis in time: what the temptation promises you in a phantom, the word of truth has already made us in reality. The word of truth, *i. e.*, the word which is truth (*Genit. Appos.* [cf. Jno. xvii. 17: ὁ λόγος ὁ σὸς ἀλήθεια ἐστι—M.)], but also the expression and life of truth (1 Pet. i. 23; cf. Eph. i. 13; Col. i. 5=εὐαγγέλιον; 2 Tim. ii. 15). The whole Epistle shows that James meant the mediation of this word by Christ, but the idea is more general because by this completion he comprehends into one whole the entire Old Testament as Christianity in process of being (or becoming). [These words are also susceptible of a different interpretation. According to it the λόγος is personal and denotes the ETERNAL WORD, the Second Person in the Holy Trinity, by WHOM we have been born again (cf. 1 Pet. i. 23), "WHO for our sakes became Incarnate and by being Incarnate gave "to those, who *receive* Him power to become *sons of God*," who are born, not of *blood*, nor of the *will of the flesh*, but of God (Jno. i. 13), and through whom we cry "*Abba, Father*" (Rom. viii. 15; Gal. iii. 26), and become "partakers of the Divine nature." Wordsworth. The noble array of authorities, in favour of this interpretation, will be found under "DOCTRINAL AND ETHICAL."—M.].

That we should be; not that we should *become*. But the teleological mode of expression is probably chosen in order to indicate that the Jews should *become* what Christians already *are*.

A (kind of) **first fruit.**—Calvin: *τινὰ similitudinis est nota; nos quodam modo esse primitias.* So Huther, Wiesinger, Gebser and al. But James hardly needed to give prominence to this symbolical mode of speech in an Epistle, symbolical throughout. It was self-evident. But on that account we are hardly prepared to understand the reference in the word with Bengel: "*quædam habet modestiam, nam primitiæ proprie et absolute est Christus.*" Christ is here included as Mediator of the Christian first fruit. But James, using this expression, might well recollect that the angels of God are a different kind of first-fruit of the creation. It has been inferred from this passage that Christians are also superior to the angels; at all events they are coördinated with them as a different type of celestial first-born. The frequent occurrence of this word in a symbolical sense (Lev. xxiii. 10; Numb. xviii. 12; Deut. xxvi. 2) removes all doubt that ἀπαρχή alludes to the God-consecrated first-fruit in the Old Covenant (Laurentius: *allusio est ad ritum legalem in V. T. de consecratione primogenitorum, frugum, jumentorum et hominum*). The word therefore involves also the idea that Christians are a people consecrated to the service of God, even as the first-consecrated in relation to the future conversion of the Gentiles and "the glorification of the world." (Huther.) But this does not warrant the inference drawn by Huther and Wiesinger that the first-born in point of time settles the idea of first-fruit in point of dignity. Even in the province of nature the idea of the first-born or matured is more or less connected with the idea of the excellent. In the New Testament, however, this idea of the word in a spiritual sense, is repeatedly made prominent (1 Cor. xv. 20, 23; xvi. 15; Rev. xiv. 4). But there is yet another element of the idea, which has to be decidedly held fast. As the first-fruit was at once the prophecy and surety of the whole subsequent harvest, so Christ as ἀπαρχή of the resurrection is surety for the subsequent stages of the resurrection, so the Holy Ghost in believers is surety for the subsequent glory (Rom. viii. 23); so the first believers of Israel in their unity are sureties for the future conversion of the whole nation, Rom. xi. 6. We see no reason for abandoning any one of these three elements, 1. The God-consecrated first-fruit people, 2. the first dignity of the real children of God involved in it, 3. the living security for future conversions, even for the glorification of the world. Huther ojects to the second element that instead of τινὰ we ought to have κτισμάτων followed by νέων or καινῶν. But the difficulty with regard to τινὰ has been settled above, and Huther's exposition, not ours, would require a νέων. Even the taking of πρῶτοι in the sense of τιμιώτατοι or some similar word (in Oecumenius) is not against the Apostle's idea; it only presents modifications and consequences of πρῶτοι.

Of His creatures.—This expression which relates generally to the whole creation but particularly to God's moral institutions in mankind, brings out primarily the second sense of ἀπαρχή, as in Ps. viii.; Rom. viii.; 1 Cor. vi. 2, 3; but also the third sense. Christians as God's ἀπαρχή are not only superior to the doings of the moral world and to the propensities of the natural world, but they are also as God's ἀπαρχή sureties for the glorification of the world. The κτίσματα τοῦ θεοῦ, although they are not really the καινὴ κτίσις (Olshausen), but the ἀπαρχὴ θεοῦ belongs also to them, as a surety that they will ripen into the καινὴ κτίσις, just as the first-fruits are an ἀπαρχή of the ripening fields. The depth of Christian knowledge contained in this passage has been admirably set forth by Wiesinger, p. 88, etc., to which the reader is referred. [We give it below under "Doctrinal and Ethical." —M.]. Particular note should be taken of the striking accord of this passage in James with the fundamental ideas of the doctrine of Paul, in βουληθείς, election, free grace; in ἀπεκύησεν the doctrine of regeneration and the new creature, in the λόγος ἀληθείας the antithesis of law and symbol, in the ἀπαρχή not only the relation of Christians to the world, but in particular the relation of the Jewish Christians to the Jews (Rom. x.), and in the κτίσματα his doctrine of the glorification of the world by Christ, Rom. viii.; Eph. i.

DOCTRINAL AND ETHICAL.

If there is *one* question, which for centuries has engaged and exhausted the reflection of the most celebrated philosophers, it is this: whence is moral evil? Moral evil, disorder in the dominion of a God of order and justice, a discord in the harmony of creation, an ever-flowing spring of misery by the side of so many and copious fountains of happiness opened for us by a higher Love. Who is the author of its disastrous existence? Does it come from God? If so, how could God be just and holy? And if it does not come from Him, how could it originate, continue and rule from the world's first dawn until now? There is no thinker who has not stood in silent contemplation of the riddle and there is also no thinker who has been able to resist the temptation of making at least an effort towards its solution. The various schools of Greek philosophy exhibit the most contradictory principles. The most different gnostic systems of the second century we see revolve round this problem as if it were their immutable centre. And even the speculative philosophy of our century, no matter how often its idealism departed from the maxims of experience, found it impossible wholly to overlook this dark back-ground of all human self-consciousness and had to include the investigation of evil in the course of its contemplations, if for no other purpose than that of denying the reality of sin as constituting the guilt of mankind. The most important efforts of human thought to explain the origin of moral evil have been discussed in a masterly manner by Julius Müller in his classical work, "*Die Christliche Lehre von der Sünde*" (new edition, 1844.)

2. The principal features of the doctrine, which James here presents concerning the origin of sin, may be compressed into one sentence, viz.: Sin is in no event God's fault but altogether our own. Every explanation of the origin of sin which makes God directly or indirectly the *causa efficiens mali*, James condemns *in toto* (as to its inmost ground), as does also Paul, Rom. iii. 8.

3. Nothing is more common than the endeavour to charge God directly or indirectly with the guilt of our transgressions. Even the heathen sought shelter in the subterfuge that some divinity or irresistible demon had impelled them to evil and the Jews asked "Why does he yet find fault?" Rom. ix. 19. The most ancient art of sinful mankind was the sewing of fig-leaves (Gen. iii. 7), and also the modern rationalism of our century in this respect seems neither to have learnt nor to have forgotten any thing. Sin, in the opinion of modern rationalists, is a relative, yet an altogether unavoidable evil. Is God not the Almighty who creates light and darkness, the Infinite from whom, by whom, and to whom are all things absolutely, the Omniscient, who foresaw the abuse of moral freedom and might easily have prevented it? It is therefore plainly thus: man could not but altogether fall and he falls not only with the high sanction but also according to the will and arrangement of God. Sin is a wholly indispensable part of our earthly plan of education just as a child would never have learned to walk without having previously stumbled. Sin is the inseparable shade-side of the light of perfection, which as it shines is inconceivable without a shadow. Sin is a want of development, an imperfection, grounded *nolens volens* in the organization of our race, for which we can no more be held accountable than for having feet but no wings. Thus sin, which is free choice and a daring opposition to God, is fundamentally made to be a rule and what might yet be wanting to the fair-seeming theory, appears in still more glaring colours in practice. Even the dullest mind becomes inexhaustible in wit and understanding if it is necessary to excuse the commission of evil. There is nothing more difficult even to infant lips than the admission of personal guilt. Now it is the fault of others or of circumstances in which we find ourselves placed, again it is the fault of our temperament or the natural infirmity of an originally excellent heart. Aye, how many a Christian seeks to lessen his guilt with the pious sigh that God had let go his hand for a moment, that the Lord had hidden His countenance from him so that now he could not evince himself as a child of light; that the flesh had proved too strong for him and it was really not he that kept on sinning, but the invincible principle of flesh within himself. If James were to revisit us, he would not

have any occasion to withdraw his exhortation as superfluous: "Let no man, being tempted, say, I am tempted from God."

4. It is only necessary to enter somewhat more profoundly into the idea that God in the most absolute sense of the word is ἀπείραστος κακῶν in order to perceive the infinite superiority of the Christian conception of God to the ethnical. James, in this respect, occupies not only a lofty religious but also a purely ethical standpoint. Just as the conception of God with many is obscured by sins, so on the other hand, the Christian conception of God corrects many confused or one-sided theories of the origin of sin.

5. In order that we may thoroughly understand the teaching of James respecting the origin of sin, we must in particular not lose sight of the point, that it is not so much his intention to account for the origin of sin among mankind as to describe it in the human individual: in other words that he here treats of the matter rather psychologically than metaphysically. Rationalistic commentators who consequently use James i. 14, 15 as a weapon against Gen. iii. and Jno. viii. 44, act most arbitrarily. The matter has two sides only one of which is touched by James, while he does not invalidate the other, no matter how true it may be in itself. Cf. Jas. iv. 7. What he describes is the history of sin in every individual man, and that in three different periods: in its beginning, its progress and its end.

6. James in declaring that lust, having conceived, brings forth *sin*, does by no means imply that ἐπιθυμία *per se* is not altogether sin. The *concupiscentia* in this case is already *prava*, but it is here expressly set forth not as the mother of the sinful principle but of the sinful *deed*. The Protestant Church at every period has rightly opposed to the pelagianizing tendencies of [Roman] Catholicism the assertion that also the ἐπιθυμία of man, which eventually becomes deed-sin, is sinful in itself (*per se*). Paul also denies that the law is sin, not that lust is sin, Rom. vii. 7. Besides the history of every more signal sin, *e. g.*, that of Adam or Pharaoh, David, Ahab and many others furnishes the most striking proofs of the correctness of the delineation here given. "This passage is greatly abused if it is cited as a proof that evil desires are not sin, provided man withhold his consent. For James does not discuss the question when sin begins, when it is sin before God and imputed as sin, but when it breaks forth. Thus he gradually progresses to show that the completion of sin is the cause of eternal death, but that sin is rooted in a man's own lust; whence it follows that men shall reap in eternal ruin the fruit which they themselves have sowed." *Chrysostom.*

7. The idea of guilt, which is here so emphatically expressed by James, is of the utmost importance to the whole development of scientific theology. Not until sin in its true nature is acknowledged as guilt, are we able to appreciate the depth of the doctrines of the atonement and of redemption. But then it must be equally acknowledged that only a Redeemer, who was really *God*-man, was able to deliver us from eternal ruin. The right conception of Soteriology and Christology is thoroughly rooted in the deeper insight into Hamartology.

8. It is impossible that God should be at variance with Himself, that His holiness should conflict with His love. The same God whom James describes in v. 17 as ἀπείραστος κακῶν he sets forth in v. 17 as the eternal source (German *primal* source) of light from whom *all* gifts and only good gifts flow to us. This declaration also reminds us of the Sermon on the Mount, Matth. vii. 11. God is here called the Father of lights, as elsewhere He is described as the Father of spirits, the God of the spirits of all flesh, Heb. xii. 9; Numb. xvi. 22. James describes the inexhaustible riches of the goodness and the glory of the immutability of God in a form at once poetical and metrical "πᾶσα δόσις ἀγαθὴ, καὶ πᾶν δώρημα τέλειον," in order to show also thereby that the inference "that such a God could yet be the cause of sin" contains the strongest *contradictio in terminis.* For it is impossible that the Father of lights should love darkness; He, with whom there is no change, cannot possibly cause to-day the evil which yesterday He did forbid or punish; detestable sin, so often condemned by Him, in no event can belong to His good and perfect gifts. "The New Testament positively opposes the repulsive assertion of a self-development of God." Heubner.

9. The greatest proof of the absolute impossibility of God being the cause of sin lies in the opposite experience of believers themselves (v. 18), where the greatest and most glorious of all good gifts (v. 17), although stated in general terms, is yet specifically named. The history of the birth of sin (v. 15) is opposed (v. 18) to the spiritual history of the birth of Christians in order to shed thereby the brightest light on the fact that God who effects regeneration, cannot possibly be the author of its contrary—evil. Those who attach but little importance to the Epistle of James in a dogmatical point of view would do well to give their earnest and thoughtful attention to his *dictum classicum* concerning regeneration, v. 18. We have here in fact the depth and riches of Paul in a brief compendium. See the exegetical notes on the passage. James' mode of statement exhibits also a surprising agreement with that of Peter (1 Pet. i. 23).

[v. 15. The progressive development of temptation is thus stated by Bede: 1. *Suggestio.* 2. *Delectatio.* 3. *Consensus. Suggestio est hostis, delectatio autem vel consensus est nostræ fragilitatis. Si delectationem cordis* partus *sequitur pravæ actionis, nobis jam mortis reis victor* hostis *abscedit.* For further illustration see Wordsworth.

v. 16. Bp. Andrewes (*Sermons*, 3, p. 374). "Though of man it be truly said by Job, "he never continueth in one stay" (Job. xiv. 2); though the *lights of heaven* have their parallaxes; yea, "the *angels* of heaven, he found not steadfastness in them" (Job. iv. 18); yet for *God*, He is subject to none of them. He is "*Ego sum qui sum*" (Ex. iii. 14); that is, saith Malachi, "*Ego Deus et non mutor* (Mal. iii. 6). *We* are not what we were awhile since, what we shall be awhile after, scarce what we are; for every moment makes us vary. With God it is nothing so, "He is that He is; He is and changeth not." He changes not his tenor; He says not, before Abraham was, *I was*; but "before Abraham was, *I am*" (Jno. viii. 58).

Yet are there "varyings and changes," it cannot be denied. We see them daily: True, but the point is *per quem*, on whom to lay them? Not on God. Seems there any recess? It is we forsake Him, not He us (Jer. ii. 17). It is the ship that moves, though they that be in it think the land goes from them, not they from it. Seems there any variation, as that of the night? It is *umbra terræ* makes it, the light makes it not. Is there anything resembling a shadow? A vapour rises from us, and makes the cloud, which is as a pent-house between, and takes *Him* from our sight. That vapour is our lust, there is the *apud quem*. Is any tempted? It is *his own lust* doth it; that enticeth him to sin; that brings us to the shadow of death. It is not God. No more than He can be tempted, no more can He tempt any. If we find any change, the *apud* is with us, not *Him;* we change, He is unchanged. "Man walketh in a vain shadow." (Ps. xxxix. 6). His ways are the truth. He cannot deny Himself.

Every evil, the more perfectly evil it is, the more it is from below: it either rises from the steam of our nature corrupted; or yet lower, ascends as a gross smoke, from the *bottomless pit*, from the prince of darkness, as full of varying and turning into all shapes and shadows, as God is far from both, who is uniform and constant in all His courses. —The *lights* may vary, He is invariable; they may change, He is unchangeable, constant always and like Himself. Now our lessons from these are—

1. Are they *given?* Then, *quid gloriaris?* Let us have no boasting. Are they given, why forget the Giver? Let Him be had in memory, He is worthy so to be had.

2. Are the *"giving"* as well as the *"gift"* and the "good" as the "perfect," of gift, both? Then acknowledge it in both; take the one as a pledge, make the one as a step to the other.

3. Are they from somewhere else, not from ourselves? Learn then to say, and to say with feeling, *Non nobis, Domine, quia non a nobis.* (Ps. cvi. 1).

4. Are they from on high? Look not down to the ground, then, as swine to the acorns they find lying there, and never once up to the tree they come from. Look up; the very frame of our body gives that way. It is nature's check to us to have our head bear upward and our heart grovel below.

5. Do they descend? Ascribe them then to purpose, not to time or chance. No table to fortune, saith the prophet. Is. lxv. 11.

6. Are they from the "Father of lights?" (Jer. x. 12) then never go to the children, *a signis cœli nolite timere*: "neither fear nor hope for any thing from any light of them at all."

7. Are His "gifts without repentance?" (Rom. ii. 29). Varies He not? Whom He loves, doth "He love to the end?" (Jno. xiii. 1). Let our service be so too, not wavering. O, that we changed from Him no more than He from us! Not from the light of grace to the shadow of sin, as we do full often.

But above all, that which is ex *totâ substantiâ*, that if we find any want of any giving or gift, good or perfect, this text gives us light, whither to look, to whom to repair for them; to the "Father of lights." And even so let us do. *Ad patrem luminum cum primo lumine:* "Let the light, every day, so soon as we see it, put us in mind to get us to the Father of Lights." *Ascendat oratio, descendat miseratio*, "let our prayer go up to Him that His grace may come down to us," so, to lighten us in our ways and works, that we may in the end come to dwell with Him, in the light which is φῶς ἀνέσπερον, "light whereof there is no eventide," the sun whereof never sets, nor knows tropic—the only thing we miss, and wish for in our lights here, *primum et ante omnia.* [A part of the above really belongs to "HOMILETICAL and PRACTICAL" but I doubt not that the reader will be thankful to me for not having attempted to sever the practical element from the doctrinal—M.].

[V. 18. WORDSWORTH:—With reverence be it said, in the work of our *Regeneration*, God is both our Father and Mother; and this statement well follows the declaration of the Apostle that *every good giving and every perfect gift* is from above, coming down from the *Father* of lights. He is a *Father*, the *Father* of lights, and He is like a *Mother* also, and gives birth to us by the Word of truth.

Compare the use of the maternal word ὠδίνω, *parturio*, used by St. Paul in one of his tenderest expressions of affectionate yearning for his spiritual children, Gal. iv. 19.

By this word ἀπεκύησεν, *He brought us forth*, St. James declares God's *maternal love* for our souls. Is. xlix. 15. Ps. xxvii. 12.

—The view which makes ὁ λόγος *personal* is not in conflict with the common view; it is based on the recognition of the two senses in which St. James and St. Paul use it. Cf. Heb. iv. 12; Eph. v. 26; Tit. i. 3; Gal. iv. 19. The comparison of this verse (James i. 18) with i. 21 shows that James passes by a natural transition from the *Incarnate Word* to the reception of the *Inspired Word.*

ATHANASIUS (*contra Arianos* iii. § 61, p. 483): "Whatsoever the Father determines to create, He makes and creates by Him (the Word), as the Apostle says. *By His will* he brought us forth by the *Word.* Therefore the will of the Father, which concerns those who are born again, or which concerns those things that are made by any other way, is in the *Word*, in whom He makes and regenerates what He thinks fit."

IRENÆUS (ii. 25, 3):—"Thou, O man, are not uncreated, nor wert thou always coëxistent with God, like His own *Word*, but thou art gradually learning from the *Word* the dispensations of God who made thee."

TERTULLIAN (c. *Praxean.* c. 7) illustrating the word ἀπεκύησεν says: "*Christus primogenitus et unigenitus Dei proprie de vulva cordis Ipsius.*"

NOVATIAN (*de Trinit.* 31):—"There is one God, without any origin, from whom the Word, the Son was born. He, born of the Father, dwells ever in the Father."

THEOPHILUS of Antioch (§ 10): "God, having His Own Word indwelling in His own bowels (σπλάγχνοις), begat Him, having breathed Him forth before all things, and through Him He hath made all things; and He is called the Beginning, because He is the Principle and Lord of all things which were created through Him."

Hippolitus (*Philos.* p. 334):—"The One Supreme God generates the Word in His own mind. The word was in the Father, bearing the Will of the Father who begat Him; and when the Father commanded that the world should be created, the Word was executing what was pleasing to the Father,—The Word alone is of God, of God Himself; wherefore He is God. The Word of God regulates all things, the First-born of the Father. Christ is God over all, who commanded us to wash away sin from man; regenerating the old man, and having called man His image from the beginning; and if thou hearkenest to His holy commandment and imitatest in goodness Him who is good, thou wilt be like Him, being honoured by Him, for God has a longing for thee, having divinized thee also for his glory."

Bp. Bull (*Def. Fid. Nic.* III. ch. ii.) says: "The Son of God, born from *Eternity*, is said by the Fathers to have certain other births in *time*. He was born into the world when He came forth to create the world. He was born again in a wonderful manner, when He descended into the womb of the virgin and united Himself to His creature. He is daily born in the hearts of those who embrace Him by faith and love."

Bp. Pearson (p. 219) says: "This use of the term *Word* was familiar to the Jews, and this was the reason that St. John delivered to them so great a mystery in *so few words*." Wordsworth adds that the same remark is applicable to the language of St. James.

Bp. Bull (*Def. Fid. Nic.* I. ch. i. § 17-19, and *Harm. Apost. Diss.* 2. ch. xv.). In the latter passage he declares the meaning of St. James to be that our Christian graces proceed from "the good pleasure of God through Christ, and from the regeneration which the Holy Spirit works in us through the Gospel."

Wordsworth:—"They whom St. James addressed, being born again by adoption and *created* anew in *Christ Jesus*, the Eternal Word (Eph. ii. 10), might well be said to be designed by God to be *a first-fruit of His creatures*, for they were *new creatures* in Christ (Gal. vi. 15; 2 Cor. v. 17), who is the *first begotten* of every creature (Col. i. 15), the beginning of the creation of God (Rev. iii. 14), by whom all things were created (Col. i. 16). By virtue of His incarnation and of their incorporation and filiation in Him, who is the *first-born* among many brethren (Rom. viii. 29), they were made the *first-fruits* of creation, being advanced to a high preëminence and primacy, beyond that which was given to Adam before the fall (Gen. i. 28) and even above the angels themselves. Cf. Heb. i. 5-13; ii. 5, 7-16."——"This higher sense of λόγος includes also the lower one, God brought us forth by the *Word* of truth, *preached* to the world."—M.].

[The Note of Wiesinger, referred to under "*Exegetical and Critical*" is as follows: "this passage is among those which reveal the depth of Christian knowledge in which the practical and moral exhortations of the writer are grounded: lying as it does expressly (διό v. 19) at the basis of them. We will here bring together in a few words the teaching of the passage, for the sake of its important bearing on the rest of the Epistle. It teaches us

1. As a positive supplement to vv. 14, 15, that the life of man must be renewed, from its very root and foundation;

2. It designates this renewal as God's work, moreover as an imparting of the life of God (ἀπεκύησε), as only possible by the working of the Spirit, only on the foundation of the objective fact of our redemption in Christ, which is the contents of the λόγος ἀληθείας;

3. It sets forth this regeneration as an act once for all accomplished (ἀπεκύησεν, Aor.) and distinguishes it from the gradual penetration and sanctification of the individual life by means of this new principle of life imparted in the regeneration.

4. It declares also expressly that the regeneration is a free act of God's Love (βουληθείς) not induced by any work of man (Eph. ii. 8, 9; Tit. iii. 5), so that man is placed by God in his right relation to God, antecedently to all works well-pleasing to God: for this the expression ἀπεκύησεν involves: cf. ἐξελέξατο, ch. ii. 5, and in so far as this ἀπεκύησεν necessarily implies the justification of the sinner (the δικαιοῦσθαι of St. Paul), it is plain also, that St. James cannot, without contradicting himself, make this δικαιοῦσθαι, in the sense of St. Paul, dependent on the works of faith.

5. λόγος ἀληθείας is specified as the objective medium of regeneration; and herewith we must have πίστις as the appropriating medium on the part of man himself: of the central import of which πίστις in St. James we have already seen something (ch. ii. 5, 14, etc.).

6. Together with this act of regeneration proceeding from God, we have also the high destination of the Christian, which the Apostle gives so significantly and deeply in εἰς τὸ εἶναι κ. τ. λ. And that which God has done to him, is now in the following verses made the foundation of that which the Christian on his part has to do: by which what we have said under 3, and 4, receives fresh confirmation. This passage is one to be remembered, when we wish to know what the Apostle understands by the νόμος τέλειος (i. 25; ii. 12) and what he means, when (ii. 14, etc.) he deduces δικαιοῦσθαι from the works of faith. As regards the dogmatical use, which we make of this passage, wishing to show that regeneration is brought about by the word, as distinguished from the Sacrament of Baptism (Tit. iii. 5-7), we may remark, that seeing that λόγος ἀληθείας designates the Gospel, as a whole, without any respect to such distinction, nothing regarding it can be gathered from this passage. The word of the Lord constitutes, we know, the force of the Sacrament also. "*Accedit verbum ad elementum et fit Sacramentum.*" And it is meant to be inferred that the readers of this Epistle were *not baptized*."—M.].

HOMILETICAL AND PRACTICAL.

It is impossible to pursue the course of life while we regard God in any way the cause of sin.—The attempt of charging God with the guilt of one's transgression: 1, The traces of this perverseness: a, in the Jewish world, b, in the heathen world, c, in the Christian world. 2. The springs of this perverseness; *a*, in a darkened understanding, *b*, in a proud heart, *c*, in a sinful will.

3, The sad consequences of this perverseness; by it a, God is insulted, b, our brother offended, c, and our own sanctification and salvation opposed.—God in opposition to moral evil.—The ethical excellency of the Christian conception of God, also a proof of its heavenly origin.—No excuse for sin, cf. Gen. iii. 12; Jno. xv. 22.—The history of the development of sin in every individual man: 1, beginning, 2, progress, 3, end.—How very different sin appears *a posteriori* from what it appears *a priori*.—Sin should never be contemplated in the light of speculative understanding only, but always in the light of conscience, the Bible and experience.—The erring Christian also should still be addressed as a beloved brother.—Error manifold, truth only one.—The errors of men in morals are mainly the effect of their not looking up sufficiently to the Father of light.—The riches of God: 1, all good lights come from Him; 2, only good gifts come from Him.—God cannot be tempted to evil but He is never supplicated in vain for good.—The exaltation of the Creator above the most exalted work of His hands.—The constant alternation in the natural world contrasted with the immutable order in the moral world.—The immutability of the Father of lights viewed 1, on its heart-stirring and consoling side, but also 2, on its solemnly-admonishing and warning side.—The miracles of regeneration: 1, God has begotten us, 2, according to His free decree, 3, by the word of truth, 4, that we should be etc.—On the whole lesson v. 13-18. Sin not God's fault but solely our own, a truth, 1, which man is only too prone to forget (v. 13), 2, which confirms the history of the development of sin (vv. 14, 15), 3, which a glance at the being of God (vv. 16, 17) and at the work of God (v. 18), removes beyond all doubt.—On the conclusion: "Do not err," v. 16. "Do not err," how James here cautions us against a threefold error: 1, Do not err, ye who expect the highest good from beneath (the earth): all good giving is from above, 2, Do not err, ye who dwelling on the goodness of God, forget His holiness: the Giver of all good is also the Father of lights. 3, Do not err, ye who think that His holiness in your case would cease to be just: with the Father of lights is neither variableness, nor a shadow of turning.

STARKE:—Man as long as he lives in time is liable to temptations.—Every man has a lust and bias peculiar to himself and carries the origin of all his temptations within himself, Jno. xii. 6.

QUESNEL:—We ourselves are our own worst enemies by our own lusts, Prov. xv. 27.—Man becomes gradually sinful.—Whatever we receive from above should take us back from below upward to God.—The rivers of God's grace flow from on high into the deep valleys; the lower the heart, the more gentle the supply [influx= the flow of God's grace into the heart.—M.].—If God is the Father of light, then sin cannot be His child. For what communion has light with darkness? 2 Cor. vi. 14.—If believers are God-begotten, they are of Divine descent [a Divine race—M.]. O, what high nobility!

LUTHER:—The lying word of the serpent has corrupted us but the true word of God makes us good again, Jno. xvii. 17.

STIER:—Nothing good comes from below; not even outward help for outward need (cf. Sir. 38, 8, 9).—Good gifts in general are of no avail without the perfect gift, which restores to us light and life in a regeneration (out of) God.

HEUBNER:—Being tempted refers not only to solicitations to apostasy from Christianity, from religion by adversities, but James manifestly speaks of sin in general.—Desire remains barren without the will.—All the woe of mankind is the fruit of sin.—Deriving evil from the Being of God is much worse than Parseeism with its dualism.—

PORUBSZKY:—The nature of temptation [*i. e.* its essence—M.], 1, lies not in the outward assault but rather within ourselves; 2, it should not be combated from without but from within.—Of the holy power needed for pious deeds: 1, of the necessity of this power; 2, of its communication.

[V. 13. God permits and overrules the temptation, but is not the Author of it.—God is neither temptable by evil things, nor versed in evil things.—Lust, the enchantress and temptress, cf. Prov. vii. 5-27. See also the admirable portrait of the gossamer approaches of sin in *Southey's* Thalaba, Book 8, 23-29.—God, the Father of lights is not the Author of evil; contrast "Father of lights" and "Prince of darkness."—

Vv. 14, 15. The way to death. 1. Man drawn by his evil inclinations out of the safe asylum of virtue (ἐξελκόμενος); 2. entrapped by the fascinations of vice and evil (δελεαζόμενος); 3. into the commission of voluntary sin (ἐπιθυμία συλλαβοῦσα τίκτει ἁμαρτίαν), and 4. ripening in sin, hurried to ruin (ἡ δὲ ἁμαρτία ἀποτελεσθεῖσα ἀποκύει θάνατον).—

V. 16. The duty of Christian pastors to caution their flocks against error.—

V. 17. God the Author of good—he cannot therefore be the Author of Evil.—God is the perennial fountain, whence gush in perpetual streams good gifts and perfect gifts.—Good *living* denotes not only temporal blessings but also spiritual—it comprehends the bestowal of every blessing accorded us by the munificence of our heavenly Father in this our *imperfect* state of existence; while *perfect gifts* are those eternal possessions laid up for us in heaven, of which *regeneration* is the beginning and pledge.—God is the *Father* of the lights, not only of heaven, not only of the lights of reason, wisdom, conscience, truth, inspiration and prophecy, but also the Father of the children of light (Luke xvi. 8; Jno. xii. 36; Eph. v. 8; cf. also Matth. v. 14, 16).—M.].

[WORDSWORTH: v. 13.—St. James delivers a caution against errors, which afterwards showed themselves in the heresies of *Apelles, Hermogenes, Valentinus, Marcion* and the *Manichæans*, which represented God as the *Author* of evil, or as *subject* to evil, and unable to resist and overcome it.—v. 14. Concupiscence is the womb of sin, and the offspring of sin is death. All these are evil and none of these are from God, who is the Author of all good.—M.].

[DIDYMUS: v. 16.—The ministry of *good* is directly and indirectly *from* God; but *evil* comes only *per accidens*, indirectly and mediately, for the correction of man, who is chastened by suffering.—M.].

[WORDSWORTH: v. 18.—Here is an Apostolic protest against two errors prevalent among the Jews, 1. that men are what they are either by *necessity*, as the Pharisees held, or else 2, as the Sadducees taught, by the unaided action of their *own will*, independently of *Divine grace*. See Maimonides in his Preface to *Pirke Aboth*, and Josephus *Ant.* xiii. 5, 9; xviii. 1, 3. Bp. Bull, *Harm. Apost. Diss.* 2, ch. 15. Thus they disparaged the dignity of the *Divine Will*.

[Man in Christ is the *wave-sheaf* of the harvest. See 1 Cor. xv. 20–23—M.].

[RABBINICAL: v. 13.—This is the custom of evil concupiscence; to-day it saith, Do this; to-morrow, worship an idol. The man goes and worships. Again it saith, be *angry*.—Evil concupiscence is, at the beginning, like the thread of a spider's web; afterward it is like a cart-rope. —M.].

[MACKNIGHT: v. 15.—The *soul*, which the Greek philosophers considered as the seat of the appetites and passions, is called by *Philo* τὸ θῆλυ, the *female* part of our nature; and the spirit, τὸ ἄῤῥεν, the *male* part. In allusion to this notion, James represents men's *lust* as a *harlot*, who entices their understanding and will into its impure embraces and from that conjunction *conceives* sin. Sin being *brought forth*, immediately acts, and is nourished by frequent repetition, till at length it gains such strength that in its turn it *begets* death. This is the true genealogy of sin and death. *Lust* is the *mother* of *sin* and *sin* the *mother* of *death;* and the *sinner* the *parent* of both." —M.].

[BP. SANDERSON: v. 13.—St. James therefore concludes positively, that every man's temptation, if it take effect, is merely from his own lust. It is then our own act and deed, if we are Satan's vassals: disclaim it we cannot; and whatsoever misery or mischief ensueth thereupon, we ought not to impute to any other than ourselves alone.—M.].

[ABP. SECKER: v. 14.—Temptation has no power, the great tempter himself has no power, but that of using persuasion. *Forced* we cannot be, so long as we are true to ourselves, our own consent must be our own giving: and without it the rest is nothing.—M.].

[DR. JORTIN: v. 17.—The unchangeable nature of God suggests very powerful dissuasions from vice. The Scripture contains no decrees concerning the reprobation and salvation of particular persons, without regard to their moral qualifications. But there is a law which declares that obstinate and impenitent vice shall end in destruction. This law is as eternal and unchangeable, as the nature of good and evil, or the nature and perfections of God. Heaven and earth shall pass away, but this decree shall not pass away: and therefore a fearful thing it is to fall into the hands of the everliving and immutable God. Yet this unchangeable nature of our Creator, considered in another view, affords no less comfort and peace to the greatest offenders, if they will repent and turn to Him. Their offences cannot be greater than His mercy and goodness, which endures to all eternity, ready to receive those who by an effectual repentance and reformation, through the satisfaction of Christ, make themselves proper objects of His mercy.—M.].

[SERMONS and Sermon themes:

v. 13. SHARP, ABP.: *How far God is concerned in temptations to sin.* Works 6, 263.

vv. 13, 14. TILLOTSON ABP.: *The sins of men not chargeable to God.*

vv. 13–15. *Apology for Providence in sin.*

SIMEON, CH. *Sin, the offspring of our own hearts.* Works 20, 27.

v. 15. SAURIN, *La manière d'étudier la religion.* Sermons 4, 1.

vv. 16, 17. SIMEON, CH. *God the only source of all good.* Works 20, 32.

v. 17. BLAIR, H. *On the unchangeableness of the Divine Nature.* Sermons 2, 85.

v. 18. CHARNOCK, STEPHEN, *The instrument of regeneration.* Works 5, 521.

HALL, ROBERT, *The cause, agent and purpose of regeneration.* Works 5, 186.

DODDRIDGE, PHIL., *Address to the regenerate.* Works 2, 536.—M.].

IV. SECOND ADMONITION WITH REFERENCE TO THE SECOND FORM OF TEMPTATION—FANATICISM.

CAUTION AGAINST YIELDING TO THE WRATH OF MAN (*SEXUAL*), WHICH THINKS ITSELF COMPETENT TO ADMINISTER THE JUSTICE OF GOD BUT IS INCOMPETENT TO DO IT. THE INSTRUMENT OF DELIVERANCE AND PRESERVATION FROM THIS ZEAL: THE CULTURE OF INNER LIFE IN FAITH AND THE VERITABLE RELIGIOUS PROOF OF THIS FAITH IN ACTS OF MERCY.

CHAPTER I. 19–27.

(V. 22–27. *Epistle for 5th Sunday after Easter*).

19 Wherefore,[1] my beloved brethren, let every man be swift to hear, slow to speak, slow
20, 21 to wrath: For the wrath of man worketh[2] not the righteousness of God. Wherefore

lay apart all filthiness and superfluity of naughtiness, and receive with meekness the
22 engrafted word, which is able to save your souls. But be ye doers of the word, and
23 not hearers only,[3] deceiving your own selves. For if any be a hearer of the word,
24 and not a doer, he is like unto a man beholding his natural face in a glass: For he
beholdeth himself, and goeth his way, and straightway forgetteth what manner of man
25 he was. But whoso looketh into the perfect law of liberty, and continueth *therein*,
he being not a forgetful hearer, but a doer of the work, this[4] man shall be blessed in
26 his deed. If[5] any man among you[6] seem to be religious, and bridleth not his tongue,
27 but deceiveth his own heart, this man's religion *is* vain. Pure religion and undefiled
before God[7] and the Father is this, To visit the fatherless and widows in their affliction, *and* to keep himself unspotted from the world.

Verse 19. [1] ἴστε is the most authentic reading. A. B. C. Vulg. al. ὥστε found in G. K. [Rec. L. Sin.] is evidently a correction designed to establish a clearer connection, which has however obscured the peculiar import of this section. De Wette and Wiesinger, indeed advocate the retention of ὥστε on internal grounds against Lachmann, Huther and al., but the internal grounds are also in favour of ἴστε and even Tischendorf's reädoption of the reading of the Text. Rec. cannot affect the question. We also read with A. δὲ after ἴστε and καί before ἔστω. Tischendorf now decidedly favours ὥστε; so does Bouman p 84 sqq.

Lange: Know however .... also let every man etc. [ye know it .... but let etc.—M.]

Verse 20. [2] ἐργάζεται A. B. [C.[3]] Sin., Lachmann; κατεργάζεται C.* G. K. al. Tisch. The former seems to preponderate, but ἐργάζεται has here surely a peculiarly emphatic meaning.

Lange: For the man's [*vir*] wrath doth not accomplish [execute] etc.

Verse 21. Lange: Wherefore, removing all filthiness and all out-flowing [communication of life] of malice [malignity] acquire in gentleness the word implanted in [and among] you, which etc.

Wherefore putting off all filthiness and superabundance of maliciousness, receive in meekness the innate Word, which etc.—M.]

Verse 22. [3] μόνον *before* ἀκροαταί Rec. A. C. K. L. Theile; *after* B. Vulg. Alford.—M.]

Lange: But become ye doers .... as those who ensnare themselves. [But become ye ....deceiving etc.—M.]

Verse 23. Lange: For if ....this man is like to a man who observes the countenance [image of appearance] of his birth [of his development-image, of his life-form, the momentary formation of his continual development] in a mirror.

Because (ὅτι) .... this man is like to a man considering the face of his birth in a mirror—M.].

Verse 24. Lange: For he observed himself and went away and forthwith forgot of what manner he was.

For he considered himself and is gone away .... what he was like (ὁποῖος ἦν, *i. e.* how he looked in the mirror)—M.].

Verse 25. [4] A. B. C. Sin. and al. *omit* οὗτος before ἀκροατής, so Lachmann; Tischendorf following G. K. [and Rec. —M.] *inserts* it. The omission may have arisen from the supposition that the word was superfluous, its pregnant force having been misapprehended.

Lange: But he, who became absorbed in the completed law, that of liberty, and remained thus, who became not a hearer unto forgetting, but a doer of the work, the same shall be blessed in his doing.

But he who looked into the perfect law, that (τὸν) of liberty, and perseveres doing so, being .... in his doing—M.].

Verse 26. [5] δὲ after εἰ, inserted by Lachmann following C., has the most important Codd. against it. It weakens also the recapitulatory character of the sentence.

[6] A. B. C. omit ἐν ὑμῖν.

Lange: If any man [among you] fancieth himself to be a religious man [one theocratically zealous of the honour of God] etc.

German for religious man, "*Gottesdiener*"=a servant of God, one observant of God's outward service; religion "*Gottesdienst*"=outward service of God.—M.]

Verse 27. [7] τῷ before θεῷ recommended by A. B. C.* Sin. al. and Lachmann. This reading is also in consonance with the thought, the reference being to the God of the Christian revelation.

Lange: A pure and unprofaned religion [outward service—M.] before the God and Father is this: to be careful of the orphans and widows in their tribulation [to have the oversight of them, and not to be engrossed with politics], to preserve himself unspotted from the world.

.... before our God and Father (τῷ θεῷ καὶ πατρὶ) etc.; παρά=with, in the estimation of Alford.—M.]

EXEGETICAL AND CRITICAL.

Analysis. Caution against the second form of temptation—fanatical, angry zeal. The clemency of the man who is called to be the child of God or who is already begotten, should be in conformity to the clemency of God v. 19.—The wrath of man [sexual] is not adapted to the ministering of the righteousness of God, v. 20.—They were to purify themselves from this temptation, by acknowledging said sin as a pollution (not peradventure as zeal for Judaistic purity) and as natural maliciousness and putting it off, and on the other hand, by thoroughly appropriating with meekness the word of Christian truth unto the furthering of their salvation, v. 21.—Such an appropriation of the word will be most readily accomplished by their becoming doers of the word and by ceasing to be mere hearers, v. 22-24.—The real doer of the word has two distinguishing marks: he is absorbed with the eye of faith in the contemplation of the perfect law, the free law of Christian truth and proves his perseverance in this contemplation by the full consistency of Christian activity (as described more particularly). By such full energy of life he attains the enjoyment of blissful life v. 25.—Whoever imagines that he is a real worshipper of God and a zealot for the honour of God and corrupts his heart in giving the reins (in fanatical zeal) to his tongue, his religious service is vain. But the counterpart, true worship of God corresponding to the true image-of-God-the-Father, is Christian care of the helpless members of the Church accompanied by a decided shunning of polluting worldly-mindedness. vv. 26, 27.

The clemency which shuns fanaticism and conforms to the clemency of the Father in heaven.

VER. 19. **Know however, my beloved brethren.**—The connection indicated by the reading ὥστε (see *App. Crit.*) deduces from the clemency of God the exhortation that the Christian also should exhibit corresponding clemency. But that reading makes this verse dependent on what precedes, as if it were simply an application, which is not correct. On the contrary we have here the beginning of a new leading thought, viz.: the guarding of Christians against the temptation of fanatical zeal by fully yielding to the spirit of meekness and liberty in Christianity. Hence the reading ἴστε is also preferable on internal grounds. Huther's observation is correct: "v. 18, connects primarily with the exhortation *to hear*—and then with the further exhortation in v. 22 to be not only hearers but doers of the word." "But the hearing here insisted upon must evidence itself as decided, (according to Matth. xiii. 23) as a full and unreserved yielding to the word of truth and consequently as the foundation and not as the contrast of doing. Semler takes ἴστε as an Indicative; *non ignoratis istud carmen* Sir. v. 11, but apart from the difference in expression there and here, the indicative sense weakens without reason the energetical tone of the exhortation. Huther remarks that ἴστε answers to the μὴ πλανᾶσθε v. 16, which view is further confirmed by the use of the same address: ἀδελφοί μου ἀγαπητοί here and there; cf. also ch. ii. 5. [But it is not necessary to connect the ἴστε taken indicatively with the exhortation at all: it therefore cannot weaken its energetical tone, on the contrary it strengthens it by its very abruptness. Adopting the indicative sense of ἴστε I connect it therefore with the preceding, as follows: Ye know it, my beloved brethren, but let every man, etc.; or paraphrasing: Ye know that these things are so, but possessed of this very knowledge let every man, etc. ἴστε is used in this sense in Eph. v. 5; Heb. xii. 17.—M.].

Also let every man.—καί (see App. Crit.) indicates that the conduct of man should be in conformity to the conduct of God. It remains to be ascertained in what sense we are to take this sentence. Laurentius and al. make it a general direction; Gebser, Wiesinger and al. give it a distinct reference to "the word of truth;" Huther, Theile and al., say that the general direction had primarily the specific aim of inculcating upon Christians the right conduct also in respect of the word of truth. But all this hardly does full justice to the double antithesis in the words: *slow to speak, slow to wrath.* The Apostle indicates the point in which Christ and Christian religiousness should evidence itself as humanity, but true humanity also as piety —even the centre of faith and humanity as contrasted with inhuman and impious conduct. Hence the express declaration: πᾶς ἄνθρωπος. It is a fundamental law of humanity, which is here described by the antithesis ταχύς and βραδύς (found in Philo, but in no other place of the New Testament, and expressed by Rückert thus: "thou hast two ears and *one* mouth.")—*Being swift to hear* denotes entire readiness, constancy and thoughtfulness of hearing (Matth. xiii. 23) and shows that such real hearing contains the germ of obedience to the truth, just as real "tasting and seeing" involves the experience "that the Lord is good." *Being slow to speak* of course does not exclude all speaking but rash, immature, thoughtless and immoderate talking (λαλεῖν), especially dogmatical speaking ch. iii. 1, although the expression is not confined to it (Pott and al.). The Apostle demands cautious, thoughtful speaking, a speaking flowing from an inward calling and therefore a weighty speaking. *Being slow to wrath* applies in like manner to anger, which is consequently not absolutely disallowed (as Hornejus has truly remarked). Eagerness in speaking by warmth leads one easily to eagerness of passion [Alford: The quick speaker is the quick kindler.—M.]. Huther justly rejects the reference of this wrath to God (Calvin, Bengel, Gebser: "impatience towards God on account of persecution"). For in that case James ought not to have allowed any slowness to wrath. Huther capitally explains this wrath of "carnal zeal aiming at the mastering of our neighbour, the fruit of which is not εἰρήνη but ἀκαταστασία ch. iii. 16; the caution is directed against Christians, who—as did the Pharisees in respect to the law—instead of using the Gospel for their own sanctification, were abusing it in gratifying their love of condemnation and quarrelsomeness." Thus our exhortation in its particular direction is addressed not only to the Jewish Christians but to all the twelve tribes, whose ancestors in fanaticism, Simeon and Levi (Gen. xxxiv.), disapproved by their father (ch. xxxiv. 49), were afterwards mentioned as patterns worthy of imitation (Judith ix.).

The wrath of man not a suitable organ of the righteousness of God.

VER. 20. **For the wrath of man worketh not.**—Our verse gives the reason of the preceding one, but contrasts the two modes of conduct, the right one there and the wrong one here. We attach importance to the distinction that in the former verse reference is made to the wrath of man in general and here to the wrath of man sexually. Thomas perceives in the expression an antithesis between the man and the child, Bengel one between man and woman but neither does conform to or satisfy the historical significance of our expression. We agree with Huther that this sentence must not be referred to the state of being righteous before God (Gebser, Grashof), and with Wiesinger that it must not be to the personal doing of men which is well-pleasing to God (so Huther following Luther—δικαιοσύνη=τὸ δίκαιον a meaning of frequent occurrence in both Testaments); but we cannot stop with Wiesinger at the interpretation of Hofmann that "the wrath (zeal) of man is unable to effect in *others* (*i. e.*, as a zeal of conversion) the righteousness of God, *i. e.*, that "state of being righteous" [*Rechtsbeschaffenheit**], which God begets by this word of truth. For James evidently has respect to the fanatical delusion of wrath, which imagines to administer and work out in the world the righteousness of God especially with reference to unbelievers by passionate words and deeds, in that it only gives reality to

*We consider this term, which through Hofmann has crept into theology, as an abortive improvement on the term "righteousness" (German: *Rechtschaffenheit* or *Gerechtigkeit*).

its unamiable ebullitions. Such was specifically the Judaistic delusion, which begot Ebionism and the Jewish war and which also found afterwards its expression in Mohammedanism and even in the Christian crusades, in the ecclesiastical persecutions of heretics and also in several fanatical heretics (Eudo de Stella, Thomas Münzer, etc.). But that the subjects of this delusion at the same time believe that their wrath (zeal) is the true way of converting men, that thus they are doing a work well-pleasing to God and that thus they will become righteous before God are features which, although we cannot set them aside, must remain subordinate to the leading idea of passionate ebullitions *in majorem gloriam Dei, i. e.*, here *justitiæ Dei.* Our translation would be more strongly expressed by the reading κατεργάζεται than by the better authenticated ἐργάζεται; but the latter taken in a pregnant sense, does also give the force of the former.

Shunning the temptation to unholy and hypocritical wrath (zeal) by means of true sanctification, negatively and positively.

VER. 21. **Wherefore removing** etc.—James bidding his readers purify themselves from the false zeal for their imaginary Jewish purity sounds like an oxymoron; for it is just their kind of zeal for purity which he characterizes as impurity and their imaginary piety as inhuman maliciousness. But true purifying is to him sanctification, that is, it is on the one hand the result of a negation (putting off impurity, etc.), and on the other, the result of a positive act, viz., the full receiving of the word of truth. However the two acts do not absolutely succeed one another (*remove* and *receive*), but with the removing of impurity (take note of the Participle) the real appropriating of the evangelical word of God is to take place. The negative element, however, has here a conditional precedence, repentance before faith (Mark i. 15); hence it is here subordinated by the Participle to the positive element on which it depends (cf. Rom. xiii. 12; Eph. iv. 22, 23). But the Participle must also be noted as enforcing constancy in purifying.—ἀποθέμενοι we cannot translate "*putting off*," for the reference is not figuratively to the putting off of filthy garments and to the opposite putting on of clean ones. The antithesis is: to remove, do away with; and to acquire, appropriate (see Eph. iv. 25 and other passages).

All filthiness (impurity).—ῥυπαρία (in the New Testament only here) is doubtless a stronger expression than ἀκαθαρσία (Rom. vi. 19). It denotes filth in a religious, theocratical sense like the filthy garment ch. ii. 2, like ῥύπος 1 Pet. iii. 21, and ῥυπαρός and ῥυπαρεύειν Rev. xxii. 11. To take the word in a general sense of *moral uncleanness* (Calvin and al.), is inadequate; still less apposite are the specific renderings "avarice" (Storr), "whoring" (Laurentius), "intemperance" (Heisen); but least of all its reduction to an attribute of the following κακία (Huther: putting off all uncleanness and abundance of malice; similarly Theile, Wiesinger and al.). It is sufficiently manifest that James sees in the carnal wrath (zeal) exerted in the interest of piety an antithesis, viz., impurity towards God (on the Atheistical in the heart of fanaticism see Nitzsch *System*, p. 39), and malice towards man.

All out-flowing (communication of life) **of malice.**—Huther: περισσεία, foreign to classical Greek, denotes in the New Testament "abundance," really superabundance. The substantive and the corresponding verb περισσεύειν signify in the New Testament the overflowing of a fulness of life, on the one hand as a development of life (a passing over into the life which continues to procreate itself Matth. v. 20; Rom. xv. 13, etc.), on the other hand as a communication of life (a passing over upon others, Rom. v. 15, 17; 2 Cor. viii. 2; ch. x. 15, etc.). Here the word is evidently used in the latter sense. This follows also from the proper definition of the term κακία, which here is not synonymous with πονηρία (1 Cor. v. 8)=*vitiositas* (Semler, Theile and al.), but according to the connection as the opposite of ἐν πραΰτητι, as Eph. iv. 31; Col. iii. 8; Tit. iii. 3; 1 Pet. ii. 1. A more specific idea, namely the inimical disposition towards one's neighbour, which we express by "animosity" (Pott)! Huther.—(Wiesinger: ὀργή, Rosenmüller: *morositas*; Meyer: malice). The overflowing of maliciousness is therefore the malicious, hateful communication which passes from the fanatical wrath (zeal) of the propagandists on those whom they influence, according to Matth. xxiii. 15; Rom. ii. 24 and according to ecclesiastical history, especially the history of the persecution of the Donatists, the Paulicians and the Camisards, etc. The definition of περισσεία = περίσσωμα (Bede); outgrowth, efflorescence (Schneckenburger, de Wette):=the remnant surviving from former times (Gebser and al.=περίσσευμα), are thus set aside. [Alford joins ῥυπαρίαν with περισσείαν, as belonging to the Genitive κακίας and remarks that "it seems better for the context, which concerns not the putting away of moral pollution of all kinds, but only of that kind, which belongs to κακία. And thus taken it will mean that κακία pollutes the soul and renders it unfit to receive the ἔμφυτος λόγος. It is very possible that the agricultural similitude in ἔμφυτος may have influenced the choice of both these words, ῥυπαρία and περισσεία. The ground must be rid of all that pollutes and chokes it, before the seed can sink in and come to maturity; must be cleaned and cleared. περισσεία, if the above figures be allowed, is the rank growth, the abundant crop."—M.].

Receive (acquire, appropriate) **in meekness.**—*In* meekness, in virtue of a meek disposition, and not only with meekness. Meekness stands first in a pregnant sense. *In meekness acquire, i. e.* a meek demeanour, the opposite of wrathfulness, exhibited towards their brethren of different opinions is not only the condition, the vital element of the reception of the Gospel on the part of the Jews but also of the right appropriation of the same on the part of the Jewish Christians. Although the word denotes not directly the *docilis animus* (Grotius, similarly Calvin and al.), yet the first condition and proof of the same. The reference, to be sure, is not to meekness as the fruit of the reception of the word (Schneckenburger), although the morally calm and gentle spirit engendered under the influence of Christianity must be manifested in its highest perfection as its fruit. Want of meekness destroys the power of the Gospel (Matth.

xviii. 23, etc.); the fourth and the seventeenth centuries prove this in a remarkable manner *Receive.* δέξασθε is emphatic and denotes the right attitude under right hearing with right doing. The rooting and growing of Paul is here strikingly described as a fuller making one's own [appropriation], because the Jewish-Christians were in great danger of again losing their own (property) and the Jews were on the point of losing their ancient title to it (cf. 1 Thess. i. 6).

The word implanted in [and among] **you.**—This word is the objective Gospel (Huther: neither "innate or connate reason" [Oecumenius], nor the inner light of the mystics, for δέχεσθαι forbids that) as in v. 18, but in its subjective form of life, as the spiritual and vital principle in believers or as the seed of regeneration (1 Pet. i. 23). In this form it is implanted in believers but likewise implanted as a principle of conversion in the Jews as a whole; the latter meaning must not be not passed over. Hence the δέξασθε is relevant both with reference to the first reception and the further appropriation of it. In consequence of the difficulty arising from the idea of *receiving* a word already implanted, Calvin made ἔμφυτος proleptic and explained it "*ita suscipite, ut vere inseratur;*" and others similarly. But the word received subjectively does not thereby cease to be objective and to be received. [It is doubtful whether Lange's solution of the difficulty will stand the ordeal of logical analysis. There is no such double sense in ἔμφυτος. Nor is the more clearly expressed exposition of Alford more satisfactory. He sees in ἔμφυτος an allusion to the parable of the sower and makes "the λόγος ἔμφυτος=the word which has been sown, the word whose attribute and ἀρετή it is to be ἔμφυτος, and which is ἔμφυτος, awaiting your reception of it to spring up and take up your being into it and make you new plants." His exposition is open to the same objection that something which is already sown in *another* soil can be *implanted* in us, if he understands by λόγος ἔμφυτος the word *written* or *preached*. Adhering however to the real meaning ἔμφυτος=*innate*, τὸ ἐν φύσει (Hesych.) we may remove all difficulty. Then the λόγος ἔμφυτος is=the *innate Word*, that is, the *Word* which has been *born in our nature, i. e. Christ.* So Wordsworth who produces much illustrative matter of the use of ἔμφυτος and thus sums up the whole: While it is true, that Christ by his Incarnation is properly said to be ἔμφυτος *innate*, born in us, and to be indeed *Emmanuel, God with us, God manifest in our flesh,* God dwelling forever in the nature of us all; or, if we adopt the other sense of ἔμφυτος, while it is true, that Christ is indeed *grafted* in us as our *Netzer* or *Branch* (see Matth. ii. 23), yet will not this avail for our salvation, unless we *receive* Him by faith. We must be planted in Him and He in us by Baptism (Gal. iii. 27), we must *dwell* in Him and He in us, by actual and habitual communion with Him in the Holy Eucharist, we must abide and bring forth fruit in Him, by fervent love and hearty obedience. Christ, who is the Branch (Zech. vi. 12), is *engrafted* on the stock of our nature; but a scion grafted on a tree will *not grow* unless it is *received* and *take root* in the stock; so His Incarnation will profit us nothing, unless we *receive* Him in our hearts and drink in the sap of His grace and transfuse the life-blood of our wills into Him, and grow and coalesce with Him and bring forth fruit in Him."—M.].

Which is able to save your souls.—The idea of individual salvation is allied here with that of the national deliverance of the Israelites as in Jno. x. 28. Hence stress is here laid not only on the salvation of the soul but also on the salvation of the life and τὰς ψυχὰς ὑμων is stronger than simply ὑμᾶς. [Alford says: "It is the ψυχή which carries the personality of the man; which is between the πνεῦμα drawing it upwards and the σάρξ drawing it downwards; and is saved or lost, passes into life or death, according to the choice between these two. And the λόγος ἔμφυτος, working through the πνεῦμα and by the Divine πνεῦμα, is a spiritual agency, able to save the ψυχή."—M.]. It is *able* (cf. Rom. i. 16, δύναμις θεοῦ), but you are unable, incompetent for the carrying out of your judaistic plans of salvation. [Calvin: "*Magnificum cœlestis doctrinæ encomium, quod certam ex ea salutem consequimur. Est autem additum, ut sermonem illum instar thesauri incomparabilis et expetere et amare et magnificare discamus. Est ergo acris ad castigandam nostram ignaviam stimulus, sermonem cui solemus tam negligenter aures præbere, salutis nostræ esse causam. Tametsi non in hunc finem servandi vis sermoni adscribitur quasi aut salus in externo vocis sonitu inclusa foret, aut servandi munus Deo ablatum alio transferretur. Nam de sermone tractat Jacobus qui fide in corda hominum penetravit: et tantum indicat, Deum salutis auctorem evangelio suo eam peragere.*"—M.].

But you will really appropriate the word by becoming doers of the word and by ceasing to remain hearers only, vv. 22–24.

VER. 22. **But become ye doers of the word.**—γίνεσθε=*be* ye (Huther against Wiesinger, Theile and al.) who render=*become* ye. Huther refers to Matth. vi. 16; x. 16 and other passages. We take it with Wiesinger, of course not in the sense of Semler, as if the word indicated *perpetuam successionem horum exercitiorum*, but in the sense of a perfect development of their Christian life. This demand on the Jewish Christians and the Jews was the cause of the martyrdom of Simon, the brother of James under the reign of Trajan; it was also the cause of the early martyrdom of James, not long after he wrote this Epistle, and this is just his idea of the deed, the doing and the work, as it here for the first time takes a distinct shape: you must become wholly consistent Christians, if Christianity is to effect your salvation. As the warning against apostasy forms the negative side of his Epistle, so this exhortation to consistency constitutes its positive side. For the word is more clearly defined in vv. 18, 21 as the Gospel. They must become doers of the same in respect of its organic unity: this cannot be done by isolated acts, but only by one general act of practical life. Cf. ch. iv. 11; Rom. ii. 13. The ποιητής, who as such is the real ἀκροατής, is contrasted with the μόνον ἀκροατής. To the theocracy in its practical direction the ἀκροατής as such is insufficient, while the Greek school understood by ἀκροατής *per se* a praiseworthy hearer. Cf. Matth. vii. 21; Luke xi. 28; Jno. xiii. 17.

As those who ensnare themselves.—See v. 26; Col. ii. 4; Gal. vi. 3; 1 Jno. i. 8; παραλογίζεσθαι—to reckon beyond the mark, to reason falsely, to use fallacies,—in its practical tendency becomes deceiving, cheating and ensnaring by fallacies. Thus the "hearer only" deceives and ensnares himself. Huther refers παραλογιζόμενοι to γίνεσθε in opposition to Gebser and Schneckenburger who connect it with ἀκροαταί; but the latter are right, because the imaginary merit of *hearing* is the fallacy whereby they deceive themselves and thus properly ensnare themselves.

VER. 23. **For** [because] **if any is a hearer.**—Demonstration of the preceding by means of a simile, which is not, however, a mere figure.

Is like to.—The οὗτος emphatically repeated.

A man.—There must be some good reason for the recurrence of the specific *man* (sexual) and not only of man in general. Huther ought not to have despatched as *curious* the exposition [of Paes—M.] "*viri obiter tantum solent specula intueri*" [*muliebri autem est curiose se ad speculum componere.*—M.]. The exposition of the word ἀνήρ is connected with that of κατανοεῖν which according to Rosenmüller, Pott and al. is here used in the secondary sense of hasty observation, but is disputed by Wiesinger and Huther. Now it is correct that in Luke xii. 24, 27; Acts vii. 31, 32; xi. 6, the word denotes attentive contemplation or consideration. Primarily it signifies simply, to observe, perceive, contemplate, understand, and if the expression is opposed, as is the case here, by the more important contemplation παρακύπτειν, and we have in narrative form the statement, that the man observed himself, went away and forthwith forgot etc., the reference is only to a somewhat imperfect, momentarily-sufficient self-contemplating, such as before the mirror is rather peculiar to man than to woman. It is moreover to be borne in mind that the ideas "to hear the word," and "to contemplate oneself in a mirror" do not exactly coincide; it is only in the moment of a knowledge of oneself, of an incipient repentance that the word, which *per se* however is a mirror throughout, becomes efficient as a mirror. The *countenance* or πρόσωπον, although it need not denote the whole figure (so Pott and Sckneckenburger), is not necessarily confined to the face (so Huther); the addition τῆς γενέσεως renders the word more expressive. Γένεσις denotes according to Wiesinger and Huther only the sphere of sensuous perception as distinguished from the ethical sphere, the face, such as a man has by natural birth. That is, James is again made to remind his readers that he only refers to a figure. We consider such an interposed explanation of the figure here also not only superfluous but inappropriate to symbolical diction. For what is the real meaning of τροχὸς τῆς γενέσεως ch. iii. 6? According to Wiesinger, to be sure, "the wheel revolving from a man's birth;" but that would be an unintelligible expression and the exposition of Grotius and al. "*cursus naturæ*" has more in its favour. For life is also a genesis in a higher degree, and the fluctuating πρόσωπον is just the signature of the stages and states through which this genesis runs. This would also enable us to fix the reference of αὐτοῦ here to γένεσις (Huther), as opposed to its reference to the general idea (Wiesinger). The Jews, as Jewish-Christians, for a while attained self-knowledge, in that they saw [knew, recognized—M.] themselves in the mirror of the Gospel according to their national and individual course of development, and thus they saw also the *maculas* of this development and appearance, hence the allusion to this circumstance (Wolf) must not be rejected with Huther. In a more general sense, πρόσωπον etc., can neither denote the natural corruption of man *per se* (Pott), nor the ideal form of the new man (Wiesinger). To stop at the figure itself (with Huther) would be tantamount to making the figure unmeaning. But it simply signifies the image of the inner man's appearance as to his sinful condition modified now this way, now that way by his actual conduct. On the mirrors of the ancients see the respective article in Winer.

VER. 24. **For he observed himself.**—The narrative form represents as in v. 11, an incident quickly accomplished in the rapid succession of the fleeting stages of its brief duration. The εὐθέως ἐπελάθετο is the most important point, as Huther remarks, but each separate stage has a meaning of its own. The stage of self-knowledge in the mirror of the word, believing hearing, is followed by speedy departing, the averting of the mind from the objective fulness and depth of the word (not only from what had been heard subjectively, as Huther explains); the departing is attended by the forgetting of the mirror-image, *i. e.*, the loss of self-knowledge conscious of the necessity of salvation which would have impelled the man to the consequence of Christian renovation of life. The loss accruing from such a course, is referred to by James in v. 26, but especially in ch. v. [The Perfect ἀπελήλυθεν standing between the Aorists κατενόησεν and ἐπελάθετο is striking and imports that the *departing* denotes a permanent neglect and disuse of the mirror.—M.].

The real doer of the word according to his marks of distinction: his being absorbed in the contemplation of the free-making word, his constancy, the blessedness.

VER. 25. **But he who became absorbed.**—The pure antithesis of the former figure. Huther: "παρακύψας corresponds with κατενόησεν, παραμείνας with ἀπελήλυθεν, and οὐκ ἀκροατὴς ἐπιλησμονῆς with ἐπελάθετο." The Participles have the effect of strengthening the already strong expressions, especially in the Aorist, while taken together they indicate: γενόμενος, that it is only by constancy that a man becomes a real doer of the word. This passage must not be construed as if James wanted to distinguish the doing of the word as something separate from the looking into and abiding in it. The παρακύψας and παραμείνας, as such, is ποιητὴς ἔργου γενόμενος. This has an important bearing on the right understanding of the passage and is also very—Pauline. Constant looking into the word of salvation by faith is preeminently *the* doing which is followed by outward proof. This construction therefore must not be altered by resolving γενόμενος into γίνεται (Pott), or by saying with Wiesinger that right hearing and appropriating leads to doing and (thereby) to the blessedness of doing. Even Huther, who rejects Wiesinger's exposition, does not strictly adhere to the full energy of the idea, for he says that the doing of the law is the necessary consequence of persevering looking into the same; although prominence must be given to the fact that he characterizes the consequence as *necessary*.—Παρακύπτειν to stoop aside, to stoop over a thing in order to examine it closely (Luke xxiv. 12; Jno. xx. 5, 11; 1 Pet. i. 12); to sink into it, to be absorbed in its contemplation. Schneckenburger thinks: perhaps *ad imaginem speculi humi aut mensæ impositi adaptatum.* But this is not the most fitting way to look into a mirror. The remaining, persevering in it, Wiesinger explains as appropriating. But it is just the remaining in the yielding oneself to the object by contemplating it, whereby the appropriating of it is effected. [One of the best illustrations of the force of παρακύψας is given by Coleridge, *Aids to Reflection*, p. 15, *note:* "It signifies the incurvation or bending of the body in the act of *looking down into;* as, for instance, in the endeavour to see the reflected image of a star in the water at the bottom of a well. A more happy and forcible word could not have been chosen to express the nature and ultimate object of reflection and to enforce the necessity of it, in order to discover the living fountain and spring-head of the evidence of the Christian faith in the believer himself, and at the same time to point out the seat and region where alone it is to be found. *Quantum sumus scimus.* That which we find within ourselves, which is more than ourselves, and yet the ground of whatever is good and permanent therein, is the substance and life of all other knowledge."—M.].

Into the completed law.—We translate *completed* because of the weighty adjective τέλειος, which here again makes prominent the N. T. completion of the O. T. (cf. the τέλειοι and the ἔργον τέλειον v. 4, and the ἁμαρτία ἀποτελεσθεῖσα, v. 7; the Sermon on the Mount, the πληροῦν Matth. ii., etc.). It is not therefore the *lex naturalis* (Schulthess), or in general the λόγος ἀληθείας, inasmuch as it is the means of regeneration and the norm of the new life (Wiesinger, Huther: the norm of the new life), or on the one hand the O. T. law as simply perfect, or on the other the Gospel in a general sense; but it is the Gospel conceived as that completion of the law which transforms the outward, enslaving law into a new principle of life communicating itself to the inner man and absolutely liberating him. And just as the expressions of Paul: the law of the Spirit (Rom. viii. 2), the law of faith (Rom. iii. 27), always contain an oxymoron alluding to the higher unity of the antithesis: law and spirit, etc., so likewise in the expressions of James: the perfect law, the law of liberty, although an imitation of Pauline modes of expression is out of the question (Kern). The law as law made men servants (slaves); in its N. T. completion it makes them free. In the same sense it is also called the νόμος βασιλικός which is fulfilled by love (ch. ii. 8), and again the law of liberty (v. 12). The passages of the Old Testament, which speak of the glory of the law (Deut. xxxiii. 2, 3), or of its sweetness (Ps. xix. 8), denote the prophetical transition from the Sinaitical standpoint to the Evangelical, which was decidedly foretold by the prophets (Jer. xxxi. 33). Those who attribute to James an Ebionite glorification of the law, put him back behind Jeremiah or rather remove him even out of the Old Testament. But James had special reasons for calling the Gospel a law of (liberating) liberty inasmuch as his people were tempted to seek in their O. T. zeal for the law the means of chiliastico-revolutionary liberation (cf. Jno. viii. 32, etc.). The Gospel is moreover a law of liberty in that it asserts, along with the Christian's liberty of faith, the liberty of conscience of those of a different mind and in this form also breaks the fetters of fanaticism.

Not a hearer unto forgetting.—Properly a hearer of forgetfulness (ἐπιλησμονῆς, ἅπαξ λεγ. in the N. T.), stronger than a forgetful hearer. The antithesis ποιητὴς ἔργου brings out the idea that forgetfulness was, as it were, the object of hearing ("*in futuram oblivionem*"). The expression "doer of the work" (as follows from the construction as stated above) cannot signify here a work-activity separated from, or only clearly distinguished from faith, but it denotes the perseverance of the life of faith, which owing to its oneness of energy leads of its own accord to a consistent exhibition of corresponding outward deeds.

The same shall be blessed.—See the beatitude v. 12.

In his doing.—(ποίησις in the N. T. ἅπαξ λεγόμ., occurs only, besides here, in Sir. xix. 20), not in his deed. In the ever diligent (efficient) energy which is the soul of his deeds. Schneckenburger: "*ut ipsa actio sit beatitudo.*"—The *striving* spiritual life-motion or the doing becomes a *festive* spiritual life-motion, perfect joy. This factual becoming blessed lies according to circumstances in confession, and Rom. x. 9, 10 exhibits a near affinity with this passage. It is noteworthy that Paul also in that passage was particularly referring to Jewish Christians and that James above all things felt anxious that the Jews should confess Christ and that the Jewish Christians should make full and common cause with their Gentile brethren.

False and true religious service or zeal for religion and the glory of God. vv. 26, 27.

Ver. 26. **If any man fancieth himself.**—Δοκεῖν denotes primarily to suppose with reference to appearance and without any higher ground of certainty (Matth. xxiv. 44; hence 1 Cor. vii. 40, an expression of modesty), hence according to the connection also to imagine erroneously (Matth. vi. 7) or as here to be spiritually conceited, [*i. e.*, the man thinks, fancies that he *is* religious.—M.].

To be a religious man.—Θρῆσκος is peculiar to James. The sense of the adjective is clear from Acts xxvi. 5 and Col. ii. 18. James has formed the adjective in a masterly manner: one who plumes himself (seeks his being in) on his pretended serving of God. The word certainly implies the exhibition of a presumed εὐσέβεια in external acts of religious worship (Huther), not exclusively however in the outward observance of religion, but in the permanent soldier- or knight-service for the glory of God. So the Jews supposed that they were *the* servants of God among the nations (Rom. ii. 17), so did the Mohammedans and Crusaders at a later period and so the Jesuits suppose now. But at that time the

Jewish Christians, conceited of their God-serving, in various ways separated themselves from intercourse with Gentile Christians and in preparing for the Jewish war, the Jews supposed they were making ready for "the glory of God." [There is no one word in English which gives the exact meaning of *ϑρῆσκος* and *ϑρησκεία*. The words *religious* and *religion* at one time were used in the sense of outward ceremonial worship. An example from Milton and another from the Homilies may prove serviceable. Some of the heathen idolatries Milton characterizes as being

——"adorned
With gay *religions* full of pomp and gold."
Par. Lost. 61.

"Images used for no *religion*, or superstition rather, we mean of none worshipped, nor in danger to be worshipped of any, may be suffered." *Homily against Peril of Idolatry.* See Trench, *Synonymns of the N. T.*, p. 233. *A propos* of this *θρησκεία*, Coleridge (*Aids to Reflection*, p. 14) has these beautiful remarks: "The outward service of ancient religion, the rites, ceremonies and ceremonial vestments of the old law, had morality for their substance. They were the letter, of which morality was the spirit: the enigma, of which morality was the meaning. But morality itself is the service and ceremonial (*cultus exterior, θρησκεία*) of the Christian religion. The scheme of truth and grace that became (*ἐγένετο*) through Jesus Christ, the faith that looks down into the perfect law of liberty, has *light for its garment:* its very *robe is righteousness.*" —M.].

Not bridling his tongue.—Not *exempli causa* (Rosenmüller); nor must we with the majority of commentators resolve the Participle into "although," as Huther rightly remarks, adding: "James wants to censure those to whom zeal in talking was a sign of *ϑρησκεία*." That is: those who by their fanatical zeal wanted to make good their pretensions of being the true soldiers of God. *Χαλιναγωγεῖν*, an expression found only in profane authors of the later period has been added by James to the fund of N. T. language (cf. Acts. iii. 2).

But deceiving his heart.—*Ἀπατᾶν καρδίαν αὐτοῦ* is not exactly synonymous with *παραλογίζεσϑαι ἑαυτόν* (Huther), but denotes the same act of self-deception in a much higher degree. From the inward self-deceit of the thoughts protrudes false zeal and this has the effect that the zealot completely deceives his heart by false self-excitement (*échauffement* and bad consequences). The fanatic, by false exaggerations outwardly, at last makes himself inwardly a false and bad character.

His religion (in the sense as defined above, his zeal for the imaginary cause of God) **is vain.**—The blinding effects of his blinding passion yield no fruit of blessing to himself and others and pass as follies (*Quixotisms* in a higher style) from history into the judgment.

VER. 27. **Religion pure and unprofaned.**—The two adjectives are not strictly synonymous (Theile, Huther), nor do they simply denote the contrast of the outward and the inward (Wiesinger and al.). The expression "*pure*" requires the Christian realization of the symbolical, theocratical purity; the sequel shows that it is to exhibit itself in the pious life of merciful love. The expression "*unprofaned*" (we supply this rendering in order to give more marked force to its literal meaning; the difference between *ἀμίαντος* and *ἄσπιλος* also must be brought out in the translation) requires in the same sense real preservation of purity and purifying. The legal Jew became unclean by natural and pagan uncleannesses, the Christian must keep himself clean and cleanse himself from worldly-mindedness and vain worldly doings. Such a Divine service, therefore, denotes here the true life and work for the glory of God.—

Before the God and Father.—This again lays stress on the Christian conception of God, as in vv. 5, 17 and *παρὰ τῷ ϑεῷ* refers not only to the Divine judgment (Huther) but more especially to the attitude of the servant before the face and mouth of the commanding Lord. (Huther rightly observes concerning *καὶ πατρί* "God in virtue of His love can only consider *pure* that religious service which is the expression of love." [Chrysostom in *Catena* says: *οὐκ εἶπεν ἐὰν νηστεύητε, ὅμοιοι ἐστὲ τῷ πατρὶ ὑμῶν, οὐδὲν γὰρ τούτων παρὰ ϑεὸν οὐδὲ ἐργάζεταί τι τούτων ὁ ϑεός· ἀλλὰ τί; γίνεσϑε οἰκτιρμονες ὡς ὁ πατὴρ ὑμῶν ὁ ἐν τοῖς οὐρανοῖς· τοῦτο ϑεοῦ ἔργον· ἐὰν οὖν τοῦτο μὴ ἔχῃς, τί ἔχεις; ἔλεον ϑέλω, φησί, καὶ οὐ ϑυσίαν.*—M.].

To be careful of the orphans and widows.—We translate thus because it brings out the antithesis *to be careful of worldly affairs*, which James has doubtless before his mind's eye, like Peter in his *ἀλλοτριοεπίσκοπος*, 1 Pet. iv. 15. Although the verb is frequently applied to visiting the distressed (Huther: Matth. xxv. 36, 43; Jer. xxiii. 2 etc.), it has also in this form a wider meaning (Theile: the *species pro genere*). The wider sense: to be careful of, to care for, to protect one, is directly brought out in Acts. xv. 14; Heb. ii. 6 and elsewhere; Philo calls *ἐπίσκεψις providentia.* "The *ὀρφανοί* are named first as those in want of help, as in Deut. x. 18; Job xxix. 12, 13 etc." Huther. This Divine service answers to the fatherhood of God; those who engage in it do His work in love and compassion, because He is a Father of the orphans and a Judge (a Protector of the rights of) the widows, Ps. lxviii. 6 and other passages. Now according to the book of Tobit it was the ideal of a true Israelite to protect the distressed among the captives of his people and Tobit i. 6, 7 we read that it was an integral part of the religious service of Tobit that every third year he gave the tithe to the strangers, the widows and the fatherless. In this manner the Israelite of the New Testament was called upon to help his poor people especially the distressed in their affliction. The state of affliction in its concrete form is most frequently and most touchingly exhibited in the distress of widows and orphans. In this direction we may have to seek the sense of keeping oneself unspotted from the world; and this probably explains the asyndeton of the two sentences (cf. Huther). They are not strictly coördinate, but the second is the reverse or the sequence of the first, its pure antithesis. Hence *ἄσπιλον* comes emphatically first. Cf. 1 Pet. i. 19; 2 Pet. iii. 14. The expression ought really to be resolved into two ideas, firstly, to keep oneself from the world, secondly to keep oneself unspotted from the world; that is, *from the world* is connected with the two elements of the sentence: to keep oneself unspotted. The ethical idea of κόσμος is everywhere the personal totality of life converted into the Impersonal, *i. e.* mankind as to its ungodly bias. The peculiarity of this idea in James comes out more clearly in ch. iv. 4. What heathenism was to the Jew, the antithesis of the holy people, to which it might apostatize by spiritual idolatry, such was to the apostolical mind, the ungodly doing of the world, whether manifested in Judaistic visionariness or in a heathen form. Oecumenius's idea of the δημώδης καὶ συρφετὸς ὄχλος, ὁ κατὰ τὰς ἐπιθυμίας τῆς ἀπάτης αὐτοῦ φθειρόμενος was consequently not far from the image of the excited condition of the world, which was floating before the Apostle's imagination; but the Judaistic ὄχλος assumed a prouder and more spiritual shape. This specific reference, of course does not exclude the more general. [Alford: "*The whole earthly creation*, separated from God and lying in the sin, which, whether considered as consisting in the men who serve it, or the enticements which it holds out to evil lust (ἐπιθυμία) is to Christians a source of continual defilement."—M.]

DOCTRINAL AND ETHICAL.

1. The purity of the moral teaching of James also is conclusive from what he says concerning *wrath.* James is far from holding a quietistic or ascetico-rigoristic view which did approve of all anger absolutely, as unworthy of man or the Christian. He recognizes with Christ (Matth. v. 22; Mark. iii. 5) and Paul (Eph. iv. 26) lawful anger as opposed to unlawful. As in the case of the Master, so also in that of the disciple anger should be the extreme point of the flame, with which love strikes. But although anger is permitted up to a certain degree, it is nevertheless restricted within fixed limits by the limiting direction βραδὺς εἰς ὀργήν. One has only to look at the deplorable mischief that may be produced by excessive anger in order fully to justify the necessity and wisdom of this precept. Peculiarly Christian is the *triplex officium*, which in v. 19 is commanded in so brief and pithy a manner. The exhibition of such a frame of mind affords proof that the regeneration spoken of in v. 18 is a reality. The natural man is the very opposite: he is slow to hear, swift to speak and swift to wrath. It is also note worthy that v. 19 contains properly the *text*, the exposition and development of which are treated of in the remainder of the Epistle. The exhortation to be *swift to hear* is expounded from v. 21—ch. ii. 26 with simultaneous reference to a fruitful hearing; the admonition to be *slow to speak* is emphatically urged in ch. iii. and that to be slow to wrath in ch. iv. and v.

2. Because on the Israelite standpoint no justification before God was possible without the fulfilling of the law, the chief demand of which is *love*, while wrath is the very expression of the most unbridled *selfishness*, there are no ideas more decidedly opposed to one another than ὀργὴ ἀνδρός and δικαιοσύνη θεοῦ.

3. Slowness of hearing was, it would seem, an evil not peculiar to the first readers of this Epistle, but also common to others, and particularly to Jewish Christians. Cf. Heb. v. 11; x. 25. The emphatic urging of the opposite quality is therefore not superfluous. Here also the words of James echo the words of Christ. Luke xi. 28; Matth. vii. 24–27; xiii. 23.

4. Real *inward* hearing is ever to receive anew the word, implanted and already extant within us as the seed of regeneration, which in an inexhaustible richness of forms is ever brought home to us as a new word of life. What would the preached word avail unless it had hidden points of contact in the hearts and consciences of Christians? cf. 1 Thess. i. 6. The forgetful hearer, whom James describes in vv. 22–24 fully corresponds with the second class of men depicted by our Lord in the parable of the sower (Matth. xiii. 20, 21).

5. James' view of the connection of faith and hearing is identical with that of Paul. Rom. x. 14–17.

6. The representation of the Gospel as *the perfect law of liberty* is as correct as it is important. Paul, who contrasts generally the law and the Gospel, acknowledges a law of the spirit of life in Christ Jesus, Rom. viii. 2. This law is *perfect* because it presents at once the most perfect and most judicious directory of the life of believers; it is the *law of liberty* because the faithful practice of it leads men to true, moral liberty. Here the saying is fully valid *legum servi sumus est liberi esse possimus.* Cf. Jno. viii. 36; Matth. v. 17–20.

7. Care must be had that James be not misunderstood in the description of the pure and unspotted religious service (v. 23), as if these words contained an exact definition of the inner side of true religious service in general. Any one somewhat philanthropically inclined and at the same time keeping himself outwardly free from worldly contamination is on that account far from being entitled to say that in so doing he is practising the pure and unspotted religious service in the sense of James. In order to prevent any possible misapprehension of his language we have to notice that he refers not indefinitely to *the* Divine service, but to *a* pure and unspotted service (θρησκεία without the Article) and states merely in a general way what is above all things essential to the being and efficacy of a practical religiousness in its outward manifestation. "As if one addicted to drink were to boast of his morality and were to be told in reply that a moral man does not get drunk, it would not be the latter's purpose to represent thereby the sum-total of a Christian conversation." *Chrysostom.* The great and principal condition is taken for granted, viz.: repentance and faith; besides, this exhortation is also addressed to Christians already regenerate, v. 18. James insists upon the duty we owe to our *neighbour*, who is here represented by widows and orphans as those most in want of help, and upon the duties we owe to *ourselves* by the practice of self-denial and vigilance. These two points reveal at the same time the true disposition toward God. Besides James does not say that the man who applies himself to the discharge of these duties shall be blessed *by* this his

doing but that he shall have even here a taste of bliss *in* this his doing (ἐν τῇ ποιήσει) so that this doing as such is to him the highest bliss. v. Gerlach: "In this doing of the law he will feel himself truly blessed, as he must be esteemed blessed. To fulfil the commandments of God, to progress in holiness, is an ever-growing enjoyment of blessedness, granted more and more to the believer and the faithful already here on earth."

8. Widows and orphans so highly favoured even by the Mosaic law (Ex. xxii. 22-24 and elsewhere), are also emphatically protected by Christian morality. The difference between the philanthropy of the Church and that of a mere humanism.

HOMILETICAL AND PRACTICAL.

Christians are called constantly to adopt the prayer of David, Ps. cxli. 3.—It is impossible that the bitter root of wrath can produce the sweet fruit of righteousness.—Difference between holy and unholy anger.—*Ira furor brevis.*—The causes and excuses of the frequent dulness of hearing.—The development of spiritual life ever conditioned by the use of the means of grace.—The preaching of the Gospel a constant watering of the seed of regeneration already planted in us.—What we have to lay aside and what we have to bring with us in order to serve God in public (*i. e.* make a public profession of religion).—Many hearers put rigorous demands on the preacher but hardly any on themselves; it ought to be the reverse.—True meeekness in the hearing of the word.—The Gospel a power of God unto salvation etc. Rom. i. 16.—The self-deception of the hearer of the word who becomes not a doer, cf. Prov. xvi. 25; 1 Cor. iii. 18.—Three classes of men: 1, those who neither hear nor do the word; 2, those who hear it but do it not; 3, those who both hear and do it.—Even Herod heard John the Baptist gladly and for his sake did many things, but not the one thing needful, Mark vi. 20.—The word of God a bright mirror which must be attentively looked into, would we attain true self-knowledge. The true hearer of the Gospel looks as carefully into the mirror as do the angels into the plan of salvation, 1 Pet. i. 12.—The Gospel 1, a law; 2, a perfect law; 3, a perfect law of liberty.—The blessedness of the doer of the word, Ps. cxix. 1 etc.—The absolute incompatibility of the service of sins of the tongue with a truly religious life.—The Christian life a service of love.—Only that Divine service is the true, which is a Divine service before "God and the Father," 1 Sam. xvi. 7.—The practice of the duties of love must be joined with conscientious watchfulness of ourselves.—The Christian's relation to the world: 1, to its distressed ones; 2, to its temptations.—The fruit of righteousness is a tree of life, Prov. xi. 30.—How eloquently James has recommended his instruction concerning active fear of God by his own example.—(vv. 19-27). A direction for and eulogy of the right hearing of the Gospel. James urges us 1, to devout hearing (vv. 19, 20), 2, to meek receiving (v. 21), 3, to active practice (vv. 22-24), and 4, to constant searching of the word (vv. 25-27).—(vv. 25-27) 1, What one enjoys (v. 25), 2, avoids (v. 26), and 3, practises in the way of active piety.—True Christianity the most practical matter in the world.

STARKE:—Believers are more eager to learn than to teach, for the cause of regeneration makes us real hearers of the word. Jno. viii. 47.

LUTHER:—Blessed is the man whose mouth is in his heart and whose heart is not in his mouth; the one is wisdom, the other folly.

STARKE:—He who along with other sins does not overcome his carnal anger, cannot enter into the Kingdom of God, Gal. v. 20, 21.—Sins are also in believers, who must more and more cleanse themselves from them, Heb. xii. 1.

QUESNEL:—He only loves the word of God in truth, who performs it by love, 1 Jno. v. 3.

LANGII OP:—To deceive others is bad, to deceive oneself worse, and the latter is more common than the first, Prov. xxiv. 8.

STARKE:—The word of God is here compared with a mirror not only on account of its intrinsic brightness and purity, but chiefly because of its use and benefit. For it not only shows us (according to the law) the detestable and sinful form of our souls which we derive from the first Adam and wherein alas, we resemble Satan, but it shows us also (according to the Gospel) the beauteous, glorious and lovely form which we may receive from Christ, the second Adam, and His Spirit by means of the new birth and wherein we resemble Him.

QUESNEL:—He that doeth not what he heareth, forgetteth more than he heareth and his latter end will be worse than the beginning, 2 Pet. ii. 20, 22.—Blessed is the man who receives his own testimony against himself. 1 Cor. xi. 31.

STARKE:—Fear not, believers, if you hear the Gospel called a law and that it enters as much and more into hearts of poor sinners with lightning and thunder than the old law of Sinai; for it is a law of liberty. Such a liberty which is more valuable than all treasures, more pleasant than life itself and more precious than all the goods of the world; none know what it is worth but those who have lost it and those who have it, although they esteem it most highly, yet do they not esteem it according to its value, Gal. v. 1-13.—Whoso truly serves God in the spirit, his tongue also is governed by the Spirit of God, Ps. xxxix. 2.—Many whose mouth is full of the praise of the truth and who are proud of their Divine service are their own worst deceivers and seducers, Rom. ii. 23.—Many a service is well-pleasing to God which is despised and even rejected by men, Acts xxiv. 14.

CRAMER:—Widows and orphans are privileged individuals before God.—He that keeps himself unspotted before the world, does the will of God and is greatly blessed, 2 Cor. vi. 17, 18.

Vv. 16-21. *Epistle for the 4th Sunday after Easter* (Cantate).

LUTHER:—Because the Epistle of James ch. i. has been read from of old on this Sunday, being also good for instruction and exhortation, we will also retain it for those who would have it continued and say something concerning it, lest it be thought we wanted to reject it, although the Epistle has not been written by an Apostle nor does set forth everywhere the manner and stamp of apostolical teaching nor quite conformable to pure doctrine. Therefore James concludes:

"Let every man be swift to hear, slow to speak, slow to wrath." That is: be taught, admonished by God's word, reproved and comforted, be swift in these things; but be not fluent in speech, in murmuring, cursing and railing against God and man. Hereby he does not forbid us all speaking, reproving and being angry, if the commandment of God or necessity require us so to do, but that we for ourselves shall not rashly and vehemently engage in it, although we be irritated thereto—and the rather hearken to and suffer us to be taught by the word; which is the true and real word, which we should ever let govern and lead us, and from which should flow whatsoever we say, blame and rebuke. Hence it is said soon afterwards to receive the word with meekness, that we may not be angry if it reprove us, or murmur if we have to suffer somewhat for it.

HEUBNER:—Talkativeness the mark of a weak mind.—The word of God the best bridle for the government of the tongue and the affections.—Never act while thou art angry.—(vv. 16–21.) The Christian's belief in the presiding control of an all-good God. 1. Nature and reason, 2. Effects of this belief.—Self-deceit in the service of God.

PORUBSZKY:—Of ungodly anger. 1. What is anger? 2. What does anger? 3. How is anger conquered?

COUARD:—Contemplations on the precious gift of the Gospel.

KAPFF:—Whereto we are impelled by the absolute perfection of God.

PALMER:—Good works: 1, their inward origin (vv. 16–18), 2, their outward form (vv. 19–21).

SOUCHON:—Receive the word daily.

STANDT:—What we may expect from God: 1, what He gives (vv. 16–18), 2, what He removes (vv. 19–21).

VON HARLESS:—Who walks in the right way to the end of life?

ARNDT:—The sins of the tongue.

HERBERGER:—Like as a wagon runs in two ruts, like as a man stands on two legs unless he be a cripple, like as he consists of two parts, body and soul, so Christianity also runs in two parts, in faith and works. 1. God the good gives good gifts, 2, and expects good to be returned to Him.

LISCO:—The fountain and the vessel of all good gifts.—Spring's threefold address to us the children of God.—The holiness of God in its incompatibility with human sin.

FUCHS:—The word of truth as the perfect gift of God.

Vv. 22–27. *Epistle for 5th Sunday after Easter* (Rogate).

HEUBNER:—Other laws bind and are often burdensome to us: the law of God delivers us from the bands of sin.—Those, otherwise free from gross sins, yet sin with the tongue.—Sefishness turns even religion into an instrument of self-sufficiency.—All religion must be moral.—We should take to the necessitous not only our gifts but ourselves.—Comparison of the true and false religious service as to 1, their nature, 2, their influence and 3, their relation to God.—Caution against the abuse of the doctrine of justifying faith.

PORUBSZKY:—Be doers of the word and not hearers only!—Our Divine service is a surrender to God.

LÖHE:—There is no doer but is also a true hearer. First a hearer, then a doer; true hearers, true doers.

LANGE:—If the word seizes not thyself, it will be a burden to thy head.

STIER: v. 27.—He refers less to the work itself than to the disposition and impulse of heart which impels us to the distressed in their affliction. Hence he says nothing of our feeding, clothing and providing for widows and orphans, but he specifies our visiting them in their affliction, protecting them, assisting them and carrying to them the best of our possessions, true consolation. We understand, it is to be hoped, how much this requires, how the duty of love drives us constantly into the world and among men, and how it is incompatible with pharisaic or pietistic separateness and monkish solitariness.—How the hearing of the word is to become saving work.

VON KAPFF:—Who is blessed in his doing?

FLOREY:—How differently Christians use the mirror of the Divine Word!

SCHMID:—The apothegm of wisdom concerning self-vigilance: 1. Mirror aright and see thyself; 2. See aright and know thyself; 3. Know (thyself) aright and think thee small; 4. Who thinks him (self) small is wise in all.

HERBERGER:—The keeping of God's word makes it ours unto salvation.

COUARD:—Caution against self-deceit in Christianity.

SOUCHON:—Be doers of the word.

WESTERMAIER:—The same.

J. SAURIN:—An excellent sermon on v. 25, entitled: *Sur la manière d'étudier la Religion*, Serm. Tom. iv. p. 1–48.

LISCO:—Of true religion.—Be doers of the word and not hearers only. 1. *When* we shall be it? and 2, *Whereby* is it seen that we are it.—Of the nature of true religion.

LEDDERHOSE:—The right hearing of the word.

NEILING:—Ye shall be not only hearers of the word, but doers also [in a rhyme which hardly deserves reproduction.—M.].

[This section is already so full of homiletical matter that instead of supplying additional ones, I refer the reader to the *new* matter given under "Exegetical and Critical" and to the following standard works which will furnish him with much that is excellent and full of thought.

On verse 22. The Sermon of BP. ANDREWS, V. p. 195; also BP. SANDERSON, III. p. 366.

On verse 26. BP. BUTLER's Sermon IV.; DR BARROW, Serm. XIII., Vol. I. p. 283.—M.].

V THIRD ADMONITION WITH REFERENCE TO THE THIRD FORM OF TEMPTATION. EBIONITE CONDUCT.

CAUTION AGAINST JUDAISTIC PARTIALITY, AGAINST FAVOURING THE RICH (THE JUDAIZING CHRISTIAN) AND DEPRECIATING THE POOR (THE GENTILE CHRISTIAN) IN THEIR CHURCH-LIFE. CONSISTENT PROOF OF FAITH DEMANDED IN THE WORK OF CHRISTIAN BROTHERLY LOVE AND IN THE ACKNOWLEDGING OF UNITY OF FAITH IN THE FAITH-WORK OF ABRAHAM THE PATRIARCH AND IN THE FAITH-WORK OF RAHAB, THE GENTILE HARLOT. DEAD AND LIVING FAITH.

Chapter II.

My brethren, have not the faith of our Lord Jesus Christ, *the Lord* of glory, with
2 respect of persons. For if there come unto your assembly[1] a man with a gold ring,[2]
3 in goodly apparel, and there come in also a poor man in vile raiment: And ye have[3]
respect to him that weareth the gay clothing, and say unto him,[4] Sit thou here in a
good place; and say to the poor, Stand thou there, or sit here[5] under my footstool:
4 [6]Are ye not then partial in yourselves, and are become judges of evil thoughts?
5 Hearken, my beloved brethren, Hath not God chosen the poor of this world,[7] rich in
faith, and heirs of the kingdom[8] which he hath promised to them that love him?
6 But ye have despised the poor. Do not rich men oppress you, and draw you[9] before
7 the judgment seats? Do not they blaspheme that worthy name by the which ye
8 are called? If ye fulfil the royal law according to the Scripture, Thou shalt love thy
9 neighbour as thyself, ye do well: But if ye have respect to persons, ye commit sin,
10 and are convinced of the law as transgressors. For whosoever shall[10] keep the whole
11 law, and yet offend in one *point*, he is guilty of all. For he that said, Do not commit
adultery,[11] said also, Do not kill. Now if thou commit no adultery, yet if thou kill,
12 thou art become a transgressor of the law. So speak ye, and so do, as they that shall
13 be judged by the law of liberty. For he shall have judgment without mercy,[12] that
14 hath shewed no mercy; and[13] mercy rejoiceth against judgment. What *doth it*
profit,[14] my brethren, though a man say he hath faith, and have not works? can
15 faith save him? [15]If a brother or sister be naked, and destitute[16] of daily food,
16 And one of you say unto them, Depart in peace, be *ye* warmed and filled; notwithstanding
ye give them not those things which are needful to the body; what
17 *doth it* profit? Even so faith,[17] if it hath not works, is dead, being alone.
18 Yea, a man may say, Thou hast faith, and I have works: shew me thy faith without[18]
19 thy[19] works, and I will shew thee[20] my faith by my[21] works. Thou believest[22] that
20 there is one God; thou doest well: the devils also believe, and tremble. But wilt
21 thou know, O vain man, that faith without works is dead?[23] Was not Abraham our
22 father justified by works, when he offered Isaac his son upon the altar? Seest thou
23 how faith wrought with[24] his works, and by works was faith made perfect? And the
Scripture was fulfilled which saith, Abraham believed God, and it was imputed unto
24 him for righteousness: and he was called the Friend of God. Ye see then[25] how that
25 by works a man is justified, and not by faith only. Likewise also was not Rahab the
harlot justified by works, when she had received the messengers,[26] and had sent *them*
26 out another way? For as the body without the spirit is dead, so faith without[27] works
is dead also.

Verse 1. Lange: My brethren, do not practise the faith in our Lord Jesus, the Christ of glory [the Messiah in His glory exalted above Judaistic expectations] with respectings of persons [personal considerations, partialities.]

[. . . . . hold not ye the faith . . . . [the Lord] of glory in respecting of persons.—M]

Verse 2. [1] εἰς τὴν. A. G. K., Tischendorf; omit τὴν B. C. Sin. al. Lachmann [Alford—M.], an important variation, showing that the reference is not to particular synagogues.

[[2] χρυσοδακτύλιος=golden-ringed.—M.]

Lange: For if there had entered into your common assembly (συναγωγή) a man with a gold finger ring, in a clean splendid garment, but there had also entered a poor man in an unclean garment.

[For if there come into your place of assembly a man with golden rings, etc.—M.]

Verse 3. [3] ἐπιβλέψητε δὲ. B. C. K. Tischendorf [Alford], is more expressive than καὶ ἐπιβλέψητε A. G. Lachmann.

[4] The omission of αὐτῷ A. B. C. Sinait. keeps the expression more general and gives it more dogmatical colouring [than its insertion, Rec. K. L. Vulg. and al.—M.]

[5] ὧδε inserted in C.** G. K., is omitted by A. B. C.*—The addition of τῶν ποδῶν in A. Vulg. [Syr.—M]. Lachmann, seems to be exegetical and intensive, but may have been dropped owing to a moderation in expression.

Lange: And ye were looking upon [made a looking up, a demonstration of] him who wore the clean splendid garment and should say [to him] [thou], sit thou here on the best place, but should say to the poor, [thou] keep standing here [on the standing place], or sit [here] under [down at] my footstool.

Verse 4. [6] καὶ omitted before οὐ by A. B. C. Sinait, may have been objected to in the apodosis as a striking form

Lange: Did ye not then separate [divide] among ourselves, and become judges according to evil considerations?

[Did ye not distinguish (invidiously) among ourselves etc.—M.]

Verse 5. [7] Rec. reads τοῦ κόσμου τούτου; [A.** C.** K. L. τοῦ κόσμου—M.]; τῷ κόσμῳ A.* B. C.* Sin etc. The variations seem to be exegetical illustrations.

[8] For βασιλείας [A. and] Sin.; read ἐπαγγελίας.

Lange: .... hath not God also chosen the poor [according to the world), who are rich in faith, heirs of the [glorified Messiah—] kingdom ......

Verse 6. [[9] For ὑμῶν A. Sinait, read ὑμᾶς.—M.]

Lange: .... [But] is it not the rich who oppress you? Is it not just they, who drag you to the courts of judgment?

[Is it not they that drag you into courts of justice?—M.]

Verse 7. Lange: Is it not just they who blaspheme that fair [glorious] name, which hath been made to you a surname?

[.... that glorious name, which was invoked over you?—M.]

Verse 8. Lange: If indeed ye fulfil [complete under the New Testament] the royal law [the law of the kingdom] according to the Scripture, Thou shalt love thy neighbour as thyself, ye act beautifully [conformable to the beautiful name of Christ as Christians].

[If, however, ye fulfil etc.—M.]

Verse 9. Lange: But if ye practise respect of persons, ye practise sin, convicted by the [very] law as transgressors.

[But if ye respect persons, ye work sin, being convicted by the law as transgressors.—M.]

Verse 10. [10] τηρήσῃ and πταίσῃ, the most authentic readings. So [A. B. C. Sinait.—M] Lachmann, Tischendorf.

Lange: For whosoever should observe .... in one thing [commandment] the same hath become guilty of all.

[For whosoever shall have kept etc.—M.]

Verse 11. [11] A. B. C. Sin. have the Present μοιχεύεις, φονεύεις.

Verse 12. [.... as those about to be judged by the law of liberty.—M.]

Verse 13. [12] ἀνέλεος not ἀνίλεως, is the true reading. So A. B. C. [K. Alford—M.] Lach., Tisch. On the form, itself and variations of spelling it see Huther.

[13] καὶ before κατακαυχ, found only in minuscule codd; δὲ after κατακαυχ. is probably also a stylistic insertion; the variations κατακαυχάσθω in A. [Vulg.;—χασθε C.** M.];—χᾶτε are exegetical efforts to render the text more easy.—ἔλεος instead of ἔλεον supported by A. B. Tischend. [Alford.—M.]

Lange: For the judgment is merciless to him who did not practise mercy, and mercy boasteth [triumphantly] against the judgment [thus Christian mercy triumphantly excels the judging legalistic spirit of Judaism.]

[For the judgment [will be] merciless to him who wrought not mercy. Mercy boasteth [triumpheth] over judgment.—M.]

Verse 14. [14] Τί τὸ ὄφελος, Tischend. following the majority of Codd. Lachmann: τί ὄφελος. So also in v. 16.

Lange: .... [what profit doth it bring] if any man were to say that he hath faith, but were to have no works. Faith [in such a case] surely cannot save him?

[.... can his faith [ἡ πίστις] save him?—M.]

Verse 15. [[15] ἐὰν δὲ the most authentic reading; omit δὲ B. Sinait.—M.]

Lange: But if a brother or sister were naked and bare and destitute of daily food.

Verse 16. [16] ὦσιν after λειπόμενοι in A. G. Lachmann, is unimportant as to sense. Sin. [B. C. K. Syr. Tischend. Alford.—M.] omit it.

Lange: And one of you should say to them: Depart in peace, be ye warmed and filled, but ye were not to give to them those things which are needful to the body, what would that profit?

[And some one from among you say to them ..... but ye give them not the necessaries of the body; what is the profit?—M.]

Verse 17. [17] ἔχῃ ἔργα [A. B. C. K. Tischend. Alf.—M.], is the most authentic and most emphatic reading.

Lange: So also faith, if it has not works, is dead for itself.

[So also faith, if it have not works, is dead in itself (καθ' ἑαυτήν.—M.]

Verse 18. [18] χωρὶς A. B. C. Sin. Lachmann, Tischend. [ἐκ Rec. K. L.—M.]

[19] σου after ἔργων omitted by A. B. [Tischend. Alford.—M.]

[20] μου after ἔργων wanting in Vulg. Syr. B. C. It seems to have originated in the parallelism of this sentence with the one preceding it according to its rejected readings.

[21] B. C. omit μου after πίστιν [A. K. L. insert it.—M.]

Lange: But some one will say [to a man of such faith]: thou hast faith and I have works: show me thy faith without the works [*how canst thou do it?*], and I will show thee my faith out of [by] the works.

[Nay, some one will say .... show me thy faith without [apart from] the works, and I will show thee my faith by [out of ἐκ] my works.—M.]

Verse 19. [22] Different readings, Rec. with G. θεὸς εἷς ἐστι; A. Sinait. Lachmann, εἷς ἐστιν ὁ θεός; B. Tischend. [Alford]: εἷς ὁ θεός ἐστιν. The strongest emphasis of A is also the most probable.

Lange: Thou believest [*the article of the law and of doctrine*] that God is one: that thou doest well therein; the evil spirits [*the demons*] also believe that and shudder.

Verse 20. [23] νεκρά A. C.** G. K. [Rec. Vulg. Copt.—M.], opposed by ἀργή in B. C.* etc.; the latter more probable (Lachm. and Tischend. support it) because the former seems to have been occasioned by v. 17.

Lange: But wilt thou know it, O empty man! that faith without works is useless [inefficient]?

[.... that faith without [apart from] the works is useless [bootless. Alford]?—M.]

Verse 21. Lange: .... justified [proved righteous] by works [out of works] when he offered Isaac, his son, on the altar of sacrifice [Gen. xxii.]?

[... When he offered Isaac, his son, on the altar.—M.]

Verse 22. [[24] συνέργει A. Sinait.—M.]

Lange: Thou seest that his faith was energetically joined with his works [was manifested as one with his works] and that faith was completed by works [out of works].

[Thou seest that faith was working together with his works and that by [ἐκ] works faith was made complete.

Verse 23. Lange: And thus also was fulfilled .... righteousness [in justification proper Gen. xv. 6.]

Verse 24. [25] τοίνυν wanting in A. B. C. Sin. [Tisch. Alf.—M.] etc.

Lange: Ye see [therefore] that by [out of] works man is justified [proved righteous as man] etc.

Verse 25. [26] κατασκόπους, C. G. seems to be taken from Heb. xi. 31.

Lange: ..... and sent them forth by another way.

Verse 26. [[27] χωρὶς ἔργων. B. Sinait.—M.]

Lange: For as the body without spirit etc.

§ 1. CHAPTER II. 1–13.

EXEGETICAL AND CRITICAL.

ANALYSIS: Caution against partiality in the Christian Church-life, that is against the Ebionitizing preference of the Jewish Christian and putting back of the Gentile Christian, in connection with the demand of the proof of faith in the exhibition of brotherly love.—Leading points: Reference to the abolition of respect of persons by the Christ of glory.—Ebionite conduct in a parable, vv. 1–4.—Reference to the faith of the poor (in a symbolical sense) as well as to the unbelief of the rich (cf. Matth. xxii. 1–10), vv. 5–7.—True fidelity of the law or the fulfilling of the whole law in the royal commandment of love, as well as the damnable transgression of the whole law in sinning against this commandment, vv. 8–13.—The true life of faith or faith evinced by the mercy of brotherly love and dead faith illustrated by heartless demeanour, vv. 14–17.—The proof of faith by the works of faith or the believer's justification before the consciousness of the Church; vv. 18, 19.—The two examples of the proof of faith by works as a general example of the unity of the living faith of Jews and Gentiles, vv. 20–26.

Caution against partiality in Christian Church-life, that is against Ebionitizing demeanour. The parable of such demeanour. vv. 1–4.

VER. 1. **My brethren, do not practise.**—The Apostle does not, as is generally supposed, pass from the doctrine of charity to a particular example of charity. If this were so, the example would be ill-chosen, for respect of persons does not violate primarily the duty of charity but the law of justice and equality. He rather passes on to a new form of the temptation.

This clause is not (as Schneckenburger and Kern take it) interrogative, not because the fact in question is beyond all doubt (Huther), for the interrogative form would express this more definitely (is it not so that ye, etc.), but because the form of a warning exhortation makes it imperative. The interrogative construction is inadmissible not only because of the analogy in ch. i. 16 but also on account of the parable which shows the form of the temptation to which they were exposed.

Do not practise:—ἔχειν denotes not only, "do not hold your faith as if it were shut up in προσωποληψίαις" (Huther); still less, "do not detain your faith" (κατέχετε Grotius), but still stronger "do not hold, cherish it in this form." The faith of fanaticism is not only allied with particularisms but the particularisms constitute its very glory. The Plural προσωποληψίαι points to the ever returning and diversified occurrences of this kind.

The faith in our Lord Jesus, the Christ.—Different constructions: 1. The faith in our Lord of glory, Jesus Christ (de Wette, Wiesinger, and al.; reference to 1 Cor. ii. 8). This construction is inadmissible on account of the position of τῆς δόξης. 2. δόξα taken in a different sense from its ordinary signification=opinion (Calvin: the knowledge of Christ obscured by the respect paid to wealth). Wholly inadmissible, because this mode of expression would be most remarkable and because the faith of Christ itself could not be thus disfigured. 3. τοῦ κυρίου etc. Genitive of the subject: the faith, derived from our Lord Jesus Christ, on the glory (Huther). 4. Bengel: τῆς δόξης is in apposition to Christ *ut ipse Christus dicatur ἡ δόξα. Gloria.* Luke ii. 32; Eph. i. 17 etc. Christ, the glory not sufficiently developed, although the idea that Christ is the Schechinah would otherwise be quite suitable. 5. Laurentius unites δόξης with Χριστοῦ, *Christus gloriæ*, but Huther objects that this construction would require the Article before Χριστοῦ. This would however occasion an error as if a twofold Christ were conceivable. In German however we have to emphasize the Article, as far as it is in τῆς δόξης. The sense is plain: faith in the Christ of glory is incompatible with estimating persons according to carnal respects. See the analogous idea 2 Cor. v. 16 and Eph. ii. 16, 17. Christ in virtue of His exaltation has also acquired the κυριότης of the unbelieving Jews. See Matth. xxvi. 64; Rom. ix. 5. [But on the whole it seems best, because it is the least forced construction, to govern τῆς δόξης by κυρίου, see 1 Cor. ii. 8.—M.]

VER. 2. **For if there had entered;** γάρ gives the reason not of the whole exhortation as such, but of the reference (connected with it) to the glory of Christ, which Luther has made prominent in his free translation; Do not suppose that faith in Jesus Christ, our Lord of glory, suffers respect of persons. The construction which makes the antecedent extend to the end of v. 4 and then makes the consequent begin (Michaelis, Herder etc.) has been justly set aside by Huther; v. 4 is the consequent. The reference of the following exhortation to misconduct in worship has led to the opinion that James is primarily addressing the Church-wardens (Grotius etc). We have already shown that this view over against the grand prophetico-symbolical expression of the Apostle is inadequate. The misconduct to which James refers is so general and important as to preclude the literal acceptation of what follows. In the first place it cannot be assumed that such a grievance as that of assigning bad places to the poor had spread throughout the entire Jewish Christian dispersion and in the second, it is even more improbable that James should have received reliable information concerning a disorder so universally prevalent. The ἐάν also and the Aorist indicate a relation which has become historical and is still in course of development.

Into your common-assembly.—Schneckenburger and al. interpret the Jewish synagogue, Huther, the place of the Christian assembly, de Wette, with reference to Heb. x. 25, the religious assembly. But the Article indicates that the *one* synagogue of the entire Jewish Christian dispersion is meant, that is their religious community symbolically described by the name of the Jewish place of worship. The symbol is the more appropriate in that it characterizes the family-bias to union in Judaism. The reference to civil judicial assemblies, which Herder and al. find here, is altogether unfounded. We have endeavoured to bring out in the translation the uniting element of Christianity.

If there had entered a man.—The Aorist not only aids the imagination by its picturesque force but indicates the historical fact that believers with Judaistic pretensions had already entered the Church.

With a gold finger-ring.—The character of the parables delineating and censuring on the one hand the factious conduct of the Jewish Christians towards the Judaizers proper and on the other towards the Gentile Christians, comes out in the most decided manner. According to Wiesinger and Huther our text gives only an example *instar omnium* for the representation of that sinful προσωποληψία, while many older commentators see in it only a figure of the preference of the rich to the poor, and these are the common views. These views give only rise to the question whether the rich and the poor are to be considered members of the Christian commonwealth (Knapp, Theile, de Wette), or unbelievers or *hospites* (Pott, Kern, Schneckenburger). Wiesinger, in support of the former view, alleges that the Epistle being addressed to Christian readers, the oppressive disparities between rich and poor should be taken as introcongregational (ch. iv. 1; vv. 13—15; v. 1); Huther, in support of the latter, that the rich are distinguished from the brethren etc.; Weiss (*Deutsche Zeitschrift für Christliche Wissenschaft*, 1854, No. 51) makes the rich a non-Christian, the poor a Christian. Schwegler is altogether wrong in making the rich the Gentile Christian and the poor the Jew, for it would follow from this that the Jewish Christians did exhibit partiality towards the Gentile Christians. But he is on the right track in that he sees in the Epistle a reflection of the circumstances of the time. Now we hold that the rich here and throughout the Epistle is not less symbolical than the rich in the Gospel (Matth. xix. 24 etc.) and just so the poor. But the attributes of the rich indicate whereof he is proud. He is in the first place a χρυσοδακτύλιος (the word ἅπαξ λεγ.). That rings with the ancients, especially among the Jews (as a signet-ring) were highly esteemed is evident from Gen. xli. 42; Esther iii. 10; viii. 2; Luke xv. 22. Received as a gift it denotes the prerogative of representing the donor; in the parable of the prodigal doubtless the restoration to the filial state. But the man with the gold ring cannot be any other than the Judaist priding himself in and boasting of his covenant-right and sonship (which to the humble was indeed a veritable gold-ring see Rom. ix.), as a χρυσοδακτύλιος, *a gold-finger-ring-wearer by profession.* He is further described by *wearing* a splendid garment (λαμπρός) which according to Rev. xv. 6 involves in particular the idea of purity and connected therewith denotes the Jewish pretensions to purity and holiness or glory. In like manner the garment of the poor, that is, of the Gentile Christian, is not stained in the ordinary sense but from a religious point of view, as is proved by the ῥυπαρός Zech. iii. 3, 4. In Rev. xxii. 11 also it denotes the opposite of the Holy in a symbolical sense. According to the Jewish conception of purity the Gentile Christians had entered the Church in such a garment; but that James notwithstanding accords to them the wedding-garment is evident from v. 25. Raphelius on λαμπρός, "*nullum certum colorem declarat, sed splendidum, clarum, nitidum, seu rubrum sit, seu alius generis.*"

VER. 3. **And ye were looking upon.**—Ἐπιβλέπειν is emphatic (*Pott*). Upon the ὁ φορῶν τὴν ἐσθῆτα, also very significant, he who *wears that* and carries himself in wearing it. Instead of experiencing disgust at the spectacle of vanity which manifestly looks out of that proud dress, they suffer themselves to be deceived by that glitter, which in their estimate should have been valueless, and to be awed by the haughty claims to it. This rich man is first looked at, contemplated in astonishment, then complimented, he also stands first; meanwhile the eye is averted from the poor man, who is furthermore despatched in a hurry. "The difference of speech to the one and to the other strongly marks the contrast; they are first distinguished by σύ—σύ, then κάθου and στῆθι, ὧδε and ἐκεῖ, καλῶς and ὑπὸ τὸ ὑπόδιόν μου are opposites" (Huther). The addition "or sit thou here, etc," as allowing him to be seated, is intended to modify the hardness of the word "keep standing there," but becomes a further humiliation, "sit here under my footstool." This means certainly "down at my footstool." but the expression involves contempt; as it were under one's feet. Not *on* the footstool. The Judaist either wanted to acknowledge the Gentile Christian merely as *hospes* in the Church, or to concede to him at most an inferior right of communion. As the reading ἐπί [for ὑπό B**—M.] indicates a tendency to soften the harshness of the expression, a similar tendency may have omitted τῶν ποδῶν before μου.

VER. 4. **Did ye not then separate among yourselves.**—The comments on this passage are wide apart. Some plead οὐ as a declaration, others as a question. 1. Those who take it *declaratorily:* then, partly ye would not have distinguished (according to sound judgment) among yourselves, partly ye would have judged after an evil manner of thinking (Grashof); or, "then ye are not any longer distinguished among yourselves, *i. e.*, godly and ungodly" (Oeder); or, "then ye have not rightly judged among yourselves" (Oecumenius, Bengel); or, "then ye have not yet judged yourselves" (Heisen); "not *yourselves* but your garments" (Cajetan). But the construction is decidedly in favour of the interrogative form, particulary the hypothetical form and the brevity of the consequent. Hence 2, *interrogatively: a.* διακρίνεσθαι=to doubt in the sense of having scruples concerning a thing. "Ye had no scruples, etc.?" (Theile). *b.* to doubt in the literal sense: "have ye not become doubters in your faith? or similarly (de Wette, Wiesinger, Huther); *c.* the verb=to *judge:* do ye then not judge among yourselves?" (Augusti); or the Verb *passive:* "Do ye not condemn yourselves? (Paraeus). *d.* to make difference; did ye not make differences (in a bad sense) among yourselves?" (Grotius, Knapp and al.). This interpretation passes into *e.* to separate, to divide in a Passive or Middle sense. But the Middle sense lies nearest: do ye not separate, divide yourselves in or among yourselves? (Semler, Gebser, Schneckenburger). We hold with Schneckenburger that the beginning of dissension in the Church primarily takes rise in the minds of those factious Christians. They are also at schism in themselves, which schism although it begins with doubting (ch. i. 6) means more than doubting, as is the case in our time with those confessional zealots [confessional= pertaining to a confession, used in German almost as the synonyme of denomination—M.], who suspend the communion of the Lord's Supper with other Evangelicals while they are willing otherwise to hold fraternal intercourse with them. Creating dissensions reacts on the zealots themselves so that they become divided in themselves. Wiesinger and Huther allege in favour of their exposition that *διακρίνεσθαι* in the New Testament constantly signifies to doubt, which it does in many passages. But the Middle of our verb occurs in our sense in Jude 5, 22 and the transition from the Active (Acts xv. 9) to the Middle lay quite near. *καί* intensifies the question. We have endeavoured in our translation to bring out the paronomasia of *κριταί* and *διακρίθητε* [In German: *zerschieden* and *Schiedsrichter*.—M.]. From the evil schism in the heart springs evil judging in the life. Richter: *after* (according to) evil considerations (motives), not the evil, etc. That is, according to the motives of national preferences, claims and prejudices, outward position, etc.

Reference to the faith of the poor in a symbolical sense as well as to the faith of the sick vv. 5–7.

VER. 5. **Listen, my beloved brethren.**—The painful earnestness of the Apostle's mind in view of the dangerous symptoms he had described may be seen in his animated exhortation, his lively address (see ch. i. 16) and his questions.

Did not God choose the poor?—Cf. 1 Cor. xii. 26. Huther: "poor to the world" [Germ. *for* the world.—M.]. Wiesinger: "poor as regards the world." In the latter sense reference may be made to the analogous *τῷ πνεύματι* Matth. v. 3. But that condition of poverty as to the Spirit, simultaneously expresses a longing for the Spirit. But such an element would be out of place here, hence the sense "to the world" is more appropriate. These persons whom you call poor, because they are Gentile Christians, are rather poor *to* the world according to their relation to the world; but to you they ought to be rich, seeing they are rich in faith. The fact that the Ebonites afterwards called themselves poor as regards this world, presents no obstacle to this exposition. Their *usus loquendi* was doubtless rather formed after the pattern of James than *vice versa*, just as the Gnostics did probably borrow many of their expressions from Paul, not Paul from them. [But the sense "poor as regards the world" is after all at least as good as that given by Lange; it is general, and there is no reason why even Lange's interpretation may not be included in it: the Dative of reference here simply shows that these persons were poor with reference to the world objectively or subjectively or both.—M.].

Rich in faith.—Not rich in the possession of much faith [*nicht reich an Glauben*. GERM.—M.], but they are rich in virtue of their faith. Still the stress lies not only on the general being rich, the result of the general condition of believing, but also on the particular measure of their being rich as contrasted with the false being rich of the Judaists. *Who are rich in faith.* Huther: *Πλουσίους ἐν πίστει* not in apposition with *τοὺς πτωχούς* (Erasmus, Baumgarten, etc.), but the complement of *ἐξελέξατο*, stating whereto God did choose the poor (Beza, Wolf, Wiesinger, etc.). But taking James' choosing as exactly synonymous with Paul's we consider to be not proven. Here the word evidently signifies rather calling, with reference to ethical good behaviour to the Divine revelation. That is: "the decree (more definitely the election), of God is here viewed (indicated) in respect of temporal manifestation." Wiesinger. Still an essential element of the idea of election is held fast. The nearer definition of the election lies in *καὶ κληρονόμους* sc. *εἶναι*. That is: Did not God choose these poor according to the world (from among the Gentiles) who prove themselves rich in faith, that they also may be heirs of the kingdom? Cf. Acts xv. 14, etc.; Eph. ii.—It is to be borne in mind that only the poor to the world were also the "rich" among the Jews. But this characteristic was not enough here, while the correction "poor to the world, rich in faith" was sufficiently definite. James therefore here utters the same idea, on which Paul laid peculiar stress as the characteristic of his evangelization, Eph. iii. 3–6, etc.—*κληρονόμους* here, points not to the kingdom as future (so Huther), but as *καὶ κληρονόμους* to the joint participation in the true *υἱοθεσία* of the Jews.—

Heirs of the kingdom.—It is the kingdom of God, the real theocracy completed in the New Testament, progressing towards eschatological completion, not the latter only, as Huther maintains. James separates from this kingdom whatever is particularly Jewish, describing it as *the* kingdom, that peculiar kingdom which God has prepared for those who love Him. The common construction gives a proposition not limited like 1 Cor. i. 26–28, and not sufficiently proven by Matth. xix. 23, 26; viz.: "chosen the poor in this sense that those whom God did choose belong to *this* category, while those belonging to the category of the rich have not been chosen." (Huther). It is impracticable to take the *one* expression literally, the *other* figuratively.

VER. 6. **But ye dishonoured the poor** (man).—*δὲ* denotes the antithesis of *θεός*, *ἠτιμάσατε* the antithesis of *ἐξελέξατο*, as Huther rightly observes. Still the Aorist is used, not only because reference is made to vv. 2 and 3, and because the case is general, but its historical force points to a historical fact, in which Judaizing Jewish Christians have already taken part with the Jews, viz.: the dishonouring of the Gentile Christians.

But is it not the rich?—These rich, who *use violence towards themselves*, i. e. the Christians, (cf. the expressions Matth. xx. 25). The reference here is not any more to the rich in general than before to the poor (both according to Huther). The populace took as much part in the persecution of the Christians as the nobility, the former indeed were conspicuous in it. Nevertheless it was with the Judaists who fancied themselves theocratically rich, that the impulses to the persecution of the Christians did then still originate. So *e. g.* the first persecution of the Apostles, the execution of Stephen. *καὶ αὐτοί*, it is just they. All sympathizing of Christian ultras with Judaistic Jews contained the germ of want of self-respect, as is the case nowadays with all sympathizing of the evangelical ultras with the ultramontanists and that of pietistic ultras with the confessionalists. Is it not just they who excommunicate you? one might ask in the latter cases.

VER. 7. **Is it not just they who blaspheme that fair name?**—Favouring those rich ones would involve not only want of self-respect but even a participation in the guilt of their blasphemous conduct in respect of the fair name. This blaspheming cannot be taken figuratively as if it did denote insult heaped on that fair name by the evil works of the Christian rich men themselves, as Huther rightly observes in refutation of the views of several commentators (also of Wiesinger, whose citations, *e. g.* Jer. lii. 5: *δι᾽ ὑμᾶς τὸ ὄνομα μου βλασφημεῖται* and similar ones, do not prove that *βλασφημεῖν* has the direct meaning "to dishonour"), nor can the reference be (according to Hensler) to the Christian name, for that is just the transfer of that name to them; the name of the poor is altogether out of the question. It is only the name of *Christ* to which reference is made, whether believers were already called *χριστιανοί* (which was the case, in part at least, Acts xi. 26), or not. The name of Christ was transferred to them as a surname denoting at once their peculiarity and to whom they belonged. [They were *Christ's χριστοῦ*, 1 Cor. iii. 23.—M.]. The expression is formed after the Hebrew model שֵׁם נִקְרָא עַל (Deut. xxviii. 10; 2 Chron. vii. 14; cf. Is. iv. 1; Gen. xlviii. 16 and Acts xv. 14, 17). In virtue of the fact that once the name of Jehovah was called over Israel, Israel was described the people of Jehovah; in like manner Christians are now the Christian people (the people of Christ—M.] in virtue of the name of Christ. His name is called fair, in opposition to the insulting blaspheming; it is the fair, the glorious name *κατ᾽ ἐξοχήν*; the name of the Lord of Glory (ch. ii. 1), in which is all salvation (Acts iv. 1; Phil. ii. 10, Wiesinger). The Christian rich men could not any more be reproached with the sin of blaspheming the name of Christ (*βλασφημεῖν* always denotes abusive *language*, Huther), than the non-Christian rich men in general (the names even of Pilate, Gallio, Agrippa, Festus and al. may here be called to mind); the reproach fitted solely, if the Judaists were the rich in a figurative sense; to them it was wholly applicable.

True fidelity of the law or the fulfilling of the whole law in the royal commandment of love, as well as the damnable transgression of the whole law in sinning against this commandment, vv. 8–13.

VER. 8. **If, indeed, ye fulfil the royal law.**—The connection, by the introduction of *μέντοι*, is difficult, but only, if doubts remain as to what precedes. James had just now reproved his readers for being partial to Judaists, proud of the law and fancying themselves rich, *i. e.* because they themselves were not free from legal onesidedness. The progress of the thought fully accords therewith: "The whole consistency of true fidelity to the law, to be sure, ye ought to exhibit, according to the commandment, thou shalt love, etc.; but your partiality is a breach of the law." According to Huther and many others (Calvin, Theile etc.) James wants to meet the excuse of his readers that their respect of the rich was the outgoing of love; but surely no Jew could have thought of representing *προσωποληψία* as love. Although in this case *μέντοι* is rendered *certainly* (*indeed*, German *freilich*) the sense is different: *igitur* (Schneckenburger) and *yet* (de Wette) are also set aside by our explanation. [Whichever particle be chosen, *μέντοι* is clearly *adversative*.—M.].

The royal law.—The law denotes here not a single commandment (as *Huther* maintains with reference to Jer. xxxi. 33, Heb. viii. 10; x. 16), for the commandment cited immediately afterwards embraces the whole law as completed in the New Testament. It is *royal* not only because it is supreme and the most excellent (so Wiesinger with reference to Philo, Plato and also Theile, Schneckenburger and al.). Although Christ, placing Himself on the Jewish stand-point calls it *first* and *great*, immediately afterwards He describes it as *all-embracing* and *principial* (Matt. xxii. 39), and this New Testament conception of it is found also in Paul, Rom. xiii. 8-10; Gal. v. 14. Now if this *principial* [*i. e.* original, initial, elementary—M.] nature of the law and this its *oneness*, Mark xii. 32, are inferred from the Oneness of God, the Giver of the Law, the explanation that it is called royal because it proceeds from God its Author, is not so far-fetched (Raphelius, Wetstein and al.), as Wiesinger supposes, who says that this is true in respect of the whole law; but this objection lacks point, inasmuch as the cited commandment is really the whole law; but it leads to the exposition that the "royal commandment is the commandment of Christ" (Grotius). Its applying to kings as well as to other men (Michaelis) its being a *via regia* (Calvin), are explanations which do not reach the fundamental idea; its *making* kings (Thomas) is less remote; but it is probably called here the law royal and the law of the kingdom, because of the authority of rich men and the contrast between rich and poor must completely vanish before the authority of the king. Before Christ, the Lord of Glory, who has comprehended all laws in this one law, the rich are low and the poor rich (ch. ii. 1; i. 9 etc.) *Negatively*, the law completed in the New Testament is a principle of perfect liberty (Acts i. 35), *Positively* it is a royal principle exacting perfect obedience to the Lord. Hence we have here once more the word *τελεῖν* conformably to the previously repeated allusions to the New Testament *τέλος*. [But why not take *νόμον βασιλικόν* in its plain and obvious sense, the law *royal*, "the law which is the *king* of all laws" (Alford)? This rendering (with reference to Rom. xiii. 10) suits the context well.—M.]—*κατὰ τὴν γραφήν* refers not only to *τελεῖτε* but to the whole sentence *νόμον βασιλικόν τελεῖτε* for the *νόμος* Ex. xx in its higher royal form is already traced beforehand, Lev. xix. 18, while that discursive form of the law is referred to the ministration of angels (Gal. iii. 19).

Ye do well. (German: "*ye act beautifully*",

—That is: conformably to the beautiful name, which those men blaspheme. Christianly beautiful, answering to the spiritual beauty or the glory of the name of Christ. Huther's remark that here something is to be conceded, not without irony, to the opponents, lies outside of the context.

VER. 9. **But if ye respect persons.**—προσωποληπτεῖν is ἅπαξ λεγ. and admirably chosen by James to denote Judaizing Christianity. By such conduct they suppose to avoid sin, but he tells them: by this very thing ye are working sin (ἐργάζεσθαι is stronger than ποιεῖν, Matth. vii. 23, etc.).

Convicted by the law.—The reference here is certainly to the specific prohibition of prosopolepsy [respect of persons—M.] Deut. xvi. 19 and similar interdictions (Huther denies it), inasmuch as it formulates the commandment of love literally and at the same time in the light of it acquires a more general sense; that is, the law of love in its oneness, as applied to the question under notice, runs into an express prohibition of prosopolepsy. The very law therefore on which the Judaist plumes himself, convicts him as a transgressor. The choice of the word παραβάτης has here, as in Rom. ii. 25, and like παράβασις ch. v. 14, a peculiar emphasis; the Judaistico-Ebionite transgression of the law as completed in the New Testament is, as it were, a second fall. Cf. Gal. ii. 18.

VER. 10. **For whosoever shall have kept the whole law.**—Hypothetical case, put so as to apply at once to the Jewish stand-point in its full consequence and to the Christian, without being ambiguous, because the full consequence of Judaism leads to Christianity. The uniform solidarity of the law is also acknowledged by the Jews; hence Rabbi Jonathan says; "*quod si faciat omnia, unum vero omittat, omnium est singulorum reus.*" ἐν ἑνί is to be taken agreeably to the preceding. Not the *one* definite commandment of love (Oecumenius, Semler), which embraces the whole but any one point of the law. Since νόμοι is rarely used to denote the Mosaic commandments one might feel inclined to take ἑνί as a neuter (with Schneckenburger and Kern), but since the following πάντων, according to Huther and al., renders the construction difficult, it is better to assume James entering into the Jewish mode of view which he potentiates in saying that every separate ἐντολή has also the full force of a νόμος. Wiesinger says that James takes the most favourable case in order to make his statement as convincing as possible. But James is hardly willing to yield this most favourable case to the reader. The point to be made is the demonstration of the absolute inviolability of the law. The πταίειν may be understood as well of a slight offence as of a gross offence, the declaration holding good in either case; but the context seems to require the latter construction which is also favoured by the preposition ἐν. Whosoever offends in *one point* so as to fall, is preëminently a transgressor of all laws, *i. e.*, he is an apostate. This sense follows more clearly from the sequel. Such an one is ἔνοχος, *i. e.*, held fast in guilt [Germ. arrested—M.] for satisfaction by the suffering of punishment. Each separate law becomes as it were a judge who arrests him.

VER. 11. **For He who said.**—The unity of all commandments lies primarily in the unity of the Lawgiver, Mark xii. 32. This implies of course the One Spirit of all commandments according to which all commandments are included in each separate commandment and the *one* sense: the requirement of love and the *one* recompense.

Thou shalt not commit adultery.—Different explanations have been given of the selection of these two commandments. Baumgarten: Because their transgression was punished with death; Wiesinger: because the readers are nowhere charged with μοιχεύειν (see for the contrary ch. iv.), whereas μὴ φονεύσῃς has the commandment of love as its kernel, because these are the first duties under the law of love to one's neighbour. However we have here once more to call attention to the symbolical character of this Epistle. To the Israelite the prohibition of adultery was at once the prohibition of religious apostasy to heathenism (which probably accounts for the transpositions Mark x. 19, etc. of which Huther makes mention), and the prohibition of murder at once that of lovelessness [coined from the German *Lieblosigkeit*, for want of a current English equivalent—M.] towards our neighbour. The sense therefore is probably as follows: the same God to whose commandment you appeal in your fear of intermingling with heathenism, has prohibited murder, of which you may become guilty by your hatred of men. We have no doubt that also 1 Jno. iii. 15 refers primarily to Ebionite conduct towards Christian fellowship (ch. ii. 19). The connection of the words with Matth. v. 17–19 is clear.

VER. 12. **So speak ye and so do ye.**—Application drawn from what has gone before, but not a new section (Semler). Huther wants to connect οὕτως with what follows, not with what has gone before. But the double οὕτως as well as the anteposition of λαλεῖτε refer strongly to what has gone before. The readers of the Epistle are charged not only after the manner of laymen to judge according to the anti-judaistic conception of the law, which had been laid down, but also to assert it in their respective spheres as witnesses of the truth (see ch. iii). Thus they were first to speak and to testify but then of course also to act accordingly.

As those about to be judged by the law of liberty.—This is not the explication but the reason of the preceding exhortation. The question comes up why here again James calls the New Testament the law of liberty as in ch. i. 25 and not, as above, the royal law? The law of liberty is the New Testament principle of the new life in the Gospel of Christ, which frees us from the restraint of the law. Conscious that according to their faithful or unfaithful conduct with reference to this law they are to be judged, true Jewish Christians and Israelites must cheerfully testify against Judaism and its legalism and exhibit Christian fellowship. It is true that this νόμος, as such, admits least a non-observance of this or that commandment (Huther), but this is hardly the reason why it is called νόμος ἐλευθερίας.

VER. 13. **For the judgment is [will be] merciless.**—*Unmerciful* is inadequate. Cf. Matth. v. 6; ch. xviii. 23; xxv. 35. The saying is primarily true objectively. The judgment will be rigidly enforced according to the love displayed in our life by mercy shown to the poor, the suffering and the despised. But the saying holds also good subjectively. A hard, merciless man reacts by his conduct upon his own consciousness; he makes himself a hard self-tormentor, who cannot but see the judgment in all his experience and a merciless judicial decree in all judgment.

Mercy boasteth over judgment.—The asyndeton intensifies the antithesis. Since κατακαυχᾶσθαι with the Genitive denotes *boasting oneself against* or *over* (see Rom. xi. 8; Jas. iii. 14), ἔλεος must not be completed by θεοῦ (so Calvin, Bengel and al.), nor interpreted as the triumphant exaltation with which mercy by its assurance of grace *confounds* (*puts to shame*) the terrors of the judgment (so Wiesinger), or transforms them into signs of redemption, as says our Lord (Luke xxi. 38); but it rather signifies the triumphant assurance with which the evangelizing mercy of believers, especially that of a James, a Peter or a Paul or the Gentile world excelled the judging spirit of the Judaists, the cheerful Gospel excelled the gloomy Talmud, the Church of the world the synagogue of the Jewish quarter and the evangelical confession the inquisition of the Middle Ages, to say nothing of the triumph of Christian philanthropy over modern particularism.

DOCTRINAL AND ETHICAL.

1. Against the genuineness of the Epistle of James there is probably not raised an objection apparently more just than that the person of Christ is less prominent in it than in other Epistles and that the author occupies a comparatively lower Christological standpoint than the most famous Apostles. It certainly does not contain the richly developed Christology which characterizes the writings of Paul and John. The Christology of James in general is on a level with that of his brother Jude and not essentially different from that of the synoptical Gospels. The mind of James is rather practical and ethical than dogmatical and speculative. Even in respect of insight into the nature of Christ there was among Apostolical authors doubtless a diversity of gifts, cf. 1 Cor. xii. 7. It is also very probable that James in his wisdom as a teacher deemed it more judicious to refer the readers whom he addressed, more to the moral precepts of the Gospel than chiefly to the Person of the Redeemer. On this account the comparatively few passages in which he speaks of Him with decision, as *e. g.* in ch. ii. 1, deserve the greater attention. On the sense of the remarkable expression τοῦ κυρίου ἡμῶν Ἰησοῦ Χριστοῦ τῆς δόξης see under *Exegetical and Critical.* This single passage proves conclusively how far James was from conceiving Christ (as some maintain) according to the old-Ebionite manner to have been a ψιλὸς ἄνθρωπος. Describing himself as the *servant* (bondman) of Jesus Christ (ch. i. 1) shows unmistakably how far he places the Master above himself, and describing Him as κύριος τῆς δόξης, he not only attributes to Him a royal rank but, indirectly at least, a higher Divine nature far exalted above all creatures. Cf. Ps. cx. 1; Heb. i. 13. Nor must we overlook his mentioning the Lord Jesus Christ at the very beginning of his Epistle in immediate connection with God Himself, and his constant reference to God as the *Father* shows not indistinctly that in doing so he had before his mind's eye the high and holy relation of God the Father to the *Son.* Of equal importance in estimating the Christology of James is the circumstance of his unequivocally calling *Christ* the *Lord,* that is transferring to Him the Old Testament name of God with which he was familiar from his earliest childhood; ch. v. 7, 8. Such an appellation was only possible on the conviction that He, who in the Old Testament is universally called *Jehovah* (Jahve), has revealed Himself in the New Testament as God (the Father) *and* as Christ. Cf. Wiesinger's Commentary on James, p. 65, and Dorner's *Entwicklungsgeschichte der Christologie,* 2d ed., I., p. 95.

2. We should wholly misunderstand James' reproof of the sin of respect of persons, were we to infer from it that he was aiming at the establishment of a perfect equality in daily life or even in the assemblies of the Church. God Himself sanctions difference of rank and station, Prov. xxii. 2; Matth. xxvi. 11. But it is contrary to the will of God, if men overstep the line of demarcation which He in wisdom has drawn, turn it into an impassable gulf and with the existing difference overlook the higher unity. The arrangement therefore, which especially in former times was so frequently prevalent in many evangelical churches, of assigning splendid seats of honour to the distinguished and of putting back the poor as much as possible, would surely be contrary to the spirit of James. It is one thing to recognize a Divinely appointed difference, but it is another to make arbitrary distinction in the public worship of God.

3. James also teaches the doctrine of God's eternal election of grace irrespective of wealth or poverty or any outward prerogatives whatsoever. Although it is true that poverty *per se* is no recommendation and wealth *per se* presents no insuperable obstacle (cf. Matth. xix. 25, 26; Jno. xix. 38, 39), it is on the other hand not less indubitable (and also a real compensation for so many things of which the poor are deprived in this world), that comparatively by far the greatest number of those who are rich in faith and heirs of the kingdom are found among the poor.

4. The idea of Christian Church-life involves among other things the non-existence of law-suits among believers, or at least the settling of their differences among themselves. Cf. 1 Cor. vi. 1-4. The readers of the Epistle of James appear however to have been far from realizing this ideal, and as a rule it was just the rich who in this respect most oppressed their poor brethren. This is therefore an additional reason for not showing them any greater honour than that to which they were legitimately entitled.

5. David was held guilty of having caused the enemies of God to blaspheme in consequence of his sin with Bathsheba and Uriah, 2 Sam. xii. 14. Equally guilty are in James' eyes those who by their oppressive conduct cause the goodly name of the Lord to be blasphemed to the

Church, the name which in Baptism was invoked over His people. This is again an indirect proof that he ascribes to the Lord Jesus Christ a really Divine dignity.—

6. "The giving of the law on Mount Sinai took place mainly by the Son of God, who as the Angel of the Lord had led the children of Israel through the wilderness and is on that account called by the prophets King of Israel (Jer. xxiii. 5, 6; Numb. xxiv. 17; Jer. xxx. 21; Jno. i. 49; Rev. xvii. 14; xix. 16), and King of all kings; hence the words *royal law* refer particularly to Christ, who in His sayings and sermons did so strongly inculcate the duty of love (Matth. xxii. 38, 39; Jno. xv. 12, 17; 1 Jno. ii. 5; iv. 20, 21). To love oneself, that is in a well-ordered manner, is nothing else than taking care of one's temporal, spiritual and eternal welfare, so that one's spiritual welfare may also promote one's temporal prosperity. This is done, if we are truly the servants of God, believe on Him and love Him. Now where this love of oneself is well-ordered, it is also a rule of a well-ordered love of one's neighbour; see Matth. vii. 12." Starke.

7. "A single sin against the commandment of God (though he have kept all others) condemns the sinner and burdens him with the curse. If it is presumptuous and intentional, it deprives him of spiritual life, destroys faith, etc., as in the case of David by adultery, in that of Peter by denial and in that of Adam by eating the forbidden fruit. If it is committed through infirmity and haste, sin as sin carries within itself the venom of damnableness, although preserving grace and forgiveness prevent its execution. The law is, as it were, a garment, which is torn altogether, although you only take away a piece thereof; it is like harmony in music which is wholly spoiled if only one voice is out of tune." Starke.

8. "If a man transgress only one commandment and, if it were possible, should keep all the other commandments of the law, he would still be guilty of the whole law, because he has offended the same God who gave the whole law and insists upon its being kept not according to one commandment only, but wholly according to all its parts; whence every man may abundantly know that there is not any single sin so trifling and bad as not to be liable to damnation, since also the most trivial offence against the law is a transgression of the whole law. But God forgiving the penitent even the grossest offences in their justification, is done for Christ's sake, just as in the case of the converted their daily sins of infirmity, although damnable in themselves, for Christ's sake are not imputed unto damnation." Starke.

9. The moral life of the Church of Christ was at all times exposed to the peril of two opposite rocks; moral rigorism on the one hand and antinomian latitudinarianism on the other. The doctrine of James (vv. 10–12) concerning the indivisible unity of the Divine Law is admirably adapted powerfully to counteract both maladies. In no event does he favour ascetical rigorism which only too frequently degenerates into soul-killing formalism. The law for which he is zealous, is a law of *liberty* in the loftiest acceptance of the term, yea the entire antithesis of authority and liberty is converted on his standpoint into a higher unity. The Divine law by no means opposes the Christian as *heteronomy*, but if he has received it through faith and love into his inmost consciousness, it becomes to him daily more and more an *autonomy* [*heteronomy* literally another law, then, living according to another law; *autonomy* literally one's own law, then, living according to one's own law, self-goverment.—M.]. But if on the other hand latitudinarianism arrives only too soon at being rigid in some points and yielding and lenient in others, James stands up with inexorable severity and administers the unity of the Divine law as that of an indivisible whole. Even the best Christian involuntarily is easily inclined pharisaically to overrate some commandments and to underrate others (cf. Matth. xxii. 36; xxiii. 23). Many a man, *e. g.* who would fear and tremble at the thought of murder would little hesitate in bearing false witness against his neighbour. Here comes in the admonition, "Whosoever shall have kept the whole law yet offend in one point, has become guilty of all." It is self-evident that James here does not speak of sins of haste, ignorance or infirmity but of intentional, presumptuous or principled transgressions (transgressing on principle) of one of the commandments. Whosoever has thus become guilty, has disturbed the harmony of the Divine law. Of course not in the sense that a murderer is therefore also a thief, an adulterer or a defamer, but because the transgressor of any one commandment disgraces love, which is the key-note and sum-total of all the commandments. The favourite notion of many people that the province of morals recognizes a greater or a smaller number of *adiaphora* therefore is here emphatically denied. He who obstinately transgresses one commandment without actually violating the others, omits doing so only because at that instant he does not feel himself incited to a definite act of disobedience. For did he feel it, he would doubtless withdraw himself with equal swiftness from the restraint of any other commandment. But where is then his respect of the Divine law in its totality? Whichever commandment be transgressed, such transgression always reveals *selfishness* opposing on principle the chief requirement of *love*.

10. The passage, "Mercy boasteth over (against) judgment" (v. 13) is not any more isolated than that it contradicts the evangelical doctrine of free grace. In the Old Testament also the idea is repeatedly expressed that love and mercy disarm to a certain degree the severity of that Divine judgment. See *e. g.*, Is. i. 17, 18; Dan. iv. 27. John the Baptist described and insisted upon actual exhibitions of love as one of the marks of a repentance by which men might flee from the wrath to come, Luke iii. 8–11. Our Lord described the blessedness of the merciful (Matth. v. 7) and set forth love as the standard in the last judgment, Matth. xxv. 34–40. This is also the spirit in which James thinks and speaks and no further intimation is needed to show that he refers to no other Christian mercy than to that which is the fruit of living faith and genuine renovation of the heart. Not only he, who loved much, may therefore hope for forgiveness but also he who asked for

much forgiveness, will now also love much, and may look forward to the judgment with greater calmness because this love of faith supplies to him and to others unequivocal proof that he has passed from death unto life. Cf. 1 Jno. iii. 14.

HOMILETICAL AND PRACTICAL.

The glorified Christ, the Lord of the Church, the object of faith. Sincere faith may still be very imperfect. Love and faith are indissolubly united, but love is irreconcilable with partial respectings of persons.—Agreement of the love insisted upon by James and that described by Paul, 1 Cor. xiii.—Rich and poor should appear in the house of prayer at unity among themselves.—Christian liberty, equality and fraternity.—The catchwords of the revolution only caricatures of a Gospel watchword.—The communion of saints is disgraced by lovelessness and party-spirit. — Loveless judging of others ill-becoming to one who will be judged himself.—The prerogatives of the believing poor! 1, They are the elect of God; 2, they are rich in faith; 3, they are heirs of the kindom of heaven which God has promised to them who love Him.—The Gospel opposed both to mobocracy [German '*Proletariat*,' a word always used in a bad sense; this must be my apology for the hybrid mobocracy. — M.] and despotism. — "He that oppresseth the poor, reproacheth his Maker, etc." Prov. xiv. 31. — Poverty evangelically considered.—It is, 1, a great sin, 2, a great shame, 3, a great harm, that the goodly name of Christ, which was invoked over us in Baptism, is dishonoured for our sake; cf. Rom. ii. 23, 24.—Love the foremost requirement made by the royal law of Christianity, Jno. xiii. 34, 35.—The inviolable unity of the Christian code of morality. —"Whosever shall have kept the whole law, but have offended in one point, etc." This saying 1, is apparently strange 2, but nevertheless perfectly true and therefore 3, calculated to solemnize our minds in the judgment we pass on ourselves and to render us careful in that which we pass on others.—The Christian must not consider the commandments of the second table to be less holy than those of the first.—We shall be judged by the law of *liberty*; the meaning, the truth, the solemnity and consolation of this thought.—The connection between faith, love, judgment and acquittal.—The thought of the impending judgment—1, wherein it may alarm the Christian and 2, wherein it may again calm his fears.

On the whole pericope, vv. 1-13.—Of respect of persons. 1. The *character* it discloses: it manifests itself *a.* among Christians (v. 1), *b.* in religious intercourse (vv. 2, 3) and *c.* it springs from impure foundations (v. 4). 2. The *wrong* it inflicts: *a.* on the poor (v. 5), *b.* on the rich (vv. 6, 7), *c.* on ourselves (vv. 8, 9). The *judgment* it deserves; this is *a.* terrible (v. 10), *b.* just (vv. 11, 12), *c.* inevitable (v. 13).—

STARKE:—The Jews had the regulation that if the rich and the poor had a cause before a tribunal, both had either to stand or to be seated.

QUESNEL:—Godliness forbids not the difference of posts of honour but simply disapproves of the rich only being respected and the poor despised, 1 Cor. xi. 22.—Whoso on account of his occupation has outwardly to wear a vile garment, let him so much the more wear the beautiful garment of Christ's righteousness. Is. lxi. 10.

STARKE:—The masses always look more at those who are splendidly attired before the world than at those who are gloriously attired before Christ.

LUTHER:—The rich enjoy greater privileges than others in things temporal, but not in things spiritual, Luke vi. 24.

LANGII OP.:—There are rich in the world who are also rich in God, but there are also poor in the world who are likewise poor in God and these are most miserable for time and for eternity, Gen. xiii. 2.

HEDINGER:—To be a beggar but a true Christian is more than being emperor or king without it.

CRAMER:—Bodily poverty should not hinder but promote one's salvation Luke xvi. 22.—Those who do not honour Christ in His members are not worthy to be honoured themselves, Luke x. 16; 1 Sam. ii. 30.

QUESNEL:—There is nothing greater than the name of Christ, but nothing more to be feared than to bear it unworthily.

STARKE:—The royal law of love makes all to be kings, who are however the subjects of the King of kings, 1 Pet. ii. 9; Rev. xviii. 6.

CRAMER:—By seeming trifles also the law may be transgressed, Numb. xv. 32, etc.

NOVA BIBL. TUB.:—The law exacts perfect obedience.

HEDINGER:—Like as the believer fulfils all the commandments of the law, so the ungodly transgresses all the commandments, 1 Jno. iii. 22.—If any man will allow only one sin to have dominion over him, he cannot receive forgiveness of sins, Ps. xxxii. 2.

STARKE:—It is as culpable to be silent when we ought to speak as to speak when we ought to be silent, Is. lvi. 10.

LUTHER:—The Divine law is the only rule of conduct in whatsoever we do in word or deed, Ps. cxix 9, 15, 22.

QUESNEL:—To be unmerciful, especially towards the innocent and believers, is a sign of men being merely natural and consequently exposed to the wrath of God, Ps. xxxvii. 26.

LUTHER:—The unmerciful will be damned without mercy and the merciful will be saved of mercy, Jer. xv. 6; Hos. i. 6.

LISCO (ver. 1-9):—True faith is remote from all sinful partiality.—(vv. 10-13). Of disobedience to the Divine law.—Christianity aims at equalizing the differences among men.

HEUBNER:—All haughtiness is a denial of faith. Unchristian distinguishing between sins.—What a contradiction! to see Christians dishonour the poor whom God honours.—Without esteeming and keeping all the commandments alike the keeping of this or that is worthless *in the sight of God.*—The assurance which love gives in the judgment.

VON GERLACH:—The Apostle calls Christ the Lord of glory in order to show the nothingness of all human distinctions in His sight.—The law of liberty has freed us from the bondage of sin, from mercenary work-holiness; we should consider therefore what a testimony there will arise against us in the judgment if we make exceptions and do not keep it in voluntary and childlike love.

STIER:—The Christianity of the rich is more frequently ungenuine and not proof than that of the poor.—If a father setting out on a journey lays down ten commandments to be observed by his child during his absence, and the child reserves one to be transgressed by him—dares such a child appear before his father and say: Father I have obeyed thee, nine of the ten commandments I have well kept! Every sin, thus reserved and remaining, every continuing transgression of one commandment given by the same God cancels our righteousness before the law, so that all its fair numbers turn into so many ciphers.

NEANDER:-Diversities and inequalities founded on the natural relations and organizations of society were not to be abrogated by Christianity but rendered less burdensome, they were to be equalized by the common bond of love and to become matter for the exercise of that Christian love.

VIEDEBANDT:—The devil has well succeeded in a double trick: 1. In making the rich think that faith is the disturber of all enjoyment and pleasure, 2. In convincing the poor that faith brings no help.

G. NITZSCH:—We do not call a negro a white man because his teeth are white; so none may be called righteous, who only speaks of *righteousness* or otherwise puts into practice some other part thereof. David says: "I keep all thy commandments."

PORUBSZKY:—Faith in Jesus Christ tolerates no respect of persons.—The moral harmony in the kingdom of God (vv. 10-12).—The taking to heart of Christian mercy (v. 13).

JACOBY (v. 12):—Speaking also is subjected to the royal law of love.—It amounts to the same whether our judgment be bribed by riches in money, in intellect or worldly education.

Vv. 8-13—Pericope on the 21st Sunday after Trinity in the Grand Duchy of Hesse and elsewhere.

BAUR:—Love as to its being and working.

J. MÜLLER:—Love the being of the Christian life.

R. KROMM:—The Christian is *able* and *bound* to keep *all* the commandments of his God.—Of the riches of Christian love.

[V. 1. *Social* differences are allowed among Christians, Rom. xiii. 7; but invidious distinctions and partiality in *spiritual* matters are disallowed and unchristian. In the use of the Sacraments, in prayer and praise, in the hearing of God's Word Christians are on a level. The pew-system is unprimitive and unchristian. The Church is the *Lord's* house, as its name implies (κυριακόν), and in the Lord's house the rich and poor alike ought to be provided with equal accommodation for worship without any invidious, unchristian and worldly reference to their pecuniary ability.—Ecclesiastical preferment of personal *friends* and *relatives*, as such, is another form of respectings of persons.—M.].

WORDSWORTH:—Contemplate the *Lord of glory* (1 Cor. ii. 8), who humbled Himself, and took the poor man's nature, and joined all in Himself, and promises glory to humility (Luke xiv. 11; Jas. iv. 10). This consideration is the groundwork of the Apostle's argument and exhortation. This is the *glory* which Christ Himself offers to you—not the *vain glory* of *this world*, which ye seek by preferring the rich to the poor, and by having men's *persons* in admiration for the sake of advantage to yourselves (Jude 16).

[V. 2. Christian places of worship true synagogues (cf. συναγωγή and ἐπισυναγωγή Heb. x. 25).—M.].

[V. 4. WORDSWORTH:—There are two distinct grounds of censure—

1. That by this partiality they become like *disputants* in a law-suit (cf. 1 Cor. vi. 6), instead of being brethren: this is the rebuke in *this* clause.

2. That they thus constitute themselves into *judges*; this is developed in what follows.

V. 7. The name invoked over Christians in Baptism and in the Benedictions (Matth. xxviii. 29; Acts ix. 14, 21; Rom. x. 12; 1 Cor. i. 2; 1 Pet. i. 17).—In the Jewish synagogue that godly name was *blasphemed* (1 Cor. xii. 3); in the Christian synogogue it was *invoked*. ἐπίκλησις in the language of the Church denotes the act of solemn *invocation*. See Bingham, *Eccl. Ant.* 15, 1.—M.].

[V. 13. CHRYSOSTOM:—"Mercy is dear to God, and intercedes for the sinner, and breaks his chains, and dissipates the darkness, and quenches the fire of hell, and destroys the worm and rescues from the gnashing of teeth. To her the gates of heaven are opened. She is the queen of virtues, and makes man like to God, for it is written, Be ye merciful as your Father who is in heaven is merciful. She has silver wings like the dove, and feathers of gold, and soars aloft, and is clothed with divine glory, and stands by the throne of God; when we are in danger of being condemned, she rises up and pleads for us, and covers us with her defence and enfolds us in her wings. God loves mercy more than sacrifice." —M.].

[SHAKSPEARE, Merchant of Venice, Act iv. Scene 1.

The quality of mercy is not strain'd;
It droppeth, as the gentle rain from heaven
Upon the place beneath: it is twice bless'd;
It blesseth him that gives, and him that takes:
etc.—M.].

---

§ 2. CHAPTER II. 14-26.

EXEGETICAL AND CRITICAL.

The true life of faith or faith evinced by the mercy of brotherly love and dead faith illustrated by heartless demeanour. v. 14-17.

VER. 14. **What doth it profit, my brethren, if a man were to say etc.?**—James, having illuminated outward legality as lacking the principle of love, now takes it up as outward faith (*Gläubigkeit*) lacking both love and the energy of practical demonstration (*Thatbeweis*). The sequel shows what he means by practical demonstration; it is the full communion with believing brethren in love and life. The following section (vv. 14-26) supports his demand by examples from the Old Testament. Here it is to be remembered "that with James πίστις is the necessary ground of σωτηρία, which is evident from ch. i. 18–21, but of course that πίστις which is not without works. In disputing the former delusion, James adopts his characteristic mode of first stating in clear and well-defined language the fundamental thought on which all the rest depends and he does it by the introduction of brief interrogative sentences, which reject that false opinion." Huther.

What doth it profit? The Article makes ὄφελος emphatic; what is the use, what profit does it bring? That is, all the blessing of the theocratic faith, ultimately also in Jesus as the Messiah, is lost if this faith does not lead to vital fruit. That faith itself is then not true; hence: "IF A MAN WERE TO SAY, THAT HE HATH FAITH. λέγῃ is emphatic, so also Gataker, Stier, de Wette and al. Although de Wette's rendering "IF A MAN PRETENDS," be probably too strong, the assertion of Huther, that the sequel does not give the lie to λέγειν, is incorrect. This is certainly done conditionally in v. 18 where it is maintained that the existence of faith cannot be proved without works. Only thus much may be admitted, that James allows the faith which is merely outward and traditional to pass as a kind of faith, on account of its objective truth he cannot call it false, but on account of its subjective untruth he calls it dead and the contrast of dead and living shows that he distinguishes faith from faith. Now the faith which he calls living needs no further complement; it is a unit as to its living energy, while the faith without works, lacks owing to the absence of works the demonstration of energy of life. If we say "the dead body is without the soul," it does not follow that we think also: "The living man consists of body and soul." Schneckenburger with reason sees something significant in the absence of the Article (ἐὰν πίστιν). Huther rightly asserts that πίστις does not denote here *nuda notitia* or *professio*, because this idea is identical with real faith in the opinion of the speaker; but he is wrong in supposing that πίστις always denotes the same thing in the mind of James. For saying, that πίστις in one is different from πίστις in another, amounts to nothing and it is false to affirm that *fiducia* cannot be denied even to dead faith. Why then is the subject of this faith uniformly the δίψυχος? [The distinction is manifestly between *theoretic belief* unaccompanied by the practice of good works and *vital faith* abounding in good works. Faith is the inward, works the outward. Works are the outward sign and pledge, the demonstration of faith within. The man dramatically introduced in the text has faith (v. 19), but his faith is theoretic belief. There seems to be no necessity for making λέγῃ emphatic.—M.].

But were to have no works—That is, the works specifically belonging to and characteristic of faith. That James particularly refers to the works of brotherly love, is manifest from the sequel.

Faith surely cannot.—The remarkable character of this proposition as contrasted with the doctrine that faith does save is variously gotten over. Some commentators emphasize the artice ἡ before πίστις: *that* faith, such a faith [Bede, "fides illa, quam vos habere dicitis"—M.]. In reply, Wiesinger and Huther observe that the Article is used, because there is a resumption of the previous idea, as ch. i. 3 with reference to ὑπομονή, and ch. i. 15 with reference to ἁμαρτία. But the resumption of the previous idea is sufficient to settle the point that the reference is here to such a faith which has no works. The demonstrative therefore is not contained in ἡ only, but in ἡ πίστις and one might translate, "*thus* faith surely cannot save him." Huther thinks that αὐτόν is emphatic, "him who thus conducts himself, faith cannot save;" but this would make faith an abstract objectivity. The reference therefore is simply to the faith in question, and the explanations of Theile (false faith), Pott (faith only) and similar ones are epexegetical. Huther in his explication of αὐτόν returns to the definition "the faith which has no works," whereas, in order to be consistent, he ought to say, "the man who has no works."

Save him.—σῶσαι relates not to the attainment of *future* salvation, as Huther maintains, but denotes, according to the idea of the New Testament σωτηρία the present, principial salvation of the redemption already experienced and passing through progressive stages of completion to ultimate salvation.

VERS. 15, 16. **But if a brother or a sister.**—The following example in the opinion of Huther (and Wiesinger) explains the preceding proposition by explaining that compassion also without corresponding works is dead and useless. But the reference to dead love or even to dead compassion would be unheard of. The question in one example also is *dead faith*, which under certain circumstances hypocritically affects the appearance of love without however evincing the reality of its existence. The absence of the work is just the absence of love or compassion. The brother and the sister are as such fellow-believers (companions of the same faith). And this leads to take these personages also in a symbolical sense. For the duty of relieving the literally needy with food and raiment was already recognized in the Old Testament as a duty of man to man; how much more then under the sense of duty acknowledged in the Christian Church. James doubtless needed not to inculcate this duty on the believing dispersion, and if it was his intention, he could not limit its exercise to Christian brethren. But the case stood differently with regard to the relation of the Jewish Christian to his Gentile-Christian co-religionist or also to the Gentile-Christian Church. That they were not literally poor and naked does not affect the question, for on the one hand they were indebted to the Apostles, who were more merciful than the Judaists, for their spiritual prosperity, and on the other hand they would still appear as very poor to the Judaists; γύμνοι, as those wholly stripped of proper and respectable apparel, after having laid aside their vile raiment (see v. 2; Huther's pressing of γύμνοι yields no gain), and destitute of daily food (the different senses in which ἐφήμερος is construed, amount to the same thing), *i. e.* destitute of positive familiarity with the word of God according to Judaistic ideas. The Jewish Christians, to be sure, had progressed so far as not to damn the poor believers (even as the Jews already affected friendliness towards the proselytes of the gate); they acknowledged the brotherhood in a general way and perchance would unctuously express that acknowledgment in the words "Go in peace," wished them perhaps also all manner of good in the self-satisfying of their (the poor brethren's) Christian wants, but having gone to that stretch of liberality, would also dismiss them, without having any other dealings with them or entering with them into the communion of devoted care and love (just as nowadays the Confessionalists dismiss the Evangelicals with unctuous sour-sweet words). Be warmed! be filled! These words are surely not uttered optatively in the sense, "May some one else help you" (Hottinger, Grotius and al.), nor imperatively in a liberal sense (Huther), but connected with the valedictory salutation of peace they denote a cant-wish of blessing, "may you succeed in getting warmed etc." The reproach of pauperism is at the same time clothed in hypocritically sparing terms, hence "be ye warmed" not at once "be ye clothed" (Laurentius and al.), but alluding to it and in like manner "be ye filled" in allusion to their hunger.—The one who thus speaks represents the general tendency but points to the unctuous speakers who understand to couch the unsparing dismissal as much as possible in fair and sparing language. Instead of such conduct they were one and altogether to show love to the poor. But our example presupposes the case that they did not even give them necessaries.

What would that profit?—See v. 14. Such a benediction (wish-of-blessing) would purely have no value and the acknowledgment of brotherhood on which it is founded would accordingly be equally void, just as the faith on which it is founded. The whole demeanour would be unprofitable *egentibus* (Hottinger) and *dicentibus* (Semler); in general to the kingdom of God.

VER. 17. **So also faith, if it have not.**—If it does not show the life-sign of animating works, which are intrinsically its property.

For itself. [*i. e. in* itself.—M.]—As it is dead as regards the brethren, so it is dead as regards itself. Καθ' ἑαυτήν not pleonastic (Grotius), not "fides sola" (Knapp), but joined with νεκρά indicative of being dead or rather of having died, whereby the life of faith and consequently the life of the believer himself is denied. And this being dead is not only the cause of this want of works (Olshausen) but also the consequence of the reaction of that want. It dies ever more and more of not being energizing. See Matth. xviii. 23 etc.

The proof of faith by the works of faith or the believer's justification before the consciousness of the Church, vv. 18, 19.

VER. 18. **But some one will say.**—Different explanations are given for the introduction of an objection by ἀλλ' ἐρεῖ τις, although the sense of the passage especially with the reading χωρὶς τῶν ἔργων is abundantly clear. The possession of faith without works may be asserted but not be proved, since the corresponding works constitute the proof of faith, while the faith may be proved by the right works. The works therefore are the exhibition, the evidence of faith. Difficulties have been found 1. In James' introducing this proposition as the expression of another person and not as his own; 2. in his introducing it by ἀλλά. The second difficulty disappears with the first. James could not well take the place of the objector because it was remote from the mind of his readers to deny the genuineness of his faith; but many among them were inclined to deny it in the case of the Gentile Christians. Hence the sense is as follows: but some one will rise up against this dead faith and with it enter the lists in proving the genuineness of his faith by his works of faith. In this sense the passage has a grand prophetical character. The Gentile Christian world has proved by its works of faith that it had the true faith, but Ebionism with its want of consistency in Christian works of love that its orthodoxism was not a living faith. ἀλλά therefore is here not the formula of a dialectical objection, as in Rom. ix. 19; 1 Cor. xv. 35, but the introduction of an actual historical antithesis, That the speaker's faith (v. 14) is dead is primarily a mystery of an inward state of death, but there will come one who by the exhibition of the contrary will make manifest that death. James makes him express in a definite antithesis what he actually shall do, in order to elucidate the law of life that invisible faith cannot be seen without visible works, while the visible works enable us to see the invisible faith. Wiesinger therefore rightly maintains that the speaker sides with James. On the other hand the artificial explanation of Huther can only be accounted for by the embarrassment he experienced with respect to ἀλλά. "But some might say in answer to what I have just stated, defending himself: *thou* (who hast not the works) hast faith and *I*, on the other hand (who affirm that faith without works is dead), have works; my one-sided insisting upon works is not any more right than thy one-sided insisting upon faith." This, in the first place, would be no defence of the speaker (v. 14), and secondly it is nowhere said that the speaker (v. 18) has no faith; he rather wants to prove his faith by his works. Stier even maintains that the ἔργα ἔχων, who has the word, is a man of pharisaic tendencies who in the interest of work-righteousness impugns faith; but this is altogether beside the connection, for there is no reference whatsoever to pharisaic works. On the other wide-differing but otherwise unimportant explanations given of this passage compare Huther especially with reference to those of Pott, Kern, de Wette and Schneckenburger. It is proper to add that Huther himself farther on gives a tolerably correct paraphrase of this passage and is equally right in remarking that with the reading ἐκ τῶν ἔργων in Text. Rec. these words should be taken ironically.

VER. 19. **Thou believest that God is one.**—The Apostle having shown in what precedes that the existence of faith cannot be proved without works, now proceeds to the proof that faith, even if granted in such a form, has a damnable effect, that is one issuing in fear and terror of God. Huther does not justly state the force of the Apostle's thought in saying that James here shows the inadequateness of faith without works to salvation. For the example of the devils who tremble just in consequence of their manner of believing, not only along with their faith, nor even notwithstanding their faith, is not simply designed to intensify the negation that such a faith is without salvation. The condition of not being saved is connected with the state of being damned. The Apostle does not start with the concession that the objector has faith (Huther), but that his faith is worthless. Huther thinks it strange that James does not name that which is specifically Christian as the object of faith. On this account Calvin supposed that this whole section treats not of Christian faith (*de fide*) but only *de vulgari dei notitia*. De Wette holds that ὅτι characterizes the faith as being merely theoretical, in which Wiesinger agrees with him and to which Huther objects without sufficient reason. Huther and al. consider that this article of faith is simply introduced by way of example and that just this article was selected because it distinguishes revealed religion from heathenism (Deut. vi. 4; Neh. ix. 6 etc.). But this suggests the additional remark that it was selected because the Jewish Christians and the Jews not only were particularly proud of this first article of their faith (Schneckenburger), but also were wont to contrast it with the distinctly Christian dogma of the Triune God and the Son of God.—This discloses moreover the further consideration that it was their pride in this increasingly misunderstood article which kept them back as Jews from fully surrendering to Christ and as Jewish Christians from fully surrendering themselves to the Christian faith. The monarchism of the Jews which was opposed to the incarnation of the Son of God continued in the germinating monarchism of the Jewish Christians. In the judgment of James therefore the fruitlessness or worthlessness of that faith is connected with the fact that in the shape of orthodoxism it obstinately remains at a stand-still on a stage of faith which has been laid aside and that in this respect it is a heterodoxy which may become a heresy and ultimately even a devilish antichristianity. It was just by remaining at a stand-still and by resistance offered to the completed revelation that monotheism originally so rich in vitality became dead deism. In a similar way the Greek article of faith has been established in opposition to Roman Catholic development, and the Roman Catholic article in opposition to evangelical faith.* Where vital development is abhorred (*perhorrescirt?*) faith becomes false confidence in the abstract article. Wiesinger justly calls attention to the circumstance that this passage shows that this Epistle is far from being Judaizing and anti-Pauline.

Thou doest well.—It is questionable whether we are to take these words ironically (Calvin, Theile, Wiesinger and many others), or literally (Grotius, de Wette and al). They cannot be purely ironical, because the article is truth; they cannot be purely laudatory, because the true article is falsely held; Huther therefore rightly observes that the ironical lies in the whole expression; that is, in the momentary appearance as if James in conceding to the objector to believe in such a manner were therewith also conceding to him the true faith. "This irony" says Wiesinger "rises into sarcasm in the combination of *πιστεύουσι και φρίσσουσι*." It may be doubted whether this conclusion is formally sarcastic. The sarcasm lies here in the naked fact itself. Formally it only flashes out in the splendid *καὶ* which connects the greatest seeming contradiction and which Huther rightly does not like to see wiped off (Theile: *atqui* etc.).

The devils.—Although we must not think of demoniacs (Wetstein), nor of the demons in the demoniacs (Schneckenburger) they furnish the most intelligible historical proof of the otherwise more transcendental declaration. Huther thinks that the reference is to the demons or apostate spirits according to the view which makes the heathen deities demons (LXX. Deut. xxxii. 17 etc.; 1 Cor. x. 20). But the Apostle's saying is perfectly intelligible without such reference, which may easily lead here to confusion. For as far as the demons are the occasion of polytheism they impugn the Unity of God but as far as they are conscious that they are lying and that the *One* God will visit them in judgment, they just appear to acknowledge the pride of Judaism and the defeat of heathenism. Holding fast to this reference we ought to pass on to the thought that heathenism also in its deepest demon-background is not without a monotheistic consciousness, and it is just this which constitutes its misery. To give to this idea a more popular shape it would run thus: the demons which as you hold inhabit and constitute the heathen world, are all monotheists but for that very reason they shudder. But if we emphasize the heathen element, we weaken the marked emphasis of the demon element, and this is the reason why we have doubts concerning said reference. Nor do they shudder *only*, because they expect the judgment, their judgment is already involved in their relation to God. This shuddering *φρίσσειν* (ἅπαξ λεγ.) is more than trembling (Job iv. 15), a horror with the hair standing on end.—

The two examples of the proof of faith by works as a general example of the unity of living faith of Jews and Gentiles, v. 20–26.

VER. 20. **But willest thou to know (it)?**—These words denote the certainty with which the Apostle announces the convincing proof of the uselessness of faith without works from the Holy Scriptures, the source of all certainty.—The ὦ before ἄνθρωπε intensifies the censure conveyed in the address, "thou empty (not as Baumgarten has it, simply unwise and shortsighted [stupid], but empty as to faith and spirtual strength) man," and which "as applied to persons occurs only here in the New Testament" (Huther). It is not perchance the fiction of an objector but the personification of a mode of thinking which is introduced as an actor, v. 1 etc. and as a speaker in v. 15. The spiritual emptiness of such a man corresponds to the spiritual emptiness or impotence and unproductiveness of his faith. The reading ἀργή (advocated by Wiesinger against Huther) certainly deserves the preference also in respect of the sense because the Apostle passes from the idea of dead faith through the idea of unproductive faith to

* If Lange alludes to the *filioque* in the Nicene Creed it is only proper to remark that the position of the Greek Church is sustained by Oecumenical consent, while the insertion of the *filioque* in the Nicene Creed has never received the sanction of an Oecumenical Council.—M.

the idea of a faith lacking the specific effect of faith (*δικαιοῦσθαι*). [Oecumenius: *κενὸν ἐκάλεσεν ἄνθρωπον τὸν ψιλῇ τῇ πίστει αὐχοῦντα, μηδὲν τῆς διὰ τῶν ἔργων ὑποστάσεως κεκτημένον εἰς πλήρωσιν.* —M.].

VER. 21. **Was not Abraham our father.**—The first example contrasts the father of faith himself with the false orthodoxy-righteousness of Judaism, just as Paul in Rom. iv. contrasts him with their work-righteousness, or more accurately with their pride in circumcision. *Abraham,* the highest theocratical authority, which they share with him.

When he offered Isaac, his son.—In explaining this difficult passage we have to start with the preliminary statement that *δικαιοῦν* (הִצְדִּיק Sept. *δικαιοῦν, δίκαιον κρίνειν*) generally denotes in both Testaments: to *pronounce, declare, set one forth as, righteous* in any forum of justice or judgment, whether in consequence of proved innocence or surrender at discretion, expiation or pardon; although there are passages in the Old Testament in which the sense *to lead to righteousness, to make righteous* predominates, Dan. xii. 3; Is. liii. 11. The most important instances of the former kind of declaring righteous are the following passages: Luke vii. 29: *ἐδικαίωσαν τὸν θεόν* and 1 Tim. iii. 16; *ἐδικαιώθη ἐν πνεύματι* (cf. Ex. xxiii. 7; Deut. xxv. 1; Prov. xvii, 15; Is. v. 23; Matth. xii. 37; Rom. ii. 13); instances of the latter kind occur in Rom. iv. 5; iii. 26 etc. The comparison of these different passages shows that to the Old Testament with reference to man belongs especially the idea of *pronouncing the innocent righteous conformably to his innocence,* while to the New Testament belongs that of *pronouncing the sinner righteous conformably to his faith.* Matth. xii. 37 must be carefully distinguished because the last judgment shall be a judgment of the *works* of faith. But even the Old Testament knew already the imputation of faith as righteousness, Gen. xv. 16. We may say therefore that James for the benefit of his readers adopts the language of the Old Testament in allotting to true faith the imputation of righteousness by the *λογίζεσθαι εἰς δικαιοσύνην,* but to the proof of true faith the *δικαιοῦσθαι.* St. Paul, on the other hand, employs the two terms as identical (Rom. iv. 6 etc.; ch. v. 1), although he is well acquainted with the Old Testament meaning of *δικαιοῦσθαι* as applied to a human forum or even to the last judgment (see 1 Cor. iv. 4, 5). Huther, after enumerating the different interpretations of this passage (Calvin: proved righteous before men; Baumgarten: his justification has been ratified before men; Grotius: he was loved as a righteous man etc.), adds "he has been declared righteous;" but this is really saying nothing concerning our passage, for the question is, in which sense? The difference in the report is noteworthy. Gen. xv. 6 we read: Abram "believed in the Lord and He counted it to him for righteousness," without any further mention of an outward declaration of God concerning it. Both to him and to the Scripture the thing is sure in virtue of the testimony of the Spirit. Very different is Gen. xxii. 16, where the proof of Abraham's faith is followed by the the solemn declaration of the angel from heaven, "By myself have I sworn etc." Has not this declaration become a manifest deposit to the house of Abraham and the theocratic posterity? And that this is a decisive element is also evident from the other proof. So also righteousness was imputed to Rahab, the harlot also, not only in the depth of her heart but along with the proof of her faith. She did also experience a *δικαιοῦσθαι* in the congregation of God, Josh. vi. 25; Matth. i. 5. The term *δικαιοῦν* consequently is used by James according to the Old Testament mode of expression in a New Testament deeper sense and denotes that God declares righteous in the theocratical forum before the theocratical congregation conceived as permanent. It is the Divine declaration of the proof of faith in and for the kingdom of God, while the *λογίζεσθαι εἰς δικαιοσύνην* of James or the *δικαιοῦν* of Paul describes an act, which transpires solely between God and the sinner in the forum of his consciousness.

Justified by works: *ἐξ ἔργων.*—Although this Plural is selected with reference to the category in question, yet it must also be remembered that the singular work "when he offered his son" was the culminating point which comprehended all the trials of his faith. Huther justly finds this pronouncing righteous in Gen. xxii. 16; but it was not solely contained in the giving of the promise on the ground of that which he had done; he had previously received less developed promises and moreover in connection with acts of well-doing. It was rather contained in the solemn declaration with which God in consequence of Abraham's proof of his faith *now sealed* to him His promise *with an oath,* whereby at the same time *a seal was set to* the consciousness of Abraham. If the distinction which Holy Scripture draws between the degree of *justification* and that of *sealing,* had been better observed, the key to the doctrine of James in its agreement with that of Paul would thereby have also been better preserved (see Jesus Sir. xliv. 20).—

On the altar.—Offering is sacrificing as to its essential element; hence Luther's version "when he sacrificed" is not as wrong as Huther thinks; but the explanation "when he was going to sacrifice" is tautological, unless the term receive the doubtful interpretation of positive *slaughtering.*

Isaac, his son.—Emphatically describing the greatness of the offering as in Gen. xxii. 16.—The example of Abraham, however, has a peculiar significance to the Jewish Christian readers of the Epistle. As Abraham obediently offered to the God of revelation his theocratic offspring with whom the promise seemed to be indissolubly connected, so were they also to learn to distinguish their natural national feelings from the promise of God and offer them for their entrance into the New Covenant.

VER. 22. **Thou seest.**—We read the verse with the majority of commentators as an assertion and not as a question (de Wette, Lachmann and al.). And what then? Not, perchance, that the works were added to his faith, but that faith and works flow forth in one gush of the Spirit and doubly cover each other; faith was actively joined with his works as the foundation, the works were reactively the completion of his faith.

That faith was working together with his works.—Most commentators perceive here the antithesis, "neither faith was wanting nor the works" (Bengel: *quid utravis pars alteri conferat;* similarly Erasmus etc. Wiesinger.). According to the opposite view the propositions are designed to demonstrate the necessity of works. Thou seest that faith was active in works and had to be completed by works (Estius: *operosa fuit, non otiosa.* Calvin). Huther, "The second hemistich is not in antithesis with the former, but constitutes its complement: faith being active with its works, itself reached its completion." But James evidently does not wish to lay so one-sided an emphasis on the necessity of works; his object is rather to vindicate the unity of both, as is manifest from vv. 18 and 23. Primarily he demanded works as *the proof of faith*, he now demands them also with reference to the ἐδικαιώθη v. 22 as the *completion of faith.* The first proposition therefore stands for the *proof of faith*, although not as demanding the *necessity* of faith which was self-evident to him and to his readers. συνήργει certainly cannot mean "faith was auxiliary in his doing" as Huther rightly observes against Hofmann and Wiesinger; nor hardly, "it was the συνεργός of his works, it operated not by itself but with his works" (Huther), which gives not a clear idea. Kern sought to avoid this dualism by taking τοῖς ἔργοις as Dat. commod., "it operated to the production of his works." σύν joined with the verb may be construed as having *additional* force, *i. e. along with*, but also *intensivo-synthetically, i. e. united to, joined with* (not to mention that it may mean: quite, thoroughly, συντέμνω etc.) Mark xvi. 20 etc. We take the passage in the latter sense thus: "*Faith manifested itself operatively at one with the works.*" Faith aided in the completion of the work and the work aided in the completion of faith.—

Faith was made complete.—ἐτελειώθη is taken by many as completed proof, that is declaratively (Calvin, Bengel etc.), against which rendering Huther with reason insists upon the expression, "it was completed," not in the sense it had been imperfect but that it was consummated in the exercise. But here again we have to remind the reader of the significance of the term τελείωσις in this Epistle (cf. ch. i. 4, 25; iii. 2; v. 11). Abraham by his faith-offering attained typically and ideally the τελείωσις, which the Jewish Christians were to attain by the full proof of Christian love out of [as the ground and source of—M.] faith and with them all Israel was to attain it.

VER. 23. **And [thus] the Scripture was fulfilled.**—That is the passage Gen. xv. 6 here cited from the Sept. (with the exception of δὲ for καί) which gives a passive rendering to the active language of the original. So Paul quotes the LXX. Rom. iv. 3; Gal. iii. 6. James, it is evident from this declaration, was fully cognizant of the predication of that passage concerning Abraham's righteousness of faith and was far from disputing it. But on that account, as Huther rightly maintains, we are unable to adopt the definition of ἐπληρώθη which is given by the majority of commentators, viz.: then was *confirmed*, or that of Hofmann: then was *proved* that God had rightly estimated the faith of Abraham (Wiesinger, "then it was shown (*erwiesen*) that the Scripture was right"). The meaning o. πληροῦν forbids such definitions. Moreover, strictly speaking this saying cannot be referred to the written declaration of Holy Scripture but to the Divine act on which that declaration is founded, *i. e.* the λογίζεσθαι, or to the prophetical sense of believing Abraham himself. But, on the other hand, we cannot adopt the exposition of de Wette and Huther, "then was realized," for that righteousness of faith was a reality from the very first. The *fulfilling* denotes throughout the completed, decided and manifested development of a seed of faith which until then was germ-like concealed, whether it be a prophecy or a type (cf. Matth. ii. 15; v. 23 etc.; 1 Kings ii. 27 etc.). That righteousness of faith of Abraham reached its πλήρωσις or τελειωσις in its proof and verification, as it was sealed by the now openly stated Divine testimony. The act of faith itself and the subsequent sealing in the life of individual believers answer to the Old Testament Abrahamic foundation and the New Testament completion. That proof and verification of faith was on its real side τελείωσις, while, on its ideal side viewed as the completion of the prophetical word of the Spirit on which the written word is founded, it was πλήρωσις. And this πλήρωσις was manifested in his being called the friend of God. Not literally but substantially he was honoured with that appellation from the beginning Gen. xxii. 16, and afterwards also was referred to in the Old Testament as the beloved of God 1 Chron. xx. 7; Is. xli. 8. This honourable appellation has developed the epithet "the friend of God" among the Jews and the Mohammedans (Wolf's *curæ*, and Theile.) ["*El-Khalil-Allah*" or, as he is more usually called, "*El-Khalil*," simply "the friend," "is a title which has in Mussulman countries superseded altogether his own proper name." Stanley's *Jewish Church* p. 14. "Abraham is the Zoroaster of the Semitic race; but he is more than Zoroaster, in proportion as his sense of the Divine was more spiritual, and more free from the philosophy of nature and the adoration of the visible world." Bunsen, *Bibelwerk*, II., 88. See also Max Müller's Essay on *Semitic Monotheism* in the London Times of April 14 and 15, 1860.—M.]. "In Gen. xviii. 17 the LXX. add the words τοῦ παιδός μου to ἀπὸ 'Αβραάμ, for which Philo substitutes τοῦ φίλου μου." Huther. Hofmann defines the expression "*the friend of God*," by "*who* loved God," while Huther disputes that definition and gives the opposite one "*whom* God loved." But both entangle themselves in a false antithesis. The friend is at once loving and loved and indissolubly so. And although it remains a fixed fact that Abraham's love was the consequence of God's love to him, it is also evident that Abraham's good conduct, that is his self-sacrificing love, is intended to be brought out. But he was not only made "the friend of God" (Grotius ἐκλήθη=*factus est*), but he was called and honoured as such. And this was the way in which he was ἐδικαιώθη for the kingdom of God. Wiesinger's assertion is therefore incorrect that δικαιοῦσθαι refers to righteousness before God and not (as Calov and al.) to right eousness before men. But this "righteousness before men" requires to be defined in the manner indicated above.

VER. 24. **Ye see that by works a man is justified.** *Out of* (ἐξ ἔργων) *works.*—The preposition is not interrogative (Griesbach), nor imperative (Erasmus), but indicative (Luther). Recollecting that δικαιοῦται here as in v. 21 does not refer to justification by faith before God, but to the proof of faith before the congregation or the forum of the kingdom of God (in the sense of being declared righteous to the world, cf. 1 Tim. iii. 16), the seeming opposition of this passage to Rom. iii. 28 and al. is set aside. *Per se* therefore μόνον might be connected with δικαιοῦται thus "not only by faith but by works a man is justified," but firstly this would not give a pure antithesis as in v. 18, and secondly, the preposition v. 26 could then not follow. μόνον therefore must be joined adjectively with πίστεως in the sense of *bare* faith, faith without works (so Theophylact, Grotius, Wiesinger, Huther and al. cf. 1 Cor. xii. 31; 2 Cor. xi. 23 and other passages).

VER. 25. **But likewise, Rahab, the harlot.** —δέ indicates the contrast between the two examples, ὁμοίως their similarity. The contrast comes out strongly in the fact that Rahab was a harlot. The Article denotes that she was the historically known personage without intensifying the idea which however must not be weakened by the exposition "hospita" (Lyranus) or "idolatra" although she was both in reality (Rosenmüller). But the circumstance that she was a Gentile is implied. The supposition of de Wette and al. that this example was chosen with polemical reference to Heb. xi. 31, because there she is praised on account of her faith, Wiesinger rejects with the appropriate observation that there as here it is the work-proof of her faith which is rendered prominent, as indeed the whole chapter (Heb. xi) lauds faith as the power of conduct well pleasing to God. Wiesinger (following Calvin) also brings out the real motive for the selection of this example. To the example of Abraham, who was the prototype of all true faith, is now added another as remote from it as possible, "that of a woman, a Canaanite, a harlot." The Apostle's motive, however, must be taken even more concretely. Doubtless Rahab stands here as the representative of Gentile Christians in their works of faith. Just as Abraham by the sacrifice of Isaac, from being a Jew, hedged in by his nationality, became the patriarch of the spiritual Israel, a pattern to the Jewish Christian readers of this Epistle, so the case of Rahab is an example drawn from the Old Testament of the ability of Gentiles becoming by means of their work of faith the spiritual companions of Abraham and his children. Now she was justified not only in that her life was spared (Josh. ii. 6, 22 etc.) but in that she became a highly honoured mother in Israel, as tradition informs us (Matth. i. 5).

When she received the messengers.—One might always think that James selected the word ἄγγελοι instead of κατάσκοποι (Heb. xi. 31) in allusion to the circumstance that the Gentiles of his time were so ready to receive the messengers of the Gospel. Although the ὑπό of the verb may not have the secondary meaning "clam excipere," (Theile) still it suitably intensifies the idea. She hospitably received the messengers and sheltered them, she received them forthwith, as the Gentiles received the messengers of the Gospel rejected and persecuted by the Jews.

And sent them forth by another way.—Cf. Josh. ii. 15. It is not simply that she let them go, but that she thrust them off with saving haste and effort, as it were by force. So Festus the Gentile sent Paul to Rome in order to deliver him from the persecutions of the Jews and so for a time the Roman rulers in general, but especially believing Gentiles protected the messengers of the Gospel from the fanaticism of the Jews. The way of the deliverance of the messengers, however, was not only another way, but an uncommon one (ἑτέρᾳ ὁδῷ [*i. e.* διὰ τῆς θυρίδος.—M.]).

VER. 26. **For as the body without spirit.** —The spirit can only describe the constant, inward vital principle (and in its actuality), which gives motion to the living body. Consequently not the soul as a quiescent substance, nor that which animates (Wiesinger), and still less the πνεῦμα as "halitus" (Piscator and al.). The spirit in its actuality is the ἐνέργεια of the body, without which it is dead. By comparison therefore faith is dead without (corresponding) works. It is an unnatural condition for the body to exist without spirit; consequently the reference here is to a faith which has passed into an unnatural condition. James, therefore, cannot mean that works must be added to faith; he rather sees in *the* works (with the Article), the collective phenomenon, that form of life which renders visible the vitality of faith, its animating *energy* (although not absolutely love, as Theile maintains) or *entelechy.* The seeming inconcinnity of the figure, to which Huther calls attention, that while on the one hand, the body is visible and the spirit invisible, faith on the other is invisible and the works visible, disappears if it is remembered that the spirit also in virtue of its actuality effects the higher visibility of the body. Being dead and being alive is the decisive antithesis, in which, however, the separate members also are brought into comparison. James is therefore far from forming a dualistic conception of real faith, he rather takes it *really* as a productive power much as Aristotle does the idea, and with reference to public proof he will recognize it only in its expression by works which almost recalls Hegel's idea that the true in the individual authenticates itself in its process of development as fact.

James's doctrine of faith in this chapter in relation to the doctrine in Rom. iii. 28; *Gal.* ii. 16, *and al.* —We refer in the first place to the Introduction, to the foregoing exegesis, to our exposition in the History of the Apostolic Age, I., p. 171; and in the next place to Huther, p. 126, and the Supplement to his Commentary, p. 208. Huther, with reason enumerates three views. 1. James and Paul agree in thought but differ in expression. This was the prevalent view before the Reformation, and in modern times the view of Neander, Thiersch, Wiesinger, Huther, etc. 2. The doctrine of James contradicts that of Paul. So Luther, de Wette, Kern, Baur, Schwegler. 3. There is certainly a difference in doctrine of subordinate importance yet without prejudicing their higher unity. So Schmid (*Bibl. Theol.*), Lechler, Weizsäcker (see the last supplement in Huther, also the controversy with Weiss and Weizsäcker, p. 130, 131). Ad 1. Theophylact and others. The ἔργα are different in both instances, Paul mentions the *opera legis*, James the "*opera fidei.*" "This is also right," as Huther correctly observes. *Paul* deals with the ergism of the Jews, *James* with their orthodoxism. Huther moreover urges with reason that Paul does not attribute justifying power to the *opera fidei*. A second distinction in the idea of πίστις was therefore necessary. This has been pointed out by Oecumenius, Neander and al.; viz. "that James takes faith *per se* simply as the mere *notitia*, the considering things as true etc." It is evident that he knows such a kind of faith but it is equally certain that he does not acknowledge it as living faith; not any more than Paul, who was equally familiar with Jewish orthodoxy according to Rom. x, but insisted with equal firmness, that faith must work by love or authenticate itself by works (Gal. v. 6). Wiesinger (with whom Huther agrees), however, is right in maintaining against Schmid, Olshausen, Neander and al., that it is one thing to say "to become righteous by (out of) faith authenticated (proved) in works," and another "to become righteous by works in which faith authenticates itself." This brings us to the third and most important distinction, the different senses of δικαιοῦσθαι. Here Wiesinger and Huther also go asunder. Wiesinger (in connection with Hofmann) maintains that man, having been justified by faith, becomes personally righteous by his works in which faith authenticates itself: that justification in relation to God becomes a justification according to a man's behaviour towards God. Huther, on the other hand, holds that by δικαιοῦν Paul describes that declaring righteous or free [*i. e.* from guilt and punishment, German *Freisprechen*—M.] on the part of God which puts the believer into the new filial relation to God, whereas James understands by it that declaring righteous or free on the part of God in virtue of which the man regenerated into a child of God receives in the judgment σωτηρία. But the two views are not quite clear. In the first the idea of the forum is wanting, where the δικαιοῦσθαι is to take place, in the second the forum of the last judgment is improperly anticipated. It is of course understood, that according to Paul also, men will be judged in the last day with reference to their fruits of faith (2 Cor. v. 10), but in *that* judgment Abraham also has not yet stood, whereas on the other hand righteousness of faith and σωτηρία along with it, are acquired only in an ideal judgment. But between the first Divine forum in a repenting conscience and the last forum in the judgment of the world there lies as a middle forum the public attestation of the believer in the consciousness of the theocratic congregation; outwardly to the Church an authentication, inwardly to believers a sealing. By the selection of the term, therefore, James wished the Jewish Christians to understand that with the Church he could not acknowledge them as believers, if they were lacking the full consistency of Christian deeds.

DOCTRINAL AND ETHICAL.

1. Both according to James and Paul (Rom. i. 16, 17) the doctrine of the sinner's justification before God is one of the principal doctrines of the Gospel. The question of the true Israelite "What shall I do, that I may have eternal life?" (Matth. xix. 16; Mark x. 17; Luke x. 25), rightly considered, is the most vital question for every sinner desirous of salvation. It is so much the more melancholy that the dispute concerning the doctrine of justification by faith (out of faith), or of justification by (out of) works has in every century of the Christian era given rise to so much misunderstanding and called forth so many attempts to show that James and Paul are irreconcilably contradicting one another. How little the doctrine of the one differs from that of the other, if we understand the meaning which each attaches to the terms *faith*, *works* and *justify*, has been sufficiently illustrated in the exegesis of this passage. See "Exegetical and Critical."—Considering this, we cannot but regard the well-known opinion of Luther on the *epistola straminea*, which is partly based on James' doctrine of justification, as the fruit of an unfortunate misunderstanding. Nor do we find in these propositions of James any positive opposition to the doctrine of the great Apostle of the Gentiles. But we hold it to be very conceivable that Paul's doctrine of justification was either involuntarily misunderstood or designedly perverted into an excuse for the flesh by the readers of the Epistle of James and that he was on that account constrained powerfully to oppose those who degraded the doctrine of grace into a cloak of sin. He therefore contends not against Paul but against a one-sided Paulinism, which in some hands might easily turn into unchristian Antinomianism and an unholy spirit of emancipation. Both James and Paul are well entitled to a hearing and every view or consideration of the way of salvation, which silences the one at the expense of the other, is decidedly unfair. Paul's preaching is glad tidings to all who are conscious of the absolute impossibility of being saved by their own virtue and strength, and the exhortation of James is a wholesome corrective for all who are apt to forget what Paul himself did teach that true faith must work by love (Gal. v. 6). Paul sets into prominent relief the great antithesis of *grace* and *sin*, James (as well as our Lord, Jno. xiii. 17) that of *knowing* and *doing*.

2. It is of the utmost importance that while, on the one hand, *justification* and *sanctification* must be distinguished the one from the other, on the other hand the one must never be separated from the other. The true preaching of the Gospel involves the necessity of Christ in all His fulness being set forth both *in* us and *for* us. If *justification* and *sanctification* are confounded, or if the latter is made the *foundation* of the former we open the door to *self-righteousness;* if *justification* and *sanctification* are separated, we deliver an open passport to *injustice*. The true union of the "for us" and the "in us" requires that justification be put first, but that sanctification be neither put in the background nor in the foreground.

3. What James says concerning the faith of the devils (v. 19) is important on several considerations 1. As affording proof of the existence of personal, self-conscious evil spirits. 2. As affording proof of their original goodness and communion with God, which consequently shuts out indirectly all reference to dualism in the question of the origin of moral evil. 3. As affording proof of the infinite misery of the fallen angels; to have a faith which yields no consolation but only excites terror and shuddering, must probably be the highest degree of misery. 4. As indicating the low and sad standpoint occupied by one who confesses the Gospel without the exhibition of love-working Christianity; his standpoint is not Christian but devilish.

The way of acquiring the favour and friendship of God in all great essential features was virtually the same under the Old Covenant as under the New. The example of Abraham, in particular (Gen. xv. 1–6), which is also used by Paul (Rom. iv.) exhibits this unity of the way of salvation under both Testaments in the clearest manner.

5. The case of Rahab, the harlot, who is introduced as a pattern to the believers in Christ Jesus (cf. also Heb. xi. 31), affords a striking proof that God exalts the mean and regards the miserable and exhibits a lofty memorial of the spiritual emancipation and exaltation of woman by Christianity. It is wonderful that just the most fallen and disgraced women of the Old Testament are preferred to honour in the New. Do not even Thamar and Bathsheba shine in the genealogy of our Lord? Matth. i.

6. "Whatever is transitory is only a similitude." Nature the symbol of grace, the body permeated by the spirit the figure of living and active faith, but the cold corpse also is the representative of a merely outward form of spiritual life, from which life itself has vanished.

7. "If James calls faith without works a dead faith, he surely cannot mean that the works, the outward and the visible render faith living and that they constitute the life of faith but he had to presume that true faith includes [carries within itself] life, the animating principle, from which the works must emanate, and that this must make itself known in the works. He considers the want of works as proof of the want of vital faith and therefore he calls such faith a dead faith." Neander.

8. Luther (in his Exposition of 2 Pet. Ed. Irmischer, Vol. LXX., p. 223 sq.) excellently says concerning the fruits of faith: "although they belong to our neighbour, in order that they may redound to his benefit, yet does that fruit not fail *because it makes faith stronger.*—It is therefore altogether a very different strength than bodily strength for it decreases and is consumed; but this spiritual strength, the more we exercise and practise it, the stronger it grows, and it decreases if it is not practised."

[V. 14. On the error which James combats, compare the following passage from Tertullian ('de Poenit' c. 5): "Some persons imagine that they have God if they receive Him in their heart and mind and do little for Him in act; and that therefore they may commit sin, without doing violence to faith and fear; or in other words that they may commit adulteries, and yet be chaste, and may poison their parents, and yet be pious! At the same rate they who commit sin and yet are godly, may also be cast into hell and yet be pardoned! But such minds as these are offshoots from the root of hypocrisy and sworn friends of the evil one."

V. 16. There is *opus fidei*, the work of faith; *fides quæ operatur*, faith that worketh; *that* is St. Paul's faith (1 Thess. i. 3; Gal. v. 6), and faith that can *show itself* by working, that is St. James's faith (ii. 18). And without works it is but a dead faith, the carcase of faith; there is no spirit in it. No spirit, if no work; *spectrum est, non spiritus:* a flying shadow it is, a spirit it is not, if work it do not. Having wherewith to do good, if you do it not, talk not of faith, for you have not faith in you, if you have wherewith to show it and show it not. Andrewes.

V. 20. Beveridge (on Art. 12 "of good works"): "Though it be for our faith only, and not for our works that God accepts us, yet our works as well as faith are acceptable unto God, yea, and they necessarily spring out from a true and lively faith, so that it is as impossible there should be true faith without good works, as that there should be good works without true faith; for as without faith our works are bad, so without works our faith is dead. And therefore a true faith may be as evidently known by its works, as a tree is clearly discerned by its fruit [Article 12 of the Articles of Religion established in the Church of England and Prot. Episc. Church in the United States reads as follows: "Albeit that good works, which are the fruits of faith and follow after justification, cannot put away our sins and endure the severity of God's judgment: yet are they pleasing and acceptable to God in Christ, and do spring out necessarily of a true and lively faith; insomuch that by them a lively faith may be as evidently known, as a tree discerned by the fruit."—M.]. If I see fruit growing upon a tree, I know what tree it is, upon which such fruit grows. And so if I see how a man lives, I know how he believes. If his faith be good, his works cannot but be good too; and if his works be bad, his faith cannot but be bad too; for wheresoever there is a justifying faith there are also good works, and wheresoever *there are no good works there is no justifying faith.*" To this last statement Wordsworth adds the following judicious modification. "Suppose the case of a person who has been baptized, and has a *lively faith* and earnest resolve to serve God, and that he is suddenly taken away from this life, without having time to show his faith by his works. Or suppose the case of an *infant* dying after baptism. Then *Faith saves.* No man can do *good* works without Faith; but faith without works saves a man, if God thinks it fit to remove him out of this life, without giving him time for working, and if God knows that he *would* have worked, if he had had time for working. Indeed in such a case *Faith* itself *is work;* according to our Lord's saying, This is the *work* of God, that ye believe on Him, whom He sent" (Jno. vi. 28, 29).

V. 25. Wordsworth. "Rahab received the spies, who were sent before Joshua, the type of Jesus, and who were types of the Apostles of Christ, and hearkened to their message and sent them forth in speed (ἐκβαλοῦσα) by a cord, by *another way* (other than that by which *they had come*), viz. *by the window*, from which she tied the scarlet cord by which they were let down (Josh. ii. 15–18), and thus obtained deliverance for herself and family by her faith, when her city was destroyed. Thus she was an example very applicable to those whom St. James addressed, who, by receiving the Gospel preached by the Apostles, might escape the woes impending on Jerusalem, as she escaped those which fell upon Jericho (cf. Heb. xi. 31), and who would be overwhelmed in that destruction, if they neglected so great salvation."—M.].

HOMILETICAL AND PRACTICAL.

The Christian utility-principle.—Faith without works.—A faith that cannot save us, cannot possibly be the true faith.—Love the touchstone of faith.—Pious works behind which lurks not seldom hardness of heart.—Those who unwittingly communicate to other their temporal goods prove thereby that they received of their God only little or nothing of spiritual goods.—The contention of dead and living faith.—Unfruitful monotheism.—The faith of devils in its infinite diversity 1, from the faith of good angels and 2, from the faith of believing Christians.—Abraham the true friend of God: 1. God calls and Abraham obeys, 2. God promises and Abraham confides, 3. God tries and Abraham stands fast.—The friendship of God compared with the friendship of the world. What the friend of God shuns, enjoys and expects. Why is it just faith, provided it be living and active, which makes the sinner so well-pleasing to God? Answer: 1. Because of the honour it gives to God, 2. because of the struggle it costs us, 3. because of the fruit it bears for the benefit of others.—Rahab, the harlot of Jericho a guide to the heavenly Jerusalem.—What the sight of a corpse suggests to a believer of the Gospel.—According to James also the sinner is justified not *propter*, *sed per fidem*.

On the Pericope. Commendation of a living faith; 1. The sense in which James exhorts us thereto, 2. The connection of his doctrine with the doctrine of the Gospel, and in particular with that of Paul. 3. The importance it will always have and has now. *a.* There are men who have neither faith nor works; *b.* others who have works without faith; *c.* others again who have faith without works; and *d.* many whose faith and works leave much to be wished for. For each one of these diseases and one-sidednesses the ever-repeated consideration of James' doctrine is wholesome medicine.

STARKE:—To boast of faith without having it, is very common, Tit. i. 16.—Neither true faith nor true love consists in bare words, 1 Jno. iii. 17, 18.—We usually refer the poor to the Providence of God and it is just this Providence that refers them to us, 1 Tim. vi. 18.—A rich man ought to rejoice in being God's hand, whereby to do good to the poor;—Prov. iii. 27, 28.—Saving faith is not either dead or living, but it is only and always living and this is properly true faith; whereas dead faith is properly not true but false faith. But apart from the article of justification both agree in this respect, that just as true and living faith consists of three parts, viz. knowledge, assent and trust, so false and dead faith consists of these three parts but its knowledge is only historical, its assent only human and its trust only carnal or a conceit of God's grace drawn in carnal assurance, Matth. vii. 21, 22; Luke xiii. 25.—Works are not the life or soul of faith but only an infallible mark of the same, Heb. xi. 8, 17.—The devils believe and know in particular four articles of our faith, Matth. viii. 2, 9. They know 1. that there is a God, 2. that there is a Christ, 3. that there will be a final judgment, 4. that they will then be tortured. But this knowledge does not minister to their peace and salvation, but to their alarm and damnation.

HEDINGER:—If true faith consists only in knowledge and outward assent, the devil also is a believer and consequently blessed, 1 Jno. ii. 3, 4.

LUTHER:—Not fear and terror, but joy, peace and consolation in the conscience work true faith, Rom. v. 1.

QUESNEL:—Even the devil is not an atheist; what then are we to think of those who boast that they believe nothing and are not afraid of anything? Ps. xiv. 1.—Some hope to be saved by a faith which does less to them than the faith of devils, Job xxi. 12, 13.

LANGII OP.:—The emptier a vessel, the more does it sound and resound; just so the hypocrite who lacks faith, Ps. xciv. 4.

QUESNEL:—Works live by faith as by the spirit which animates them, Rom. xiv. 23.

LUTHER:—Works do not make us righteous but cause us to be declared righteous, Luke xvii. 9, 10.—All the world has admired the offering of Abraham; what may not come to pass, since God has offered His own Son? Rom. v. 8; viii. 32.—Faith is the mother who gives birth to the virtues, as her children.

STARKE:—All true believers are the friends of God and this is the peculiar prerogative of believers of the New Testament, Jno. xv. 14, 15.—The faith of converted Jews and Gentiles is uniform, Acts xv. 19.—The grace of God does not charge us with past transgressions, if we are converted, 1 Tim. i. 13.—The weak faith of a Rahab must be as active as the most perfect faith of Abraham, Rom. iv. 19, 20.

LANGII OP.:—This is the only right and safe way to seek righteousness, which enables us to stand before God, solely by faith in Christ out of His merit so that that faith be also actively shown by love, Phil. iii. 9; Gal. v. 6.

HEUBNER:—Unfruitfulness betrays the ungenuineness of faith.—Love never complains of want of ability; the stronger love, the greater the ability.—Dead faith is no faith.

AUGUSTINE:—Such faith is a palsied hand.—The faith of Abraham was imputed to him for righteousness, before it had brought forth works, but it was a living faith, in which the works lay as to the germ.—Works *per se* are not the spirit, but the faith moving in the works, is spirit.

VON GERLACH:—What James calls faith without works is properly speaking no faith at all; not any more than a love which deals only in pleasant words, is love (v. 15).—Paul opposes the antithesis of dead work-holiness, James the antithesis of a pharasaic pride in empty intellectual knowledge.—Paul met the Pharisees with precisely the same argument, cf. Rom. ii. 6–11; xiii. 27.—Man is not justified by (out of) faith separable from works, not any more than fire (*e. g.* painted fire) separable from heat and light is able to warm and light us.

LUTHER:—O, faith is a lively, busy active thing, so that it is impossible for it not to be ceaselessly working good! It does not ask either if good works are to be done, but before it asks, it has done them and is ever doing. But whoso doeth not such works, is an unbelieving man, gropes and looks out for faith and good works, and neither knows what is faith nor what are good works, but for all chatters and talks much of faith and good works. Faith is a living, well-weighed assurance of the grace of God, so sure, that he would a thousand times die for it, and such assurance and knowledge of Divine grace renders men glad, daring and merry before God and all creatures, which is the work of the Holy Ghost in faith. Hence man becomes without constraint ready and glad to serve everybody, to suffer many things to the praise of God and from love of God who has been so gracious to him, so that it is impossible to separate works from faith, yea as impossible as it is to separate burning and shining from fire.

STIER:—James by no means affirms that works give life to, produce or create faith; for faith comes by the power of the word, entering into and received by us and by nothing else. But faith grows complete in works, that is the same as Paul's saying or rather the Lord's saying to Paul, that the strength of God may be completed in weakness (2 Cor. xii. 9). The strength of faith, indwelling from the beginning and already received along with the first seizing of grace, becomes fully proved, verified and its operation completed. Thus our calling and election are made sure in the diligence of living and doing (2 Pet. i. 10). Thus Abraham's first call was made sure in his last works and the word concerning justification by (out of) faith already before accorded to him, was lawfully and actually confirmed as a truth.

VIEDEBANDT:—A faith which helps not our neighbour, neither helps ourselves, for it has not helped us to love.—Before faith are the tears of Peter and after faith the following after of Paul.

JAKOBI:—A sacred author tells us of true faith that it is the firm confidence of things hoped for. But the faith of the devils is an assurance not of what they hope for, but of what they fear.

PORUBSZKY:—Dead faith cannot save. This is evident 1. from the being of blessedness, 2. from the nature of dead, 3. from the experience of daily life.—Living faith justifies and saves (Reformation-Sermon). Cf. art. 20 of the Augsburg Confession.

LISCO:—Faith and works.—Operative faith justifies us before God.—True Christian faith a sanctifying power of life.

[v. 17. HALL:—As that is a vain and idle charity, which bids a man be warm and filled, yet gives him nothing to feed or warm him with, so is that a vain and dead faith, which, professing an adherence to God, yet is severed from all good works and is void of charity.—M.].

[v. 21. HAMMOND:—Abraham was the father of the faithful, the great example of faith and justification; but it was not upon his bare belief of God's promise that he was justified, but upon that high act of obedience to God, in being ready to offer up his only son, in whom the promises were made to him.—M.].

[v. 23. ADAM CLARKE:—As among friends everything is common, so God took Abraham into intimate communion with Himself, and poured out upon Him the choicest of His blessings; for as God can never be in want, because He possesses all things, so Abraham. His friend, could never be destitute, because God was his friend.—M.].

[v. 24. HORNE:—In this instance of the father of the faithful, as in a common centre, are the doctrines of both Apostles met: one says a man is justified by faith working; the other by working faith; and this is really and truly all the difference between them.—M.].

[v. 26. BRIGHT:—Justification then by faith, or according to the Christian doctrine as opposed to the law, must be that all men being sinners are justified, and particularly receive remission of sins, the Holy Spirit, and everlasting salvation, from the free and undeserved goodness of God; upon the consideration of the perfect righteousness and the meritorious sacrifice of Jesus Christ, and upon the condition or qualification of a pious temper of heart for the future, to obey the will of God, and consequently to do what is right and just in whatsoever way He is pleased to declare it, but particularly as it is declared by the Lord Jesus Christ; which same condition too we had never been able to perform without the assistance of the grace of God.—M.].

[TAYLOR:—Let a man believe all the revelations of God; if that belief ends in itself and goes no further, it is like physic taken to purge the stomach; if it do not work, it is so far from bringing health, that itself is a new sickness.—M.].

[EPIPHANIUS:—Faith hath in it the image of godliness engraven and infidelity hath the character of wickedness and prevarication.—M.].

[SALVIANUS:—*Hominem fideliter Christo credere est fidelem Deo esse, h. e. fideliter in Dei mandata servare.*"—M.].

[LACTANTIUS:—"*Christianorum omnis religio sine scelere et macula vivere.*"—M.].

[TAYLOR:—There are but three things that make the integrity of Christian faith; believing the words of God, confidence in His goodness, and keeping His commandments.—Believing is the least thing in a justifying faith; for faith is a conjugation of many ingredients, and faith is a covenant, and faith is a law, and faith is obedience, and faith is a work, and indeed it is a sincere cleaving to and closing with the terms of the Gospel in every instance, in every particular.—M.].

[Compare also on v. 23. JOHN HOWE, Friendship with God, 10 Sermons. Works, 8, 376.—v. 24. TAYLOR, Faith working by love. Sermons.—BULL, *Doctrina D. Jacobi de justificatione ex operibus explanatur et defenditur*, Works, 3, 1.—M.].

VI. FOURTH ADMONITION WITH REFERENCE TO THE FOURTH FORM OF TEMPTATION—PROPAGANDISM.

CAUTION AGAINST THE JUDAISTIC BIAS TO FANATICAL ACTIVITY OF TEACHING. REFERENCE TO THE POWER OF THE TONGUE AND TO THE DEPRAVITY, LICENCE AND DUPLICITY OF THE FANATICALLY EXCITED TONGUE. THE CONTRAST OF FALSE AND TRUE WISDOM IN SPEECH ACCORDING TO THEIR OPPOSITE OPERATIONS.

Chapter III.

My brethren, be not many masters, knowing that we shall receive the greater con-
2 demnation. For in many things we offend all. If any man offend not in word, the
3 same *is* a perfect man, *and* able also to bridle the whole[1] body. Behold[2], we put bits
in the horses' mouths, that they may obey us; and[3] we turn about their whole body.
4 Behold also the ships, which though *they be* so great, and *are* driven of fierce winds[4], yet
are they turned about with a very small helm, whithersoever[5] the governor listeth[6].
5 Even so the tongue is a little member, and boasteth great things[7]. Behold, how great a
6 matter a little[8] fire kindleth! And the tongue[9] *is* a fire, a world of iniquity: so[10] is the
tongue among our members, that it defileth the whole body, and[11] setteth on fire the
7 course of nature[12]; and it is set on fire of hell. For every kind of beasts, and of birds,
and of serpents, and of things in the sea, is tamed, and hath been tamed of mankind:
8 But the tongue can no man tame[13]; *it is* an unruly[14] evil, full of deadly poison.
9 Therewith bless we God[15], even the Father; and therewith curse we men, which are
10 made after the similitude of God. Out of the same mouth proceedeth blessing and
11 cursing. My brethren, these things ought not so to be. Doth a fountain send forth
12 at the same place sweet *water* and bitter? Can the fig tree, my brethren, bear olive
berries[16]? either a vine, figs? so *can* no fountain both yield salt water and fresh[17].
13 Who *is* a wise man and endued with knowledge among you? let him show out of a
14 good conversation his works with meekness of wisdom. But if ye have bitter envying
15 and strife in your hearts[18], glory not, and lie not against the truth[19]. This wisdom
16 descendeth not from above, but *is* earthly, sensual, devilish. For where envying and
17 strife *is*, there[20] *is* confusion and every evil work. But the wisdom that is from
above is first pure, then peaceable, gentle, *and* easy to be entreated, full of mercy and
18 good fruits, without partiality, and[21] without hypocrisy. And the fruit of[22] righteousness is sown in peace of them that make peace.

Verse 1. Lange: Become not many teachers, my brethren, since ye know, that we shall [as such] receive a greater [a more severe] condemnation [judicial sentence.]

[. . . . knowing that we shall receive greater condemnation.—M.]

Verse 2. [1 Cod. Sin. has δυνάμενος for δυνατός.—M.]

Lange: For manifoldly we offend all: if a man offendeth not in word *he* is a perfect man, able even to bridle the whole body.

[For oftentimes we all offend . . . . word, this man is a perfect man, able to bridle also the whole body. —M.]

Verse 3. [2 Rec. reads ἰδού against the most authentic codd. C. and Griesbach read ἴδε. A. B. G. Sin. and al. Lachmann and Tisch. have εἰ δέ. [So Alford, Wordsw. *Ecce enim*, Syr. *Si autem*, Vulg.—M.]

[3 B. C. εἰς τό. [So Cod. Sin. Alf. Rec. πρὸς with A. K. L. (?)—M.]

Lange: But if we put bits into the horses' mouths, in order that they may obey us, we guide also their whole body.

[. . . . . . the bits into the mouths of horses in order to their obeying us, we also turn about their whole body.—M.]

Verse 4. 4 [ἀνέμων σκληρῶν. B. C. K. Cod. Sin. σκληρ. ἀνέμ. Rec. A. L.—M.]

5 [ὅπου ἄν Rec.—ὅπου Sin. B.—M.]

6 [Cod. Sin. B read βούλεται for βούληται.—M.]

Lange: Behold even the ships, although they are so great and are [moreover] tossed about by fierce winds, even they are guided with a very small rudder, whithersoever the direction [course] of the steersman [guide] may wish.

[. . though so great and driven by . . . are turned about by a very small rudder, whithersoever the will of the steersman may wish.—M.]

Verse 5. 7 The reading μεγάλα αὐχεῖ A. C.* recommended by Tischend. is preferable to μεγαλαυχεῖ.

8 The difference between ἡλίκον and ὀλίγον keeps balancing between the authorities and the critics. In point of sense both amount to the same thing with the exception that ἡλίκον, the more difficult reading, gives also the stronger expression: what a fire, *i. e.* what a little fire. [ἡλίκον is decidedly the more authentic reading. It is in A.** B. C.* Cod. Sin. Vulg. received by Lachmann, Tisch., Alford, Wordsw., de Wette, Huther and others. Alford maintains that ἡλίκος is "*quantulus*" as well as "*quantus*" and cites Lucian, Hermot. 5.—M.]

Lange: Thus also the tongue is a little member and boasteth great things.—Behold what a little fire—what a forest it doth kindle [Jerusalem on fire.]

[. . . Behold how small a fire kindleth how great a forest.—M]

Verse 6. [9] [Cod. Sin. omits καὶ before γλῶσσα.—M.]
[10] οὕτως before the second ἡ γλῶσσα is wanting in [A. B. C. K. Cod. Sin.—M.]
[11] [Cod. Sin. reads καὶ σπιλοῦσα for ἡ σπιλοῦσα. Rec. and many others.—M.]
[12] [Cod. Sin reads ἡμῶν after γενέσεως.—M.]
Lange: The tongue also is a fire; it, the world [the adornment of the world, worldliness [Germ.: "*Weltförmigkeit*"] of unrighteousness. The tongue steppeth forth [rules] among our members, it, which defileth the whole body and inflameth the [revolving] wheel of the development of life, and itself is inflamed by hell.
[And the tongue is a fire, that world of iniquity. The tongue makes itself in our members the polluter of the whole body [Wordsworth], and setteth on fire the wheel of nature, and itself is set on fire by hell.—M.]

Verse 7. Lange: For every nature of the wild beasts and of the birds, of the creeping creatures and of sea-creatures is tamed and hath been tamed by human nature.
[..... of beasts and birds [lit. *winged things*], of creeping things and things in the sea. . . . . —M.]

Verse 8. [13] [δύναται δαμάσαι ἀνθρώπων. Cod. Sin. A. K.—M.]
[14] ἀκατάστατον is on good grounds preferred by Lachm. Tisch. according to A. B. Vulg. and Cod. Sin. to ἀκατάσχετον, Rec. C. G. K.
Lange: But the tongue no one of men is able to tame, the [causing restlessness and disquiet; Germ: "*unruhstiftend*"—] evil full of death-bringing poison.
[. . . it is a restless evil, full of death-bringing poison.—M.]

Verse 9. [15] A. B. G. Tisch. Lachm. [and Cod. Sin] read τὸν κύριον.
Lange: With it praise [bless] we the Lord and Father [also as Father] and with the same curse we men, who after the image [similitude] of God are created [have become, destined to become His children.]
[Therewith bless we the Lord and Father, and therewith . . . . . . have been created after the likeness of God.—M.]

Verse 10. Lange: . . . praising and cursing.
[. . . goeth forth [Stier, de Wette, Allioli and al.]—M.]
Lange: It shall not be thus, my brethren, that these things come thus to pass.

Verse 12. [16] οὕτως is opposed by the most important witnesses. The immediate sequel in Text. Rec. becomes modified into οὔτε ἁλυκὸν γλυκὺ ποιῆσαι ὕδωρ. Cod. Sin. favours οὕτως etc. [Syr. "*ita etiam aqua salsa non fieri potest dulcis.*"—M.]
[17] [Cod. Sin. omits καὶ before γλυκὺ.—M.]
Lange: Doth the fountain, perchance, bubble out of the same opening sweet and bitter [water]? A fig-tree, my brethren, surely cannot produce olives, or the vine figs? [Thus] nor can [any fountain] salt [water] give sweet water.
[Doth a fountain, perchance, out of the same chink [Alford] send forth the sweet and the bitter? Can a fig-tree, my brethren, yield olives . . . , nor can salt [water] yield sweet water.—M.]

Verse 13. Lange: Who is wise and intelligent among you? Let him show through good conduct his works [that is] in gentleness of wisdom.
[. . . intelligent among you [Bengel, Stier, de Wette, al] . . . out of a good conversation his works in meekness of wisdom.—M.]

Verse 14. [18] [Cod. Sin. ταῖς καρδ.—M.]
Lange: But if ye harbor bitter zeal and quarrelsomeness in your hearts, boast not yourselves. . .
[But if ye harbor bitter emulation and party-strife . . . boast not.—M.]
[19] [Cod. Sin. κατὰ τῆς ἀληθείας καὶ ψεύδεσθε.—M.]

Verse 15. Lange: For this wisdom is not that which cometh down from above, but an earthly, sensuous [soulish (Germ. *seelisch*, almost impossible to render in English without a circumlocution), passionate], devilish one.
[This wisdom is not that which is coming from above, but earthly, sensuous, devilish.—M.]

Verse 16. [20] [Cod. Sin. has καὶ after ἐκεῖ; so A.—M.]
Lange: For where is emulation and quarrelsomeness, there is seditious work and all manner of evil doing.
[. . . emulation and party-strife, there is perturbation and every evil deed.—M.]

Verse 17. [21] A. B. C. Sin. and al. omit καὶ after ἀδιάκριτος.
[22] τῆς before δικαιοσύνης is omitted in A. B. C. L. [and Cod Sin.—M.]
Lange: But the wisdom from above is first of all consecrated [theocratically pure or chaste, free from apostasy], then peaceable, equitably disposed [philanthropical, humane], gladly yielding, full of compassion and good fruits, without separatism, without hypocrisy.
[. . . first pure, then peaceable, equitable, compliant, . . . undistinguishing, without hypocrisy.—M.]

Verse 18. Lange: But the [future] fruit of righteousness is sown in peace by them. . . .

EXEGETICAL AND CRITICAL.

Analysis: Caution against the Judaistic bias to fanatical activity of teaching, vv. 1. 2.—The power of the tongue vv. 3, 4 (first half). The depravity of the tongue vv. 5, 6.—The untamableness of the tongue, vv. 7, 8.—The duplicity (German "doubletonguedness," *Doppelzüngigkeit*) of the [fanatically excited] tongue, vv. 9–12.—The contrast of false and true wisdom in speech according to their opposite operations, vv. 13–18.

Caution against the Judaistic bias to fanatical activity of teaching.

Vers. 1, 2. The exhortation progresses from Judaistic visionariness (ch. i.) and from Judaistic particularism and exclusiveness (ch. ii.) to Judaistic, fanatical activity of teaching, to the evil, exciting and pernicious tongue-sins of bitter emulation, cursing, envying and party-strife exhibited in a false, devilish wisdom in contrast with true and heavenly wisdom. That this section is an essential point peculiar to the entire Epistle, is evident from the fact that it has been announced already in ch. i. 17, 26. The fanatical, proselyting and polemical mania for teaching, which is here described by James, had previously been delineated by the Lord Himself, Matth. xxiii., and by Paul the Apostle in Rom. ii. 17; it is here and there illuminated in Acts (ch. xv.) and in the Pauline Epistles (2 Cor. xi. 13; Phil. iii. 2; Gal. ii.), and it is finally condemned in Rev. ii. 9. Wiesinger heads this chapter "against the itch of teaching" and adds the observation—that "the author passes on to the ready-tongued teaching and finding fault with others, because this is the false actualization of the πίστις of his readers, whereby they think themselves warranted to dispense with genuine actualization [*i. e.* the practical exhibition of living faith by good works.—M.]. Nothing is nearer to a faith which consists in knowledge only than conceit of teaching and dogmaticalness (cf. Rom. ii. 17 etc.). Thus ch. iii. is the carrying out of the censure James had already passed on his readers in ch. i. 19, 20 and similarly as in ch. i. 26, 27, where the author had indicated inability to bridle the tongue as the characteristic of a purely imaginary religion and the exhibition of compassionating love as the characteristic of true religion, he now returns to [we ought to say: he now takes up in earnest] this subject, and represents to his readers that the human inability, so strongly developed in them, of taming the tongue, ought to cure them effectually of the desire to teach others." Huther: "Words had taken the place of works."

VER. 1. **Do not become many teachers.**—The exposition of Huther (and of de Wette, Wiesinger) "be not teachers in great numbers," gives hardly a satisfactory sense. For if reference were made to ecclesiastically ordained offices of teaching (as Wiesinger maintains with reference to 2 Tim. iv. 5), the language of the Apostle would hardly convey the rebuke he intends to administer. It is evidently his purpose to censure the false mania for teaching, the dogmatizing contentiousness, which is thoroughly characteristic of the Judaizing Christian. We therefore connect (with Gebser and Schneckenburger) πολλοὶ with γίνεσθαι and so that πολλοὶ and διδάσκαλοι form one idea. Do not end with being a great host of teachers. Luther: "Let not every one dare to be a teacher." The expression has consequently an ironical colouring and even stronger than the μὴ πάντες of Grotius.

Knowing that we.—They know it and they ought to be conscious of it. [Huther remarks that εἰδότες, being closely joined in the Imperative, is itself hortatory: "knowing, that ye might know:" James says here "*we* shall receive" and in v. 2 "*we* all offend" and thus forcibly practises his precepts vv. 2, 17, 18. Cf. 1 Cor. vi. 12.—M.].

A greater condemnation.—Although κρίμα cannot signify "responsibility" only (so Hottinger and Augusti) the ordinary N. T. usage does not necessitate us to insist with Wiesinger (who remarks however that a *sententia damnatoria* is out of the question) and Huther on the meaning "*punitory sentence.*" The fact that James includes himself is certainly against the latter construction. "The humility of love" (Wiesinger) surely could not cause him to assert something, which was inapplicable to Himself, and Huther's observation that the punitory sentence might be postponed, does not by any means settle the difficulty. κρίμα denotes primarily *judgment,* then more definitely a *judicial sentence* and it generally becomes a *punitory sentence* by the connection, just as the connection here does not make it so. Moreover, how were the readers of the Epistle to know that all teachers as such have to expect heavy punishment (German, punitory sentences). The increased measure of the sentence may be gathered from various sayings of our Lord (Matth. xxiii. 13 and elsewhere). The increased measure, to be sure, indicates that the severer sentence agreeably to nature may easily turn into a punitive sentence.

VER. 2. **For manifoldly we offend all** (ἅπαντες).—This assertion is absolutely valid. The Apostle includes himself without any qualification, just as Peter (Acts. xv. 11), Paul (Phil. iii. 12) and John (1 Jno. i. 8) include themselves in similar assertions. Although πταίειν does not bear directly on the *errores, qui docentibus obvenire possint* (Grotius), but comprehends moral offences in the widest sense (Huther), the word is so chosen as forthwith to point to moral errors and offences and these occur for the most part in the sphere of teaching (*Lehrrede*=didactic utterance).

If a man offendeth not in word.—The asyndeton indicates that James progresses in the same sphere of thought and hence aims not at an antithesis, as Wiesinger rightly observes. Although the ἐν λόγῳ may not have to be limited to ἐν διδασκαλίᾳ (cf. ch. i. 19), as Pott maintains, the context requires us to think of didactic offences which were the soul of Judaizing proceedings.

He is a perfect man.—Supply ἐστί. Every word is here significant; οὗτος denotes the rarity of such a man, ἀνήρ indicates that the Apostle refers in particular to a sphere of males and their doings, τέλειος describes once more the N. T. maturity of faith, principial completion. The proposition may easily be generalized and made to denote the ideal of the Christian life which none can attain here on earth (see de Wette); but James manifestly refers to something attainable, which is evident from what follows.

Able even to bridle the whole body.—This inference is founded on the thought that the tongue is that member of the body over which man finds it most difficult to establish the mastery and that he who does not offend in word, shows that he has established that mastery. Consequently: he who offendeth in no word and thereby shows himself to be the master of his tongue, has obtained the mastery over his whole body. But just as the inference is here not to the physical tongue as such but only as the organ and symbol of readiness of speech, so James does not "set the body as such in opposition to man" as a relative independent power which offers moral resistance to the will of the "Ego" (Wiesinger, Huther), but the body denotes here the organ and symbol of all human action with the exception of speech. The sense in brief is therefore as follows: he who truly masters his words, will also master his works. Life under the law of liberty is most difficult to be evidenced in the mastery of one's speech. Huther also afterwards acknowledges the figurative in the language of James: "The καρδία indeed is the fountain of evil deeds (Matth. xv. 19), but the lust which is rooted therein, has so thoroughly appropriated the members of man and *as it were* fixed its dwelling in them, that they appear as lusting subjects and may be represented as such in living-concrete language." But the figures of the horse and the ship, which follow, prove that the reference is not only to opposing sinfulness (the seeming law in the members Rom. vii. 23), but also to the naturalness itself which is subordinated to the spirit and needs guiding; for the horse does not resist its rider, and the ship its helmsman, as the old man resists the new. Huther moreover sets here aside several explanations ("the whole connection of the acts and changes of man" Baumgarten, etc.), which are more or less well suited to define the idea on which the "*as it were,*" in connection with the body needing to be guided, is based. But the organic concretion and membering (Gliederung=articulating) of the lusts of the heart in the sinfully untuned corporealness must be held fast.

The power of the tongue, vv: 3, 4.

James illustrates the power and import of the tongue by two comparisons. In v. 2 he had set it forth as being relatively the most mighty member among the members of the body, he now develops the thought that it is the ruling member, the control of which involves the control of the whole body. He takes for granted that it is only the spirit which can control the body; but the organ of its rule, the instrument to be controlled for the control of the body, is just the tongue. The word is the disposer of acts. "This whole discussion of the wild power of the tongue is not 'bombast' (Schleiermacher), but designed to make clear to his readers their perverseness." Wiesinger. Right, but James knows also a power of the tongue in a good sense.

First figure. VER. 3. **But if we put the bit into the mouths of horses.**—The Apostle introduces first the figure of horses, because he had already before borrowed therefrom the figurative expression χαλιναγωγῆσαι (v. 2; ch. i. 25). Hence the Genitive τῶν ἵππων should probably be joined with τοὺς χαλινοὺς (Theile), and not with τὰ στόματα (Oecumenius and al. Huther). [τῶν ἵππων appears to stand first for the sake of emphasis. Translating literally "But if of horses we put the bits into the mouth" is not English. (Alford). We have therefore expressed the idea in idiomatic English; the distinction of Lange to connect τῶν ἵππων with τοὺς χαλινοὺς instead of joining it with τὰ στόματα is really a distinction without a difference. We put *bits* into the mouths of horses, that is real, material bits; of course, *such* bits we do not put into the mouths of men. The sense is really the same on either construction. The similitude contains the application.—M.]. The bits [Lange throughout uses the word *Zaum*=bridle, but χαλινός is not the *bridle*, but its metal mouthpiece. I have therefore uniformly rendered *Zaum*=bit.—M.] of horses as literal bits are contrasted with the figurative. But both kinds belong to the respective mouths: the horse-bit belongs to a horse's mouth, the man-bit to a man's mouth. Thus the principal accent lies certainly on τὰ στόματα. These constitute the *tertium comparationis*, not "the smallness of the χαλινοί, as the majority of commentators suppose" Huther. The apodosis begins with καὶ ὅλον (Wiesinger, Huther); it is not contained in v. 5 (Theile); nor does it require us to supply something in thought (de Wette). μετάγειν occurs in the N. T. only here and v. 4.—

Second figure.—VER. 4. **Behold even the ships.**—The organ of guiding, probably connected with the natural unruliness of the horse to be guided, was the principal idea of the first figure: the mouth, the tongue; in the second figure it is the contrast between the smallness of the organ, the fine touch required to influence it and the greatness as well as the storm-tossed condition of the ship to be turned. The small rudder on which the will of man with almost the stillness of spirits, exerts its impulse, governs the whole great ship with all the fearful reaction of the wind and the waves, which like infuriated elementary spirits oppose the firm spirit of the steersman. Hence the first καὶ, as well as ἰδοὺ, denotes intensification. The participial sentence ὄντα brings out the immense weight which the rudder has to overcome; *which are so great*, or *though so great*.—ἐλαύνειν to drive on, set in motion, is used elsewhere in the N. T. of navigating proper [cf. Mark vi. 48; Jno. vi. 19, LXX. for שַׁיִט, Is. xxxiii. 21.—M.], but then also of restless agitation 2 Pet. ii. 17. Fierce winds are the wild navigators of the ship whom the human navigator opposes with his rudder. They have doubtless a symbolical import, as Bede did think, not however as the *appetitus mentium* originating within, but as the great temptations (πειρασμοί) of the world, coming from without, the place of whose nativity, to be sure, is within (see ch. i. 6). The little rudder is here obviously the antitype of the little tongue. [Bede's exposition may be found useful in point of *application*, although it is hardly sound in point of *exegesis*. "Naves magnæ in mari, mentes sunt hominum in hac vita, sive bonorum sive malorum. Venti validi, a quibus minantur, ipsi appetitus sunt mentium, quibus naturaliter coguntur aliquid agere etc."—M.].

Whithersoever the direction.—Although ὁρμή hardly denotes the *impulsus externus*, the steersman's pressure on the rudder (Erasmus and many others), the translation "eager will, desire of something" (Bede, Calvin, Huther etc.) is hardly sufficient; ὁρμή always indicates active will developed into an effort or onset; hence here the direction, the course of the navigator, kept in action by the rudder. On similar comparisons among the classics see Gebser, Theile. [ὁρμή signifies primarily *any violent pressure onwards* (ὄρνυμι), then *the first stir* or *move* towards a thing, then impulse, eager desire in the sense of will. I render "will," because the will of the steersman directs the impulse given to the rudder and thereby to the ship.—M.].—"The two similitudes of the bit and navigation have often been connected by the ancients in a similar manner, so that Pricæus even thought that James might have borrowed them from Plato or some other Greek writer." Gebser. Huther further calls attention to the circumstance that the reference here is to the actual εὐθύνων, not to the technical or official εὐθυντήρ.

VER. 5. **Thus also the tongue.**—A little member like the little rudder.

And boasteth great things.—Since μεγαλαυχεῖ describes absolutely haughty and overbearing conduct, the reading μεγάλα αὐχεῖ seems to be preferable (see note in Appar. Crit. above). For James had spoken of a great and praiseworthy doing; he could not with οὕτως pass at once from the figure of the rudder to the pernicious doing of the tongue. The ἰδού moreover separates the thought under notice from the contemplation of the pernicious operation of the tongue, which follows. The selection of the term simply intimates that the tongue not only does great things, but boasts of the great things. Bede: "*Magna exaltat.*" The explanation "accomplishes great things" Luther (similarly Oecumenius, Calvin and al.), gives tone to the fundamental idea without preserving the shading [*i.e.* the gradual shading off—M.]. Persevering to the idea μεγαλαυχεῖ (Huther, similarly Wiesinger) is not based on the context.

The pernicious doing of the tongue.

v. 3 (second half), v. 6. **Behold how small a fire.**—ἡλικὸν gives prominence to the quantity according to the construction, either in point of greatness or smallness; here in point of smallness (Cajetanus, Huther). de Wette understands it as denoting a great fire; but the Apostle's design was not so much the aesthetic contemplation of a forest-conflagration, as to point to the wicked origin thereof in a little spark; against this Wiesinger justly lays stress on ἀνάπτει [which is not=consumed, but=lighteth up, kindleth. Seneca (*Cont.* v, 5) employs very similar language "*quam lenibus initiis quanta incendia oriantur.*"—M.].—Huther, adverting to corresponding descriptions in Homer, Pindar, Philo etc., points out that the concrete sense of ὕλη=forest, is preferable to the vaguer *materia* =combustible etc. [The classical descriptions are found in Homer, *Il.* xi. 115: Plutarch, *Sympos.* viii. p. 730; Pindar, *Pyth.* iii. 66; Virgil, *Georg.* ii. 303.—M.].

VER. 6. **The tongue also is a fire.**—The figure of a spark or a very small fire producing the conflagration of a forest, is now applied to the incendiary ravages of the tongue. The tongue is fiery as to its nature in general, *i. e.* the organ of speech, easily inflamed by spiritual fire, by passionate, vehement and consuming impulse. James here passes over the fact that the tongue is destined to become an organ of heavenly fire, Acts ii., for his eye is fixed on the pernicious fire of fanaticism which begins to inflame the Judaistic spirits throughout the world.

It the world of unrighteousness [that world of iniquity].—Not an elliptical clause, requiring ὕλη to complete it in the sense "the tongue is the fire, the world is the forest."—Morus and al. This cosmos then is a further designation of the tongue. According to Wiesinger κόσμος in general, denotes the sum-total of what is created (Matth. xiii. 35; Eph. i. 4), "the cosmos of unrighteousness," hence here "the sum-total of unrighteousness." So Huther citing ὅλος ὁ κόσμος τῶν χρημάτων LXX. Prov. xvii. 8. Calvin: "*Acsi vocaret mare et abyssum.*" Olshausen and al., "it is as it were the unrighteous world itself, which has its seat in the tongue." See the interpretations of Theile, Estius, Herder, Gebser, Clericus (who with others holds the words to be spurious), in Huther. Oecumenius and many others read κόσμος=adornment of unrighteousness: the tongue adorns unrighteousness by rhetorical arts. Wiesinger objects 1. that κόσμος is a passive idea, 2. that the sense would be too feeble. The word need not be taken in the sense of "adornment," but we may nevertheless suppose that James here, as frequently, returns to the original signification of the Greek word. In point of fact it is the tongue which sophistically, rhetorically, poetically, parenthetically and imperatively gives to unrighteousness its worldly, apparently respectable and even splendid form. We therefore suppose that James wanted to say that "the tongue is the form of the world, worldliness, worldly culture, the seemingly beautiful world of unrighteousness." At all events he could have described it as the sum-total of unrighteousness only in a highly figurative sense. We therefore hold with Tischendorf and Neander against Huther and the majority of commentators, that ὁ κόσμος τῆς ἀδικίας does not belong appositionally to what goes before, but belongs to what follows. The addition "the sum-total of unrighteousness" would not explain the proposition "the tongue is a fire." But it is to be understood that the tongue is prominent among the members as the world of unrighteousness. It is however matter of inquiry what is the meaning of καθίσταται? The following interpretations are idle, to say nothing of their incorrectness: it *stands*, it *is placed*, it *is set;* that of Huther also is inadequate: it *sets itself, appears* in connection with what follows, as that which polluteth the whole body. In agreement with the full meaning of καθιστάναι and with the context, the word according to the analogy of Heb. viii. 3 and other passages, taken absolutely, denotes the presidency, the domination of the tongue among the members. In virtue of its worldly culture, which understands even how to beautify unrighteousness, the tongue rules among the members. But what a contrast between its works and its position! And it is just *it*, which from its prominence *pollutes the whole body.*—Before the world it washes all unrighteousness clean, before God or truth it stains and pollutes the whole body, *i. e.* the tongue, by the preceding, sinful word paves the way to all the sinful acts of all the members. Although σπιλοῦν does not suit πῦρ (notwithstanding Bengel's explanation "*ut ignis per fumum*"), it suits the saying "the tongue is the κόσμος" as its perfect antithesis. Apparent comeliness is the most essential deformity of life. How it pollutes the life is apparent from what follows. [But there seems really to be no objection to the rendering "*makes itself,*" which is preferable to Lange's, because it is founded on better grammar than his and gives a good, clear and unforced sense. καθίσταται is used here as in ch. iv. 4. Huther. "The tongue by acting in and upon the members, makes itself to be the defiler of the whole body. It is so made ἐν τοῖς μέλεσιν ἡμῶν, which, as their name intimates, ought to move in harmonious *melody* and amicable concert with each other; and so glorify their maker. But the tongue mars their music by its discord. It is even like an intestine volcano; and sends forth a dark stream of lava, and a murky shower of ashes and smoke, and is thus a source of pollution, *sullying* and *staining* as with foul blots (σπιλοῦσα) the beauty of all around it; and *also* like a volcano, it emits a flood of fire." Wordsworth.—M.].

And inflameth.—Wiesinger takes καὶ, καὶ in the sense "as well as," and sets both in the relation of logical subordination to ἡ σπιλοῦσα. We object with Huther, because the following words are not only explanatory but intensive. The tongue inflames

The wheel of the development of life —That τροχός denotes a *wheel* requires no further proof (see 1 Kings vii. 30 etc.; Ezek. i. 15, 19, 20). But the question is what is the meaning of γένεσις and what is therefore the meaning of τροχὸς γενέσεως? According to Huther γένεσις denotes here "as in ch. i. 23" (see the passage), *birth*, the wheel of birth; that is: the wheel revolving from our birth, *i. e.* life. Similarly Oecumenius. Taking the separate features differently, Calvin and al. reach the same idea: the wheel is the *cursus*, the genesis is the *natura*; the two united—life.—Wiesinger (after Kern) passes from the interpretation "it inflameth the revolving wheel," the spherical course of being (Pott, Schneckenburger), to another: "it inflameth the circumference of our corporeal being" (literally "of that which has become"). As the axis or centre of the circle it diffuses its fire over the whole circumference. However, genesis, taken in the sense of birth, is not life itself but itself only the first revolution of the wheel. Although we need not think (with de Wette following more ancient commentators) of the orb of creation absolutely, or of the cycle of the self-renovation of mankind (תּוֹלְדוֹת גַּלְגַּל, Wolf and al.); it does not follow that genesis here should be taken as birth only, and life only as individual life. The genesis of man rather progresses in an ethical sense through the whole of his earthly existence, and if it is said that the tongue setteth on fire the wheel or the revolution of the development of life, the word in this generality applies not only to individual life, but also to the life of humanity, primarily of course, to the life of the Jewish people, but in its widest sense even to the development of the life of this (earthly) cosmos. The fanatical fire, which at first made the development of the life of individual Jews a continuously growing fire of a burning and revolving wheel, at last seized the development of the life of the whole Jewish nation (for chiliastic worldliness lay at the bottom of the crucifixion of Christ and of the Jewish War) and imperceptibly communicates itself to all mankind and to the earthly κόσμος as the causality of the fiery day, the last day—immanent in the world. James is fully right in saying that it is the tongue which changes the wheel of the human development of life into a burning fire-wheel; or we might say: a ship on fire entering the port. Perhaps every man may find in his course of life a proportionate quantity of this feverish fire-impulse (see Ps. xc.) "This verb φλογίζειν is ἅπαξ λεγ, in N. T.; it occurs in the LXX. Ex. ix. 24. Huther, with whom we should interpret the word of the fire of passion and not with Morus "*de damnis quæ lingua dat*," although the self-consumption of this sin of burning passion is also alluded to, and the reference is not to a mere kindling (Michælis). [Alford renders "the orb of creation," and Wordsworth "the wheel of nature." The idea in both is really the same. The note of the latter will doubtless be prized; "The τροχὸς γενέσεως is the wheel of nature, the *orbis terrarum*, the world itself in its various revolutions; in which one generation follows another, and one season succeeds another; and so τροχὸς γενέσεως is used by Simplicius in Epict. p. 94, and other like expressions in authors quoted here by Wetstein, p. 670.—In a secondary sense, this τροχὸς γενέσεως is the *wheel of human nature*, of *human life*, of *human society*, which is compared to a *wheel* by Solomon Eccl. xii. 6; and so Greg. Naz. (*in Sentent. ap.* a Lapide), and Silius Ital. 3, 6, "rota *volvitur ævi*," and Bœthius (*de Consol.* 2, pr. 1), "*hæc nostra vita est* rotam *volubili orbe versamus*." This wheel is ever rolling round, ever turning apace, whirling about, never continuing in one stay, seeking rest and finding none. So these words of the Apostle are explained by Oecumen., Bede, and Bp. Andrewes, 1, 361; 2, 294, 319.—The functions of a wheel, set on fire by the internal friction of its own axis, are deranged, and so the organization of human society is disturbed and destroyed by the intestine fire of the human tongue; a fire which diffuses itself from the centre and radiates forth to the circumference by all the spokes of slander and detraction, and involves the social framework in combustion and conflagration.—M.].

And itself is inflamed.—Not only once, but habitually (φλογιζομένη Part. Pres.). It is as unwarrantable to change the participle into the preterite as to explain it of the future, as a prophecy of hell-fire (Grotius and al.).

By hell. Gehenna itself uniformly and throughout to be distinguished from Sheol (besides the synoptical gospel found here only), as a symbolically described fire-region (γέεννα τοῦ πυρός) will not be wholly completed before the end of the world. The positive primitive fire of Gehenna is brought about by the immanent heat of devilish passions which proceed from the devil through his kingdom. This devilish heat, therefore, is here described as the causality of that fanatical heat of men (cf. v. 15). That fiery heat of fanaticism the origin of which the Judaists wanted to refer to God (ch. i. 13). James refers directly to the devil. And in this manner it exhibited itself by hatred, lying and death and particularly by frenzy. The strongest utterance concerning the evil tongue excepting the sayings of our Lord of the blasphemy of the Holy Ghost and the apocalyptic saying of the blasphemies of the beast (Dan. vii. viii.; Rev. xiii.)! Approximating descriptions are produced by Huther, Ps. lii. 4; cxx. 3, 4; Prov. xvi. 26; Sir. v. 15. Wiesinger in addition to the specification of sin according to the members of the body, as here indicated, cites also Rom. iii. 13; Col. iii. 5. But the latter passage belongs to another chapter; the seeming members (Scheinglieder) of the old man.—But Rom. vi. 13, 19 belongs hither.

The untamableness of the tongue. vv. 7, 8.

VER. 7. **For every nature of the wild beasts.**—γὰρ creates difficulty. Huther thinks that it substantiates, especially with reference to v. 8, the foregoing judgment expressed concerning the tongue. But the assertion concerning the untamableness of the tongue does not substantiate the assertion concerning the depravity of the tongue. Wiesinger makes γὰρ substantiate even the preceding μεγαλαυχεῖ, while Pott holds that it simply indicates the transition. In our opinion the γὰρ substantiates the words immediately preceding: "itself is imflamed by hell." Whereby will he prove that assertion? By the untamableness of the tongue. If the nature of the tongue were only animal, man, the power of human nature could tame it as well as every thing animal. But the untamableness of the tongue shows that there is something devilish in its excitement, over which human nature left to itself has no power. Only by the wisdom which is from above v. 15, can be conquered the wisdom which is from beneath, *i. e.* devilish wisdom, v. 15, and that not in the form of taming, breaking in and enslaving, but in the form of free transformation by regeneration. James first specifies what can be tamed,—universal animal nature, then what can tame it—human nature. Man as man is a match for a beast, but if the animal element in man is strengthened by the devils, he can acquire the superiority of the *ἀνὴρ τέλειος* only by Divine grace. James divides the animal world into four classes. He first mentions together quadrupeds (not beasts in general, Pott, or wild beasts in particular, Erasmus etc.) and birds, that is the higher and more noble species of beasts. Then the dismal creeping beasts (not "animalia terrestria" in general [Pott], not only serpents in particular [Luther, Calvin], but amphibia and worms as in Gen. xxiv. 25), and the stupid sea-animals (not only fishes in the literal sense [Huther], nor sea-wonders [Luther], nor sea-monsters [Stier]). Huther: "The classification is here the same as in Gen. ix. 2, which passage may have been before the Apostle's mind." James doubtless thought of serpents as the representatives of creeping beasts, with reference to the conjurers of serpents, of trained fishes, dolphins or the like as the representatives of sea-animals. We see here, moreover, that even menageries or the art of taming beasts have some reference to apostolical truth. The opinion of the Apostle really amounts to this: all *φύσις*, every *φύσις*, as further specified is subjected to human *φύσις*; the condition only, that man understand the natures, which are subjected to him and seize them at the right spot of want, docility or dependence. Huther rightly observes that James does not describe the relation of man the individual to individual beasts, but the relation of human nature to animal nature in general.

By human nature—So we must take the Dative [it is the Dative of the *agent*—M.], not as a *dativus commodi.* Human nature is here the whole power of mankind, as it is made to depend on itself in dependence upon God, Gen. i.; hence not only the "ingenii solertia" (Hottinger), but that ingenuity regarded as the most proper characteristic of human *δύναμις* in its superiority to animal power.

Is tamed and hath been tamed.—For this is a process which beginning with the most remote past continues to the most distant future. The beasts are more and more subjected to human nature, while the diabolically excited tongue (to which in the modern world must also be reckoned the pen, so that Satan now speaks more to men by the goose-quill [or the steel-pen—M.] than by the mouth of the serpent) becomes increasingly untamable (see Rev. xiii. 6). *δάμαζεσθαι δύναται* is by this process illustrated as a fact, and consequently assumed in the two tenses of the verb, and not limited to the present only (Schneckenburger and al.); *δαμάζειν* moreover denotes not the conquest of our resistance (Huther) which also takes place in conversion, but the translation into a coerced-psychico-physical dependence by the use of appropriate means. If it is said therefore that the tongue cannot be tamed by human nature, this implies also that it cannot be tamed in the form of taming. This expression may also affirm with reference to the animal world that man's original relation to the beasts has not altogether remained the same (see Gen. ix. 2; cf. Gen. i. 28; ii. 20). Wiesinger: "In the opinion of James also man's dominion over the creatures is not lost (cf. Ps. viii. 7, 9) but it has been modified like his relation to the earth itself." v. 9 also furnishes a parallel to this verse.

VER. 8. **But the tongue no one of men.**—Estius and al.: the tongue of *others*; Huther, one's *own* tongue. Doubtless *primarily one's own* tongue, for the taming of the tongue must proceed from the heart; but the more general sense must not be lost sight of. Before the human tongue diabolically grown wild natural humanity stands as before a dragon, for whom there is not found a Knight St. George among men as they are. Bengel, who interprets: "*nemo alius, vix ipse quisque,*" overlooks that the antithesis between the natural power of man and a higher power is here postulated. But that which still causes James to utter an expression of indignation, is the pernicious working of the tongue in the Judaistic world of his time.

The turbulent evil.—We interpret *κακόν* in the positive ethical sense as wickedness or evil and the adjective *ἀκατάστατον* (see App. Crit.) with reference to ch. i. 8 and *ἀκαταστασία* ch. iii. 16 according to the meaning of the word in Luke xxi. 9; 1 Cor. xiv. 33; 2 Cor. vi. 5; xii. 20. The revolutionary conduct of the Judaistic tongues became at that time more and more inflamed in order to prepare for the Jewish people nothing but evil, death and ruin. [Alford thinks that the figure here seems to correspond nearly to what is related of Proteus, that he eluded the grasp of Menelaus under many various shapes. Cf. Hermas, *Pastor* 2, 3, *πονηρὸν πνεῦμά ἐστιν ἡ καταλαλία, καὶ ἀκατάστατον δαιμόνιον.*—M.].

Full of death-bringing poison.—The diabolical nature, the death-bringing serpent-virulence of the strife of tongues; contains substantially the same idea, as the opinion expressed in the preceding verse; "inflamed by hell," Ps. lviii. 5; cxl. 4.

The duplicity of the (fanatically excited) tongue, vv. 9–12. The new element which is introduced (but not noticed by Huther and Wiesinger) in v. 9, is the falseness, the duplicity, the self-contradiction and consequently the self-judgment (*i. e.* self-condemnation) of the tongue. The serpent-like nature of the tongue, v. 8, forms an apt transition to the duplicity of the same, inasmuch as it is simultaneously deceitful and venemous.

VER. 9. **Therewith bless we the Lord.**—(See Appar. Crit.) *ἐν* is instrumental. *Blessing* and *cursing* constitute a familiar antithesis; the blessing, *εὐλογεῖν*, בָּרַךְ, as applied to God, denotes however *praising Him.* The unusual connection "*the Lord and Father*" appears to have been stated not without design. Although *the Lord* here does not directly designate Christ, yet it describes God as the God of revelation, who has finally revealed Himself in Christ as Father. In Him even the Jew praises unconsciously and reluctantly the revelation of God in Christ. (Rom. ix. 5).

And therewith curse we men which.—A difficulty, insufficiently noticed by many commentators, arises from the circumstance that the Apostle includes himself in *we.* In order to escape it, Benson, Gebser and al. suppose that the reference is solely to those who set themselves up as teachers. To be sure the reference is primarily to them, but then also in general to the Judaistic element as a whole. Is the proposition a general confession of sins concerning the abuse of the tongue? or a hypothetical judgment; if we curse men, we do so with the same tongue wherewith we praise God? The design of a particular reproof forbids the former, and the premising of the fact the latter. The difficulty may be solved either by taking the second clause as a question expressive of surprise or by hearing James speak as the representative of his people in the name of his guilty people. [Alford recommends the retention of *which* instead of *who,* which would personally designate *certain men* thus made, while *which* is generic. This distinction, he continues, which some modern philologists are striving to obliterate, is very important in the rendering of Scripture, and has been accurately observed by our English translators.—M.]. The latter is probably the most natural solution.

Have been created after the likeness of God.—That is, the subjects of this Lord, the children of this Father according to their destination, or also the images representing this Lord and Father. This is the glaring contradiction. Wiesinger and Huther (the latter with reference to Bengel's "*remanet nobilitas indelebilis*") here observe that sinful man also remains created in the likeness of God (Gen. i. 26). Without detracting from the general application of the proposition the Apostle may be thinking of such men, in whom the likeness of God (ὁμοίωσις) *i. e.* the actuality and visibility of the image, has *reappeared* [Germ. "has become again," *wieder geworden*—M.], *i. e.* Christians, and particularly according to their majority, Gentile Christians. With regard to them, the contradiction of the cursing Judaists, was perfect; they praised the Father of revelation, they cursed the children of revelation.

VER. 10. **Out of the same mouth goeth forth.**—It is the sinful mouth as to its fanactical excitement in general, but the mouth of Judaism in particular as at that time it continued traditionally to praise God in the Old Testament and began with talmudical rancor (the source of the later Talmud) to curse the Gospel and its adherents.

It shall not be thus. [οὐ χρή, ἀδελφοί μου, ταῦτα οὕτως γίνεσθαι. These things, my brethren, ought not so to be."—M.]. This address to the brethren hardly means only: it is not right that these things (denoting the substance) are done thus (denoting the form). χρή has its full weight and denotes at once that the thing must not be done according to the oracle [here of course with reference to the revealed will of God—M.] and that the thing itself is unprofitable (with reference to χράομαι). Moreover the Plural ταῦτα and the emphatic οὕτως are to be noticed. [χρή is ἅπαξ λεγ. in N. T.—M.].

VER. 11. **Doth a fountain perchance out of the same chink send forth the sweet and the bitter?**—βρύειν, ἅπαξ λεγ., to bubble over, overflow [Lange renders "bubble" with an evident attempt to find a word as nearly intransitive as possible. βρύειν is generally *intransitive,* but it is used transitively by Anacreon, 37, 2 ἴδε πῶς, ἔαρος φανέντος, χάριτες ῥόδα βρύουσιν. It means therefore "to cause to burst forth," and this is the reason why I render "send forth."—M.], ὀπή, the opening of the fountain [ὀπή is probably connected with ὄψ, ὄπτομαι, to see; Wordsworth adds that so the word *Ænon* (the place of *springs*) is derived from the Hebrew עַיִן (*ayin*), an eye, Jno. iii. 23.—M.]; the *sweet* and the *bitter* describe the heterogeneous waters applied to blessing and cursing. Such an occurrence is unknown in nature, hence in the moral world also it only appears as something monstrously unnatural. The fountain is not exactly man, but the disposition, the heart. Out of the abundance of the heart, the mouth (the chink of the fountain) speaketh (*Germ:* Whereof the heart is full, the mouth overfloweth.—M.]. However here again the reference is not to the moral unnaturalness of this duplicity in general but the concrete bearing of the reproof on Judaism becomes increasingly apparent. It is not the Divine purpose and law that the fountain of Judaism in its historical *going forth* for the world should send forth such a contradiction between praising God and cursing the children of God. The application to the end of the Christian Middle Ages lies near.

VER. 12. **Can a fig-tree, my brethren, yield olives?**—The figurative statement of the preceding verse is continued in the figures taken from nature, *i. e.* the idea that nature does not bring forth that which is contradictory and inconsistent. But if the former figure was meant to say: "your duplicity [double-tonguedness] is like a fountain which sends forth at the same time sweet water and bitter, if it were possible to find such a fountain," the figures which now follow set forth with still greater distinctness the impossibility of such a contradiction in nature. And this certainly brings out not only the reprehensible and morally unnatural character of duplicity, but it also expresses the idea that one of the two must be false, either the cursing or the blessing; so that if their cursing the images of God be true, their praising God must be lying and hypocrisy (Huther). To this must be added that in the metaphors which follow the reference is to the character itself, as is the case in the saying of our Lord Matth. vii. 16.—Thus we infer their double-mindedness of character which is false on the side of godliness (δίψυχος) from their duplicity of speech. It may however seem strange that James should use several examples in order to corroborate the thought that as nature is always at unity with itself, true and consistent, so also ought man to be true and consistent. The multiplying of examples has primarily the effect of illustrating more forcibly the general application of the law of life, which the Apostle had laid down. But the supposition might occur that the examples may have also a symbolical import. The fig-tree, the symbol of a luxurious natural life cannot bring forth olives, the symbols of spiritual life. The vine, the symbol of theocracy and ultimately of Christianity, cannot produces figs, happiness [*i. e.* outward], the fulness of the Jewish natural life. The meaning whereof would be as follows: if you want to be natural Jews you cannot bring forth the fruits of the children of the Spirit; but if on the other hand, you want to be Christians, you must not cherish Jewish ideals, sit under the fig-tree of outward prosperity and expect to enjoy its fruit. This would explain the last figure after this manner: as the salt-spring or the salt-current is a mixture which cannot yield pure and drinkable refreshment of life, so a mixture of Jewish severity and hardness and Christian vitality cannot produce the pure water of life of the New Covenant. We leave this symbolism undecided as a whole, but maintain at all events that the salt water is designed to denote a mixture, in which the two elements pure by themselves, have been stained and corrupted. Salt water cannot be drunk. This would give a train of thought which beginning with duplicity in speech passed on to double-mindedness and thence again to its final cause, doubleness of belief, the mixture of legalism and evangelical vitality. On similar biblical figurative modes of speech among the ancients, see Gebser, p. 290; Theile, p. 196.

The contrast of false and true wisdom in speech as to their origin, character and opposite operations. vv. 13–18.

VER 13. **Who is wise and intelligent among you?**—The same words occur in LXX. Deut. i. 13; iv. 6. Heb. חָכָם וְנָבוֹן. Wisdom is the knowledge of ends acquired by enlightenment; intelligence (or understanding, German, *Einsicht*—M.), the knowledge of relations acquired by experience and practice [Wisdom is the gift of God, intelligence and knowledge are the results of education.—M.]. The Apostle's question sounds like an exclamation of the greatest anxiety; it characterizes the desperately bad spiritual situation of Israel. Their few wise and experienced men are to rise and conjure the storm by the wisdom of gentleness.

Let him show out of a good conversation.—James is here more explicit and definite in describing the works to which he had referred as evidences of faith in ch. ii. Such as flow from a good or beautiful life, in which it develops itself. And in order to remove all doubt concerning the main object he has at heart, he adds emphatically: **in meekness of wisdom.** We refer this clause to the whole proposition which precedes it: all the works of this good conversation are to culminate in meekness of wisdom.—The deviating construction of Neander: let him show it by his good conduct; "his works in meekness of wisdom" is recommended by a certain vivacity and pregnancy, but requires the verb to be mentally repeated; the *αὐτοῦ* also would be rather in the way while the demand of the exhibition of works, so common to James, would be rather obscured. *αὐτοῦ* is based on *τίς*, who wants to advance true claims to being wise. Every weakening of the expression *ἐν πραΰτητι σοφίας* either by reading "meek wisdom" (Bede and al.), or "wise meekness" (Laurentius), affects the full sense of the words: the meekness wherein wisdom evidences itself (Wiesinger somewhat different: which is proper to wisdom and proceeds therefrom), see ch. i. 19, 20. [Alford: "in that meekness which is the proper attribute of wisdom"—M.]. Wiesinger thinks that it describes the disposition attending the doing; but James obviously calls for the activity of meekness, for meekness itself in corresponding acts. It alone was able to deliver the Jewish Christians as well as the Jews from fanaticism, conjure the storm and save the hope of Israel. See the promise Matth. v. 5.

VER. 14. **But if ye have bitter zeal [emulation].**—This was the real situation of affairs and on this account James addresses them personally on the subject. We render *ζῆλος* not jealousy but zeal, for doubtless the reference is primarily to a religious and not to a moral passion. James means the specifically Jewish emulation which was considered by those who exhibited it as enthusiasm for the glory of God, as Paul describes it Rom. x. The adjective shows that it was a false, unholy zeal; *πικρόν* indicates passionateness and animosity; this certainly turns zeal into jealousy, for religious zeal becomes zealotical and fanatical through the admixture of jealousy and hostility. *Ἐριθεία* is really the envy, rivalry and party-strife rooted in venality; so Paul frequently uses the word (Rom. ii. 8; 2 Cor. xii. 20 etc.). *ἔχετε* denotes not only an active having but a real fostering.

In your hearts.—"In contrast with the *word* of the readers who make boast of their wisdom." Huther.

Boast not.—The offence of their excited teaching, striving, judging and cursing was twofold: firstly a haughty self-elevation or proud demeanour against others, secondly a more or less conscious lying suppression of their better consciousness. But both sins were more aggravated from being directed against the truth itself. According to Wiesinger *ἀλήθεια* denotes Christian truth (because otherwise *ψεύδεσθε* would be tautological: to lie against the truth). Huther seems to understand by it only the real fact that the condition of the heart is in opposition to the word. But with James theocratical truth and Christian truth converge into *one truth of the revelation of God*, the effect and import of which are in the lives and consciences of men. The boasting and lying therefore was directed not against a mere object and against a mere fact; but it was a haughty and hypocritical insurrection against the very truth which the zealots, with an evil conscience, professed to protect (see Rom. ii. 23). It becomes more and more evident that James addresses not only the Jewish Christians, but his nation in general.

VER. 15. **[For] this wisdom is not that.**—"*Negatio cum vi præmissa*" Theile. *αὕτη* must be taken in connection with *ἡ σοφία*, the latter is therefore introduced ironically here as in Matth. xi. 25; 1 Cor. ii. 6; false wisdom the opposite of the true. Luther's translation: "This is not the wisdom which cometh down from above" must be corrected accordingly. The participle *κατερχομένη* emphatically denotes the continual coming down, as in ch. i. 17; it has therefore adjective force and must not be resolved into the Indicative as do Schneckenburger and al. The expression is a little difficult, but it ceases to be so if we consider that it is the purpose of James to give the most emphatic negation to the false pretence that it was ἄνωθεν κατερχομένη. Hence he gives his judgment: it is on the contrary (described false by the use of three adjectives) *earthly, sensuous, devilish.* It is earthly as to its earthly nature and origin and thus opposed to the heavenly (Phil. iii. 19); it is sensuous or properly speaking psychical (Luther has the improper rendering "human;" the Vulgate better "*animalis;*" Allioli following it "animal;" Stier and de Wette: "sensuous," which in consideration of the modern idea of "sensuousness" may pass [for want of a better term—M.], having its origin in a psychically restrained passionate constitution deprived of the rule of the Spirit (1 Cor. ii. 14: iii. 3; Jude 19) and is opposed to the spiritual [pneumatical] wisdom—of the spiritual life excited by the Holy Ghost; it is devilish (δαιμονιώδης is ἅπαξ λεγ.), proceeding from the devil or inspired by accursed devils and is opposed to the Divine. Hornejus has not wrongly delineated the moral sides of these evil characteristics: "*terrena, quia avaritiæ dedita est, quæ operibus terrenius inhiat; animalis, quia ad animi lubidines accomodatur; dæmoniaca, quod ambitioni et superbiæ servit, quæ propria diaboli vitia sunt.*" These were surely also the characteristics of Judaistic and Ebionite zealotism. The earthly was peculiarly exhibited in their chiliastic claims to the rule of the earth, the psychical in their fanatical and hateful passions, the devilish in their great errors nourished by haughtiness and hypocrisy.

VER. 16. **For where is emulation [zeal] and party-strife.**—γάρ makes this assertion the proof of the one preceding it. In what goes before James describes a wisdom properly animated by evil zeal and party-strife, and designates it as earthly, sensuous and develish. The proof is that that spirit of emulation and party-strife is so disastrous in its consequences. He does not say "*where is such wisdom,*" for he has torn the mask of wisdom from this evil spirit of emulation. In its nakedness it is carnal and devilish conduct. ζῆλος occurring here without the adjective πικρός might lead one to think at once of jealousy, but the zeal is sufficiently characterized as evil from being connected with rivalry and party-strife. Everywhere is exhibited the rebellious element. ἀκαταστασία is not only mere disorder but the dissolution of order; in the theocratic sense it denotes rebellion (Numb. xvi.; Prov. xxvi. 28), in church-life a seditious spirit opposing the order of God, who has constituted civil order (Rom. xiii. 1, etc.) and church order (1 Cor. xiv. 33).

And all manner of [every] evil work.—φαῦλον might be rendered "*foul*" (German "*faul*") in an ethical sense. [Shakspeare uses the word in the sense of wicked, abominable. "A *foul* fault:" "*Foul* profanation." The current value of '*faul*' in German is *rotten, lazy,* its ethical value denotes moral rottenness, evil.—M.]. Such was the situation of Jewish affairs at that time. The rebellious attitude broke out everywhere in insurrections against the Christians, which were the prelude of the insurrection against the Romans, with numerous episodes of evil work, and all proceeding from the same fountain of diabolical fanaticism.

VER. 17. **But the wisdom from above.**—See Proverbs; the Wisdom of Solomon; Sirach; Matth. xi.; 1 Cor. viii. Its first characteristic is distinguished from the others, as its principle.

Consecrated [pure].—ἁγνή. Really *consecrated* [or *hallowed*—M.], *i. e.* not only *pure* from the influence or even from the inspiration of worldly, carnal and devilish motives, but only **chaste**, free from the spirit of apostasy into which the fanatical zealots fell, but also animated by the Divine Spirit and therefore wholly consecrated to the service and glory of God; consequently full of a dignified and priestly character. From this principle flow its social virtues. It is **peaceable**, *ironical* (Matth. v. 9), **equitably disposed** (1 Tim. iii. 3), **gladly yielding** ([*compliant*—M.]. Εὐπειθής the opposite of stubborn, ἀπειθής Tit. iii. 5; not "easily persuaded," but well inclined to enter into the views and reasons of others, compliant). All this as opposed to the contentiousness of false zeal. But it not only resists evil, but overcomes evil with good; it is **full of compassion** (in the widest sense, in its sympathy with the necessitous ch. i. 27; ii. 13) **and good fruits,** in which compassion is evidenced. The contrast is exhibited in the seditious character and the foul doings of false wisdom. So stood in those days Christianity over against its enemies and so it was to show itself also in the Jewish Christians over against Judaism. This attitude of wisdom induced James still further to add in its praise ἀδιάκριτος, ἀνυπόκριτος! de Wette, Wiesinger and Huther render the first word '*without doubting;*' that is, consequently, *confident, decided.* This would give a good sense if 1. the reference here were not to social conduct and 2. if a certain correspondency between ἀδιάκριτος and ἀνυπόκριτος were not necessary.—Now since the word (as well as that which follows) has to be taken in an active sense, although its primary meaning is passive (not distinguished, undecided, so that the first word might mean "*undivided,*" "being a unit" [*einheitlich*], there being only *one* wisdom—"*non duplex*" Wetstein; "simple" Neander—and the second *undivided, i. e.,* without any false admixture) the idea "not *separatistic,* not *sectarian*" seems to lie nearest (so Baumgarten, Schneckenburger and al.: "*quæ non discernit homines;*" Luther, Grotius, etc.: "without partiality;" Vulgate: "*non judicans;*" Semler: "*non temere judicans*"): With this corresponds then ἀνυπόκριτος, without hypocrisy, without dissembling, sincere Rom. xii. 9; 2 Cor. vi. 6. [The reader is referred for further information on ἀδιάκριτος to notes on ch. i. 6–8; ii. 4; on ἀνυπόκριτος to ch. i. 22, 26; ii. 1].

VER. 18. **Fruit of righteousness.**—This difficult expression might be taken literally as follows: the fruit which consists in the righteousness as just described (*Genit. appos.* not only justification, Schneckenburger), is once more turned into seed, it is sown in the world, primarily among erring brethren, in peace, *i. e.,* in the form of peace, in the exhibitions of a peaceful demeanour [not εἰς εἰρήνην, *i. e.,* unto eternal life, de Wette), and then becomes the lot of the children of peace as the harvest of peace and the kingdom of peace. But Wiesinger rightly calls attention to ch. i. 20. "For the wrath of man worketh not, accomplishes not the righteousness of God," and adds "that which the readers pretend to realize by their contentious wisdom, can only prosper under the quickening influence of peace." The righteousness of God in its full manifestation in the world, for which Christians are yearning and for which at that time the Jews in particular were yearning also, is a harvest-fruit which has to be sown by the peaceful demeanour of the peacemakers (τοῖς ποιοῦσιν εἰρήνην *Dat. actionis.* Huther). The term καρπός, etc., would be therefore "a pregnant expression for: the seed, which yields the fruit of righteousness, is sown." (Huther). This construction is also favoured by the remark of Huther, made elsewhere, that James is fond of beginning his speech with the teleological leading idea. Huther rightly observes that the sowing is not only teaching proper (Schneckenburger), still it remains a fundamental form of evangelical peace-making. The *dat. comm.* in τοῖς ποιοῦσιν "for the children of peace," is reluctantly given up and Wiesinger would like to connect this meaning with the *Dat. actionis.* It must be observed, however, that the world-historical harvest of righteousness will affect all men, although it will be a kingdom of peace only to the children of peace. The words of the Apostle therefore were primarily an exhortation addressed to his readers, *i. e.*, to the twelve tribes to this effect: if you really seek the righteousness of God, then prepare the future harvest of righteousness in such wise that as children of peace you scatter the seed by a peaceful behaviour (which includes, to be sure, the peace of the Christian righteousness of faith). Sow peace and you will reap rightousness to your joy. But the idea must be so construed that the Apostle is made at the same time to lay stress on the fact that the harvest of righteousness is prepared under all circumstances. Whether you join in or not: that righteousness, for which you suppose to contend in zealotical party-strife, is now sown with the patience of the sower (see ch. v. 7) by the peacemakers who are really in the world, by Christians in their exhibitions of peaceful demeanour (ἐν εἰρήνῃ hardly denotes mere mode, but rather the form of the seed, evangelical peace), and at the time of harvest it will appear in its full maturity.

DOCTRINAL AND ETHICAL.

1. The fault which James reproves in the greater part of this chapter, is nothing but a natural manifestation of the egotism of sinful human nature, a fault which, although suppressed, is by no means fully overcome even in Christians. It would seem that, as elsewhere, there were many among the first readers of this Epistle in particular, of whom the author knew or at least was afraid that they were more fond of speaking than of hearing, more fond of teaching others than of receiving instruction themselves. He therefore seizes the fault, described in ch. i. 19, 26 by the root, at the same time pointing out, that those who set themselves up as teachers, are in the greatest danger of bringing on themselves greater condemnation than their hearers. His doctrine in this respect is in perfect agreement with that of our Lord, Matt. xii. 36, 37.

2. There are not a few in our day who set up as teachers and leaders of the congregation without being sufficiently prepared for this important and difficult work, who thus render more difficult the work of the duly appointed servants of the Gospel and scatter the flock without cause; and there are others who suffer themselves to be duly led and to be prepared for the holy ministry, but whose desire to enter the ministry springs from very impure motives. How desirable that both would seriously lay to heart the teaching of James on this subject! [Ministerial preparation is not sufficiently appreciated by the uneducated portions of the laity and not unfrequently made light of by the ecclesiastical authorities. In a new country, like America, the supply of ministers is not equal to the demand and owing to this circumstance men morally and spiritually fitted but intellectually and educationally unfitted, are frequently put in charge of churches, whose best interests are apt to be grievously affected in such incompetent hands. The moral and spiritual qualifications of candidates for the holy ministry is a *conditio sine qua non*, but their possession cannot cover or supply intellectual and educational deficiency. How can a man preach the Gospel intelligently and beneficially, if he is ignorant of the first principles of correct interpretation, completely at sea in scientific theology and void of all knowledge of Church History and other cognate branches of a theological education? If these lines are read by any minister, who is conscious of his intellectual deficiency, the writer would affectionately entreat him to remember that he ought to be *thoroughly* equipped for the study of God's Holy Word and that he cannot *teach* his people aright, if he does not understand aright. The *cacoethes docendi* is a great evil in our days and has ruined many a man, who had he only been content to sit awhile on the students' bench might have been eminently successful in the ministry.—M.]. It is of course self-evident that the Apostle's warning is not directed against a great number of teachers as such, which on the contrary is in many respects useful and desirable (cf. Eph. iv. 11), but rather against an eager pressing into the Ministry of the Word, when men touch the Holy *illotis manibus*. The language of Homer: "ουκ αγαθὴ ἡ πολυκοιρανίη, εἷς κοίρανος ἔστω." ["The rule of many is not good, let there be one ruler"—M.], applies also to Church government.

3. The familiar saying of James "manifoldly we offend all" is frequently but erroneously taken and used as a *dictum probans* of the doctrine of the universal sinfulness of human nature. The author speaks not of men in general, but of Christians in particular. He considers not so much gross transgression as sins of infirmity and haste; and particularly the danger to which the hearer is less exposed than the teacher, namely the danger of offending in word. The preacher of the Gospel may very easily offend in word, on the one hand by setting forth his own perverse notions instead of the objectively given truth of salvation, or on the other by onesided preaching or by want of clearness and simplicity. Thus he may even involuntarily give offence and estrange his hearers, or on the other hand, he may lull them into a false sleep of peace and thus

do infinitely more harm than good with his preaching. How urgently ought he therefore to press the exhortation that men should not prematurely set themselves up as teachers, since probably they would do much better to continue disciples a little longer! Cf. Heb. v. 12. But this warning ought not to deter any one who sincerely desires to serve God in the ministry of the Word and truly loves the Lord and His Church. By watchfulness and prayer the servant of the Gospel may preserve himself from many sins of the tongue. The best corrective, in this respect, is doubtless the petition Ps. xix. 15; cxli. 3.

4. In order to form a correct estimate of the magnitude of the sins which Christians also commit with the tongue, first of all it must not be forgotten that the faculty of speech is originally a *Divine* gift bestowed on man. Compare Herder's *Origin of Language* (1770), a work which is still very valuable. This idea was not unfamiliar even to the pagans. Cf. Hesiod: ἔργα καὶ ἡμ., v. 79; Horat. *Od.* 1, 10, vv. 2, 3; Ovid, *Fastor.*, v. 667. See also Dr. J. C. Amman's *Dissertat. de loquela*, Amsterd. 1700, and especially Schubert, *History of the Soul*, 3d ed. 1839, p. 153–163. "The word uttered is only the outward sound of the begetting inward language of ideas through the corporeal medium." Ennemoser.

5. No Christian moralist may omit to bestow the greatest possible attention on the doctrine of James concerning the sins of the tongue. For speaking is also a doing and a doing of such daily and manifold occurrence, that its good and its evil consequences are all but incalculable. Compare the familiar French proverb: "*le style c'est l'homme*," and the motto of the well-known diplomatist Talleyrand "*le langage est donné* pour cacher *ses pensées*." No wonder that the Old Testament abounds in warnings against the perverse use of the tongue; see *e. g.* Ps. xv. 24, 34, and other passages.

5. In saying that "if any man offend not in word, he is a perfect man," James of course takes for granted, that such a mastery of the tongue is not solely the fruit of a politic wisdom, but rather the fruit of Christian self-control as the product of faith and love. He who has learned from this principle to set a watch before his lips, may with certainty be supposed to have attained so high a degree of discretion and life-wisdom, that to him the performance of any other duty cannot be particularly difficult, still less impossible. Cf. Prov. x. 19; xiii. 3; xvii. 27. But in order to obtain and to preserve the mastery of one's tongue, one must before have become master of one's most violent emotions and remain collected in one's intercourse with friends and enemies. Ps. xvi. 32. Cf. the language of Plutarch on this head: "*de capienda ex hostibus utilitate*," opp. ed. Reiskii, Tom. 6, p. 355 sq; also "*de garrulitate*," Tom. 8, p. 13 sqq.

7. "Plutarch (*de Auditione*, p. 137, and *in conviv. Sept.* p. 556, vol. 6, ed. Reiskii) relates that Amasis, King of Egypt sent a sacrifice to Bias and requested him to send back the best and the worst part thereof: Bias sent back the tongue." Heubner.

8. James who wrote his Epistle as a warning to believers, from the nature of the case could only advert to the *harm* caused by the abuse of the tongue, not (or only slightly) to the *profit* that might accrue to the cause of the Lord by the well-ordered use of the power of speech. To realize this *light-side* of the matter ought to be the daily effort of every Christian, but more particularly that of the Christian teacher.

9. The words of James (v. 9) would be unmeaning, if he meant that only the first man bore the likeness of God, which by the fall was wholly and eternally *lost* to his descendants. The ravaging power of sin is manifested not in the *potentiality* but in the *actuality* of man's likeness to God, and the *Conf. Belg.* art. 14, is therefore right in speaking of small remnants (*scintillulæ*) of the Divine image in fallen man, which are perfectly sufficient to take away all his excuses. [Art. IX. of the Articles of Religion in the Church of England and the Prot. Ep. Church in the U. S. says: "man is *very far* gone from original righteousness."—M.]. Lange (*Positive Dogmatik*, p. 299) is perfectly right in saying that "man is the image of God, *i. e.* the visible form of the Infinite in the totality of his being. The Being of God consists in His eternally embracing Himself perfectly in the clearness and liberty of His Being, in that He is the Absolute Spirit. And in like manner the being of the image of God consists in man's living in himself as a spirit, in his continually taking back the whole manifoldness of his existence into the unity of his consciousness and out of it re-forming it anew."

10. The doctrine of James (vv. 11, 12) exhibits a remarkable agreement with the sayings of Christ in the Sermon on the Mount (Matth. vii. 16–19; Luke vi. 43-45); a new proof that the publication of the fundamental law of the kingdom of heaven could not be forgotten by this servant of the Lord.

11. The bearing of James concerning the wisdom, which is from above (v. 13 etc.) is remarkable for its recalling not only many of the proverbs of Solomon but also many cognate ideas in Jesus Sirach and the Book of Wisdom. James, although occupying a purely evangelical standpoint, is nevertheless full of the ethical portion of the Old Testament, and in part even of the deutero-canonical writings. However it is impossible to examine the doctrine of this entire chapter more closely without discovering that the author himself has and exemplifies that heavenly wisdom, which in vv. 16, 17 he has so admirably and beautifully delineated as contrasted with earthly wisdom.

12. Very important is the connection of knowledge and life, on which James here insists. He who does not prove his wisdom by works, which have the seal of a meek disposition, contradicts himself and gives the lie to his confession of the Lord, which he is constantly making. He may boast in the possession of the truth but he is an opponent of the truth, if he does not receive it as the principle of his life; cf. 1 Jno. iv. 20, 21. His wisdom, as contrasted with that from above, is purely *earthly*, as contrasted with that of the pneumatical man purely *psychical*, as contrasted with that of good angels (cf. 1 Pet. i. 12), even *devilish*.

13. "The peaceable scatter in peace the seed of genuine Christian wisdom, which grows into

the harvest of righteousness. This applies not only to teachers but to every one who has received from God wisdom and the gift to influence others." Von Gerlach.

14. The seven qualities which James attributes to the wisdom from above (v. 17) are nothing but the seven colours of the one ray of light of heavenly truth, which has been revealed and has appeared in Christ Himself. He is therefore supremely entitled to the name "the Wisdom of God" (Luke xi. 49).

15. Even the closing sentences of this instruction reëcho notes from the Sermon on the Mount, Matth. v. 8, 9.

HOMILETICAL AND PRACTICAL.

A. vv. 1–12.

The lust of rule one of the most ancient diseases in the Church of Christ.—Even the manifold warnings of Christ (Matth. xviii. 1; Jno. xiii. 12–17 and other passages) have been insufficient hitherto to prevent disputes about precedency among those who confess Him.—The higher the position we hold before others, the greater will be our responsibility.—"Manifoldly we offend all." The remaining infirmity of the elect.—The truth, solemnity and comfort of this saying.—The use and abuse which may be and at different times have been made of this saying. —How the knowledge of our own, manifold infirmities ought to make us judge others leniently. —No matter how much the Christian may offend, he ought nevertheless to advance.—Christian self-control.—Man, lord of the animal creation but not lord of himself.—Even the bravest sailor suffers each time ship-wreck on the rocks of the tongue.—The power of the tongue evident 1, from the harm it can do, 2, from the utter impossibility of wholly subduing it.—The faculty of speech which makes man superior to the beasts is not seldom the means of making him inferior to them.—The sad part acted by the evil tongue in every century of the history of the Christian Church.—The sinful tongue is the sinful man. Sinful man is able to raise himself above every other irrational creature but he is unable to raise himself above his own nature.—That which is impossible with men, is possible with God.—The sad want of many men's conformity to their proper being.—How extremes meet also in the use of the tongue.—That which is never seen united in nature, is often simultaneously found present in men.—Man at once a lord and a slave (v. 5. "Behold how small a fire kindleth how great a forest.") Suitable text for a Reformation-sermon. [That is a sermon preached on the festival of the Reformation, which in Germany is kept October 31, the anniversary of Luther's fastening the 95 theses to the door of the Castle Church of Wittenberg A. D. 1517—M.].—There is not a thumb's breadth between our strong side and our weak side.—The melancholy inconsistency and the still sadder consistency of the abuse of the tongue.

Starke:—He who wants to teach others in spiritual things, ought to be first well established himself. A man must be a pure and obedient sheep of Christ before he can become a shepherd. Hos. iv. 6.—Many, although they have not Divine wisdom and experience but possess only a literal knowledge, acquired not in the school of the Holy Ghost, but from the books and writings of men, straightway presume to be guides of the blind etc. Rom. ii. 18.

Quesnel:—If all men have to observe caution in speech, how much more those, whose office requires them frequently and religiously to discourse of holy things? Rom. xv. 18.—Men must fairly strive to attain evangelical perfection, especially if they seek to be employed in the Ministry, 2 Tim. iii. 17.—

Osiander:—If a man is able to govern his tongue so effectually as not to utter any thing censurable, he is doubtless equally able so to govern and guide his body as not to indulge in any vice, Job xxvii. 4, 5.—Many men are more unruly than a horse—men whom God by the infliction of severe punishment has to make somewhat orderly. David cautions us against this disposition Ps. xxxii. 9.—If irrational creatures suffer themselves to be guided and ruled, how much rather ought rational creatures suffer it likewise? Is. i. 3.

Luther:—The tongue guides men either to virtue or to vice, 1 Cor. xv. 33.—The tongue of a Christian is ruled only with the bridle of faith and love, Ps. cxvi. 10.

Quesnel:—Who knows not how to govern his tongue, is like a passenger on a ship without rudder in the open sea exposed to the fury of the storm.—If the rudder of our body is controlled by the Spirit of God, we sail in safety on the sea of the world, Rom. viii. 14.

Cramer:—Many have fallen by the edge of the sword, but infinitely more by evil tongues, Sir. xxviii. 21.

Langii op.:—How easily may an uncircumcised and untamed tongue cause discord in a whole family, so that the best of friends fall out with one another! Sir. xxviii. 15, 16.—God has distinguished us from the brutes by the use of the tongue, and we are distinguished from one another by the good or evil use we make of it, Ps. cxix. 23.

Hedinger:—Evil tongues and bad lungs have caused the death of many. The former spiritually and mostly. How much murder is committed with the tongue? how forward and swift is this poor member to wound the conscience? Whoso is wise puts a lock to his lips. Sir. xxii. 33—O God, create us a new tongue, that we may praise Thee! Prov. xviii. 21.—

Quesnel:—There is no sin, of which the tongue may not be the cause and instrument, and which as a poisoned seed it may not contain, Matth. xv. 18.—Think, O ye liars and slanderers, how shameful and hurtful a member ye carry in your mouth! Ps. lvii. 5.—Whoso desires to be delivered from the sins of the tongue must particularly apply himself to work in faith at the bottom of his heart by repentance and renovation, Matth. xii. 33.—As the Holy Spirit did set on fire the tongues of the Apostles with godly zeal, so contrariwise the spirit of hell sets on fire the tongues of the ungodly with venom and great malice to crush the good name and reputation of their neighbour, Acts ii. 3, 4, 11.—The diligence of men is able to change the wildest natures of beasts! but none is able to change the sinful nature of men, save the Wisdom and Omnipotence of God, Ez. xxxvi. 26.—God must needs take a coal from His altar and touch our tongue or it cannot be tamed. We stammer by nature like Moses, until God makes us eloquent, Is. vi. 5.—The tongue of the hellish serpent has thrown us into the greatest confusion, but the tongues of the Holy Ghost show us again the way to eternal peace, Acts ii. 4, 38.—We shun serpents, yet consort with people that carry poison in their mouths, Ps. xliv. 4; lv. 22.—How ill-suited it is that those should engage in the praises of God, the whole of whose lives dishonours God! A golden collar cannot be so ill-becoming to a sow covered with filth and dirt as the praise of God to a filthy sinner, Am. v. 23.—

LANGII OP.:—The nobility of human nature is very exalted and no man may offend it in word or deed without sinning against God, Gen. ix. 6. —We ought to honour the image of God in every man be he never so bad, 1 Jno. iv. 12.

STARKE:—Man is so perverse, that there is nothing left in the world which is like him. He wants to render impossibilities possible, to do good and evil at the same time, which is contrary to the whole order of nature, Eccl. i. 15; Ps. lviii. 4.—If we want to show others their follies and sins, we must not do it in boisterous scolding, but in compassionating brotherly love, 2 Tim. ii. 24, 25.—Words are fruits enabling us to form an estimate of the heart, *i. e.* the tree which bears them; if this is pure, the others are not bad, Matth. xii. 23.

STIER:—Future accountability is solemn and difficult even in the case of our own soul. Who would lightly undertake to be accountable for the souls of others? Indeed is it not written, "Many are called but few chosen"—who will call himself in order to fall with so much more surety into condemnation? Many did it then, and alas! many do it now. "But howsoever, let me, I pray thee, also run after Cushi," said Ahimaaz the son of Zadok, and would not be dissuaded when he was told "thou hast no good tidings ready." He stuck to his "let me run." (2 Sam. xviii. 19-23). There are many such teachers and runners, who are not sent. They surely are not the true teachers and masters that shall shine as the brightness of the firmament (Dan. xii. 3),—but they will stand illy.— "Manifoldly we offend all"—James includes himself in this confession in order to put to shame the proud brethren. Not indeed that he intended to expose the supposed errors of his Divinely-inspired Epistle to their criticism or now to ours, but he rather meant solemnly to assert respecting life in general apart from the sacred office, that the perfect man who does not even trip in a word, cannot be found anywhere. Even the Apostles were assuredly not sinless, holy and infallible in their daily and hourly private life; the promise of the Holy Ghost to guard them from all error related only to their sacred office, just as it was with reference to their office and the principal and fundamental truths of their message that the seventy as well as the twelve were told "He that heareth you, heareth me."—Although the proud tongue may boast, I can be silent, or I can thoroughly dissemble myself—it is a thing beyond its control, there it is brought to shame. The most expert hypocrite can never reach such a point of dissembling as to prevent its failing him even in a word; the heart runs over, the hell within bursts out on the tongue. Our speech is and remains the nearest, surest and most irresistible effluence of the heart. What follows lastly from James's sermon against the sins of the tongue? Whither they lead—to the world full of unrighteousness, whence they come—from the inward abyss of corruption —he has shown; it is not difficult to apply here the only remedy.

HEUBNER:—We are more on our guard with respect to sins in deed than with respect to sins in word.—Whoso fails to govern his tongue is like a rider on an unruly horse, or like a sailor in a ship without a rudder.—The tongue is a channel which transmits the evil of hell.—An *unconditional* impossibility to tame the tongue does not exist. If thy tongue is cursing, it is unfitted for praise.

VIEDEBANDT:—The rule of the tongue is more important than the rule of the world.—What an evil full of deadly poison is many a newspaper tongue!—If Satan has your heart, he also rules your tongue. The tongue and the heart are only a span apart.

NEANDER:—James attacks the being of mock piety at all points. Such is that pious cant which while it utters the praises of God in words, hatefully censures and condemns men, in whom the image of God ought to be honoured, aside. —Thus James points out the fundamental idea of this whole Epistle, that everything depends on that disposition which gives direction to a man's whole life, the recognition of which truth was as remote as possible from that tendency, attacked by him at all points. which only considers the outward, single acts, and the appearance of things.

JAKOBI:—The Apostle shows from the harmony, visible in universal creation, that it is unnatural and therefore ungodly and therefore displeasing to God if the same tongue is used in the service of heaven and hell, and if praises and curses proceed out of the same mouth God, says another Apostle, is a God of order. Because the fig-tree, the olive tree and the vine bear fruit each according to its kind, figs, olives and grapes, and because sweet fountains and salt fountains always send forth the same kind of water and because of this order in nature, God rejoices in all his works (Ps. civ. 31), and looking down from heaven upon the earth, behold, all things are very good. Therefore it cannot be good and well-pleasing to God, if contrary to the Divinely appointed order the gifts and faculties intrusted to man are employed in opposite uses, if the same tongue which has just stammered the praise of God, utters shameful words, folly and unseemly jests. Therefore as long as this continues to be done among Christians, so long as we who have just had on our tongue the sweet word of God, indulge in bitter revilings of those who share with us the greatest of all blessings, as long as out of the same opening of the mouth there flow such sweet and such bitter streams, so long the sad dissension of sin continues in us and we do not yet stand in the unity and truth of the Divine life.

LISCO:—The sins of the tongue: 1. They are of all sins the most corrupt; 2, They are of all sins, the most difficult to be avoided.—He who governs himself solves the problem of the Christian life.—The tongue 1, is the communicator of our thoughts and 2, ought to be solely the mediator of good.

PORUBSZKY: (vv. 1, 2):—Religious conversation in social life.—(vv. 3–12). The tongue of scandal.

BECK:—Three golden rules for a Christian's life: 1, have humility in your heart (vv. 1, 2), 2, have truth in your mouth (vv. 3-9), 3, practise faithfulness in your life (vv. 10-12).

W. HOFACKER (Sermons p. 635):—Our speaking tongue one of the greatest gifts of God's grace.

Vv. 1-10. Epistle for the 16th Sunday after Trinity in the Grand Duchy of Hesse and elsewhere.

GEROK:—Watch thy tongue: 1, It looks so little and so small 2, Yet worketh such great things for all; 3, Kindles many a fire of hell, 4, Yet heaven has ordered it so well [German: 1, *Sie ist nur klein und scheint gering* 2, *und richtet an so grosse Ding;* 3, *sie hat manch Höllenfeuer entflammt* 4, *und führt doch ein so himmlish Amt.*—M.].

RUPERTI:—Several oft-forgotten duties to be practised by the Christian in order that he may become master of his tongue in his intercourse with others.

ALT:—The evil word towards one's neighbour.

B. vv. 13-18.

VV. 13-18. Epistle for Quinquagesima Sunday in the Grand Duchy of Hesse and elsewhere.

The difference between abstract knowledge of Christian truth and true life-wisdom.—The tree is known by its fruit.—Meek wisdom the crown of Christian virtue.—The intimate union of truth and love on Christian ground. The wisdom which is from above, and the wisdom which is from beneath; the sevenfold more exalted character of the former and the threefold baseness of the latter.—The wisdom from above: 1, how it is evidenced, 2, how it is rewarded, 3, how it is learned.—The harvest feast of the peaceable: 1, the seed, 2, the fruit, 3, the harvest-joy; here in its beginning, hereafter in its perfection.—James himself is in his Epistle a continuing proof of the truth of what he says, vv. 13–18.

STARKE:—The possession of a natural, wise, prudent understanding is a great gift of God, but to be truly enlightened with the light of truth is invaluable, Prov. iii. 13; 2 Cor. iv. 6.

CRAMER:—Our Christianity is then inseparable, for a good understanding have all they that do His commandments, Ps. cxi. 10.—Many men's meekness is a worm-eaten fruit of nature. They are rather tamed lions than meek sheep of Christ, Matth. xi. 29:—

NOVA BIBL. TÜB.:—Wisdom and meekness are noble virtues which ought to regulate the whole of our conversation; they are the springs of all other virtues, Prov. xix. 2.—Those who are ready to dispute and quarrel and are ever at odds with their neighbour, exhibit an infallible token that they are still lacking true wisdom, Prov. xviii. 6; xx. 3.—

QUESNEL:—A teacher above all things should be an enemy of all disputing and contention, 2 Tim. ii. 24.

CRAMER:—Cunning is not wisdom. Hence little wisdom in the fear of God is better than much wisdom allied to contempt of God, Sir. xix. 21.—

QUESNEL:—The wisdom of the world is very different from the wisdom of the Gospel. It is only cunning wisdom whose end is to rule on earth, but which is ruled itself by nothing but brutal lusts, 1 Cor. i. 21; ii. 7, 8.—Sin punishes itself even in this world, because man in the service of it does not enjoy his life on account of the great trouble and annoyance to which sin puts him, Ps. xxxii. 10.—

CRAMER:—As smoke causes pain to the eyes and prevents their seeing distinctly, so it happens to reason and wisdom, for if it is disturbed by the passions, it cannot see any thing and decide what is white or black, right or wrong.—The most simple Christian who practises these seven qualities of virtue will be wiser than the seven sages of Greece. Remember only one for each day of the week.—Those who scatter the poison of their evil heart in anger, contention and brawling, will reap from it the unhappy fruit of eternal trouble, tribulation and anguish, Rom. ii. 8, 9.—Be content, ye peacemakers, if your souls are afraid to dwell with those that hate peace, (Ps. cxx. 6), remember that ye shall hereafter dwell forever in a peaceable habitation, Is. xxxii. 18.—

STIER:—To be only prudent and understanding does not amount to much and is a very doubtful and suspicious thing, but to be wise and prudent, that is the right thing.—Every good gift as well as true wisdom is from *above*, but that which is passed off for it with lying against the truth, all false wisdom is not from heaven, but earthly; not from the Spirit of God but human, from man's soul, flesh and blood; not from Christ the King of the kingdom of God, the destroyer of the works of the devil, but rather devilish still, from the influence and seduction of evil spirits. Indeed on this profound saying of James might be written a history of all knowledge falsely so called, of all so-called philosophy or even theology.—All the trouble and confusion in the Church, all the disorder and unruliness or rebellion of self-will opposing the Spirit of God originates in the brawling of carnality; hence schism, factions, sects, hence other evils and particularly also evil hypocrisy under coërced unity. Even in the world and in things earthly a family and many a city give unceasing testimony that good cannot mature under the influence of envy and contention, but that these conduce to nothing but evil. Still more lamentable and ravaging are the contentions concerning God's Word in the house and city of God, the carnal wrangling of brethren and members in Christ.—Many are officiously engaged in imparting to others opinions, which are their truths and in disputing away errors—but where is the good fruit of all these efforts? whom have they improved thereby, converted and won for the kingdom of heaven? On the other hand look at many quiet people in the land: they make no noise, they do not deal in great things, they walk everywhere in meekness and gentleness—but wherever they go they carry something along with them, which passes from them like a breath of life;—the words which they utter at the right time, are seeds—all their walk and work burst into fruitfulness around them with a silent, deep power, and many things are recorded on high as the fruit of their righteousness, whereof men know and suspect nothing. Grace works by them, they live in love and this is their deep power.—"*Fruits*, gentlemen, fruits that shall make men whole." It was this which the king of Prussia demanded of the University of Königsberg, and truly it was a great royal word, a Solomonic word, in its time. Wholesome, healthy fruits will grow where healthy seed has been sown, but the seed itself had before grown as the produce of ripe fruit; thus righteousness is sown and transmitted from one to another.

HEUBNER: (v. 15).—This is a description truly applicable to those who by their writings,—either immoral, provoking vice, or irreligious, undermining the faith of Christians—especially if they exhibit skill and genius, have exerted the influence of devils upon the world. The subtle and disguised ones are the worst; subtle poison insinuates itself most thoroughly.—Earthly wisdom effects nothing good for eternity.—

NEANDER:—Holy Scripture often designates, by the name of the flesh, all evil, whatever is opposed to the Spirit of God, to the Divine life. If the word is used in this general sense, it includes also man's spiritual nature, reason and the soul, as far as it has not been made subject to the Divine Spirit, but persists in its selfish being, pretends to be something by itself, independent of God, without (*extra*) God and hence opposed to Him. The term flesh in this biblical sense includes all these ideas. Its meaning is by no means restricted to what we call flesh, sensuality in the narrower sense of the word. Now if we take *flesh* in this more general sense, biblical usage distinguishes it from that which in the narrower sense is designated as psychical, *i.e.*, the spiritual [part of man], as far as it is made not to conform to God, but to conform to the world [German: "In sofern es nicht vergöttlicht ist, sondern verweltlicht."]. Reason however cultivated remains still within the sphere of the psychical [*i. e.* the rational soul not only not influenced by the Divine Spirit but rather influenced by the physical and the cosmical. The German for psychical is *seelisch*, as stated before.—M.]. The seed of whatever is truly good in action, proceeding from righteousness, can only prosper where peace reigns and with those, the end and aim of whose actions is peace. Where all is strife, nothing truly Christian can prosper.

JAKOBI (on the feast of the ingathering of the harvest):—What a description of wisdom! Truly such wisdom cometh from above, from the Father of Light with whom every thing is light, and pure and holy; thence it cometh as the best and most perfect light, communicated by Him, in whom is treasured up the fulness of all good, communicated by the Son of Eternal Wisdom and Love to all those, who renouncing earthly, human and devilish wisdom, and looking to Him alone in simplicity of faith, suffer Him to create in them a pure heart and receive a new sure spirit, the spirit of truth, which is also for this very reason the spirit of true wisdom.

PORUBSZKY:—Wisdom in action.—Envy sets us at variance 1, with God, 2, with man, 3, with ourselves.—

BECK:—Heavenly wisdom the fountain of earthly peace.

SCHMALTZ: The fire of discord.

KÖSTLIN:—Of true, Christian wisdom as contrasted with false, earthly wisdom.

ALT:—With the wisdom of Christians we will overcome the evil of time.

[v. 2. BARROW:—To *offend* originally signifies to *impinge* (*infringe*), to stumble upon somewhat lying across our way, so as thereby to be cast down, or at least to be disordered in our posture, and stopped in our progress: whence it is well transferred to our being through any incident temptation brought into sin, whereby a man is thrown down, or bowed from his upright state and interrupted from prosecuting a steady course of piety and virtue. By an opposite manner of speaking (Ps. xxxvii. 23, 24) our tenor of life is called *a way*, our conversation *walking*, our actions *steps*, our observing good laws *uprightness*, our transgression of them *tripping*, *faltering*, *falling*. By *not offending in word*, we may then conceive to be understood such a constant restraint and such a careful guidance of our tongue, that it doth not transgress the rules prescribed by the Divine law, or by good reason; that it thwarteth not the natural ends and proper uses for which it was framed, to which it is fitted; such as chiefly are promoting God's glory, our neighbour's benefit, and our own true welfare.—

— A constant governance of our speech according to duty and reason is a high instance and a special argument of a thoroughly sincere and solid goodness.—

— The offences of speech are various. 1. Some of them are committed against God, and confront piety; 2. others against our neighbour, and violate justice, charity, or peace; 3. others against ourselves, infringing sobriety, discretion, or modesty; 4. some are of a more general and abstracted nature, rambling through all matters, and crossing all the heads of duty.—

Cf. on this subject Dr. Barrow's sermon on this text; Bp. Butler on the Government of the Tongue, an abstract of which is here given; Bp. Taylor's Sermons on the Good and Evil Tongue: On Slander and Flattery; On the Duties of the Tongue.

Abstract of Butler's Sermon on the Government of the Tongue. (Bohn's edition.)

"One of the most material restraints under which virtue places us in the obligation of 'bridling the tongue.'" Let us then ask

1. What vice is opposed to this precept? and

2. When can a man be fairly said to act up to it?

1. The vice alluded to is not evil-speaking from malice, nor from selfish design. It is *talkativeness* or a disposition to talk at random without thought of doing either good or harm. Now talkative persons, when other subjects fail them, will indulge in scandal or divulge secrets; or, further, they will go on to invent matter, and all in order to engage attention; and if a quarrel ensue, they will defame and revile their enemy, but without malice.

As all our faculties may be made instruments of evil, so also the tongue. Deliberate and wilful falsehood, indulged in from malice or revenge, does not arise from having no government of the tongue. But there is a vicious habit, without malice, which arises from a desire to arrest attention; and in these people the very least thing excites the tongue, and so gives birth to innumerable evils, especially to strife. Its effects are often as bad as those of malice or envy; it wrongly distributes praise and blame, and, being used at random, always does harm.

2. In what does the government of the tongue consist? We are to measure our faculties by the end for which they have been given to us. The end of speech clearly is to communicate our thoughts to each other, either for real business or for enjoyment. In this secondary use, it contributes to promote friendship, and so is serviceable to virtue and its tendency is to general good.

Corresponding to these two uses is the abuse of speech. As to its primary end, *deceit in business* does not come within our scope. It is in its secondary sense that it becomes the object of our inquiry, for the government of the tongue relates chiefly to what we call *Conversation*. Certain cautions are to be observed in governing the tongue. First, that there is a fit time to speak and a time to keep silence. This rule is too often forgotten; and they who forget it, too often, if they amuse at all, amuse at their own expense. The times for silence are when they are in company of their superiors, or when the discourse is of subjects above themselves; and these obvious rules are generally passed over by those who in their talkative mood forget that the very essence of conversation is that it should be mutual, and talkative persons are generally disregarded. Men, then, should be silent, both when they have nothing to say, or nothing but what were better left unsaid.—

In talking on indifferent subjects, the first rule is not to spend too much time on them; the second, to be quite sure, that they *are* indifferent. Conversation about other people and their matters is often very dangerous; as in such cases we cannot always be indifferent and neutral, or escape being drawn into rivalry. But as we cannot entirely avoid speaking of others, we should take care that what we say, be true. It is important to know the characters of the bad as well as the good, and abuse will scarcely follow, if these two rules be observed: 1st, That to speak evil of a man undeservedly is worse than to speak good of him undeservedly, for the former is a direct injury to the person as well as to society. 2nd, That a good man will always speak all the good which he can of his fellows, and never any harm unless he has some positive reason for so doing; for example, just indignation against villany, or to prevent the innocent from being deceived. For we must always study justice: and we do justice to society at large by exposing bad characters.

Those who observe the above cautions and precepts have due government over their tongues. —M.].

[v. 3. WORDSWORTH:—St. James follows up the metaphor of the preceding verse with an argument *a fortiori*. We can rule irrational animals with a bit; how much more ought we to be able to govern ourselves! And if we rule our *tongues*, we do in fact govern the whole man; for the tongue is to man what a bit is to horses, and a rudder is to ships; it rules the whole; let it therefore be governed aright.—M.].

[v. 5. VIRGIL, Georgic 2, 303.

"Nam sæpe incautis pastoribus excidit ignis,
Qui furtim pingui primùm sub cortice tectus
Robora comprendit, frondesque elapsus in altas
Ingentem cœlo sonitum dedit; inde secutus
Per ramos victor, perque alta cacumina regnat
Et *totum involvit flammis nemus*; et ruit atram
Ad coelum piceâ crassus fuligine nubem;
Præsertim si tempestas à vertice sylvis
Incubuit, glomeratque ferens incendia ventus."

For the benefit of those not familiar with Latin, I subjoin Davidson's translation. The quotation itself *mutatis mutandis* forcibly illustrates the incendiary ravages of the tongue.

"For fire is often let fall from the unwary shepherds
Which at first secretly lurking under the unctuous bark,
Catches the solid wood, and shooting up into the topmost leaves,
Raises a loud crackling to heaven: thence pursuing its way,
Reigns victorious among the branches and the lofty tops,
Involves the whole grove in flames, and darts the black
Cloud to heaven, condensed in pitchy vapor;
Chiefly if a storm overhead rests its fury on the woods,
And the driving wind whirls the flames aloft."—M.].

[v. 6. WORDSWORTH:—*That world of iniquity*, that universe of mischief, as containing within it the *elements* of all mischief; as the world contains within itself mineral combustibles and volcanic fires, and electric fluid, which may blaze forth into a conflagration.

— By the faculty of speech man is distinguished from the rest of creation: by it his thoughts are borne, as upon eagles' wings, to the remotest shores, and are carried to distant ages; by it they are endued with the attributes of omnipresence and immortality; by it men are reclaimed from savage ignorance; by it cities are built and are peopled, laws promulgated, alliances formed, leagues made; by it men are excited to deeds of heroic valor, and to prefer eternity to time, and the good of their country to their own; through it the affairs of the world are transacted; it negotiates the traffic of commerce, and exchanges the produce of our soil and climate for that of another; it pleads the cause of the innocent, and checks the course of the oppressor; it gives vent to the tenderest emotions; it cheers the dreariness of life. By it virtuous deeds of men are proclaimed to the world with a trumpet's voice; by it the memory of the dead is kept alive in families. It is the teacher of arts and sciences, the interpreter of poetic visions, and of subtle theories of philosophy; it is the rudder and helm by which the state of the world is steered; it is the instrument by which the Gospel of Christ is preached to all nations, and the Scriptures sound in the ears of the Church, and the world unites in prayer and praise to the Giver of all good, and the chorus of Saints and Angels pours forth hallelujahs before His throne.

Such being the prerogatives of speech, it is a heinous sin to pervert the heavenly faculty, to insult the Name of the Giver Himself, or to injure man, made in the image of God. All true Christians will put away profane and impure language, calumny and slander, injurious to God's honour, the welfare of society, and their own eternal salvation. They will abhor it worse than pestilence, and they will pray to Him from whom are the preparations of the heart, and who maketh the dumb and the deaf, the seeing and the blind, who quickened the slow speech of His servant Moses, and put words of fire into his mouth, and whose Spirit on the Day of Pentecost descended in tongues of fire on the Apostles, and filled them with holy eloquence, so to direct their thoughts and words, that both now and hereafter they may ever sing His praise. —M.].

[v. 10. VAYIKRA RABBA: § 33:—"Rabbi Simeon, the son of Gamaliel, said to his servant Tobias, Go and bring me some *good food* from the market: the servant went and brought *tongues*. At another time, he said to the same servant, Go and buy me some *bad food*: the servant went and bought *tongues*. The master said, What is the reason that when I ordered thee to buy me *good* and *bad* food, thou didst bring *tongues?* The servant answered, From the *tongue* both *good* and *evil* come to man: if it be *good*, there is nothing *better;* if *bad*, there is nothing *worse*."—M.].

[v. 13. PYLE:—Whatever Christian convert or Jewish zealot, therefore, would be indeed a master of religious wisdom, let him show his wisdom first in the suppression of this wretched habit, and in reducing himself to a meek and charitable disposition towards his brethren.—M.].

[v. 14. BP. HALL:—Never brag vainly that ye are Christians: and do not shame and contradict that truth which ye profess, by a real denial of the profession thereof.—M.].

[v. 16. WORDSWORTH:—Strife and party-spirit would destroy Sion, and can build up nothing but Babel. Cf. Bp. Sanderson I. pp. 214, 350; and see Clemens Rom. I. capp. 3–9.—M.].

[HERBERT:—

Be calm in arguing, for *fierceness* makes
Error a fault and *truth discourtesy*:
Why should I feel another man's mistakes
More than his *sickness* or his *poverty?*
In *love* I should: but *anger* is not *love;*
Nor *wisdom* neither; therefore *gently move.*
—M.].

[—*Fortiter in re, leniter in modo.*—M.]

[On the meaning and use of the term "*wisdom from above*" see Schoettgen; illustrations:

1. SOHAR, *Yalcut Rubeni* f. 19: "*The wisdom from above* was in Adam more than in the supreme angels: and he knew all things."

2. *Sohar Chadath*, f. 35: "The angels were sent from above and taught him (*Enoch*) the *wisdom that is from above*."—Ibid. f. 42, 4. "Solomon came, and he was perfect in all things, and strongly set forth the praises of the *wisdom that is from above*."

For particular texts consult the following, besides the above:

v. 1. BP. BULL: The priest's office difficult and dangerous. Visitation Sermon. Works 1, 137.

v. 2. BARROW: Not to offend in word, an evidence of a high pitch of virtue. Works 1.

vv. 14–17. ABP. WHATELY: Party-spirit. Bampton Lecture 33.

v. 16. SOUTH: The nature, causes and consequences, of envy. Sermons, 5, 389.

v. 17. LEIGHTON: The nature and properties of heavenly wisdom. Works, 3, 86. —M.].

VII. FIFTH ADMONITION.

REFERENCE TO THE INFALLIBLE TOKEN OF AN UNSPIRITUAL (FANATICAL) MENTAL CONSTITUTION FOUNDED ON WORLDLY-MINDEDNESS, VIZ.: THE WARS AND FIGHTINGS IN THE JEWISH CHRISTIAN WORLD AND PARTICULARLY IN THE JEWISH WORLD BOTH INWARDLY AND OUTWARDLY.—THE CONSEQUENCE THEREOF: FAILURE AND FRUSTRATION OF THEIR STRIVING, THEIR MURDEROUS ENVYING, THEIR WARRING AND EVEN OF THEIR PRAYING.

CHAPTER IV. 1–3.

1 From whence *come* wars and[1] fightings among you? *come they* not hence, *even* of your
2 lusts that war in your members? Ye lust, and have not: ye kill, and desire to have, and
3 cannot obtain: ye fight and war, yet[2] ye have not, because ye ask not. Ye ask[3], and
receive not, because ye ask amiss, that ye may consume *it* upon your lusts.

Verse 1. [1] A. B. C. Cod Sin. and al. insert a second πόθεν.
Lange: Whence then [are] wars and whence fightings among you? Is it not hence: from your lusts, which [especially] wage war in your members.
[Whence *are* . . . ? Are they not . . . —M.]

Verse 2. [2] Rec. and some minuscules read δὲ after ἔχετε. A. B. G. K. οὐκ ἔχετε; C. Cod. Sin. Vulg. Griesbach and al. καὶ οὐκ ἔχετε.
Lange: Ye desire it and ye have it not, ye murder and ye strive and ye cannot obtain it; ye fight and ye make war, and ye get it not, because ye ask not.
[Ye desire and ye have not: ye commit murder and ye envy, and are not able to obtain; ye fight and make war, and ye have not, because ye ask not.—M.]

Verse 3. [3] Notice the interchange of αἰτεῖτε and αἰτεῖσθε. Cod. Sin. intensifies the last word of this sentence into καταδαπ.
Lange: Ye ask and receive it not, because ye ask illy [desirable in your interest] that ye may waste it in your lusts.
[Ye ask and receive not, because ye ask amiss, that ye may spend *it* in your lusts.—M.]

EXEGETICAL AND CRITICAL.

ANALYSIS:—See above in summary of contents. The Apostle comes now to worldly-mindedness [*i. e.* the lust of the world—M.] which lies at the bottom of the fanatical zeal of teaching and wrangling described in the preceding chapter. He began with the appearance of visionariness (ch. 1), passed on to party-spirit (ch. ii.), then portrayed fanatical striving in its outward aspect (ch. iii.) in order to come now to the inward disruptions and breaches among the readers of his Epistle and to worldly-mindedness, which is really the root from which they spring. By and by (ch. iv. 4 etc.) we shall meet it in the shape of selfishness and a bias to apostasy (ch. v.), as self-righteousness ripe unto judgment. The Apostle moreover passes more and more from the Jewish Christians to the Judaizing Christians and from these to the real Judaistic Jews themselves. *This suggests the remark that James put this Epistle into the hands of the Jewish Christians in order that it might influence all Jews, as it were,* as a missionary instruction to the converted over against the unconverted, and to the rightly-converted over against the badly-converted. Notice the rapid transition from the thought immediately preceding, viz.: that righteousness can prosper only *in peace*, to the impressive question: *πόθεν πόλεμοι*, the answer to which is contained in a second question appealing (Wiesinger) to the conscience of the readers (Huther).

VER. 1. **Whence then are wars and whence fightings?**—Not only dogmatical disputes between the teachers (Schneckenburger), or civil contentions concerning "*meum*" and "*tuum*" (de Wette). It is a true picture of the hostile dissensions of the Jewish people. Pharisees, Sadducees, Essenes, Alexandrians, Samaritans—on this basis sprung up nothing but new dissensions; believing or Christian and unbelieving Jews. The former contained as yet in the germ the opposites of Nazarenes and Ebionites, of Essene-gnostic and Pharisaic-vulgar Ebionites, the latter the shocking discord which appeared in the Jewish war and during the siege of Jerusalem. The *πόλεμοι* were the basis: *the condition of war* [warlike attitude], the *μάχαι*, single quarrels and fightings, which certainly partook occasionally of the character of skirmishes and at a later period even of battles; this is denied by Laurentius: "*non loquitur Apostolus de bellis et cædibus, sed de mutuis dissidiis, litibus, jurgiis et contentionibus.*" [Alford renders "*militate.*" To act the soldier is the real meaning of *στρατευομένων*.—M.].

Is it not hence?—The explanation; for *ἐντεῦθεν* is not a separate question: from hence? (Michaelis).

From your lusts.—*ἡδοναί* are more than *ἐπιθυμίαι* (Huther); they are desires actualized, a life of sensual indulgence (Luther: voluptuousness, *Wollüste*). These wage war chiefly *in the members.* The members need hardly be emphasized as being the camp of the lusts (Wiesinger); nor is the idea that they war against the soul (Rom. vii. 23; 1 Pet. ii. 11; de Wette) the leading idea. Theile, Schneckenburger and others rightly apply the term to the war of the lusts among themselves. Huther thinks it denotes an *inward* warfare against our fellow-men, but *ἡδοναί* would hardly be the most suitable word to bring out that idea. We might however think of the members in a restricted and in a wider sense; the members of individuals and the members of the people. From the individual Jew, whose lusts become inimically opposed in his members, the division and dissension between spiritual selfishness and vain worldly-mindedness are communicated to the members of the whole nation. Wiesinger thinks the fightings denote opposition of the *ἐπιθυμεῖν* and the *οὐκ ἔχειν*. The fruitless struggling however is only an appearance and a judgment of this fighting. It is described in four gradations: 1, desiring; 2, murdering and envying; 3, fighting and warring; 4, praying and not receiving. To the first corresponds not having, to the second not obtaining, to the third an increased not having, to the fourth an increased not receiving. The first grade denotes Judaism full of chiliastic worldly-mindedness up to the time of the New Testament. The second grade describes particularly the attitude of the Jews towards the Christians. The third grade comprises the development of the Jewish war. The fourth is mainly the history of Judaism after the destruction of Jerusalem. Such a definite mapping out of periods was of course not intended by the Apostle, but it describes the process of the development of Judaism as unfolded by history. The common construction that the reference here is either to the desire of individuals or of entire churches, and the limitation of the object of that desire to worldly riches and glory are inadequate to the prophetical relation in which James stood to his people. [Alford cites a remarkable parallel from Plato, *Phædo.* p. 66, c: *καὶ γὰρ πολέμους καὶ στάσεις καὶ μάχας οὐδὲν ἄλλο παρέχει ἢ τὸ σῶμα καὶ αἱ τούτου ἐπιθυμίαι.*—M.].

VER. 2. **Ye desire it and ye have it not.**—The indefinite object at all events is implied; in the most general sense the object of the chiliastico-judaistic longing for the world [*Weltsehnsucht, i. e.* longing for the dominion of the world—M.], in the utmost variety of form and colour, nominally the fruit of righteousness, ch. iii. 18. The antithesis pregnantly expresses the fruitlessness of the struggle. *Ye have not* has of course also the sense: ye receive not (de Wette); but it declares at the same time that they receive not, because they have not, because they are empty (Luke xix. 26). [Desire is not possession; there is many a slip between the cup and the lip. —M.].

Ye murder and ye envy.—This strong expression has induced commentators to submit various modifications of it arising from their supposition that the Apostle here addresses only Christians and refers as yet only to the internal dissensions among the members themselves. Ye kill your own soul (Oecumenius), *ye envy* (according to the conjectured reading *φθονεῖτε*, Erasmus, Calvin and many others), *ye hate* (according to the doctrine that hatred is murder in thought 1 Jno. iii. 15. Luther, Estius, Wiesinger, Huther) ye strive even to murder and death (Carpzov, Schneckenburger). Winer rightly advocates the literal sense of the term. That *ζηλοῦτε* is not mentioned first proves nothing: for the two terms are not intended to a stronger and a weaker degree of conduct, but the negative and positive sides of their conduct. They committed murder because they thought they were zealous for the glory of God. With their striving they were hunting for the fleshly ideal of the glorifying of their religion. On that account also *murder* must come first. The twelve tribes, however, who had already killed the Lord Himself and Stephen, who were in part responsible for the death of the Baptist and James the son of Zebedee, who had already shown the disposition to kill Paul, and who soon after did kill the author of the Epistle himself, had to submit to this address; the Christians among them were at least sympathizing with these national offences. But their acts of murder and strife were wholly in vain, as were afterwards the acts of the inquisition, the hierarchical judicial murders and religious wars of the zeal of the middle ages from the Crusade against the Albigenses to the Thirty years' War. Ye do not attain your terrible, hypocritical end, the Babel of conscience-monarchy in the pseudo-glory of Zion.

Ye fight and ye make war.—These words are not merely explanatory of πόλεμοι v. 1 (Huther), for the primary reference is no longer to the quarrels among the Jews themselves. Their individual words become at last open fighting, and this leads to open warfare. Hence οὐκ ἔχετε is repeated here, and, as we read with Griesbach and Lachmann, with καὶ preceding it, "and yet ye have not, *i. e.* ye get it not." We join this with what goes before in order to constitute the third antithesis, not with what follows (Huther) to introduce the specification of the cause of all their disappointments.—Not till then follows the reason, not only of the frustration of their warring, but also of their murderous striving and desiring. All lacks the true life of prayer, which purifies, hallows and adjusts our efforts to the Divine disposition of affairs. But the probable protestation of the Judaists: "we pray much," prompts the Apostle to add an ironical self-correction which brings out the fourth and most terrible antithesis. Their asking (αἰτεῖν) is evil praying (αἰτεῖσθαι. The Apostle having introduced an interchange of Active and Middle—see Winer, p. 297: Matthiä II. p. 1097.—he may here either take the Active as denoting importunate asking or the Middle as denoting egotistical praying for oneself. The latter is probably intended.), and for the reason that they pray for the help of Jehovah for a fulness of prosperity which they intend to squander in the lusts of their worldly mind. We have here to remind the reader of the visionary expectations of the Jews during the destruction of Jerusalem, of their gloomy lamentations in the post-christian synagogue (how they make God Himself weep over the unhappiness of His people) and of their vain, worldly striving and their description of the most sensual carousals in the future Kingdom of God.

DOCTRINAL AND ETHICAL.

1. It is indeed a sad contrast if we oppose the name of Christ as that of the Prince of Peace (Is. ix. 6) to the wretched quarrels and disputes of those who call themselves Christians and yet not uncommonly carry on such quarrels in His name. The question of James "Whence are wars and whence fightings among you?" may be addressed with equal pertinence to the countless sects and parties in just as many Christian communities in every age of the Church's history. The cause is really still the same now which it was in the Apostolic age, viz.: the carnal mind which exhibits the selfishness of the natural man, after he has been baptized. The Church of Christ, which ought to be a Zion of peace, has in consequence become a Babel of confusion. But the serpent-seed of discord bears even now the same unhappy fruit which it did then. The sword which the loveless man turns against his brother, wounds his own hands, and in proportion as men covet what is their neighbour's, they themselves grow poorer in true peace.

2. There is no greater enemy of the true spirit of prayer than the spirit of quarrelsomeness and contention, cf. 1 Pet. iii. 7. It is impossible to find faith where love is wanting; how then can the unbelieving prayer of an ἀνὴρ δίψυχος (cf. ch. i. 6–8) obtain any thing at the Lord's hand? Many a complaint of prayers not answered would surely cease, if men did not confine themselves to hearing their hearts only concerning the disappointment they have experienced, but would also examine their consciences concerning hidden guilt, which renders the hearing of prayer on the part of God morally impossible. Cf Is. i. 11-15.

3. Prayer in order to be well-pleasing to God must ever go hand-in-hand with a God-consecrated life. There is no greater horror in the sight of God than prayer which irreconcilably contradicts the inward and outward life. Cf. Prov. xxviii. 9; Ps. xxxiv. 16, 17.

4. The Christian is permitted to pray also for outward things, provided it be done in the spirit of absolute submission and resignation to the Divine Will, to the glory of His name and in the name of Christ. The rule Matth. vi. 33, applies also here. If this mind is wanting, prayer will not be followed by peace filling the heart, and this very want of true peace consequent upon prayer is an intimation that we need not expect the fulfilment of the desire uttered by us in prayer. Cf. *Conférences sur la prière, par* J. Martin, Paris, 1849, p. 111 etc.

5. Prayer is evil first respect of the object, if we pray for some vain, unprofitable or foolish thing; secondly in consideration of the disposition, if we pray in a vain, covetous and boisterous spirit, that is without submission and filial trust, without leaving every thing at the disposal of God. Heubner.

HOMILETICAL AND PRACTICAL.

The disputes and quarrels in the Christian Church—a great proof how little the wisdom which is from above is understood and practised, ch. iii. 16.—Every sensual and selfish lust which is not killed in the heart of the Christian, sooner or later must work disastrously to the detriment of fraternal communion.—Disappointed hopes should not fill us with bitterness and hatred against one another, but rather prompt us to humility and believing, confiding prayer.—It is not sufficient to pray only, all depends upon the manner *how* we pray and in what spirit.—God not a God of disorder, but a God of peace in all churches of the saints, cf. 1 Cor. xiv. 33.—The history of prayers that have not been heard. Examples: Deut. iii. 26; Jno. xi. 3-6; 2 Cor. xii. 8, 9 etc.—Prayer the true thermometer of the spiritual life.—He who prays illy need not expect more than he who prays not at all.—What our Lord said to Salome applies to many a praying man, Matth. xx. 22.—In prayer we must not think first and foremost of ourselves, but chiefly of the glory of God and the welfare of our neighbour.—A Christian prays not that he may bend the will of God according to his will, but in order that he may shape his will according to God's.—No prayer without work, no work without prayer.—

By caring and by fretting,
By agony and fear,
There is of God no getting,
But prayer He will hear.

Mit Sorgen und mit Grämen
Und mit selbsteigner Pein,
Lässt Gott sich gar nichts nehmen,
Es muss erbeten sein. cf. Ps. cxxvii. 1, 2.

STARKE:—Even with believers Satan attempts to bring about all manner of evil. He sows tares among the wheat, Matth. xiii. 25.

LANGII, OP.:—The wars of the world are nothing but outbreaks of the evil heart, in which the evil lusts fight against God, against man and also among themselves, Ps. cxl. 3.

CRAMER:—Many a man rakes and scrapes and strives to get everything for his own use to no purpose, and labours tooth and nail but only hinders himself therewith.

QUESNEL:—It is a great mercy of God not to hear men if they offer unjust prayers, Ps. lxvi. 18.

STIER:—It is natural that the heathen, before Christ teaches them peace, break the battle-bow (Zech. ix. 10) and live fighting and warring with one another; but where Christendom knows and confesses the name of God, peace ought surely to be there. To be sure, this so-called Christendom upon earth, inclosing (not contrary to the Divine purpose) as a net many nations, is far from being the Church of Saints, the Body of the Lord, animated and occupied by His Spirit; hence to this day bloody wars are waged even between Christian nations, and it cannot be otherwise because of righteousness against unrighteousness; the vigorous conduct of such wars is the Christian duty of rulers and ruled (kings and subjects) in the right place to which the sword put by God into hands [of lawful authority—M.] belongs. Moreover the good fight of faith must go on among Christian nations, states and churches, the sword of the spirit must be drawn against whatever is unchristian and ungodly, just as every holy man must fight for peace with the devil and with the world. But James makes no reference whatever to this good fight; he doubtless includes pure zeal for the truth in love, directed against all unrighteousness and whatever belong thereto in word or deed, in the peace in which the fruit of righteousness should be sown (ch. iii. 18). But for all, enough remains for this cutting question: "Whence are wars and whence are fightings among you, quarrelling and discord in word and deed among brethren and members of the Church of God, evil wars on a small scale like those without among the nations?"

JAKOBI:—Do not even desire that which cannot benefit thee in things pertaining to God, and whatever thou dost desire, desire it only in as far as it furthers thy eternal salvation. But if thou prayest only in order to have and to enjoy, if thou openest communication with God only in order to receive or as it were to extort from Him worldly gifts, thou dost indeed draw nigh to Him with thy mouth and serve Him with thy lips, but thy heart is far from Him.

NEANDER:—James like Paul here presupposes an inward conflict in man, the conflict between flesh and spirit. As Paul calls the powers of evil the law in the members, because the body is the outward manifestation of man and because the dominion of sinful desires exhibits itself on and in the body, so James speaks of the lusts that war in the members.

VIEDEBANDT:—The real trouble-states (*Störenfriede*=disturbers of peace) in the world are seated deep in the hearts of men—the worldly lusts.—Peace *among* men is the consequence of peace *in* men.—Who carries his point among men by quarrelling, is always the loser no matter how much he may gain besides, for he loses with God.—There is relatively little praying in the world and besides, much of that little is evil praying.—Most men desire the gifts of God, not God Himself.—Envy seeks quarrel and quarrel brings woe.—We find often many obstacles in the way by our desires. Why? Because self-will and pride present obstacles to Divine help.

LISCO:—The sinful lusts.—The dissensions of worldly life.—The nature and consequence of lusts.

PORUBSZKY:—The deepest root of all strife.

[v. 1. Harmony ought to reign in the members (ἐν τοῖς μέλεσιν. The word μέλος signifies 1. a limb, a member; 2. a song and then the music to which a song is set, an air, a tune, a melody. ἐν μέλει, in tune, harmoniously. The Greek word μέλος would suggest the double idea of member and harmony to a Greek ear and I cannot but consider the selection of the word to have contemplated such an allusion), but now they exhibit strife and discord, the confusion of the camp and the violence of an armed soldiery. The lusts act the part of soldiers (στρατευομένων), they are not only encamped within us and foraging (Alford), but they are acting the part of soldiers, engaging in all the offices of military service.—M.].

[v. 2. φονεύετε. This was especially true of those bands of λῃσταὶ, *sicarii*, robbers and assassins, who, under the name of *zealots*, infested Jewish society at this time, and at last made the Temple itself a den of assassins. See Matth. xxi. 13. Evidences of the blood-thirsty spirit of rage, which now like a fiend possessed the heart of large numbers of the people, may be seen in the murderous plots and violent and frequent outbreaks at this period, mentioned in Josephus (see below), and in the Gospel and Acts, such as that of Barabbas (Matth. xxvii. 16; Jno. xviii. 40), and of Judas of Galilee, and Theudas (Acts v. 36), and the Egyptian (Acts xxi. 38), and the conspiracy against St. Paul (Acts xxiii. 12–14). There may also be a reference here to the cry of the multitude assembled from all parts of the Jewish dispersions at the Passover, "*Crucify Him*" (Matth. xv. 13, 14). Wordsworth.—M.].

[Whitby cites the following passages from Josephus. *Bell. Jud.* IV. 10; II. 1; *Antiq.* XVIII. 1; *Bell. Jud.* II. 23; VII. 31; I. 705.—M.].

VIII. SIXTH ADMONITION.

EXHORTATION TO REPENTANCE ADDRESSED TO THE JEWISH CHRISTIANS AND THE JEWS IN REFERENCE TO THEIR BEING ON THE WAY TO APOSTASY. THEY ARE ADDRESSED AS (RELIGIOUS) ADULTERERS AND ADULTERESSES, AS APOSTATES. THEIR FRIENDSHIP OF THE WORLD, WHICH IS THE CAUSE OF THEIR IMPENDING APOSTASY, THEY WERE TO ACKNOWLEDGE AS ENMITY OF GOD, TO REPENT OF IT AND TO RETURN FROM THEIR WORLDLY RUNNING AND WANDERING TO THE QUIETNESS OF A CONDUCT MARKED BY HUMILITY AND RESIGNATION TO THE DIVINE WILL.

Chapter IV. 4–17.

4 Ye adulterers[1] and adulteresses, know ye not that the friendship of the world[2] is
enmity with God[3] whosoever[4] therefore will be a friend of the world is the enemy[5] of
5 God. Do ye think that the Scripture saith in vain,[6] The spirit that dwelleth in us
6 lusteth to envy? But he giveth more grace. Wherefore he saith, God resisteth the
7 proud, but giveth grace unto the humble. Submit yourselves therefore to God.
8 Resist[7] the devil, and he will flee from you. Draw nigh to God, and he will draw
nigh to you. Cleanse *your* hands, *ye* sinners; and purify *your* hearts, *ye* double-
9 minded. Be afflicted, and mourn, and[8] weep: let your laughter be turned to mourning,
10 and *your* joy to heaviness. Humble yourselves in the sight of the[9] Lord, and he shall
11 lift you up. Speak not evil one of another, brethren. He that speaketh evil of his
brother, and[10] judgeth his brother, speaketh evil of the law, and judgeth the law:
12 but if thou judge the law, thou art not a doer of the law, but a judge. There is one
lawgiver,[11] who is able to save and to destroy: who art thou[12] that judgest another?[13]
13 Go to now, ye that say, To day or[14] to morrow we will go[15] into such a city, and
14 continue[16] there[17] a year,[18] and buy and sell, and get gain: Whereas ye know not
what[19] *shall be* on the morrow. For what *is* your life?[20] It is[21] even a vapour, that
15 appeareth for a little time, and[22] then vanisheth away. For that ye *ought* to say, If
16 the Lord will,[23] we shall live,[24] and do this, or that. But now ye rejoice[25] in your
17 boastings: all[26] such rejoicing is evil. Therefore to him that knoweth to do[27] good,
and doeth *it* not, to him it is sin.

Verse 4 [1] A. B. Sin. etc. Vulg., Bede, Lachmann, Tischendorf and other translations read only μοιχαλίδες. μοιχοί preceding it in G. K. etc. originated probably in the O. T. symbolical sense having been abandoned and the literal sense adopted.

[2] Cod. Sin. inserts τούτου after κόσμου.

[3] Cod. Sin. reads ἔστι τῷ θεῷ for τοῦ θεοῦ ἐστιν of Rec. and al.

[[4] B. Cod. Sin. read ἐὰν for ἄν.—M.]

[[5] Cod. Sin. has ἐχθρὰ for ἐχθρὸς.—M.]

Lange: Ye [adulterers and] adulteresses know ye not that the friendship of the world is the enmity of God? Whosoever therefore willeth to be a friend of the world, standeth up as an enemy of God.

[Ye adulteresses .... is enmity of God? .... shall be minded (Alford) to be a friend of the world, is constituted an enemy of God.—M.]

Verse 5 [6] A. B. Sin. Lachmann, Wiesinger read κατῴκισεν for κατῴκησεν G. K. etc.

Lange: Or do ye suppose .... The spirit that made His abode in us, as opposed to envy, longeth upward?

[Or do ye fancy .... The spirit that He planted in us, jealously desireth? (So de Wette, and after him Alford).—M.]

Verse 6. Lange: Still greater however [than is the longing], He giveth grace: wherefore it [the Scripture] saith ...

[But He giveth greater grace: wherefore He saith, God is opposed to the proud but giveth grace to the humble.—M.]

Verse 7. [7] A. B. Sin. Vulg. etc. insert δέ after the verb. δέ is omitted probably in order to give to the sentence a more independent form.

Lange: Subject yourselves .... But resist ....

[Submit yourselves .... But resist the devil and he shall flee from you.—M.]

Verse 8. Lange: .... Cleanse the hands, ye sinners, and consecrate [make chaste unto God] the hearts, ye double minded.

[Purify your hands ...., and make chaste your hearts.—M.]

Verse 9. [8 A. and Cod. Sin. omit καὶ before κλαύσατε.—M.]

Lange: Feel miserable and mourn and weep! Let your laughter turn itself into lamentation and your joy into dejectedness.

[Be wretched and mourn and weep: ...., and your joy into humiliation.

[Alford: The old English noun *downcast*, now obsolete as a noun, is the exact equivalent of κατήφεια and ought to be resuscitated.—M.]

Verse 10. [9 Cod. Sin. inserts οὖν after ταπεινώθητε.—M.]

The omission of τοῦ does not affect the translation. [A. B. K. etc. Cod. Sin. omit it.—M.]

Lange: ..... before the Lord, and He will exalt you.

[Be humbled, therefore, before .... and He shall exalt you.—M.]

Verse 11. 10 A. B. K. Sin. etc. Tischendorf read ἢ κρίνων for καὶ [Rec. etc.—M.]

Lange: Do not calumniate [decry] one another, brethren. He that calumniateth or judgeth his brother, calumniateth the law and judgeth the law.

[Do not speak against one another, brethren; he that speaketh against a brother or judgeth his brother, speaketh against .... M.]

Verse 12. 11 καὶ κριτής omitted by Rec. [with K. L. etc.—M.], is inserted in A. B., many minuscules, almost all the versions, Tischend. Lachm. also Cod. Sin.

[17 A. B. K. L. many minusc. Cod. Sin. Vulg. Syr. Copt. al. insert δὲ after σύ, a reading by all means to be retained on account of the strong emphasis "But *thou* (almost contemptuous), who *art* thou?"—M.]

13 A. B. Cod. Sin. and many minuscules fix the readings ὁ κρίνων and τὸν πλησίον against those of Rec. ὃς κρίνεις, and τὸν ἕτερον.

[K. adds (see Ps. xxxvi. 23) ὅτι οὐκ ἐν ἀνθρώπῳ ἀλλ' ἐν θεῷ τὰ διαβήματα ἀνθρώπου κατευθύνεται—M.]

Lange: One is the Lawgiver and Judge, He, who is able ......But who art thou, thou that judgest [art judging] thy neighbour? [.... But thou. who art thou that judgest thy neighbour?—M.]

Verse 13. 14 A. G. I. etc. Tischendorf [Cod. Sin. Alford.—M.] read σήμερον καὶ αὔριον, which is also more authentic and important than ἢ αὔριον.

15 Lachmann and Tischendorf following B. etc., several minusc. Vulg., read the Future for the Subjuntive of Rec. In point of matter more suitable. A. has first two Subjunctives then two Indicates. [So Cod. Sin.—M.]

[16 A. B. Alford ἐμπορευσόμεθα καὶ κερδήσομεν. K. L. Subjunctive.—M.]

[17 A. omits ἐκεῖ.—M.]

18 B. and Lachmann omit ἕνα, but the omission is not decisive.

Lange: Well then, ye that say: to-day and to-morrow we will journey to such and such a city, and will work there one year, and do business and make gain.

[Go to now .... to-day and to-morrow we will set forth to this city and will spend there one year and will traffic [de Wette, Van Ess, Allioli etc. Alford] and get gain.—M.]

Verse 14. 19 The Plural τὰ (A. Lachmann) is in every case more telling than τὸ (G. I.) Tischendorf.

20 Lachmann, following A. Vulg. etc. omits γὰρ after ἀτμίς, which makes the expression more difficult, but also more lively. [But A. Cod. Sin. Vulg. Copt. omit not only γὰρ but ἀτμὶς γάρ.—M.]

21 ἐστε is fixed by A. B. I. etc.

22 A. B. etc. read καὶ for δέ [Rec. Vulg. Æth. Bede put καὶ before ἔπειτα: Cod. Sin. agrees with A. ἔπειτα καὶ is accordingly the most authentic reading.—M.]

Lange: Yes ye that know not [understand not] what will be to-morrow [the great tempests of judgment]. For what [of what kind] is your life? A vapour, forsooth, ye are, which appeareth for a little while, and then vanisheth [again].

[Whereas ye know not the things of to-morrow: for of what sort (Alford) is your life? For ye are a vapour which appeareth for a little while, then vanishing as it came.—M.]

Verse 15. 23 [B. reads θέλῃ.—M.]

24 A. B. Cod. Sin. read ζήσομεν and ποιήσομεν. So Lachmann, Tischendorf [and Alford. K. L al. have the Subjunctive.—M.]

Lange: Instead of that you ought to say ....

[Instead of which ye .... we shall both live and do this or that.—M.]

Verse 16. [25 Cod. Sin. has κατακαυχᾶσθε for καυχᾶσθε.—M.]

[26 Cod. Sin. has ἅπασα for πᾶσα—M.]

Lange: But now ye boast yourselves in your [vain] illusions, all boasting of such kind is evil.

[But now ye glory in your vain-boastings: all such glorying is wicked.—M.]

Verse 17. [27 (A.) reads ποιῆσαι for ποιεῖν.—M.]

Lange: To him now who knoweth ...., to him it will turn to sin.

[So that to him who ...., to him it is sin.—M.]

EXEGETICAL AND CRITICAL.

Analysis:—Reproach of the impending apostasy, v. 4.—Exhortation to a better and higher aim, vv. 5, 6.—The characteristics of their conversion to God on theocratic fundamental ideas (the new allegiance of the people of God, their purification, penitential mourning, and humiliation according to their situation) vv. 7–10.—Renovation of their conduct towards the brethren, vv. 11, 12.—Dissuasion from their restless, gain-seeking and self-willed wandering through the world in consideration of the approaching storm of judgment vv. 13–15.—Reproof of their false security and forewarning of their conscience. vv. 16, 17.

Reproach of the impending apostasy.

Ver. 4. **Ye adulteresses, know ye not.**—The fact, that the majority of commentators are in favour of the Text. Rec., the authorities to the contrary notwithstanding, and that they consequently read; "ye adulterers and adulteresses," is rightly accounted for by Huther, who says that it arises from their taking the term in a literal sense, "which is expressly done by Augusti, Lachmann and Winer." But we can hardly conceive any thing more extravagant than to suppose that James would brand all Jewish Christians as literal adulterers and adulteresses. It is however in perfect keeping with the symbolical language of the Old Testament that James here describes the Judaistic bias to apostasy from the living God of revelation, Ps. lxxiii. 27; Is. lvii. 3; Ez. xxiii. 27; Hosea; Matth. xii. 39; xvi. 4; 2 Cor. xi. 2; Rev. ii. 22 The wonder is that this passage has not led commentators to learn the symbolical character of the whole Epistle, and more particularly the symbolical character of the rich in ch. ii and ch. v. The only suprising part of this exposition is the occurrence of the feminine *adulteresses*, a term which Theile considers to be not altogether fitting, which Wiesinger calls singular as applied to individuals, while Huther remarks that the term should be referred to Churches. Besides it is noteworthy that symbolical adultery according to the usage of the Old Testament and according to the figure itself is feminine inasmuch as it describes the apostasy of the Lord's bride. To this must be added that the Apostle is not addressing now the Jewish Christian Churches in particular, but Judaism in general, such as, in the preceding section, he saw it sundered into the most diverse factions. The Plural probably denotes this disruption, not only the several synagogues but also the several factions.

Know ye not.—From your theocratical calling to the covenant with God as opposed to the ungodly world, and from your teaching and knowledge.

That the friendship of the world.—That is befriending and alliance with an ungodly world (ch. i. 27; cf. 1 Jno. ii. 15), not merely inclination to wordly goods (Theile and al.), nor worldly desires (Laurentius), nor both of these together (de Wette). The world is personified in this antithesis; it is idolatry depicted as a whole, the vanity of mankind deifying itself and deified (*i. e.*, ungodliness showing itself in its propensity for the impersonal) connected with the whole visible world frustrated by it. The Judaistic friendship for the world, which must be taken chiefly in an active sense, consisted just in the chiliastic desire of enjoying a worldly glory which at the best was only dyed hierarchically pious (in sensual enjoyment, honour and dominion cf. Matth. iv.). It is to be noticed that this vain worldliness concealed itself under the garb of a pious fleeing from the world (the hatred of heathenism, even of Gentile-christian, pretended uncleanness).

Is enmity of God.—Here also the predominant active sense must be held fast "on which account the majority of commentators interpret it straightway by ἔχθρα εἰς θεόν (Rom. viii. 7)" Huther. Lachmann following the *inimica* of the Vulgate, has even adopted the reading ἐχθρὰ [which, however, is also the reading of the Cod. Sin.—M.], which greatly weakens the weight of the idea.

Whoever therefore shall be minded to be a friend of the world.—Inference drawn from what precedes. Ὃς βουληθῇ. The difficulty which has been found in this expression, because it seems to involve an intentional choice of evil, is set aside if we distinguish between a formal and a material intention. The Apostle certainly could not suppose his readers to have the formal intention of surrendering to the world. But it was very different with the material intention of taking a direction in worldliness which involved the friendship of the world. But this was precisely the case with the rebellious chiliasm of the Jews, even with the worldly-mindedness of Judaistic Christians. And in this sense the term certainly lays stress both on the conscious intention (Baumgarten) and on the antithesis of their doing which had already become a reality. Whosoever is devoted to the world, although as yet only in his heart (not, as Wiesinger, who for the present is only inclined that way), has stood up as the enemy of God, because our attitude to God is determined by the attitude of our heart. The Lord looketh at the heart. Huther's laying stress on the construction that the world mus be taken here as an aggregate of persons, because φιλία then consists in a reciprocity, seems to be an expedient beside the mark. That the world is represented as an aggregate of persons stands to reason; but the question is whether the persons are to be honoured as persons or dishonoured as impersonal things as a means of selfishness. However he rightly observes that καθίσταται here as in ch. iii. 6, must not be weakened, but denotes "he takes the attitude." We render "he stands up," or "appears," because this brings out the as yet inward character of his attitude. [On the whole "is constituted" seems to be the best rendering of the term in English; it does not touch the inward or the outward attitude in particular but involves either and this seems really to be the Apostle's meaning. It is immaterial whether the man's purpose be latent, uttered in words or manifest in deeds, in any case he is constituted an enemy of God.—M.].

Exhortation to a better and higher aim, vv. 5, 6.

VER. 5. **Or do ye fancy that the Scripture saith in vain.**—This passage is one of the most difficult in the New Testament; we must therefore refer the reader to the Commentaries for a full discussion of the question (see Schneckenburger, *Beiträge*, p. 193: Huther, Wiesinger, etc.). We have first to set aside the really desperate expositions which aim at improving the text (see Huther's note p. 166) and then the connection of πρὸς φθόνον with what goes before. The Scripture saith against envy (du Mont), or: Think ye that the Scripture speaks in vain and *enviously* (πρὸς φθόνον adverbially, Gebser)? But in that case πρὸς φθόνον ought to precede λέγει. We consider the exposition of Beza, Grotius and al.: "The spirit of man has a natural bias to envy" as underrated by Huther. In that case the words have to be connected with what the Scripture says of the envy of Cain, and similar passages. But that exposition is inadmissible, for 1. The spirit is described as having taken up its abode in us and consequently distinguished from ourselves, 2. μείζονα κ. τ. λ. would be without a subject. The first difficulty, indeed, would be obviated if we could take πνεῦμα in the sense of πνεῦμα φθόνου according to Wisd. 2, 24.= διάβολος. Huther undervalues the similar exposition of Semler ad. v. 7, saying, "because of its strangeness we make room for Semler's note on this passage: *Jacobus, Paulus, Petrus, Judas uno quasi ore id confirmant, opus esse, ut Romanis et sic* (*!*) *Deo se subjiciant*" and further on: "*τῷ διαβόλῳ, qui per πνεῦμα φθόνου vos suscitat adversus magistratum romanum.*" But the want of a subject to μείζονα deters us from adopting this exposition somewhat as follows: even the Holy Scripture testifies that there has come among us a spirit which excites that envy which is the specific attribute of that love of the world which causes the wars and fightings described above (see the book of Jonah). Less tenable is the exposition which makes the spirit to denote the Divine Spirit but takes the respective words interrogatively, as follows, "*num ad invidiam proclivis est Spiritus Sanctus? minime*" (so Gabler and similarly Bede, Calvin and al.). Where the citation from Holy Writ introduces the subject, we hardly expect an interrogative sentence. The interpretation of de Wette, Huther and al. is at present urged more than any other. Huther: "Or do ye think that the Scripture speaks in vain? (No) the Spirit, that has taken His abode in us, enviously desires us, but gives (so much the) more grace; therefore He saith," etc.—The parentheses abundantly show how very forced is this interpretation, which is also advocated by Schneckenburger and al. Our objections to it are as follows: 1. The anthropomorphism "that the Spirit of God loves us even unto envy" is too strong. The reference to ζῆλος, the jealousy of God in the conjugal relation He sustains to His people, is allowable but ζῆλος is not φθόνος, which is uniformly mentioned in Holy Scripture as a source of evil. To this must be added 2. The postulated supplements and the defective antithesis "but He gives so much the more grace," etc. But this mode of expression at first sight grows even more dark, if we understand with Wiesinger τὸ πνεῦμα as the object of the human spirit, supplying ὁ θεός as the subject: Divine Love enviously desires the object of its Love, that is, the human spirit from God (*i. e.*, aus Gott=emanating from God—M.], which turns either to God or to the world. If we bear in mind that θεός had been named immediately before, the envious loving remains in the first place, and then appears as a loving which is only directed to the Spirit. This applies also to the similar interpretation of Theile, who supplies however ἡ γραφή instead of ὁ θεός. However, even if we wished to retain the interpretation of Wiesinger or Huther we should be obliged to go back to the passage Ex. xx. 5. The jealousy of God would be expressed in His visiting the iniquity of idolatry (=adultery) on the children of the third and fourth generation, and the antithesis "but showing mercy unto thousands, etc.," would be adequately expressed in μείζονα δὲ δίδωσι χάριν. With reference to the citation in question, we have the following conjectures which we give in brief from Huther: Gen. vi. 3, 5 (Grotius), Gen. viii. 21 (Erasmus, Beza, etc.), Numb. xi. 29 (Witsius), Deut. v. 9 (Schneckenburger), Deut. xxxii. 21 (Heisen), Ps. cxix. 20 (Clericus), Prov. xxi. 10 (Michaelis), Song of Solomon viii. 6 (Coccejus), Wisdom of Sol. vi. 12 (Wettstein). Others again have guessed at passages from the New Testament, at some lost passage in the prophets, at a passage in the Apocryphal book called the Testament of the twelve Patriarchs or at a collective statement of different passages of Holy Scripture. Huther denies the fact of a citation altogether and believes the reference to be to a statement of James and that ἡ γραφὴ λέγει adverts either to the idea immediately preceding or to the citation introduced with διὸ λέγει in v. 6: ὁ θεός, etc. After all the interpretations given, that of Luther (Gomarus, Bengel and al.) still continues to possess much weight, viz., "the spirit lusteth against hatred=invidia," (cf. Gal. v. 17); in favour of which may be produced the following passages: Ps. xxxvii. 1, etc.; v. 34, etc.; Ps. lxxiii. 3, etc. Huther can hardly dispute successfully that πρὸς φθόνον in point of language may be equivalent to κατὰ φθόνον and that ἐπιποθεῖν may be taken in the sense of ἐπιθυμεῖν. But we still want the subject for μείζονα δὲ κ. τ. λ. and we are driven to recognize it in πνεῦμα itself. Then it is the Divine Spirit in believers on the one hand, mediating in them a longing going beyond the love of the world (Rom. viii. 23–26), and on the other also a grace which is beyond all longing, praying and understanding (1 Cor. ii. 9; Eph. iii. 22). We therefore construe the passage with reference to Ps. xxxvii. 1 and Ps. lxxiii. 3 as follows: "over against and opposed to envy (which is really at the bottom of your worldliness and is the very soul of your wars, fightings and insurrections) the Spirit who took abode among us, utters a higher longing (ἐπιποθεῖ emphatic), and not in vain; for the self-same Spirit mediates also the grace which goes even beyond our longing in Him." The Jews in consequence of the envy of their worldliness became unbelieving with respect to Christianity (Acts xiii. 45; ch. xxii. 22), and rebellious toward the Romans; but the spirit which lived and acted in the true theocrats from Abel to Asaph (Ps. lxxiii.) and from him and the prophets to the Christians, coming in contact with it [envy?—M.] was longing beyond it and its objects for the immortal. And as envy shows itself in the proud whom God opposes, so that longing shows itself in the humble to whom He gives grace. We therefore give our sense of this passage by way of paraphrase. The friendship of the world of which envy is really the soul, and the friendship of God, of which the longing of the Spirit is really the soul are incompatibles and inimically opposed to each other. This may be proved from Scripture. For as to our relation to God it says not without reason that the strong longing of the Divine Spirit, who took up His abode in us (who united with our spirit, is the spirit of prayer, of our yearning for heavenly riches; while as the Spirit of Divine consolation and peace He mediates for us a grace which is even greater than our longing), bids defiance to and is opposed to envy which is the truest form of the spirit of the world. But as to the relation of God to ourselves, the Scripture saith: God resists the haughty and proud who are at one with the spirit of envy, while He gives grace to the humble who are at one with the poor in spirit. On the meaning of πρός=in *relation* or in *proportion to*, or *against*, in *opposition to* cf. the Lexica. The sentence, more clearly defined, would read thus: πρὸς τὸ ποθεῖν τοῦ φθόνον ἐπιποθεῖ τὸ πνεῦμα.—The Comparative "greater (more) grace" must consequently not be referred to the antithesis: what the friendship of the world does give (Bede, Gebser and al.), or: "*eo majorem, quo longius recesseris ab invidia*" (Bengel), or according to an obscure thought: as compared with the case that the πρὸς φθόνον ἐπιποθεῖν did not take place (Wiesinger, de Wette, Huther).

[Without reconsidering this bewildering conflict of opinions, the view which seems to harmonize best with the context and the line of James' argument, is to take πνεῦμα as the *object*, and understanding the Holy Spirit, to supply ὁ Θεός as the *subject* and to render πρὸς φθόνον adverbially. "The (Holy) Spirit that He (God) planted in us, jealously desireth [us]." The expression is highly figurative and alludes to the conjugal relation between God and the soul of believers. The Spirit of God implanted in us, jealously desireth us, jealously desires us to break entirely with the world and to be wholly consecrated and devoted to God. Any temporizing with the world would be spiritual adultery.—Then as to the citation from Scripture referred to we hold with many commentators that James gives the general sense of Scripture without specifying a particular passage. Alford takes the same view. —M.].

VER. 6. This greater grace is the greater measure of the comforting and satisfying Spirit as related to the longing Spirit. *διὸ λέγει*, that is the same Scripture, not *τὸ πνεῦμα*. [But why not refer *διὸ λέγει* to *τὸ πνεῦμα* the Holy Spirit? He speaks in us and in the Holy Scriptures—M.]. *διὸ* is very apposite: just as the Scripture speaks of our relation to God, so it speaks of God's relation to us. The passage in question is Prov. iii. 34 LXX., which has however *ὁ κύριος* instead of *ὁ Θεός*. [The same variation occurs in 1 Pet. v. 5.—M.]. *Ὑπερήφανοι* (not exactly equivalent to the idea *τὰ ὑψηλὰ φρονοῦντες* in Rom. xii. 16) are the same as the rich in ch. v. 1 etc. or in the Sermon on the Mount, Luke vi. 24 etc. In like manner the *ταπεινοί* represent the poor, the lowly, the wretched in a symbolical sense, so much comforted in the Old Testament, or the poor in spirit, the suffering, the meek and the merciful of the Sermon on the Mount.

The characteristics of conversion to God required of the readers of the Epistle, or theocratic fundamental ideas.—The new allegiance of the people of God. Their approach, purification, penitential mourning and humiliation according to their situation. vv. 7–10.

VER. 7. **Subject yourselves therefore to God.**—Now follows a series of theocratic ideas in the process of the New Testament fulfilment or completion, which significantly reflect in consecutive order the several moments of Jewish conversion; a circumstance which seems to be not sufficiently noticed by Exegesis. *Subject* yourselves to God; become once more His real subjects, as the people of God, in opposition to your leaning to apostasy. This is the first and the whole, an exhortation not exclusively addressed to the decided *ὑπερήφανοι*. Calvin emphasizes the circumstance that the reference is not to obedience to God in general, but to *submissio* in particular. Semler indeed maintained that they were exhorted "*ut Romanis se subjiciant, et sic Deo,*" but it is rather the reverse; they were first to subject themselves to God and then in consequence of it, to the power appointed to rule them. Their submission to the rule of the living God was moreover to exhibit itself in their humbly getting reconciled to the new order of things, the change of Judaism into Christianity, the unity of Jews and Gentiles in Christianity and the existing rule of pagan Rome.

But resist the devil.—Not only because he is the enemy of God and the prince of this world, by the attractions of which they suffer themselves to be enticed, but especially because he is the demon of self-boasting and envy, who assumes the garb of an angel of light, and desires them by representing that his temptation to sedition is a call from God, ch. i. 13.—Being only half-decided and doubting make the tempter bold and strong, while resolute courage in God and resistance unmask him in his impotence; for real courage and real power come from God; the power of Satan is a lying phantom-power (Matth. iv.). It is only in the self-temptation of man that the temptation of Satan can become efficient. [Huther quotes Hermas, *Pastor*, 2, 12.—"*δύναται ὁ διάβολος παλαῖσαι, καταπαλαῖσαι δὲ οὐ δύναται, ἐὰν οὖν ἀντίστῃς αὐτόν, νικηθεὶς φεύξεται ἀπὸ σοῦ κατῃσχυμμένος.*"—M.].

Draw nigh to God.—The allegiance of the people of God is followed by their drawing near to Him. נָגַשׁ or קָרַב in relation to God is a specifically theocratical idea. Ex. xx. 21; xxiv. 2; Lev. xvi. 1; Ezek. xl. 46; cf. Is. xxix. 13; Heb. vii. 19; hence the expression *Korban*, that which is consecrated or offered to God. Here drawing near is used in the N. T. real sense=convert yourselves. The particular although not the exclusive reference to prayer.

And He will draw nigh to you.—The antithesis "Resist the devil and he shall flee from you" corresponds to the antithesis "Draw nigh to God and He will draw nigh to you." (See 2 Chron. xv. 2; Is. lvii. 15; Zech. i. 3).

VER. 8. **Cleanse the hands, ye sinners.**—The first specifically theocratic act. The expression refers to the Levitical purifications, the negative part of Levitical repentance, separateness from the world. The prophets did already apply this symbolical purification to ethical purification or rather interpret it ethically according to its profound import. See Is. i. 15, 16; Ps. xviii. 21; xxiv. 4; "He that hath clean hands and a pure heart." The hands are the organ and symbol of ethical actions. To cleanse the hands signifies therefore to repent (Pott), to become separate from evil works, especially from lovelessness and wrong. This summons does not begin the summons to conversion (Huther), for it is already implied in the words "Subject yourselves to God," which branch out into two moments, the negative "to resist the devil," and the positive "to draw nigh to God." This approach to God, in its turn, branches out into purification and sanctification in the narrow sense.

Consecrate your hearts.—The real consecration of our life to God consists in the consecration of the heart, in its surrender to God (Ps li. 12, 18, 19; Prov. xxiii. 26; Jer. xxxi. 33; 1 Pet. iii. 15 etc.). The words "ye sinners" relate to the cleansing of the hands, the words "ye double-minded" to the consecration of the heart. The term *ἁγνίσατε* probably alludes more particularly to the unchastity of the heart, as the source of religious adultery. Wavering and unchastity are here alike, so are on the other hand simplicity or decision and chastity.—They are *sinners* in a particular sense according to theocratic ideas, as far as they are about to excommunicate themselves by their evil actions (ch. ii. 3), to burden themselves with the ban of the real congregation of God (publicans and sinners=those who are liable to the discipline of the synagogue); but the reason lies in this double-mindedness, their wavering (ch. i. 7, 8), their mischievous halting between God and the world, between Christianity and apostasy. Calvin's note is almost superfluous: "*non duo hominum genera designat, sed eosdem vocat peccatores et duplices animo.*" It is evident from vv. 6 and 8 that this exhortation to their own self-activity presupposes the grace of God as the source of strength.

VER. 9. **Feel miserable and mourn.**—Hardly limited to the mourning which introduces and accompanies the repentance of individuals; the type is found in the Old Testament extraordinary acts of penitence which in situations of uncommon offences and peril were performed to complete the ordinary acts of penitence, viz. purifications and consecrations or offerings, Ex. xxxiii. 4; Judg. ii. 4; Ch. xxi. 2; 1 Sam. vii. 6 etc.—The verb ταλαιπωρεῖν (ἅπαξ λεγ. in N. T.; the adjective form in Rom. vii. 24; Rev. iii. 17; the noun Rom. iii. 16; Jas. v. 1), denotes primarily to go outwardly through hard work, to endure hardship or distress, then the inward sense of misery on account of outward or inward wretchedness. Grotius and Roman Catholic theologians apply it without reason to castigations. Jewish fasting and other castigations as symbols of penitential sorrow are indeed the type, but Christian penitential sorrow must not be changed back into legal symbolism.

Mourn and weep.—See Neh. viii. 9; Mark xvi. 10; Luke vi. 25; Rev. xviii. 15, 19. The putting on of mourning-apparel or sitting in sackcloth and ashes (Grotius) can only be the type of the Gospel requirement of inward mourning (2 Cor. vii. 10).

Let your laughter be turned.—Is. lxv. 13; Luke vi. 25. "James passes from the outward manifestation (γέλως-πένθος) to the inward state (χαρά—κατήφεια)." Huther.—κατήφεια, casting down of the eyes, literally and figuratively. Hence shame and humiliation, ἅπαξ λεγ., Luke xviii. 13.

VER. 10. **Humble yourselves before the Lord.**—The fundamental idea of the leadings of the Old Testament and the O. T. fundamental rule of piety and of the promises attached to it; it has met its fulfilment in the humiliation and exaltation of Christ and must be realized in the life of believers (Rom. vi. 4; Job v. 11; Ezek. xxi. 26; Matth. xxiii. 12; Luke xiv. 11; 1 Pet. v. 6; cf. Sir. ii. 17). As this humbling must be realized inwardly in the bowing of repentance before God (ἐνώπιον κυρίου), and outwardly in the patient enduring of the humiliating state of servitude and lowliness (ὑπὸ τὴν χεῖρα τοῦ θεοῦ, i. Pet. v. 6) appointed by Him, so the exaltation also should begin with the inward consciousness of the exaltation, liberty and glory of the Divine Sonship [*i. e.* the state of being the children of God in Christ=*Gotteskindschaft*; υἱοθεσία, adoption—M.] and come to its outward consummation in the future glory, of which we have however some antepast here on earth. κύριος does not exactly signify Christ (Grotius), nor θεός as opposed to Christ (Huther and al.). James wants to see the living God of revelation recognized in Christ.

Renovation of their conduct towards the brethren. vv. 11, 12.

VER. 11. **Do not calumniate one another, brethren.**—Huther thinks that this exhortation, couched in a milder form than the preceding and exhibiting a contrast in the address, ἀδελφοί being opposed to μοιχαλίδες, ἁμαρτωλοί δίψυχοι, intimates that James now addresses, at least primarily, another class of persons, namely those "who by the worldly ways of the former felt induced to do those things against which he exhorts them." But Wiesinger takes a more correct view as the transition: "The connection is as follows: if they thus humble themselves before God, they must not deny humility in the judgment they pass on their brethren. He therefore exhorts them to put away imaginary superiority to others in judging them, which is really an arrogant usurping of the judicial functions of God. The end corresponds to the beginning. Worldly pride the source of strife, humble submission to God the end thereof." He adds however "he refers particularly to the oppressed." But really there is no reason to see here already a distinct transition from one class to another. Slander and judging were the very soul of their fanatical doings in relation to their brethren. In ch. iii. 1 also he addresses the brethren, although the sequel contains the severest kind of reprimand. καταλαλεῖν found here and 1 Pet. ii. 12; iii. 16. It denotes not only slandering (backbiting, Luther) but also evil contradiction, retorting.—

He that calumniateth or judgeth his brother.—The Participles καταλαλῶν and κρίνων are stronger than the indicative: he, whose characteristic consists in that he calumniates his brother. Huther thinks that while καταλαλεῖν always includes κρίνειν=to condemn, the reverse holds not good. This would make the former the stronger expression, but we consider the latter to be so. κρίνειν passes from a loveless and therefore from a hateful *judging* of one's neighbour to a similar *condemnation* of him. Wiesinger says indeed that "the context affords not the slightest occasion to think here of quarrels among Jewish Christians and Gentile Christians," but the spirit of the whole Epistle constrains us to think of it, although the word ἀλλήλων shows that the primary reference here is to the internal divisions of Judaism. James probably alludes more particularly to the expressions and accusations which the Jews as Judaists and unfree Jewish Christians were wont to bring against the believing and more believing Jews. This seems to follow from the sequel "He that calumniateth, etc., calumniateth the law." Schneckenburger rightly observes that the epithet brother given to the slandered persons emphasizes the peculiarly reprehensible character of calumny. But the sequel shows that the Apostle, by the use of this word, still aims at something more. Νόμος designates here, as in ch. i. 25 and ii. 9, etc., the Old Testament law in its New Testament fulfilment. Hence the idea of Huther is right that slandering and condemning one's brother is really slandering and condemning the law itself, viewed as the law of the Christian life and more particularly as the law of love, for such conduct amounts to rejecting it as an unjust law; but the Apostle's idea seems to be more comprehensive, viz., the condemnation of one's brother from the standpoint of fanatical motives is a condemnation of the essential νόμος according to its inmost evangelical import and especially as to its tendency of saving and not condemning. Thus the condemnation of one's brother in all cases is not only *without* the law and *contrary* to the law, but it falls also upon the law itself. This was perfectly clear in the case where the Jews judged the Christians; they judged the whole revelation (Jno. v. 45, 46); but in the opposite case also, *i. e.*, that is where Christians judged the Jews, judgment was passed on the heart-point of the law, viz.: the promise of grace. De Wette, who sees in the respective expression only a figurative, pointed speech indicating the disregard of the law, dilutes the idea. Surely Grotius, Baumgarten, Hottinger are not altogether wrong (as Huther thinks) in understanding νόμος as the Christian doctrine and perceiving here the idea that whosoever burdens his neighbour with arbitrary commandments, pronounces upon the deficiency of the Christian doctrine and in so far sets himself up as its judge. For this is just the manner of those who condemn; occupying a false standpoint, in particular that of illiberal legalism, they set themselves up as judges over the word of revelation, which judges no man uncharitably and is unwilling that any man should be absolutely condemned and least of all he, who has taken his standpoint in that very word.

But if thou judgest the law, *i. e.*, if thou settest thyself up condemningly over it.

Thou art not a doer of the law.—Although thou boastest, to be zealous and jealous of it to the highest degree.

But a judge.—The question is does this mean 1, a judge who from another standpoint judges and condemns the law itself, that is a God-hostile adversary of the law, an out and out *anomist* [ἄνομος, without law, a lawless man.—M.], which would require us to supply the Genitive νόμου after κριτής (so Neander, Wiesinger and al.), or 2, does κριτής denote absolutely the judge who administers the law in judging men? This interpretation is opposed by Huther to the former, with the remark that the former makes this sentence and the one preceding it tautological, that it dilutes the antithesis of doer and judge and that the sequel adverts not to a judging of the law but to a judging of men. As to tautology, it does not belong to the first interpretation, because we have then the climax, not doers but condemners of the law. The antithesis "observer and despiser of the law" is surely much stronger than that of "doer and guardian of the law." Lastly the idea "condemner of the law" is substantiated with what goes before. But the relation is such that the *anti-judge* is also always *pseudo-judge* just as *anti-Christ* is also always *Pseudo-Christ.*

VER. 12. **One is the Lawgiver and Judge.**—He is *One*, which is emphatic, not only as contrasted with all men, of whom this is not true, but also in the unity of the Lawgiver and the Judge (Morus), which does not suffer to rise a contradiction between the spirit of the law and the spirit of the judgment such as it ought to exist if the judging of the Judaists were authorized. Now His power to judge has developed itself in the first place as the power to save or to render blessed and in the second as the power to destroy or to damn. The sequel therefore is not a further predicate: "He is able to save, etc." (Luther), but states the characteristic, "He, who is able." This intimates at least that the Judge is the God of the Gospel, who saves or damns men according to their belief or unbelief, Mark xvi. 16.—He manifests Himself in fact as this δυνάμενος and thus establishes His exclusive prerogative to judge. Bengel: "*Nostrum non est judicare, præsertim cum exequi non possimus.*"

But who art thou.—*Impotent* before that judicial majesty and power of God, moreover as a sinner guilty of the judgment and in want of grace (see Rom. xiv. 4).

That judgest.—Really who makest judging thy business: ὁ κρίνων, with the Article to which Schneckenburger calls attention. But this word evidently serves to introduce the sequel, according to which a great judgment is impending on these judges.

Dissuasion from their restless, gain-seeking and self-willed wandering through the world in consideration of the approaching storm of judgment. vv. 13–15.

VER. 13. **Well then, ye that say.**—Huther, who is supported by many predecessors (Oecumenius, Bede, Semler, Pott, Hottinger and al.), thinks that James now addresses no longer members of the Christian Church, but the rich; viz., rich Jews, according to the forementioned explanation of the term rich. Gebser and al. contradict this view; Wiesinger holds that James addresses simply a particular class of his readers. But the Apostle's address really avoids every definite outward classification. His Epistle is addressed to the twelve tribes by the hands of the Jewish Christian, *i. e.*, primarily to these with the intent that they should use the Epistle for missionary purposes among their brethren. But as James looks upon Judaism as a solidary* guilt and perverseness attaching to the whole people, although mostly to the unbelieving Jews, so all his exhortations and warnings are addressed through the Jewish Christians to all Jews. Still so that the centre of gravity in his address is continually progressing from the Jewish Christians to the Jews. With respect to this section of the Epistle, while it still describes a gain-loving, trafficking Jewish wandering through the world, of which the Jewish Christians as well as the Jews might readily become guilty, at least to some extent, yet it is evidently the transition to the subsequent prophetical lamentation over the rich, *i. e.*, over the hardened part of the Jewish people, especially their leaders, and is consequently addressed more particulary to the Jews.—The interjection ἄγε νῦν (here and ch. v.; not found elsewhere in the New Testament), according to Theile="age audite," refers doubtless to the announcement of the judgment, which comes out quite clear in ch. v. 1, but is here darkly and menacingly alluded to. James is anxious to communicate to

*Trench says: "*Solidarity*, a word which we owe to the French Communists, and which signifies a community in gain and loss, in honour and dishonour, a being, so to speak, all in the same bottom, is so convenient that it will be in vain to struggle against it."—M.

his readers his sorrowful forebodings of the judgment impending on his people. Grotius renders: "*jam ego ad vos*," de Wette construes it as calling upon them to lay aside the respective fault, Huther as preparing for the κλαύσατε in v. 5.

Ye that say.—*οἱ λέγοντες*, ye that are in the habit of using such presumptuous and worldly language.

To-day and to-morrow.—See Appar. Crit. καὶ (according to Theile) certainly expresses greater confidence than ἤ; the plan of the journey of the restless traders. Wiesinger understands "*and to-morrow*" of the different plans of journey of different persons, Huther thinks that it fixed the precise duration of the intended journey. But v. 14 shows that "to-morrow" is also added for the purpose of resenting the false security of the project. "To-morrow" denotes therefore the undefined future subsequent to "to-day," not only a second day; for at that time a two days' journey did not take one very far.

We will journey; *we shall journey*, πορευσόμεθα uttered with false, prophetical assurance.

To such and such a city.—A demonstrative pronoun instead of the name of the city, with the collateral idea that the goal is now one city, now another. [I have adopted the rendering *this* city, because "such and such," "this or that" is a sense in which ὅδε is not used; at least the best Lexica do not give it, and I agree with Alford, that Winer p. 174, who refers to Plutarch. *Sympos.* I. 61 for this image of ὅδε= τὸ δεῖνα, does not make his point, and that all that is necessary, is to suppose that τήνδε τὴν πόλιν expresses in general terms the city then present to the mind of the speaker.—M.].

And will work there one year.—ποιεῖν with a definition of time may denote primarily one's stay at a place; but it probably intimates also that the respective time is spent (Acts xv. 33; xx. 3 etc.). But we take the verb "work" in the sense of "working in the conduct of business." The definition *one year* again denotes not only the false security of the calculation, but also their restless, unsteady habits; *then*, they think, *we move on or return.*

And do business [*and traffic*—M.]. The hastily following καὶ and the hastily following future are also pictorial expressions descriptive of their immoderate false security. Bengel: "*Polysyndeton exprimit libidinem animi securi.*" Huther assents to Kern's note: "Traffic is introduced only *by way of example* as characterizing man's doing calculated only with reference to earthly life and as contrasted with the life in God." But it is doubtless an example illustrating the secular aspect of the chief tendency of the Judaism of that time as it already began to develop itself; and the Apostle with a prophet's glance evidently, describes beforehand the fundamental trait of the diabolically excited worldliness of his people, as it afterwards became more and more developed.

VER. 14. **Yes, ye that know not** [*whereas ye know not* E. V. much more correct and idiomatic than Lange's rendering—M.]. οἵτινες, properly, "ye that are of such a kind." [Alford: ="*ut qui*"—"belonging, as ye do, to a class which."—M.].

What will be to-morrow.—Prov. iii. 28, xxvii. 1. The general idea that carnal security is here met by ignorance of the future and the transitoriness of life (Huther) has here also a prophetico-historical bearing. Hence not only: "Ye know not, as mortal men, whether you are still alive to-morrow," but also "ye have no presentiment of what the next future has in reserve for you with our people." It is to be remembered that these words were written by an aged Apostle a few years before that great catastrophe, which brought the greatest misery and death on many thousand people not only at Jerusalem (and James considered Jerusalem and Judea to belong also to the dispersion of the twelve tribes in the enlarged sense of the term), but previously also in many cities of the Roman Empire (Cæsarea, Scythopolis, Ascalon, Damascus, Alexandria; Josephus, *de bello Jud.* 2, 18, 1–8; 20, 2).

For what is your life?—Of what sort, ποία. It is not only fleeting and perishable physically, but as the spiritual life of the nation also it is affected with deadly disease and a deadly destiny.

A vapor, forsooth, ye are.—Better "*For* ye are a vapor."—M.]. On γὰρ see Appar. Crit. The reading ἐστέ is manifestly a stronger expression than ἐστί, applied to their life. "They themselves are thereby described as a vapor, as it is also said of the πλούσιος ch. i. 10 that he shall pass away as the flower of grass." Huther. Does ἀτμίς denote vapor of fire (smoke, as in Acts ii. 19 in connection with καπνοῦ) or vapor of water, that is, a misty formation, or is there no definite reference designed? We feel inclined to take the former view; 1, on account of the familiar reference to Acts ii. 19; Joel iii. 1–5; 2, on account of the reference to fire in ch. v. 3; 3, on account of the greater volatility of the vapor of smoke as compared with the vapor of water which in the shape of cloudy formation is apt to last longer and in reality does not vanish if it dissolves into rain. But the real *tertium comparationis* is certainly the volatility of vapor, presenting an affinity with the volatility of the shadow in Job viii. 9; Ps. cii. 12; cxliv. 4. But in the last passage the figure also contains the idea of a breath and Ps. cii. 4 the figure of smoke. Our passage is probably more nearly related to the one named last.

And then (again).—Laying the emphasis on φαινομένη, appearing in splendid extension, say like an illuminated cloud, καὶ might be rendered *even:* it not only decreases but *even* vanishes. But as objection may be raised to such an emphasis, Huther's explanation of καὶ is sufficient "as it appeared so it vanished." Thus Israel as a nation, was soon to vanish from the rank of nations.

VER. 15. **Instead of that ye ought to say.**—These words connect with v. 13, but the parenthesis v. 14 has the import of a prolonged characterizing address.

If the Lord will, we shall live.—See Appar. Crit. According to the less authenticated reading of the Text Rec. (καὶ ζήσωμεν), adopted by the majority of commentators, καὶ ζήσωμεν is generally connected with the protasis. Luther: "If the Lord will and we live, we shall do this or that;" Erasmus, Calvin, de Wette. The second καὶ then denotes the apodosis. Here the protasis is divided into two hypothetical ideas: if the Lord will and if we live. Grotius and al. take the whole somewhat differently: "if the Lord will *that* we live, then the rest also will follow, then we shall do this or that;" but this really runs into the construction of Luther. Most impracticable is Bornemann's construction, who adopting the *Text Rec.*, makes καὶ ζήσωμεν the apodosis in the sense: "let us make our livelihood." The better sense also favours the more critically sustained reading. Not only our doing depends on the will of the Lord, but also, first of all, life itself. Hence if the Lord will, we shall live and then do this or that (Wiesinger, Huther.) [I prefer the reading ζήσομεν and render "If the Lord will, we shall both live and shall do this or that," for it is evident that the hypothesis controls both our living and doing. Our life is dependent on the will of God and our doing depends on our living. Cf. Winer, p. 301. —M.].

Reproof of their false security and forewarning of their conscience. vv. 16, 17.

VER. 16. **But now ye boast yourselves in.**—But now, *i. e.* instead of their thinking and speaking. Instead of it *ye boast yourselves* etc., according to the preliminary allusion, v. 15.

In your illusions.—'Αλαζονεία denotes vaunting or bragging regarded in the light of illusion or deception.—But here we must lay more stress on the objective, vain, arrogant self-exaltation than on the boasting. The clause: "ye boast in your boastings" (de Wette), is rather tautological. Boasting being a joyous testifying of the ground of confidence, the sense is as follows: ye boast in a ground of peace, consisting in those vain illusions or castles in the air, which from their nature are multiform. Huther remarks that ἐν denotes not the object but the ground of their boasting; but in this boasting the ground is really made the object.

All boasting of such kind.—That is, grounded on haughtiness and self-illusion; whereas both James and Paul know a holy boasting (ch. i. 9—that is glorying) grounded on the most opposite qualities, not on self-exaltation in forgetfulness of God and departing from God but on self-abasement in reliance on God and resignation to God.

VER. 17. **To him now who knoweth to do good.**—This is not only a moral sentence used for the purpose of warning the readers but the concluding forewarning addressed to the Judaists, followed by the announcement of the judgments upon those who still persevere in their obduracy; the great turning-point in the Apostle's argument like our Lord's last address to the Jews Jno. xii. 35 (Matth. xxiii.), or that of Paul, Acts xxviii. 23 etc. And first we have to note that the main stress lies not on καλόν, as the sum-total of good, because this would require the Article (so Wiesinger), but on εἰδότι with which καλόν κ. τ. λ. must be connected. He therefore who, although he knows better, omits the good and *moreover the doing* of good which he knows to do, to him it is reckoned as sin. The reference here, however, is not primarily, that a single sin of omission is also sin, but the whole attitude of an impenitent religious knowledge, the whole self-contradiction of a hypocritical and unfruitful orthodoxism is here described as *a wholesale* sin of omission. As sin, according to Rom. i. 21 began with a great central sin of omission, so it is also sealed with the great, all-embracing sin of omission of impenitence. But this proposition contains also the common doctrine of the single sin of omission. Now concerning this knowledge of good the question arises (according to Huther) whether James refers to the knowledge he had imparted to his readers by his exhortations (Estius), especially by the last (Grotius, de Wette and al.); or whether this knowledge describes one already existing in his readers, as Huther assumes, observing; "the uncertainty of human life is something so palpable that those who notwithstanding talk in their audacity as if it did not exist, as if their life were not dependent on God and contrary to their own knowledge do not that which is seemly but that which is unseemly and therefore is is so much the more sin unto them." We consider this antithesis as confusing. It is surely assumed that the readers of the Epistle knew from the Old Testament the rudiments of doing good and that in this knowledge the Gospel had raised them to the full consciousness of the highest degree of doing good; but it is assumed with equal certainty that this word of the whole Epistle, as a final word of exhortation is to them matter of the greatest and most decisive importance. The word should therefore be taken as a final word with reference to their better knowledge of evangelical behaviour in general and not merely as reminding them of their previous knowledge of their dependence on God. We have still to ask what is sin to one who knows and doeth not? The *knowledge* by itself, or that knowledge as connected with *not doing?* The former would be more piquant and would mean something like this: to such an one even his Jewish prerogatives turn to ruin (Rom. x.). The Gospel proclaimed to him first, becomes to him a savor of death unto death. However we must distinguish sin from the judgment of sin, hence the reference cannot be to the better knowledge by itself but to the contradiction between *knowing* and *not doing*, which runs thrugh the whole Epistle as the object of the Apostle's controversy. This contradiction becomes sin to the perfect ἀνὴρ δίψυχος which is reckoned to or reserved for him *i. e.* unto judgment. This great forewarning introduces the subsequent passage of the judgment. It is noteworthy that James seems to foresee with assurance that the greater part or the mass of Israel would grow obdurate contrary to a better knowledge or with an evil consciousness against *doing* the truth of the Gospel and that all the Judaistic corruptions of his Christian readers, which he assails, are also connected with such a conscious perverseness in general and in the whole, although not with reference to every individual in every individual case, and although the solidarity of the judgment is suspended in the case of believing Jews.

[The real point of this saying is hardly brought out in Lange's note and not touched at all under "Doctrinal and Ethical" and "Homiletical and Practical." The reference is not to sins of *omission*, but to sinning against light and knowledge, to *doing evil* the knowledge of good notwithstanding. *καλόν* v. 17 is the opposite of *πονηρόν*; and the persons, whom James addressed *knew* well enough that they ought to do good, but they separated their knowledge from their practice and *did evil*. This verse (v. 17) contains a sharp rebuke, if not a sarcastic reflection on their inconsistencies.—M.]

DOCTRINAL AND ETHICAL.

1. One of the most important life-questions of Christian ethics is undoubtedly that of the Christian's relation to the world which surrounds him. In answering it James again fully agrees with our Lord (cf. Matth. vi. 24), and with Paul the Apostle (cf. Rom. xii. 2; 1 Cor. vii. 29–31; 2 Cor. vi. 14–18). He wants Christians neither to conform to the world nor entirely to separate themselves from it, but he insists so much the more on their being distinguished from the world and on their showing that they are governed by a very different principle and a much loftier spirit than the friends of the world. If this is omitted and on the contrary that friendship of the world is sought, which is incompatible with a harmonious and independent development of the Christian life, it must surely lead to the result, that God and His service are ultimately abandoned. The impossibility of uniting God and the world in the heart of a Christian belongs to the nature of the case; cf. Matth. xii. 30. The world demands that we should love ourselves, God requires us to love Him; the world wants self-exaltation, God abasement and humility. The friend of the world and the friend of God are diametrically opposed to each other in principle, inclination and aim. Moreover how can there exist a lasting communion among things that cannot be reconciled? Here applies the saying in Matth. xvi. 26; Luke x. 38–42.—

2. James as well as the other writers of the New Testament receive the *γραφή* as the highest authority.

3. No sin is more loathsome in the sight of God than pride. We have only to realize for a moment the light in which a holy God cannot but regard a guilty sinner in order to understand that self-exaltation is not only wicked but almost ridiculous before Him. Thus far we may say that *parcere victis et debellare superbos* is the fundamental law of the Divine government both under the Old Testament and under the New. Then countless examples taken from history prove also the truth of the saying, which is constantly heard in the Gospel. Cf. Matth. xviii. 4; Luke xviii. 14; 1 Pet. v. 5.

4. What James says here (v. 7) of the devil is at once a supplement to his doctrine of the origin of sin (ch. i. 14, 15) and a corrective of those who are wont to dilute the last mentioned passage after the manner of the Pelagians.

5. In writing "Draw near to God and He will draw near to you" James by no means wants to deny that the grace of God is prevenient and free and to teach that the sinner, for his part, must first turn to God, before God is able in grace to turn to him. This would conflict with the nature of the case and also with 1 John iv. 19. But he is here addressing Christians, whom God had already approached before (cf. Is. lxv. 1), but who, by their transgressions, had for a time departed from God and had first to return before they could again enjoy His grace and communion. It is once for all impossible to merit the favour of God by conversion and equally impossible personally to experience it without such a genuine conversion. Now all temporizing [indecision, half-work, German "*Halbtheit*"—M.], all discord between the outward and the inward life is fundamentally incompatible with such a genuine conversion. Cf Luke xi. 38–41.

6. True joy is the child of sorrow for sin Man has therefore his choice here on earth between short grief to be followed hereafter by constant joy and short joy to be followed hereafter by eternal grief. Cf. Matth. v. 3, 4; Luke vi. 21; 2 Cor. vii. 10.

7. Nothing is more sad and pernicious than that Christians also in their intercourse with each other yield themselves so often to loveless calumny and forget the words of the Lord Jesus, Matth. vii. 1–6. In this connection attention should be called to rash contradiction and hasty judging which are often the effects of ignorance or disgraceful passion; to censoriousness which contrary to men's own better conviction magnifies the faults of their neighbour and overlooks his good parts, in direct opposition to the Apostolic precept, 1 Cor. xiii. 4–7; to calumny, slander, tale-bearing, back-biting, etc., on which vices Reinhard's *System of Christian Morality*, 4th ed. I. p. 681–693 deserves to be consulted. [Also Jeremy Taylor's Sermons,—*The Good and Evil Tongue—Slander and Flattery—The Duties of the Tongue.*—M.]. He justly observes that partial and passionate reviewers are not unfrequently guilty of these vices to an eminent degree. Compare also Bayle's *Dissertations sur les libelles difamatoires*, in Vol. IV. of his Dictionnaire, and the capital sketch of an accomplished calumniator in Gellert's *Moralische Vorlesungen*, p. 647 etc.' It is self-evident how ill all this accords with the duties of Christian brotherly love. Cf. 1 Cor. iv. 5; Eph. iv. 25; Col. iii. 13.

8. "The law protects our neighbour by the precept of brotherly love; he who notwithstanding injuriously assails him, violates the protecting law itself, sets himself above the law and makes choice of that part of the law he means to observe or not to observe; but in doing so, he ceases to be a doer of the law." von Gerlach.

9. The Christian must also show in his daily life that he is influenced in all things by the sense of dependence which is the real foundation of the religious and moral life. James in concert with Solomon (Prov. xxvii. 1), with our Lord Himself (Matth. vi. 34) and with the Epistle to the Hebrews (ch. vi. 3) urges this upon his readers. Many a sinful action would remain undone, many a hasty step would not be taken, if the words "If the Lord will and we live" were not only on the lips but in the hearts of men. Compare the treatise of Morus, "*de homine submittente se Deo,*" *in Opusculis*, II p. 123. sqq.

10. There is not a more extensive region of sin than that on which James allows us to cast

a solitary glance (v. 17), the region of sins of omission, and again none in which not a few exhibit less concern. How many are perfectly satisfied if in their opinion they have not *done* any thing in thought, in word or in deed, which conflicts with the love of God and of our neighbour, although they have never accused themselves of that which unconsciously or designedly they omitted to do! Many secretly object to such simple and self-evident exhortations as those in vv. 13–16, that they have *known* it all a long time without considering that *knowing* without *doing* is altogether inexcusable, cf. Jno. iii. 17.—"The omission of good is the commission of evil. In this manner we actually may become thieves and murderers; *e. g.*, the priest and the Levite who passed by the unfortunate sufferer, offended by omitting to observe the sixth commandment. This omission of good is also connected with slackness in doing good; gradually men become more and remiss in doing until at last all love of and longing for good leaves them and this is the death of which we must be on our guard. Beware, therefore, of procrastination! By deferring a thing we ought to do from day to day, we come to lessen its importance and soon forget it altogether. Such negligences disclose to us the slothfulness of our heart, a most dangerous and critical state of disease." Viedebandt.

[v. 12. Sanderson: "The words of St. James assert that there is but *one* Lawgiver—not one selected out of *many*, nor *one* above all the rest, but one *exclusively;* that is, *one*, and but *one alone*, who is able to save and destroy. What was usually applied to the prerogatives of Kings, may be justly said of the *conscience* of every man, that *it is subject to none but God, and knows no superior upon earth.* Memorable is the observation of the Emperor *Maximilian*, "To offer to domineer over the conscience, is to assault the citadel of heaven." *That* man is a plunderer of the Divine Glory, and an invader of the authority that belongs to God, whosoever he be, that claims a *right* over the consciences of men, or usurps upon them. Let the *popes* of Rome, and the train of canonists, jesuits and sycophants, that flatter and fawn upon them, clear themselves, if they can, of this sacrilege; and let such as *submit their consciences* to the power of any creature, which only ought to be subject to God, be careful lest by transferring the honour of that service that belongs to God, to any creature upon earth, they make a god of that creature, and so, in effect become guilty of *idolatry.*

From this first *conclusion* thus proved, follows this remarkable inference, that the *proper rule* of the conscience is that which *God*, the Supreme Lawgiver, has prescribed to it; and besides that, there is no other that ought to be admitted.

Yet this hinders not, that there may be other lawgivers of an *inferior order*, who by authority *derived* to them from the *Supreme power*, may have a just right to make laws, and consequently to bind the conscience to obedience. We do not say that God has committed to the Magistrate a power to oblige the consciences of his people by laws, but rather (to speak with more care and propriety) that God has given to the magistrate a jurisdiction to make laws, which by virtue alone of the *Divine* authority, do oblige the consciences of the subject; for properly speaking, the Magistrate does not oblige the conscience to obey the *law*, but God obliges the conscience to obey the magistrate."—M.].

[v. 17. Wordsworth: This conclusion of St James is added as the summing up of the argument, in the same manner as the aphorism with which St. Paul closes his reasonings concerning a *doubting conscience*, where he says, "Whatsoever is not of faith, is sin," that is, whenever a man *does* anything without *being persuaded* in his mind that he *may* lawfully do it, he is guilty of sin. Rom. xiv. 23.

St. James appears to have his eye here on this statement of St. Paul.

St. James adds to it another maxim of general import, viz., that whensoever a man *omits* to do anything which he is persuaded in his own mind that he *ought* to do, he is guilty of sin.

Thus these two Apostolic verdicts, delivered in a similar manner, constitute two fundamental rules of human action, as to what men are *bound to forbear doing*, and as to what *they are bound to do.*

Those persons whom St. Paul addressed, were tempted to do many things, which they did not, in their consciences, approve; and the Apostle warns them, that if they do any thing against their conscience, they commit sin.

They to whom St. James wrote, were vainglorious of their religious *knowledge;* but they were not careful to show forth their religious *knowledge* by religious *practice;* and the Apostle teaches them that their knowledge will only increase their guilt, unless they *do* what they *know* to be right.

Hence, while it is sin to shun knowledge, and there is *some* sin of *ignorance* (cf. *Augustine* 6, 661), and it is a sin to shut the ears to instruction; and it is a duty to *get knowledge*, to *increase* in knowledge, to *abound* in knowledge, we must beware not to *rest* in knowledge. We must *add* to our *knowledge, temperance, patience, godliness, brotherly kindness, charity.* Without these *knowledge* is unprofitable; nay, will only increase our condemnation. See Sanderson 3, p. 232–234. Cf. Luke xii. 47; Jno. ix. 41; xv. 22; and see the woes pronounced on *Chorazin* and *Capernaum*, Matth. xi. 21.—M.].

HOMILETICAL AND PRACTICAL.

Friendship with the world, enmity of God.—The Christian's relation to the world which sursounds him.—On spiritual adultery, cf. Hos. ii. 1–19.—The Scripture should never utter a single word in vain to the Christian, cf. Jno. x. 35*b*.—The Spirit that dwells in Christians is decidedly opposed to every manifestation of hatred and envy.—God is able to do exceeding abundantly above all that we ask or think (understand), Eph. iii. 20.—God resisteth the proud but giveth grace to the humble: 1. This *is* not otherwise according to the voice of history and experience; 2. It *cannot* be otherwise, if we consider the relation of God and the sinner; 3. It *shall* not be otherwise if God is to be glorified and the sinner preserved; 4. It *will* never be otherwise and the sinner had therefore better lay it to heart.—(vv. 6, 7). How God stands to the humble Christian and how the humble Christian stands to his God.—The necessity of a constantly renewed conversion towards God after every new aberration.—The greatest *demand* of the Christian life: draw near to God, and its greatest *consolation:* He will draw nigh to you.—The insignificance of clean hands without a clean heart; the inward and the outward must be indissolubly united in conversion.—The beginning of conversion, the end of every sinful joy.—If we did not remain so far from God, God also would not remain so far from us.—The commandment of inward purification can never be fulfilled without prayer, Ps. li. 12.—(vv. 10, 11). The Christian life a union of humility and love. He who truly knows and humbles himself before God will neither have the desire nor the courage to judge his brother uncharitably.—Sinning against our brother is also sinning against God.—Slander in religious associations and Christian circles: 1, The traces, 2, the sources, 3, the fruits of this vice.—He that speaks evil of others injures thereby 1, the brother whom he calumniates, 2, the neighbour who listens to him, 3, but most of all himself.—The Christian indeed is called to be a doer of the word but not in order to be a judge of the law.—The relation in which God stands to the transgressor of the commandment of love: 1, as the Lawgiver, 2, as the only Lawgiver, 3, as the only Lawgiver who is able to save and to destroy.—(v. 13, etc.). On our dependence on God even in the actions of our daily life.—Difference between the Christian-minded and the worldly-minded merchant.—Christian and unchristian travelling. Our ignorance of the future, 1, the alarm it occasions, 2, the benefit it works.—"What is your life?" Different answers to this question from the standpoint 1, of experience, 2, of faith.—Life a vapor which is to ascend fragrant as incense.—How much cause have we not only to think but also to say: "If the Lord will and we live!" 1. Reasons for this frame of mind: *a.* death or want of ability prevent not seldom the execution of our best plans; *b.* the plans of others often conflict with ours or ours with theirs and both neutralize one another; *c.* we are often deprived of the opportunity or the desire to carry out our plans, but all under the guidance of God. 2. Fruits of this frame of mind: it will *a.* make us careful in laying, *b.* thankful for the success, *c.* submissive and satisfied with the frustration of our most cherished plans and desires.—Memento mori, cf. Ps. xc. and ciii.—The problem of life must never be considered apart from its direct connection with death.—Lawful and unlawful glorying on the Christian standpoint.—The great chasm between knowing, willing and doing.—The greatness of seemingly little sins of omission.—"He that knoweth to do good, etc." Extended application of this rule to the field of Christian philanthrophy and of Missions among the heathen.

Starke: Luther:—Envious men are not the temples of the Holy Ghost, ch. iii. 14, 15; 2 Tim. i. 7.—The proud instead of the honour, after which they run, receive shame and dishonour, Matth. xxv. 33.—The more of humility, the more of grace; if in valleys some hollows are deeper than others, the water collects in them, Luke v. 8.—Humility of heart is the most certain way not only to the love of our fellow-men but also to honour from God Himself. Luke xiv. 11.

Hedinger:—The enemy is not conquered by sleep. Take the sword of the Spirit, the helmet of hope, the shield of faith, then thou art equipped for the contest, Eph. vi. 11.—Nothing unclean is able to combine with God, the most pure Being, Is. i. 16.—Humility the surest road to constant exaltation, Matth. xxiii. 12.—To speak evil of our brother does more harm than is generally thought; as many words, so many wounds are struck in the conscience, Ps. lii. 4; cxl. 12.

Nova Bibl. Tub.:—A pious man always guards his tongue lest it judge his neighbour and defame him, Rom. xiv. 13.

Luther:—God gave us His law, not that we should censure it, but keep it. Deut. vii. 11.

Starke:—Human legislators are able to render those, who obey their commandments, to some extent happy, but they can neither save them nor themselves; God is able to do both perfectly.—The Apostle does not absolutely disallow commerce, he only blames those who are so covetous that they forget God in their business and think that every thing depends on their cunning, chasing and running, and do not remember that they cannot do any thing without the grace of God. Trading and chaffering has been peculiar to the Jews before and after the birth of Christ, especially to those who have lived out of Canaan, their country. For because they had no landed property among foreign nations, they were compelled to make their living by trade, which is the case now, if only it were done as it ought to be done.

Nova Bibl. Tub.:—O wretched man that layest out such great plans, dost thou not know that to-morrow God may require thy soul at thy hands? Luke xii. 19, 20.

Langii op.:—Nothing is more common than that the healthiest bodies of any age are all of a sudden attacked by divers diseases, Job. xiv. 2.

Hedinger:—The will of God is the sole rule of Christians in all matters relating to the body or the soul, as in the case of Christ and Paul, Jno. iv. 34; 1 Cor. iv. 19; Acts xxi. 13, 14.—The will of God permits also evil but turns it to the welfare of His children, Gen. l. 20.—An evil cause and a stubborn mind full of self-glorying go generally together, ch. iii. 14; Rom. i. 30.

Langii op.:—Ignorance is no excuse in cases where knowledge might have been had; but if a man knows better and yet is unfaithful and disobedient, he only aggravates his guilt accordingly, Luke xii. 47, 48.

(v. 11) Stier:—I must judge in my heart in order to preserve myself from evil and to retain only what is good; I owe it in love to my brother to censure and exhort him in order to make him better and to prosper his soul. But this is altogether different from haughty, angry rebuking and scolding when I converse with some one about his sin; but the worst of all, and that which uniformly begets still greater discord, is the, alas, nowhere uncommon although thoroughly concealed vice of backbiting, which Luther in his Catechism has wisely ranged under the eighth commandment. People discourse without vocation or duty, from sheer wantonness with a hateful temper of one's supposed sin to another; speak evil of their brother behind his back, as a false brother, instead of saying it sincerely to his face. Thus acted the heathen in the Apostolic age towards the Christians, wantonly refused to see their good works and preferred to backbite them as evil-doers (1 Pet. ii. 12). Thus still act nowadays baptized heathen towards the godly, saying of them and burdening them with all manner of evil falsely. If this is done also among those who pretend to be brethren, verily the Holy Spirit strongly testifies against it and rather teaches Christians for their part not to deal thus with the children of the world. Where such backbiting takes place there is never a good conscience or a courageous answer to the questions: would I say this of him, if he were present? why do I not first tell him? why and for what purpose do I now speak of it?—There is neither obedience of duty nor intent of love; here speaks and judges one's own presumptuous, haughty mind, hence it runs so soon into judging falsely or even, if the matter were really so, into *condemning*, into damning judgment, which is at any rate absolutely forbidden.

(v. 17). We are unprofitable servants before the Most Highest; that is certain, for all profitableness comes only from Him; but it is just because He makes us profitable that we are bound to do whatever is commanded us, to be diligent in doing good, as we know it, according to the will of God. James puts this lastly in the place of every self-willed doing of this or that. If we suffer ourselves to be found in good works aspiring for eternal life, then our earthly life verily has become more than a vapor, which vanishes away, then it is the seed-time of the great harvest of true gain.

JAKOBI: (v. 15):—"If the Lord will and I live." There are indeed not a few Christians who take the precept of our text literally and think that they are sinning if in speaking of the future, they do not every time employ such a pious addition. But if faith here borders almost on superstition and if we actually find the traces of such superstition even in many otherwise enlightened Christians, is it not true that this momentous saying "If the Lord will and I live" sinks down into a mere conventionalism, if we carry it on our lips on every trifling occasion? and is it not to be feared that that which we should always utter only with a profound and most living sense of our impotence and the omnipotence of God, degenerates into a mere, blind habit? Let us apply also in this respect the mighty saying of St. Paul: "The kingdom of God is not in word, but in power," 1 Cor. iv. 20.—

NEANDER:—"If the Lord will and we live." It is evident that James in saying this did not insist upon it, that we should always express such a condition in words. Such expressions might easily degenerate into mere forms and those Churches, in virtue of their whole tendency, were apt to turn every thing into a mere form. James, as we have already seen, is fond of naming the specific instead of the general thought, and instead of expressing the general thought of the uncertainty and dependence of our whole earthly life, makes use of language calculated to indicate the general thought by its application to a specific case.

HEUBNER: (v. 15):—James will appear to some as a pietist, but just from what he says we may know what genuine, sincere piety is. He is truly pious, whose piety interpenetrates also his whole heart, his whole life and his whole doing. To carry on even his earthly affairs with God characterizes the Christian: "with God" is his motto in every thing, Col. iii. 17.—The spirit of enterprise without religion is always pride.—

LISCO: (vv. 7–10):—All our doing is at the same time the work of God.—(vv. 11–17) The danger of pride: 1, It misleads us to judge others uncharitably (vv. 11, 12); 2, it seduces us to trust over much in our own strength (vv. 13–17).—The unchristian element in the conduct of temporal affairs.—

PORUBSZKY: (vv. 4–6):—Worldly and spiritual.—(vv. 6, 7) Be subject to God.—(vv. 7, 8) The greatest task of human willing.—(vv. 8–10) Three steps to genuine repentance: 1, grief; 2, faith; 3, work.—(vv. 11, 12): Our judgment of others condemns ourselves.—(vv. 13–17). Of assurance in our worldly affairs.—

WEINECK: (vv. 13–15):—In what Christian families may find comfort in the retrospect of a departing year.—

WOLF: (vv. 13–16):—Man may become the destroyer but not the architect of his happiness.

[WHITBY: v. 11:—The great exception which both the unbelieving Jews and the Judaizing Christians among them had against the believing Gentiles was this "they observed not their feasts or Sabbaths and that they were not circumcised," whence they concluded they differed little from the heathens. This was the thing for which the Christian fathers did contend against them; viz. that the ancient patriarchs of old were acceptable to God, and consequently the Christians, and especially the converted Gentiles, might be acceptable to God without the observation of these feasts and Sabbaths or of circumcision.

v. 15. It was a rule of Ben Syra (Buxt. *Flor.* p. 4) "Let no man say he will do any thing, unless he first say, If the Lord will:" who also adds, that "one died before night, for refusing to add this." And when Alcibiades had said to Socrates, "I will do so if you will," Socrates (Plat. *Alcib.* 1, *in fine*) tells him he ought to have said, ἐὰν ὁ θεὸς ἐθέλῃ, "if God will." Not that we are obliged always to say thus (Rom. xv. 28), but only still to own our dependence upon Divine Providence.—M.].

[v. 17. Εἰδότι οὖν. Menander says: "It is manifest folly to know what we ought to do and not do it.—M.].

[MACKNIGHT:—v. 8. This and other exhortations of the like kind found in Scripture imply, that in matters of religion and virtue men must coöperate with the grace of God by their own earnest endeavours.—M.].

[PYLE: v. 11. As to you, dear brethren, who are already converted to Christianity, be sure to avoid that pernicious custom of slander and rash censure. Remember, that whoever hastily and unjustly condemns another man, reflects upon religion itself, sets up for a judge and makes himself wiser than the Divine Law. And such an one must not pretend to be a true disciple of that law, while he sets himself above it.—M.].

[v. 17. Now this, or any other crime, must be greater in a Christian than in any other man; because he, by the clear revelation of the Gospel, has or ought to have better notions of his duty, and a stronger sense of his religious obligations.—M.].

[Burkitt: v. 17. Let us learn hence, that to sin against light and knowledge, is a very heinous aggravation of sin, because the knowledge of our duty lays us under the greatest obligation to do it; and that the greater advantages and opportunities any man has of knowing his duty, and the more knowledge he sins against in not doing it, the greater is his sin, and the more grievous will be his condemnation.—M.].

[v. 4. There is a sense in which a man may be a friend of the world and yet remain the friend of God, and this seeming paradox is the duty of every Christian and more especially of the minister of Christ. He must be the world's true friend by telling the world its faults, exposing its corrupt maxims in a spirit of tender love and solicitude by preaching the truth of the everlasting Gospel and endeavouring to gain the world to Jesus Christ.]

v. 8. The Father, in the parable, running to meet the returning prodigal, a Divine illustration of the words "Draw nigh to God and He will draw nigh to you."—Outward lustrations are not sufficient, the heart must be purified as well. ἁγνίσατε καρδίας, literally "make chaste your hearts" alludes to their spiritual adultery (v. 4), and the whole clause may be applied to *baptized* Christians whose hearts are in the world.

v. 13. Debarim Rabba, § 9. p. 261. 1 we read as follows: "Our rabbis tell us a story, which happened in the days of Rabbi Simeon the son of Chelpatha. He was present at the circumcision of a child and stayed with his father to the entertainment. The father brought out wine for his guests, that was seven years old, saying, *With this wine will I continue for a long time to celebrate the birth of my new-born son.* They continued supper till midnight. At that time, Rabbi Simeon arose and went out, that he might return to the city in which he dwelt. On the way he saw the angel of death walking up and down. He said to him, Who art thou? He answered, I am the messenger of God. The rabbi said, Why wanderest thou about thus? He answered, I slay those persons who say, We will do this or that and think not how soon death may overpower them: that man with whom thou hast supped, and who said to his guests, *With this wine will I continue for a long time to celebrate the birth of my new-born son,* behold the end of his days is at hand, for he shall die within thirty days."

v. 16. Clarke cites from an old English work "The godly man's picture drawn by a Scripture pencil" the words: "Some of those who despise religion say, *Thank God we are not of this holy number!* They who thank God for their unholiness, had best go ring the bells for joy that they shall never see God."

v. 13, The same author cites the following from Saady's *Gulistan*: "I knew a merchant who used to travel with a hundred camels laden with merchandise and who had forty slaves in his employ. This person took me one day to his warehouse and entertained me a long time with conversation good for nothing. 'I have,' said he, 'such a partner in Turquestan, such and such property in India, a bond for so much cash in such a province, a security for such another sum.' Then, changing the subject, he said, 'I purpose to settle in Alexandria, because the air of that city is salubrious.' Correcting himself, he said, 'No, I will not go to Alexandria; the African Sea (the Mediterranean) is too dangerous. But I will make another voyage and after that I will retire into some quiet corner of the world, and give up mercantile life.' I asked him, what voyage he intended to make? He answered, 'I intend to take brimstone to Persia and China, where I am informed it brings a good price; from China I shall take porcelain to Greece; from Greece I shall take gold tissue to India; from India I shall carry steel to Haleb (Aleppo); from Haleb I shall carry glass to Yemen (Arabia Felix); and from Yemen I shall carry printed goods to Persia. This accomplished, I shall bid farewell to mercantile life, which requires so many troublesome journeys and spend the rest of my life in a store.' He said so much on this subject, till at last he wearied himself with talking: then turning to me, he said, 'I entreat thee Saady, to relate to me something of what *thou* hast seen and heard in thy travels.' I answered 'Hast thou never heard what a traveller said, who fell from his camel in the desert of Yoor?' *Two things only can fill the eye of a covetous man—contentment or the earth that is cast on him when laid in his grave.*"—M.].

Compare also on

v. 8. Bp. Hall. The duty of drawing nigh to God. Works, v. 745.
Bp. Smalridge. Of double-mindedness. 4 Sermons. Sermons, 349.
v. 10. Robert Hall, Humility before God. Notes of Sermons. Works, v. 312.
v. 11. Barrow. Against detraction. Works, i. 523.
Sydney Smith. On Slander. Sermons, 257.
Chalmers. The guilt of calumny Posth. Works, vi. 12.
v. 12. Bp. Sanderson. Prælectiones.

IX. SEVENTH ADMONITION.

DENUNCIATION AND ANNOUNCEMENT OF THE IMPENDING JUDGMENT ON THE RICH *I. E.*, THE JUDAISTS PROPER, COUCHED IN PROPHETIC STYLE. EXHORTATION TO REPENTANCE OR TO THE PRESENTIMENT OF THE JUDGMENT.

CHAPTER V. 1–6.

1 Go to now, *ye* rich men, weep and howl for your miseries that shall come upon *you.*[1]
2 Your riches are corrupted, and your garments are motheaten. Your gold and silver is
3 cankered; and the rust of them shall be a witness against you, and shall eat your flesh[2]
4 as it were fire. Ye have heaped treasure together for the last days. Behold, the hire
of the labourers who have reaped down your fields, which is of you kept back by fraud,[3]
crieth: and the cries of them which have reaped are entered into the ears of the Lord
5 of Sabaoth. Ye have lived in pleasure on the earth, and been wanton; ye have
6 nourished your hearts, as[4] in a day of slaughter.[5] Ye have condemned *and* killed the
just; *and* he doth not resist you.

Verse 1. [1] Cod. Sin. inserts ὑμῖν after ἐπερχομέναις [so Vulg. Syr. Copt. Æth. Arm.—M.]
Lange: Well then, ye rich, weep unto howling over your calamities which are drawing near on you.
[Go to now, ye rich, weep howling over your miseries which are coming upon you.]

Verse 2. Lange: Your riches are [already] corrupting, and your garments are become motheaten.
[. . . . corrupted . . . . M.]

Verse 3. [[2] Cod. Sin. A. inserts ὁ ἰὸς after σάρκας ὑμῶν.—M.]
Lange: Your gold and the silver is rusted and their rust will be a testimony against you and shall consume your flesh [σάρκας, your carnalities] as fire. Ye have heaped up treasure in the last [these last] days.
[Your gold and your silver are eaten up with rust and their rust shall be for a testimony to you . . . . Ye heaped up treasure in the last days.—M.]

Verse 4. [[3] Cod. Sin. B. read ἀφυστερημένος for ἀπεστερημένος.—M.]
Lange: . . . . .which hath been kept back, crieth out from you, and the cries of the reapers have come to the ears of the Lord of hosts.
[. . . . have entered into the ears of the Lord of hosts.—M.]

Verse 5. [4] Cod. Sin. A. B. omit ὡς before ἐν; so Vulg. and other versions; found in Rec., G. K. and is probably an exegetical addition.
[[5] Aeth. Pell Platt's edition. "*ut qui saginat bovem in diem mactationis.*—M.]
Lange: Ye have lived high on earth, ye have lived wantonly and fattened [like flesh] your hearts [as] in the day of slaughter.
[Ye lived in luxury on the earth and wantoned (Alford); ye fattened your hearts in . . . . M.]

Verse 6. Lange: Ye have condemned, ye have killed the Just. He doth not resist you [any longer opposing and saving].
[Ye condemned, ye killed the Just One. He doth not resist you.]

EXEGETICAL AND CRITICAL.

1. *Analysis:* The Judaists exhorted to repentance or to realize a presentiment of the judgment, v. 1.—Their condition: spiritual self-delusion, the corruptness and self-consumption of their supposed riches, vv. 2, 3.—Their positive sins resulting from such spiritual self-delusion. Their sins against the reapers of the harvest in Israel.—Their unsuspecting assurance of their life of indulgence in the very day of their judgment. The crime of the murder of the Just One, vv. 4–6.

The Judaists exhorted to repentance or to realize a presentiment of the judgment.

VER. 1. **Well then, ye rich.**—Concerning the rich see Introduction, ch. i. 10 and ii. 6, 7. That the reference is not to the outwardly rich but to the rich in the sense of Old Testament (Ps. lxxiii.; Is. v.), Gospel (Matth. xix. 24; Rev. iii. 17) and symbolical usage may be expected from an Apostolical man, to say nothing of an Apostle. The ordinary construction put on this term would lead us to expect either that the Epistle ought to have driven the outwardly rich from the Church or that they would have excluded the Epistle from the Canon.. But just as the Jewish Christians themselves have ceased to be known so also the Gentile Christian Church has suffered the majestic prophetical penitential discourse of the faithful Christian Apostle to the Jews to be reduced to the conception of a severe moral lecture. The repetition of ἄγε νῦν does not prove that the reference here is to the same persons who are addressed in ch. iv. 13 (as Huther supposes). Nor is the reference at all to individuals as such; the persons addressed there are Judaists in a most perilous condition, while those addressed here are those who according to the last warning harden themselves by the self-delusion of their being theocratically rich. The entire prophetical lamentation must be judged according to its analogies in the Old Testament (Is. ii. 22; Ch. iii. 9, 19 etc.) the words of Christ (Matth. xxiii.) and the Apocalypse (ch. xviii.).

Weep unto howling.—De Wette and al. take this as an exhortation to shed the tears of repentance; Huther agrees with Calvin who denies that there is any reference to repentance and considers the passage to be "*simplex denun-*

ciatio judicii dei, qua eos terrere voluit ab spe veniæ." Wiesinger takes a middle position: that the design of James, as in the case of the prophets of the Old Testament, is nevertheless none other than that of moving them, if possible, to turn from their perverse course. Huther, who objects that James nowhere intimates such design, overlooks 1, that also the strongest menaces of judgment in the Old Testament are at any rate hypothetical (see the Book of Jonah, Jer. xviii. 7 etc.), 2, that the most assured foreseeing of the inevitability of the judgment as a whole still involves the possibility of individuals being wakened and saved in virtue of such menace, 3, that the Divine fore-announcement of such a judgment is at the same time made as a testimony of the truth for the future and designed to serve other generations as a warning and to conduce to their salvation. The strict construction of Huther is still more striking because he disputes Semler's exposition of the Imperative, viz. "*stilo prophetico imperat, ut rem certissimam demonstret,*" and maintains that the proper force of the Imperative ought to be retained. This would therefore be a command to weep without any hope of salvation. The Participle ὀλολύζοντες (ὀλολύζειν used often to describe howling with reference to the near approach of the judgment, Is. xiii. 6; xiv. 31 etc.) denotes weeping accompanied by constant howling, *i. e.* increasing unto howling.

Over your miseries.—The impending judgments, not specified by the Apostle, but further alluded to only with respect to their premonitory symptoms.

Which are drawing near on you.—There is hardly room to doubt that James refers primarily to the Jewish war and the destruction of Jerusalem; so Thomas Aquinas, Grotius, Michaelis and al. understand it. Huther cannot substantiate by any proof the remark that "they (Thomas Aquinas, etc.) are not wrong in this respect, because in the Apostle's mind the destruction of Jerusalem and the last judgment had not yet been distinguished." The ταλαιπωρίαι are rather said to be ἐπερχόμεναι, already approaching; whereas a very patient waiting is necessary with respect to the coming of the Lord, v. 7, etc., although in the light of Christian hope (not of chiliastic calculation) it is near at hand. *On you*, by which Luther and others further define the approaching judgments, follows not from the literal expression but from the connection; ἐπί also contains an allusion, favouring the construction. [See Appar. Crit. Note 1.—M.].

Their condition: spiritual self-delusion, the corruptness and self-consumption of their supposed riches. vv. 2, 3.

VER. 2. **Your riches are corrupted.**—The verb σήπω (ἅπαξ λεγ. in N. T.), to make rotten or putrid, destroy by rottenness, signifies in 2 Perf. Pass. (as here) to rot, moulder, to be rotten or also to be in a state of rotting fermentation. But it has also the more general sense, to corrupt, to consume oneself (Sir. xiv. 19). [σέσηπα is Perf. Middle.—M.]. The verb therefore does not necessitate us to understand with Gebser and al. πλοῦτος=*frumenta*. The main question here is to determine whether this and the next expression denote the natural immanent judgment of sin as portents of the positive judgments, or the latter (Grotius, Bengel), so that future events are prophetically described as having already taken place (de Wette, Wiesinger, Huther and al.). But the reference is evidently to the former; the corrupting of riches and the moth-eaten garments denote immanent, natural corruptions. But here, as in the prophets (Is. xxviii. 1, 2; ch. xxxiii. 11, 12; Jer. vii. etc.) and in our Lord's eschatological discourse (Matth. xxiv. 28) these natural corruptions, as the judgment of the self-dissolution (—consumption) of sin, are in their products the tokens of positive judgment. But the riches must be taken figuratively, not literally as is generally done. The prophetical idea of the rich corresponds to the prophetical idea of the riches. It denotes therefore externalized Judaistic righteousness with all its national prerogatives, of course connected with that outward worldly prosperity and ease which are the outward complements of such self-righteousness. It is matter of historical record that at the time when James wrote this Epistle, Jewish affairs had the appearance of spiritual prosperity (in point of orthodoxy and world-holiness), as well as of worldly flourishing in the reign (in part at least) of Herod Agrippa II. (See my Apost. Age. I. pp. 307, 312, 324).

And your garments.—Doubtless in the sense of the splendid garment ch. ii. 2.

Are become moth-eaten, σητόβρωτος, Job xiii. 28: not found in Classic Greek and not elsewhere in the New Testament.

VER. 3. **Your gold and your silver are eaten up with rust.**—κατιόω is ἅπαξ λεγ. in the New Testament. Gold and silver do not contract rust, hence Hornejus observes that it is *populariter dictum*, which is approved by Huther. Pott interprets the striking expression of the dimness of their burnish, others otherwise. According to Huther James did not anxiously calculate the difference of metals in his vivid concrete depiction; but this would be an intensely popular mode of expression. The words Is. i. 22, "Thy silver is become dross" are not a merely popular expression; on the contrary they are designed to bring out the unnatural fact that the princes of Israel are become rebellious and companions of thieves. It is then an unnatural phenomenon to which James adverts, of course in figurative language. It is as unnatural for gold and silver to be eaten up with rust as for the glory of Israel to be as corrupted as the glory of other nations corrupts, which may be compared to base metals.

And their rust shall be a testimony against you.—Wiesinger, with whom Huther agrees, proposes the following interpretation: in the consuming of their treasures, to be brought about by an outward judgment, they see depicted their own. But the loss of outward wealth under the influence of outward corruption is by no means evidence of the inward corruption of the losers. Oecumenius supposes that the rust on their gold and silver shall testify against the hardness of their heart, because they did not use them in doing good. This is correct as far as the reference is doubtless to a corruption inherent in their circumstances, but it lacks the due appreciation of the figurative sense: the rusting of your gold and silver, of your glory, represented by your leading men (see Is. i. 22, 23), shall be a token that the nation is corrupted in its rich men in general. And this was actually the case. The leading men who in the spiritual life ought to have shone like burnished silver and gold were rusted in legalism and dragged the majority of the self-righteous people into their own corruption.

And shall consume your flesh.—The Plural σάρκες is differently explained. The word stands simply for ὑμᾶς (Baumgarten), it denotes their well-fed bodies (Augusti), the fleshy parts of the body as contrasted with the bones (Huther who refers to 2 Kings ix. 36; and particularly to Mich. iii. 2, 3). But these passages contain no allusion to a consuming fire: fire consumes bones as well as flesh. We therefore assume that the term *flesh* is here used in a bad sense as in Gen. vi. 3; Jer. xvii. 5 and Jno. iii. 6, and that the Plural describes the life of the rich as exhibited in the carnalities or externals of religious, civil or individual life, in which they take delight. That consuming rust of the decayed, defunct and deadly legalism beginning at the gold and silver with which they decorate themselves, eats through the flesh of their customs, ceremonies and earthly possessions to the very destruction of their life. It is a rust which has the consuming energy of fire (Ps. xxi. 22; Is. x. 16, 17). The *rotten fixity*, described as *rust*, in its last stage transforms itself into the *fire* of a *revolutionary movement*, into a fanatical, *consuming conflagration* of rebellion (see Rev. xix. 20), or in brief: absolutism becomes revolution. It is the consummated national self-dissolution, as it fully developed itself in the Jewish war and in Jerusalem besieged. The reference therefore on the one hand, is neither to consuming grief and want (Erasmus and al.), nor, on the other, already to the real, positive judgments (Calvin, Grotius, Wiesinger, Huther and al.). With respect to ὡς πῦρ, Wiesinger, who adopts the punctuation of Cod. A and Oecumenius, and follows Grotius and Knapp, connects it with ἐθησαυρίσατε: "*tanquam ignem opes istas congessistis, et quidem ipsis extremis temporibus.*" Wiesinger cites as an analogy θησαυρίζεις σεαυτῷ ὀργήν, Rom. ii. 5, to which Huther rightly objects that in the words ἐθησαύρισατε ἐν ἐσχάταις ἡμέραις the principal stress rests on ἐσχάταις ἡμέραις. This is sufficient; his further remark that the fire denotes already positive judgment we consider, for the reason already given, to be incorrect, but this fire points to positive judgment. ὡς also is against Wiesinger's construction, and so does the over bold metaphor: ye have as it were gathered fire in gathering your wealth.

Ye have heaped up treasure.—The verb requires no definite specification of the object and the supply of ὀργήν (according to Rom. ii. 5. Calvin and al.) is superfluous and arbitrary. Moreover, the treasure, as Huther remarks, has been specified before.

In the last days.—Not perchance the last days, and the last days are neither the last days of life, nor the last days before the advent of Christ (Huther). James refers to the last days before the final national judgment, alluded to in v. 1, but not yet described. The gathering of treasure is done in the anticipation of a long happy future; this reprehensible heaping up treasure in the last days of their existence, immediately before the judgment involving not only the ruin of their treasure but also of their very existence, characterizes moreover their fearful want of apprehension (freedom from all misgiving and fear, assurance) and mad-like self-delusion. All their spiritual and worldly treasures are useless obstacles in the impending judgment, destined to vanish as the means of their self-delusion in order to make room for a fearful undeceiving. Thus the indication of positive judgment draws nearer, but the Apostle first refers to their decisive sins.

Their positive sins resulting from such spiritual self-delusion. Their sins against the reapers of the harvest in Israel. The unsuspecting assurance of their life of indulgence in the very day of their judgment. The crime of the murder of the Just One. Vv. 4–6.

VER. 4. **Behold the hire of the labourers.**—First decisive sin. Huther: "Injustice towards those who work for them;" Wiesinger: One case instead of many, a case moreover which clearly exposes the crying injustice of those rich men as the transgression of the express prohibition, Deut. xxiv. 14, 15; Lev. xix. 13; Mal. iii. 5.—And this is to be the whole meaning of this passage! But in the first place it is inconceivable that those wandering trafficking Jews of the dispersion (ch. iv. 13) should all of a sudden be transformed into large landed proprietors, and in the second equally inconceivable that James should have occasion to reproach all the rich landlords of the dispersion with literally holding back the hire of their labourers. Here also we must again insist upon the symbolical sense of the passage. The first question is to determine the sense in which the term "the harvest of Israel" is used by the prophets (Is. ix. 3; Joel iii. 18), by John the Baptist (Matth. iii. 12), and by our Lord (Jno. iv. 35; Matth. ix. 38; cf. Rev. xiv. 15, 16).—It denotes the time when the theocratic seed of God in Israel has become ripe unto harvest; on the one hand unto the harvest of judgment, on the other unto the harvest of salvation. The latter idea predominates here. The harvest of Israel was the ripened spirit-produce of the Old Testament, as manifested in the work of Christ; in the reapers we may aptly see the Apostles (according to Jno. iv. 35), and the first Christians in general. From them the rich in Israel kept back the hire in that they rejected their testimony in unbelief. And thus the voices of those reapers cried into the ears of the Lord of hosts, *i. e.*, abandoning the figure: their sin against them cried out to God, even to God, the Lord of those hosts which were already on the point of approaching in order to execute the judgment of God on Israel.—The labourers, ἐργάται, see 1 Tim. v. 18. ἀμᾶν is ἅπαξ λεγ. in N. T. The expression imports moreover that Israel's whole harvest of blessing has been brought home by these labourers into the Christian Church and that there is no other harvest besides it.

Which hath been kept back.—We construe with Huther "the hire which hath been kept back, crieth out from you," ἀφ' ὑμῶν, as we read in Gen. iv. 10. "the voice of thy brother's blood crieth unto me from the ground," because thus the injustice crying out for vengeance is laid to the charge of the evil-doers not to that of the labourers; the common construction "which hath been kept back by you" seems to be less opposed by taking ἀπό in the sense of ὑπό, than by the consideration that κράζει denotes a crying out for vengeance. Hence the connection is not: "the hire of the mowers crieth out and this crying has come to the ears of God" (Theile), but the crying out of the hire that has been kept back (Gen. xviii. 20; xix. 13) on the one hand, is completed on the other by the βοαί of the reapers or the gatherers of the harvest, first as cries of complaint and cries for help (see Heb. v. 7; Acts iv. 24 etc.; ch. xii. 5), and lastly also as cries for righteous recompense (Rev. vi. 10, 11). And these, even more than the former crying have entered into the ears of the Lord of hosts; which would yield this sense: not only the unbelief of the unbelieving Jews but also the distress of the believing Christians induce the Lord of hosts to send forth His hosts unto judgment; as indeed the destruction of Jerusalem was not only a visitation of judgment on Judaism but also a visitation of salvation on the Christian Church. The crying out of Christian blood for mercy to enemies reaches also its limit in the induration of unbelievers; moreover we should distinguish the reapers themselves from their βοαί, here made objective. The term "Lord of hosts" hardly renders prominent the power of God, as that of Lord of the heavenly hosts only (Wiesinger, Huther); He is also Lord of the earthly hosts according to the prophets (Is. vi. 3; xviii. 7; xxiv. 21; Amos ix. 4, 5), and also according to Christ (Matth. xxii. 7). [Bede suggests the following reason "*Dominum exercituum appellat, ad terrorem eorum, qui pauperes putant nullum habere tutorem.*" This is the only passage in the New Testament where the term "Lord of hosts" is used in direct discourse. Rom. ix. 29 is a quotation.—M.].

Second sin. v. 5. **Ye have lived high on earth.**—τρυφᾶν is ἅπαξ λεγ. in the N. T. It comprehends the ideas: to live softly, voluptuously, gloriously and also extravagantly. In LXX. (Neh. ix. 25 and Is. lxvi. 11) the fundamental idea is "to take delight in something to revel." σπαταλᾶν denotes living lewdly, luxuriously, especially in eating and drinking; but in LXX. (Ezek. xvi. 49 and Amos vi. 4) the idea of idle indulgence is decidedly predominant, probably also in 1 Tim. v. 6. Hence the two words would express not the definite antithesis *deliciæ et exquisita voluptas* and *luxuria, atque prodigalitas* (Hottinger), but that of positive sumptuousness in pleasure and sensuality and of negative sumptuousness in effeminate, careless indolence. We might therefore translate "Ye have had your *delight* and have *settled down* on earth," or "ye have become worldly and effeminate," or "ye have bragged and made a show." The opposite order occurs in Luke xvi. 19: the daily wearing of holiday-apparel denotes the idler, the sumptuous living, revelry. Huther strikingly points out the contrast of this sumptuous mode of life and the toilsome life of the labourers, also the contrast of such revelling on earth and the complaint which is made to the Lord in heaven. But we must not overlook in this revelling on earth the thought, that the earth, the earthly, figuratively taken, was the foundation in which their revelling struck root, and that the day of slaughter is the principal antithesis of revelling.

And fattened your hearts.—τρέφειν in the opinion of several commentators denotes *fattening*, for the evident design of this clause is to show that the rich regarded and nourished their heart as an animal existence. Hence Huther is wrong in his correction of Luther, "to pasture your hearts," better: "to satiate." Luther's rendering is excellent and we should have retained it but for the necessity of holding fast to the other meaning that fattening the heart is at the same time indurating the heart (καρδία πεπωρωμένη). The heart, however, is not a paraphrastic description of the body or individuality but denotes inward life, the kernel of spiritual life (Acts xiv. 17). Wiesinger asserts that καρδία involves *per se* the idea of passionate fondness of enjoyment, but Luke xxi. 34 is the last passage which makes good his assertion.

In the day of slaughter.—On the omission of ὡς see Appar. Crit. Nor must ἐν be changed into εἰς. The rendering "as on a day of slaughter" (Luther, Wolf, Augusti) is consequently a double weakening of the thought. The comment of Calvin, Grotius, Bengel etc., that the day of slaughter is the day of sacrifice, when the slaughter of the victims is followed by banqueting, is altogether outside of the connection with the judgment. Calvin: "*Quia solebant in sacrificiis solemnibus liberalius vesci, quam pro quotidiano more. Dicit ergo divites tota vita continuare festum.*" Huther rightly observes that the term in question is never used in this sense. De Wette sees in it a comparison to beasts, which on the very day of slaughter eat in unconcern. Huther thinks this comparison inappropriate, since beasts do not eat more greedily on the day of slaughter than at any other time. But this refutation rests on a misunderstanding. Beasts* always eat greedily; their eating on the day of slaughter may therefore be used as a figure of the inordinate feasting of the obdurate on the very day of judgment. The analogy of 2 Pet. ii. 12 only tends to strengthen the appropriateness of this construction. The thought is further intensified by the consideration that while beasts are led to pasture and fattened for the day of slaughter, these men laid themselves voluntarily out for feasting in the very day of slaughter. But we may suppose that this point of comparison must not be dissociated from the general and more lofty meaning of ἡμέρα σφαγῆς, viz. that of a day of judgment (Jer. xii. 3; xxv. 34). In the last passage also the ideas "day of judgment" and "day of slaughter" are taken together in a literal sense, so also in Is. liii. 7; Rev. xix. 17, 18. But the day on which began Israel's day of judgment which is developing itself into a day of slaughter, was the day of Christ's crucifixion

* In German "*Fressen*" and "*Saufen*" are properly used to denote the *eating* and *drinking* of beasts, *i. e. inordinate, greedy* eating and drinking. Applied to human beings the terms are offensive and insulting, although the vulgar are apt to indulge in these choice terms with reference to themselves.—M.

which connected with the day of the destruction of Jerusalem becomes in a symbolical sense *one* day of visitation. The Aorists here, therefore, are not used to indicate that the conduct of the rich is to be viewed from the future day of judgment at the second coming of Christ (Huther), but because their carnal arrogance and unconcern in the devilish revelling of their hearts culminated just on the judgment-day of Israel. Since then their day of slaughter is in process of development. Just as they had therefore collected together the treasures of legal righteousness in the last days, while the old time was on the wane, so they had reached the climax of their self-indulgent worldliness on the last day, the day of judgment.—This leads to their third and greatest sin.

VER. 6. **Ye have condemned, ye have killed the Just.**—The fact of modern commentators disputing the exposition of Oecumenius, Bede and Grotius that *the Just* signifies Christ, proves how far they have wandered from the text in the treatment of this Epistle. Only think of James, the witness of Christ, at the end of his course calling out to the obdurate of all the people of Israel: Ye have condemned and killed the Just and they not to have understood him to refer to the rejection and crucifixion of Christ! But to what or to whom else did they think he was alluding? Gebser and Huther [also Alford—M.] take *δίκαιον* collectively for *τοὺς δικαίους*; *i. e.* oppressed, suffering Christians, and Huther says: "The ground of the persecution is implied in the word *δίκαιον* itself; the Singular should be taken collectively, the idea absolutely" (similarly Theile). But then surely Christ ought to be considered as standing at the head of these slain ones. Wiesinger (and de Wette) refers the term to continued persecution *ad mortem usque* and adds that all reference to Christ is so manifestly against the whole context of the passage, that refutation is altogether unnecessary. On the contrary, proof is almost unnecessary. Wiesinger objects first, that the Epistle is addressed to the dispersion. But at the Passover, when Christ was crucified, the dispersion also was represented at Jerusalem, and symbolically all Israel was already dispersed. The most important objection is the *Present οὐκ ἀντιτάσσεται ὑμῖν*. This *Present* is certainly difficult. But is it more convenient to affirm concerning the collectively just man, that he had been killed by those rich and that he was still living than to affirm as much concerning Christ? The Vulgate probably alludes to Christ in rendering "*non restitit;*" so Luther, "he hath not resisted you." But the *Present* forbids such a rendering. But also the common explanation: "Ye have killed the Just, he does not resist you" gives a thought which is not clear, at least not very distinct. It would perhaps be easier to suppose that the readers of the Epistle understood James to say: "Christ does not resist you in His members, He still endures willingly all persecutions in His sufferings." But would this thought be a fitting conclusion of the great denunciation of those obdurate people? Nor is it the idea "the just do not resist you." We understand therefore Bentley's conjecture of reading *ὁ κύριος* instead of *οὐκ* (see Ch. iv. 6; 1 Pet. v. 5; Prov. iii. 34); still more the explanation of Benson to take the clause interrogatively. Giving to *ἀντιτάσσεσθαι* the fullest Middle sense, the question would read thus: "Does He not bring up against you His army (as the executor of the punitive justice of the Lord of hosts)?" or "does He not rise against you in combat?" At least it is easy to understand that with a predominantly ascetic turn of mind such a question might have been asked. But considering the importance of the matter, the interrogative form ought to be more distinctly marked: does he not already march against you, march against you in the tempest of war? Besides such an explanation might easily obscure the thought of the continuous suffering which Christ endures in His people. Hence one might light on the idea of rebellion, as we have it in Rom. xiii. 2. He does not rebel against you, *i. e.* you are the rebels. But this again is not sufficiently clear. We read therefore: He stands no longer in your way, He does not stop you (in the way of death); He suffers you to fill up your measure. See Matth. xxiii. 32–38. And this dark, pregnant sentence is the concentration of the announcement that the judgment impending on them, is inevitable. [The clause "*οὐκ ἀντιτάσσεται ὑμῖν*" seems to be ironical: *He* lets you alone (Hos. iv. 17).—James was called by his contemporaries "the Just" and this reference to Jesus as "*the Just One*" is a touching illustration of his character, for a delineation of which the reader is referred to the Introduction.—M.].

DOCTRINAL AND ETHICAL.

1. Both the Gospel and James are altogether free from any and every Ebionite one-sidedness that wealth, as such, is sinful and poverty, as such, meritorious. James allows the possession and use of earthly riches, but—*in majorem Dei gloriam*. While the rich are thus more privileged than others, they are also under doubly great obligations; but if they persistently acquit themselves of their discharge and use their riches only for the attainment of selfish ends which conflict with the law of love, then they are in all justice and reason liable to a *væ vobis divitibus* cf. Luke vi. 24; Matth. vi. 19–21.—

2. Earthly wealth is not an absolute but a relative obstacle to entering the kingdom of God; cf. Mark x. 23–25.—The history of many rich men, *e. g.* Nicodemus and Joseph of Arimathea shows that this obstacle may be overcome. But this is impossible where covetousness reigns supreme and adopts every means of preserving or increasing earthly possessions. Here applies the Apostolic warning, 1 Tim. vi. 17–19,—compare also Plutarch, *de cupiditate divitiarum*, and the saying of Seneca, *de benef.* II. c. 27, "*concitatior est avaritia in magnarum opum congestus,*" also Sallust, *in Catil.* c. x. 4.—A life of luxurious indulgence as the concomitant of wealth and dependence on that wealth coupled with unfeeling contempt of one's brother, according to the teaching of Christ Himself, deserves the judgment Luke xvi. 25. And the history of the destruction of Jerusalem as well as innumerable incidents taken from the history of the kingdom of God confirm the fact that such rich men are

not rarely visited already here below with earthly calamity and outward distress apart from that judgment for eternity.

3. The rejection of the Messiah, to which James clearly alludes (v. 6), as the work of the prominent Jews, as the murder of the Innocent and the Just was not only a heinous crime *per se* (cf. Acts iii. 13–15), but also the first of a series of crimes enacted on the members of the Body, after they had first laid hands on the Head, which terminated at last in the horrors of the Jewish civil war and were punished with the fall of the city and the destruction of the temple.

4. Christianity imposes upon all men, blessed with earthly goods, the duty to ascertain and, if practicable, to satisfy the wants of their subordinates and servants and to consider themselves not as the lords but as the stewards of the capital confided to them, Luke xvi. 2; cf. Col. iv. 1.—Those who neglect this duty and oppress the poor have even pursuant to the tenor of the Old Testament to bear the dreadful punishment of God. See *e. g.* Ps. xxxvii.; Prov. xiv. 31; Eccl. v.–vii.

5. "Indulgence as it were fattens men for the punishment of hell—a figure taken from the sacrificial victims—*i. e.* ripens them so much the more for torments." Heubner on v. 5.

HOMILETICAL AND PRACTICAL.

Wealth not an absolute superiority, poverty not an absolute evil.—Those who have most possessions on earth, have also to lose most in times of common suffering and tribulation.—Earthly riches from the nature of the case, are as transitory as their owners.—The true Christian an *omnia sua secum portans.*—The history of the rich fool is that of many (Luke xii. 16–20).—The degree to which the rich may be poor and the poor rich.—God's rich harvest-blessing changed into a curse through man's selfishness.—It is possible to do evil, but not to do it unpunished.—God is higher than the highest that oppress the poor Eccl. v. 8.—The worldling's short joy followed by long pain.—The murder of the Just One the most horrid manifestation of outward selfishness.—The fact that evil is suffered here on earth no guarantee that it will not be punished (vv. 4–6).—Threefold sin of the rich; 1, oppression of the poor (v. 4), 2, selfish indulgence (v. 5), 3, murder of the Just One (v. 6).—How the crime of the rejection of Christ is still continued in various ways by many among the rich of this world.—The Christian has great cause to offer the prayer of Agur, Prov. xxx. 7–9.—The love of money the root of all evil (1 Tim. vi. 10) and of idolatry, Col. iii. 5.—

Starke: Cramer:—If you get riches, set not your heart on them, Ps. lxii. 11.—A man may be very rich and yet be very wicked, Ps. lxxiii. 12.

Augustine:—*Magna pietas! thesaurizat pater filiis; immo magna vanitas! thesaurizat moriturus morituris.*—Many who do not leave even children and know not whose shall be their riches (Luke xii. 20) are so possessed of avarice, that they loathe parting even with a penny. O, unhappy rich!

Quesnel:—Thus the rich ground their hope on things which decay and perish. Foolish building! Matth. vii. 26, 27.

Langii Op.:—If there were many pious rich men, who did husband their wealth as the stewards of God, the need of the poor would be greatly lessened, Luke viii. 2, 3; xxii. 35.

Hedinger:—There are many who gather along with their gold a treasure of the wrath and vengeance of God, Rom. ii. 5.—To defraud labourers of their hire they have earned is a sin that crieth out to heaven and is sure to be followed by the curse and most fearful vengeance of God, 1 Thess. iv. 6.—The name of God "the Lord of hosts" is as terrible to the ungodly as it is consoling to the godly, Ps. xlvi. 11, 12.—Robbing the poor of their well-earned wages is murder, Ex. i. 13, 14.

Stier: (v. 6):—James refers primarily to the Lord, the Just One (Acts vii. 52) and he himself bore the honourable epithet "the Just," he here (*implicite*) humbly declines that epithet. Yet again—(here the inspiration of the Spirit affects the author of the Epistle so perceptibly and becomes here so remarkably prophetical that again)—he is unconsciously prophesying of himself. An author, who lived soon after the Apostles (Hegesippus), gives us a full account, which is doubtless correct in its main features, of the martyrdom of James the Just, the Lord's brother, shortly before the siege of Jerusalem. See Introd. p. 9 etc.; [also Excursus p. 18, etc.—M.].—(v. 4). Surely the words of James apply to many of our contemporaries, and many a proud palace ought to have the appropriate inscription.—"Woe unto him that buildeth his house by unrighteousness and his chambers by wrong."—The treatment which poor labourers experience at the hands of our money-aristocrats and merchant princes, who in their avarice are just what those names import and nothing more, who refuse to know the Lord God and our Saviour, cries *everywhere* loud enough in *our ears*, and is it likely that this crying has not also entered into the ears of the Lord of hosts? Of Him, who commanded even Moses to say in the law: "Thou shalt not oppress an hired servant, that is poor and needy—lest he cry against thee unto the Lord, and it be sin unto thee." Deut. xxiv. 14, 15.—

Jakobi:—It is not the measure of wealth, but the measure of sin, which tells; everything depends upon the manner how earthly riches, be they great or small, have been acquired and are enjoyed; and hence those whom we can by no means call wealthy, may be just as ungodly and unrighteous, just as indulgent and voluptuous as those who are really rich. Our text is therefore addressed to all that are earthly-minded, to all worldly people that do not order their lives according to the rule "to have, as though they had, and to buy, as though they possessed not." 1 Cor. vii. 29 etc.

Neander:—James describes wealth in three different respects, viz. in garnered fruits of the field, in apparel, in gold and silver. All these, he says, the rich heap up without profit. Their treasures in gold and silver, for want of use, are eaten up with rust and will testify against them in judgment, finding them guilty because they suffered to perish for want of use that which they ought to have employed for the benefit of others. The rust consumes their own flesh, reminding them of their own perishableness and of the punishment that awaits them in the judgment, because instead of gathering durable riches, they have heaped up the fire of Divine punishment in treasures destined to be eaten up with rust.

VIEDEBANDT:—A Christian, as has been strikingly said, may own worldly possessions like Abraham, David and many more, for a beggar's staff will no more take us to heaven than a golden chain or velvet fur will take us to hell. Christ says not; "Ye cannot have God and mammon," but "Ye cannot *serve* God and mammon." Riches, says Augustine, are gifts of God and therefore good in themselves. Lest men decry them as evil, they are also accorded to the good, lest they be valued as the best goods, they are also given to the evil; Holy Scripture therefore only forbids men to be proud of and to ground their hopes on uncertain riches. But although riches and righteousness are compatible with one other, yet those who are distinguished by their worldly possessions, should cherish in their souls a sacred fear of them.—Riches are snares [German rhyme "*Schätze sind Netze.*"—M.].—A man lights hell-fire with his own hands if he suffers the fire of lusts to burn in his heart.—Dr. Sauvergne, a physician, narrates the case of a miser, who had his money brought to his dying bed and expired with the words "more gold, more gold!"

LISCO:—The dangers of wealth.—Of twofold riches (earthly and heavenly).—

PORUBSZKY:—The woe uttered over the rich. 1, what it means; 2, its application to our time, 3, when it will cease.

[WORDSWORTH: v. 2.—Although they may still glitter brightly in *your* eyes, and may dazzle men by their brilliance when ye walk the streets, or sit in the high places of this world; yet they are in fact *already* cankered. They are loathsome in *God's sight*. The Divine anger has breathed on them and blighted them; they are already withered and blasted, as being doomed to speedy destruction; for ye *lived delicately on the earth* (v. 5), and have not laid up treasure in *heaven*, where neither *moth* nor *rust* doth corrupt (Matth. vi. 20).

Even while shining in your coffers, they are, in God's eye, sullied and corroded, and they will not profit you in the day of trial, but be consumed by His indignation: and the rust they have contracted by lying idle as κτήματα, and not being used as χρήματα, will be a *witness against* you at the Great Day; and will pass from them by a plague-like contagion and *devour your flesh as fire.*

v. 5.—A striking contrast. Ye feasted jovially in a day of sacrifice, when abundance of flesh of the sacrificed animals is on the table at the sacrificial banquet. Ye ought to have ruled the people gently and mildly; but ye "have fed yourselves and not the flock," ye *nourished* your *own hearts* and not those of your people; ye have sacrificed and devoured them like sheep or calves of the stall-fatted for the pampering of your own appetites. Cf. Ezek. xxxiv. 1–10. Cyril *in Caten.* p. 33.

Ye did this at the very time when ye yourselves were like victims appointed to be sacrificed in the day of the Lord's vengeance, which is often compared by Hebrew prophets to a sacrifice, see below, Rev. xix. 17. Cf. Oecumenius and Theophylact here.

This was signally verified by the event. The Jews from all parts of the world came together to the *sacrifice* of the *Passover* A. D. 70, and they themselves were then *slain as victims* to God's offended justice, especially in the *Temple*; particularly was this true of the *rich*, as recorded by Josephus, *B. J.* vi. *passim.*—Their wealth excited the cupidity and provoked the fury of the factious zealots against them, and they fell victims in a day of slaughter to their own love of mammon; what was left of their substance was consumed by the flames, which burnt the city.—Joseph. *B. J.* VII. 29, 32, 37.—M.].

X. FINAL THEME AND CONCLUSION.

FURTHER ADDRESS TO THE BRETHREN. FINAL THEME: EXHORTATION TO ENDURANCE IN LONG-SUFFERING PATIENCE UNTO THE COMING OF THE LORD.—ENCOURAGEMENT THERETO. CONDITION THEREOF. FINAL PROMISE.

CHAPTER V. 7–20.

7 Be patient therefore, brethren, unto the coming of the Lord. Behold, the hus-
bandman waiteth for the precious fruit of the earth, and hath long patience for it,
8 until he receive the early[1] and latter rain. Be ye also patient;[2] establish your hearts:
9 for the coming of the Lord draweth nigh. Grudge not one against another, brethren,[3]
10 lest ye be condemned:[4] behold, the[5] judge standeth before the door. Take, my[6] bre-
thren,[7] the prophets, who have spoken in[8] the name of the Lord, for an example of
11 suffering affliction,[9] and of patience. Behold, we count them happy which endure.[10]
Ye have heard of the patience of Job, and have seen[11] the end of the Lord; that the
12 Lord[12] is very pitiful, and of tender mercy. But above all things,[13] my brethren,
swear not, neither by heaven, neither by the earth, neither by any other oath: but
13 let[14] your yea be yea; and *your* nay, nay; lest ye fall into condemnation.[15] Is any

14 among you afflicted? let him pray. Is any merry? let him sing psalms. Is any sick
among you? let him call for the elders of the church; and let them pray over him,
15 anointing him with oil in the name of the Lord:[16] And the prayer of faith shall save
the sick, and the Lord shall raise him up; and if he have committed sins, they shall
16 be forgiven him. Confess[17] *your* faults[18] one to another, and pray [19] one for another,
that ye may be healed. The effectual fervent prayer of a righteous man availeth
17 much. Elias was a man subject to like passions as we are, and he prayed ear-
nestly that it might not rain: and it rained not on the earth by the space of three
18 years and six months. And he prayed again, and the heaven gave rain,[20] and the
19 earth brought forth her fruit. Brethren,[21] if any of you do err from the truth,[22] and
20 one convert him; Let him know[23] that he which converteth the sinner from the error
of his way shall save a soul[24] from death, and shall hide a multitude of sins.[25]

Verse 7. [1 Rec. A. K. L. al. insert ὑέτον before πρώϊμον; Cod. Sin. inserts τόν καρπόν (τόν improb.) before πρώϊμον.—M.]

Lange: Be patient therefore [endure], brethren, ... having patience with reference to it, till it hath received the early and the latter rain.

[.... being patient over (Alford) it, untill it shall have received .... —M.]

Verse 8. [2 Cod. Sin. L. al. insert οὖν after μακροθυμήσατε.—M.]

Lange: .... strengthen your hearts, for the coming of the Lord is nigh.

[.... stablish ...., because the coming .... —M.]

Verse 9. 3 A. B. Lachm. Tischend. place ἀδελφοί before ἀλλήλων. [Cod. Sin. κατὰ ἀλλήλων.—M.]

4 A. B. K. L. [Cod. Sin.—M]. al. read κριθῆτε for κατακριθῆτε.

5 Rec. omits not ὁ κριτής (as Huther asserts), but ὁ sustained by A. B. K. L. [Cod. Sin.—M.] al.

Lange: Groan (sigh) not .... that ye be not judged .... before the doors.

[Murmur not, brethren, ... that ye be not judged .... —M.]

Verse 10. 6 7 Rec. K. L. al. insert μου before ἀδελφοί, omit A. B.—Rec. has τῆς κακοπαθείας before ἀδελφοί but A. B. K. L. al give ἀδελφοί first.

8 ἐν found in B [Cod. Sin.—M.], adopted by Lachmann, is wanting in A. G. K. al.

[9 Cod. Sin. reads καλοκαγαθίας for κακοπαθείας.—M.]

Lange: Take, brethren, as an example of suffering evil and of patience the prophets who have spoken in virtue of the name of the Lord.

[Take, my brethren, ... of affliction and patience ...., who spoke in .... —M.]

Verse 11. 10 Lachmann for ὑπνμένοντας reads ὑπομείναντας A. B. Vulg. al. Cod Sin. ὑπομίναντας.

11 ἴδετε A. B. G. al. Tischend. [Alford], through an exegetical mistake appears to have been changed into εἴδετε Rec. B. al. and adopted by Lachmann.

12 ὁ κύριος omit G. K. al. Tischendorf; A. B. insert it, but B omits the Article. This ὁ κύριος was probably omitted, because it was held to be superfluous after the preceding κυρίου (Huther).

Lange: Behold, we count happy the sufferers who did endure.—Ye have heard of the endurance of Job and look at the end [the consummation] of the Lord. For very compassionate is the Lord and merciful.

[Behold, we count happy them that endure .... See also the end of the Lord [of His dealings with him]: because the Lord is very pitiful and merciful.—M.]

Verse 12. [13 Cod. Sin. has πάντων οὖν.—M.]

[14 Cod. Sin. reads ἤτω δὲ ὁ λόγος for ἤτω δὲ Rec.—M.]

[15 Luther's rendering "into hypocrisy" arose from the less authentic reading εἰς ὑπόκρισιν Rec. G. K. al. But A. B. Vulg. al. fix the reading ὑπὸ κρίσιν.

Lange: But above all things, my brethren, swear (conspire) not, neither by the heaven, nor by the earth .....But let your (Sinait.: ὁ λόγος) yea be a yea, and your nay a nay, that ye fall not under judgment.

[.... that ye fall not under judgment.—M.]

Verse 13. Lange: Does affliction happen to any among you? ...., is any cheerful, let him sing praise.

[Is any among you in affliction? .... Is any cheerful? .... —.M]

Verse 14. [16 Insert τοῦ before κυρίου Rec. K. L. omits B, which also omits κυρίου.—M.]

Lange: .... let him call to himself ....

[.... let him call for .... —M.]

Verse 15. Lange: And the prayer of faith shall help the sick .... it shall be forgiven him.

[.... save (heal) the sick man; .... M.]

Verse 16. 17 A. B. K. [Cod. Sin.—M.] Vulg. al. Lachmann [Alford] insert οὖν. [Rec. omits it.—M.]

18 τὰς ἁμαρτίας A. B. [Cod. Sin.—M.] al. Lachmann; τα παραπτώματα G. K. al. Tischendorf [Alford.—M.]

19 A. B. προσεύχεσθε; [Rec. εὔχεσθε.—M.]

Lange: Confess, therefore, your sins to one another, and pray for one another .... The prayer of a righteous man, inwardly effectual [efficiency effected] availeth much.

[.... therefore your transgressions one to another .... The inwardly effectual prayer of a righteous man is very efficacious.—M.]

Verse 17. Lange: .....of like passions with us, and he prayed a prayer that it should not rain, and it did not rain in the land for ....

[.... of like passions with us, and he prayed with prayer that it might not rain, and it rained not on the earth for .... —M.]

Verse 18. [20 ἔδωκεν τὸν ὑετόν Cod. Sin. A. al.—M.]

Verse 19. 21 Rec. G. Tischend. omit μου, A. B. K. [Cod. Sin.—M.] insert it; so Lachmann [Alford.—M.]

[22 Cod. Sin. inserts τῆς ὁδοῦ before τῆς ἀληθείας.—M.]

Lange: My brethren, if any among you should have strayed from the truth, [Sinait.: from the way of the truth] and one should convert him ....

[.... be led astray from the truth and one turn him back.—M.]

Verse 20. [23 γινωσκέτω Rec. A. K. L. Vulg. al.; γινώσκετε B. Alford.—M.]

24 ψυχὴν αὐτοῦ. A. [Cod. Sin.—M.] Vulg. al. Lachmann, [A inserts τήν—M.]; Rec. B. G. K. al. read ψυχήν.

Lange: Let him know .... cover a multitude of sins.

[Know ye, that he who turneth a sinner from the error of his way .... —M.]

25 The subscriptions: of James; Epistle of James; Epistle of St. James.

[Ιακωβου B; Ιακωβου επιστολη, A; τελος· του αγιου αποστολου Ιακωβου επιστολη καθολικη Z.—M.]

EXEGETICAL AND CRITICAL.

Analysis:—Further address to the brethren. Final theme, viz: exhortation to endurance in long-suffering patience unto the coming of the Lord, vv. 7-9. Encouragement thereto: Examples of patient suffering, vv. 10, 11.—Conditions thereof: Shunning of seditious movements. A hallowed disposition. The healing of their sicknesses. Liberation of the conscience by means of confession of sins. Exhortation to intercession. The example of Elias, vv. 12-18.—Conclusion replete with promise, vv. 19, 20.

Further address to the brethren. Final theme: viz. exhortation to endurance in long-suffering patience unto the coming of the Lord, vv. 7, 8.

VER. 7. **Be patient therefore, brethren.**—ἀδελφοί is the turning-point in the Apostle's address. He now turns primarily to the Christian section of his readers without excluding however the further design of the address for all Jews capable of conversion in contrast to the aforementioned incorrigible πλούσιοι. μακροθυμεῖν literally to have great courage, to be magnanimous, branches out into the ideas to be long-suffering or forbearing towards the erring, applicable both to Divine and human long-suffering, and to be patient in the endurance of suffering, but also with the lateral idea of patiently hoping for endurance under apparent danger, *here* under the experience of worldly and human wrong, Heb. vi. 12. Hence μακροθυμία is distinguished from ὑπομονή in Col. i. 11. And here also the term is obviously chosen instead of ὑπομένειν ch. i. 12, because the Apostle desires to lay stress on the endurance of the Jewish-Christian under the wrongs of the old situation of the world, by which the Judaists suffered themselves to be drifted into revolution.

Unto the coming of the Lord.—The Lord is Christ, as in ch. ii. 1, and the παρουσία denotes His eschatological advent according to the entire evangelical and apostolical system of doctrine (consequently not the coming of God unto judgment distinct and separate from the advent of Christ, as held by Augusti, Theile, de Wette). But this involves no reason for identifying this παρουσία with the judgments announced in v. 1. nor must we, on the other hand, limit the coming of Christ to the last and concluding event of His epiphany. The coming of Christ is the epiphany (manifestation) of Christ with all its antecedent interpositions, be they universal or individual, the greatest of which is the destruction of Jerusalem, as the type of all subsequent comings.

Behold the husbandman waiteth.—Cf. ch. iii. 18; Sir. vi. 16; 2 Tim. ii. 6.

For the precious fruit of the earth.—Which is well worth waiting for. In this the husbandman is a symbol for believers, as also in that he confides the seed to the earth, to invisibleness, to seeming death and the grave. Jno. xii. 24.—

Being patient over it.—μακροθυμεῖν probably denotes here his persevering hope of the seemingly buried seed. It is the preciousness of the fruit (which, although invisible, he sees in expectation), that gives him long-enduring, faith-like courage. He calculates on it. [ἐπί is very graphic; it depicts him, as it were, sitting over it in the confident expectation of its appearing.—M.].

Until it shall have received.—That is, the fruit in its seed, not the husbandman (Morus).

The early and the latter rain.—That is with reference to the climate of Palestine: the autumnal rain before sowing, the spring rain before harvest, Deut. xi. 14, 2; Jer. v. 24, etc. See Winer, R. W. B. Article "*Witterung.*" [The early rain πρώϊμος מוֹרֶה יוֹרֶה began to fall about the middle of October, became more continuous in November and December and turned into snow in January and February. The latter rain ὄψιμος, מַלְקוֹשׁ fell in March and lasted to about the middle of April. Thunder-gusts were not uncommon from January to March.—The singular exposition of the early and the latter rain given by Oecumenius may prove suggestive: πρώϊμος ὑετός, ἡ ἐν νεότητι μετὰ δακρύων μετάνοιά. ὄψιμος, ἡ ἐν τῇ γήρᾳ.—M.].

VER. 8. **Be ye also patient.**—As is the husbandman. It is assumed that the seed has been sown among them. Their patience, indeed, is sorely tried, hence:

Establish your hearts.—1 Thess. iii. 13; 1 Pet. v. 10. It is here understood that this must be done by seeking refuge in prayer to the Lord, who giveth strength, as has been repeatedly pointed out, ch. i. 5, 6 etc.

Because the coming of the Lord is nigh.—Literally: it has already drawn nigh in its coming nigh. It is not a fixed nearness but a constant drawing nearer and that, not in the sense of a chronological definition, but in the sense of a religious expectation and assurance, which does not calculate the time and the hour, or rather looks at time in the spirit of the Lord before whom a thousand years are as one day (2 Pet. iii. 8). In the Apostle's sense of the expression, it could be said and may be said at all times: the coming of the Lord is nigh.

VER. 9. **Murmur not, brethren, against one another.**—There is no reason why this should be limited to the mutual forbearance among "Christians" (Huther). Here again all the dissensions among the Jews must be taken into consideration. As James had already denounced their quarrels, so he now feels anxious to stop the very sources of these quarrels. Huther admits that James refers to a "*gemitus accusatorius*" (Estius, Calvin), but denies that it amounts to a "*provocatio ultionis*" (Theile and al.). But the second cannot be separated from the first; the legalism of the Old Testament, moreover, as contrasted with the thorough fidelity of the N. T. intercession, exerted as yet a powerful influence over the minds of the Jewish-Christians and might easily bias them in that direction. The believing Jews were peculiarly exposed to that temptation by the oppressive and irritating treatment they received at the hands of the rich. Huther rightly remarks that impatience in affliction has the tendency of making men irritable. [It is of course difficult to determine whether the reference is to Christians only or to those who were open to conviction, or to all whom it might concern. As the exhortation states a general moral duty, it is perhaps best to give it the widest possible application. In this sense the note of Hornejus (in Huther) will be found useful: "*Quos ad manifestas et gravissimas improborum injurias fortiter ferendas incitarat, eos nunc hortatur, ut etiam in minoribus illis offensis quæ inter pios ipsos sæpe subnascuntur, vel condonandis vel dissimulandis promti sint. Contingit enim ut qui hostium et improborum maximas sæpe contumelias et injurias æquo animo tolerant, fratrum tamen offensas multo leniores non facile ferant.*"—M.].

That ye be not judged.—According to Matth. vii. 1, because murmuring against one another is also judging. [The reference is to final condemnation.—M.].

Behold, the Judge standeth before the doors.—(Matth. xxiv. 33). *Before the door.* The Judge *i. e.* Christ. Theile sees here a reference to the disposition of the Judge to punish the oppressors and to avenge the oppressed; Huther, on the other hand, says it is intended to caution the suffering against the suspension of love and to hold out to them the promise of speedy deliverance. But it is pretty certain that the love of justice, purified from every unholy admixture, may also expect the just recompense of evil, and that the two ideas, therefore, go together. Wiesinger's remark is excellent: "Ye may with perfect calmness leave the judgment to Him and therefore ye ought not to expose yourselves to the danger of the judgment." Cf. Phil. iv. 5. [Seeing Christ will speedily execute judgment, do not murmur against one another; murmuring against one another is a species of judging and condemning, ye are brethren, not accusers and judges of one another; invading the prerogative of the Judge renders you liable to judgment and condemnation. Love, requite evil with good and leave the judgment in the hands of Christ.—The reader is referred to the Introduction for the remarkable incident recorded by Hegesippus that the religious sects at Jerusalem were wont to ask St. James "which is the *Door* of Jesus?" Wordsworth says: "The words of St. James 'Behold the Judge standeth at the *doors*' perhaps became current among them. Perhaps those words may also have excited the question put in a tone of derision, 'which is the *Door* of Jesus?' at *what* Door is He standing? By *what Door* will He come? Show Him to us and we will go out to meet Him.—This supposition is confirmed by the reply of St. James, 'why do ye ask me concerning the Son of Man? He sitteth in heaven, and *will come* in the clouds of heaven.'"—For other interpretations of that saying "Which is the Door of Jesus?" see Bp. Pearson on St. Ignatius, ad Philadelph. 9, αὐτὸς ὢν θύρα τοῦ πατρὸς, with reference to Jno. x. 7–9; Valesius and al. on *Euseb.* II. 23; Lardner, *Hist. of Apostles*, ch. 16; Credner, *Einleit.* 2, p. 580; Gieseler, *Church Hist.* § 31; and Delitzsch on *Ep. to the Hebrews*, p. 673.—M.].

Encouragement thereto. Examples of patient suffering. vv. 10, 11.

Ver. 10. **Take, my brethren, as an example.**—ὑπόδειγμα, example or pattern=παράδειγμα, representation, related to ὑπογραμμός, writing-copy (copy-head) perhaps also attestation, and τύπος, the original pattern or beginning of a thing.

Of affliction and patience.—κακοπάθεια, ἅπαξ λεγ. in N. T. although not exactly=to suffer wrong (Hottinger), or=to suffer absolutely, denotes suffering evil or affliction, which easily suggests suffering wrong. [But, as Alford remarks, the word is strictly objective and is found parallel with ξυμφορά and the like. Cf. v. 13, Mal. i. 12; 2 Macc. ii. 26, 27; and Thucyd. vii. 77, ἐλπίδα χρὴ ἔχειν, μηδὲ καταμέμψασθαι ὑμᾶς ἄγαν αὐτούς, μήτε ταῖς ξυμφοραῖς, μήτε ταῖς παρὰ τὴν ἀξίαν νῦν κακοπαθείαις (spoken by Nicias to the suffering Athenian army in Sicily): so Isocr. p. 127. c. μηδὲ μικρὰν οἴεσθαι δεῖν ὑπενεγκεῖν κακοπάθειαν.—M.].

The prophets, who spoke in the name of the Lord.—Cf. Matth. v. 12. The addition characterizes them as servants of the Lord, who endured wrong for His sake.—**Who spoke.**—In a pregnant sense as frequently in the prophets.

In the name of the Lord.—(Lange: "in virtue of the name of the Lord"). Huther makes τῷ=ἐν τῷ, claiming as much for Matth. vii. 22. But there the sense is modified and here also this peculiar expression has probably to be so explained that the name of the Lord, *i. e.* the fundamental thought of the revelation of the Old Testament, gave impulse to their speaking. [But this seems a forced construction and since B. and Cod. Sin. actually supply ἐν there is really no reason why τῷ should not be taken=ἐν τῷ.—M.].

Ver. 11. **Behold, we count happy.**—(Matth. v. 10, 11). This saying is not only a subjective judgment of James but a reference to the fixed judgment recognized in the theocratic congregation and more particularly in the Christian Church. On this account also the reading τοὺς ὑπομείναντας is preferable to ὑπομένοντας. This embraces of course also the prophets just referred to (Grotius etc.), yet not them only but besides them also the most honoured sufferers. Hence we have "ye have heard of the patience of Job," Ez. xiv. 14, 20; Tob. ii. 12–15.—Although his patience was at first shaken by the great temptation, it gradually became established even unto conquering the temptation. The Jewish Christians had heard of him not only by means of the lessons which were read in the synagogue, but the name of Job was popularly honoured among them.

The end of the Lord.—We have here once more James' uniformly significant τέλος, the import of which is wholly misunderstood if the passage is made to denote with Huther, Wiesinger and many others: "the termination which the Lord gave" (of the Lord, Genitive of the causal subject). We therefore return confidently to the exposition of Augustine, Bede, Wetstein and al. "the end of the Lord is the completing of Christ." It is objected that the context does not warrant such a construction. But the context speaks in the Plural, not in the Singular of those who did suffer. The final clause of the verse "for very compassionate is the Lord and merciful," it is supposed, ought to be restricted to the mercy of God, which gave so happy a termination to the sufferings of Job. But was Job's restitution, according to the idea of the book, merely an act of mercy? On the other hand the supposition that Christ the Lord, pursuant to His compassion, entered upon His passion and thus showed the endurance of patience, conforms exactly to the biblical idea (1 Pet. ii. 21; iv. 1; Heb. ii. 10), and this idea is actually prefigured in the book of Daniel (ch. iii. 25). Huther, moreover, thinks it improbable, that James should have connected the example of Christ immediately with that of Job. But he did thus connect the example of Abraham with that of Rahab. There the antithesis was: Abraham, the father of believing Jews, Rahab a degraded Gentile woman; the antithesis here is: the great sufferer of the Old Testament, the Great Sufferer of the New. This abandonment of the ancient interpretation of our passage we cannot regard otherwise than as a consequence of the disparaging views held with respect to this Epistle. Besides James could hardly extol to the Jewish Christians the glorious gain of patience in suffering without adverting also to the example of Christ (cf. 1 Pet. ii. 21 etc.). This might have struck some of his readers as almost amounting to a denial. And why does he employ the term τέλος, by which he understands principial completion, and generally that of the New Testament? Why does the verb ἠκούσατε not suffice him and why does he in contrast with it, use the Imperative ἴδετε "look at the completion of the Lord?" But the Lord, like Job, went through suffering to glory, and that in the highest sense; and He was moved thereto by His infinite compassion, His love, which is also designed to coöperate with the patience of Christians. And this ἴδετε seems to be the culminating point of the Apostle's missionary saying addressed to those Jews who were as yet unbelieving: "the end of the Lord, look at it;" while the common exposition: "The end, which the Lord gave, see (*i. e.* know, learn from it) that the Lord is πολύσπλαγχνος etc." (Huther), is not only very flat, but also forced.—*For very pitiful is the Lord.* Rendering ὅτι *for*, appears to Huther unsubstantiated by what goes before, but nothing can be more simple than the thought: "look at the end of the sufferings of Christ, for that He suffered need not excite astonishment, it is a consequence of His pity. πολύσπλαγχνος occurs here only; it is formed after רַב חֶסֶד (Wiesinger), the LXX use instead πολυέλεος, Paul and Peter εὔσπλαγχνος (Eph. iv. 32; 1 Pet. iii. 8).

Conditions of this patience. Shunning of seditious movements. A hallowed disposition. The healing of their sicknesses. Liberation of the conscience by means of confession of sins. Exhortation to intercession. The example of Elias. vv. 12–18.

VER. 12. **But before all things, my brethren, do not swear (conspire).**—We cannot admit the view of Kern and Wiesinger that the connection of the Epistle breaks off at this point or that the dehortation contained in this verse has no other connection with what goes before than that which arises from the conduct of the readers.* The fundamental idea which connects this verse with v. 11 and v. 13 etc., is the allaying of the fanatical excitement which was constantly growing among the Jews and was threatening through the influence of the Judaists to deprive the Jewish Christian Churches of their Christian composure. The history of the banding together of more than forty men against the life of St. Paul (Acts xxiii. 12–21) proves the bias of judaistic zealots to enter into conspiracies; subsequently towards the outbreak of the Jewish war they were doubtless of more frequent occurrence. We have employed in our translation an ambiguous word [*Verschwörung*, of which we have no current equivalent in English, *i. e.* an *ambiguous* equivalent; the German words denotes 1, to bind oneself by an oath; 2, to enter into a conspiracy. *Conjuration* is the nearest English representative of *Verschwörung*, but the sense of *conspiracy* attached to it, although current in the days of Sir Thomas Elyot (+1546), is now obsolete.—M], in order to intimate this meaning. To be sure we take it textually in the sense that all swearing accompanied by hypothetical imprecations or the giving of a pledge is conspiracy. See Comm. on St. Matth. v. 34 etc. Hence James, like Christ (Matth. v. 34), defines this swearing as swearing by heaven, by the earth, or by any other oath (ὅρκος) connected with a hypothetical curse. The Greek construction ὀμνύειν with the Accusative brings out the unseemly character of such swearing by or appeal to a created object as a witness or avenger, with greater distinctness than the Hebrew construction of the same verb with ἐν. Oecumenius, de Wette, Neander, and al. understand the prohibition to apply to swearing in general, as in Matth. v. 33 with reference to or for the ideal condition of the Church. On the other hand Calvin, Wiesinger and many others refer the prohibition to light and trifling oaths in common life. With this must be connected the remark of Huther that swearing by the name of God is not mentioned; had he intended this swearing, he ought to have mentioned it in express terms because it is not only commanded in the law in contradistinction to other oaths (Deut. vi. 13; x. 20; Ps. lxiii. 12), but also foretold in the prophets as a token of men's future conversion to God (Is. lxv. 16; Jer. xii. 16; xxiii. 7, 8). But it follows also from this contradistinction that the oath in virtue of its N. T. completion was designed to be stripped of the formulæ of cursing and imprecation which always involve the pledging of things over which man has no control. To be sure, the stress lies here not only on this idealizing of the oath but also on the total setting aside of the abuse of oaths in the reality of social life. This attitude of James respecting abitrary oaths and his recommendation of the anointing with oil mentioned in the sequel, show that he was free from all Essene prejudice, for the Essenes were wont to administer to novices the vow of their order with a strong oath, although they rejected all other swearing, and so in like manner the anointing with oil.

But let your yea be yea.—[Winer: *Grammar*, p. 92, the Imperative ἤτω for ἔστω (which in the N. T. is also the usual form) 1 Cor. xvi. 22; Jas. v. 12; (Ps. civ. 31; 1 Macc. x. 31, cf. Clem. Alex. *Strom.* 6, 275; *Acta Thom.* 3, 7\, Buttman I. 529; only once in Plato, *Rep.* 2, 361;

* On the attempt of Rauch to prove the non-authenticity of the section ch. v 12–20, see Gebser, p. 395.

d. See Schneidel p. 1. According to Heraclides (in *Eustath.* p. 1411, 22), the flexion is Doric. The other imper. form ἴσθι occurs in Matth. ii. 13; v. 25; Mark v. 34; Luke xix. 17; 1 Tim. iv. 15 (Buttmann I. 257).—M.]. The exhortation corresponding to the prohibition. Here we find two opposing interpretations; 1. Let your yea *and* nay agree with your consciousness of positive or negative facts, *i. e.* let it be according to truth (Theophylact, Calvin and al.); 2. Let your yea be a simple yea, your nay a simple nay (Estius, Neander, Huther). We think that the two ought to be connected together from the nature of the case (see Comm. on Matth. v. 34 etc.), but that the choice of the expression in Matthew along with actual truthfulness gives prominence to the assurance, while here James rather intones the perfect composure whereby the soul contents itself with the simple declaration.

That ye fall not under judgment.—On the reading εἰς ὑπόκρισιν see Appar. Crit.; on the expression see 2 Sam. xxii. 39; Ps. xviii. 39. The context requires a judgment of condemnation and this is to be dreaded not only on account of the formal, wicked carelessness with which such oaths are uttered (which carelessness moreover leads to hypocrisy) but also on account of the mutinous and perilous acts or steps by which they are frequently sealed.

Ver. 13. **Is any among you in affliction?**—In opposition to the reprehensible sealing of excited frames of mind by such imprecatory swearing, the Apostle exhorts them to calmness of disposition and points out the means of accomplishing it. Its way was under all circumstances by a religious elevation of the mind. In the case of affliction (for the rendering: "does any among you suffer?" strikes us as too weak) the depression of the mind is to be raised by prayer; in the case of prosperity the mind is to be guarded against wantonness by the sacrifice of prosperity, by thanksgiving, by the singing of psalms or songs of praise (ψάλλειν 1 Cor. xiv. 15). Cf. ch. i. 9, 10. Huther thinks that the connection of this exhortation with the one preceding it cannot be substantiated. The connection is manifestly the Christian regulation of different mental conditions.

Ver. 14. **Is any sick among you?**—Here is the culminating point of the question whether the language of James is to be uniformly taken in a literal sense, or whether it uniformly bears a figurative character. The literal construction involves these surprising moments: 1. The calling for the presbyters of the congregation in the Plural; 2. the general direction concerning their prayer accompaning unction with oil; 3. and especially the confident promise that the prayer of faith shall restore the sick apart from his restoration being connected with the forgiveness of his sins. Was the Apostle warranted to promise bodily recovery in every case in which a sick individual complied with his directions? This misgiving urges us to adopt the symbolical construction of the passage, which would be as follows: if any man as a Christian has been hurt or become sick in his Christianity, let him seek healing from the presbyters, the kernel of the congregation. Let these pray with and for him and anoint him with the oil of the Spirit; such a course wherever taken, will surely restore him and his transgressions will be forgiven him. This symbol, explained in the Epistles of Ignatius as containing the direction that the bishop, the centre of the congregation should be called in, may be founded on a wide-spread Jewish Christian custom of healing the wounds of the sick by prayer accompanying the application with oil. Most remote from the mind of the Apostle is the Roman Catholic tradition of extreme unction; for the reference here is to the healing of the wounds of the sick conducing to their recovery, but not to a ritual preparation of him for death; not any more here than in Mark vi. 13. Cf. Huther's note, p. 196.

Let him call to himself (summon, call for).—In the case of bodily sickness it is self-evident that this must be done by others than the sick man. [προσκαλεσάσθω does not necessarily mean that the sick man is to call in person on the elders of the Church, it leaves the manner of his appeal undefined, he might call on them in person or *summon* them to his side by the intervention of others. To summon in the sense of sending for seems to be the most approved meaning. Cf. the Lexica.—M.].

The elders of the Church.—We must neither reduce the Plural to the Singular in the sense: "let him summon one of the presbyters" (Estius, Wolf), nor assert confidently that ἐκκλησία denotes here the particular congregation to which the sick man belongs, although the latter is probable. The main point is that ἡ ἐκκλησία, as a local congregation did represent from the beginning the whole Church and that consequently the presbyters could be sent for primarily from the most specific ecclesiastical district but also from a more distant sphere. [If I understand Lange's allusion, I doubt whether his inference is sustained by the facts of the case. *Interloping* was not sanctioned in the primitive Church. The Apostles uniformly insist upon order and decency in the conduct of Church government. A sick man, connected with a particular ecclesiastical organization would send, of course, for the presbyters connected with it; where no such organization existed, he would send for those presbyters to whom access might most easily be had.—M.].

And let them pray over him; *i. e.* not only for him, nor only literally as standing over his bed, but with reference to effecting his salvation (Acts xix. 13). [Bengel: "*Qui dum orant, non multo minus est quam si tota oraret ecclesia.*"—M.].

Anointing him with oil.—Many commentators assume, with reference to the Jewish custom, that the oil was here intended to coöperate as a medium of cure, cf. Jer. 8, 22; xlvi. 11; Luke x. 34. The disciples also used to connect this medium with their miraculous cures, Mark vi. 13. See this Comment. in loco. Now in so far as the reference here implied lies to an apostolical method of effecting cures, we must doubtless think also of the organic connection of intercession with oil, *i. e.* of the spiritual effect accompanying that produced on the medium of the body. Huther (in opposition to Meyer) dissolves this connection without sufficient reason, by observing that the oil as such was only refreshing to the body. What such a refreshing amounts to, is not very clear; the chief point is that the two were to be united in one act, which was performed in the *name of the Lord* (Christ). But Huther rightly remarks that James did not prescribe anointing, but assumed the observance of the usage. He prescribes prayer in connection with that usage and the anointing as an anointing in the name of the Lord, which latter particular must not be referred to prayer only (Gebser), nor to both acts (de Wette), but solely to the act of anointing (Huther). In the literal acceptation of the precept, prayer would be the medium of the miraculous cure, which was then to be performed in the name of the Lord (*i. e.* not pursuant to His command, but in the power and limitation of His name). Schneckenburger adds that the presbyters had the χάρισμα ἰαμάτων (1 Cor. xii. 9). Huther calls this an arbitrary assumption and says that moreover nothing is said here of the χάρισμα. But the χάρισμα has at all times been the *conditio sine qua non* of ministerial efficiency and in the Apostolical church the office of presbyter did not involve the charisma, but rather those who had the respective charisma were generally ordained as presbyters (see 1 Cor. xii. 9, 30). Huther also sets aside without sufficient reason the connection between miraculous gifts and gifts of natural experience to which Pott, after his manner, calls attention: "*quia uti omnino prudentissimi eligebantur, sic forte etiam artis medicæ peritissimi erant.*

VER. 15. **And the prayer of faith.**—Not faith in general, but miraculous faith as a special charisma of the Christian spirit (see 1 Cor. xii. 9, 10). Prayer characterized by such faith, not in general: the prayer which faith offers. Grotius and al. rightly assume that this faith implies identity of purpose on the part of the presbyters who intercede, and on that of the sick for whom intercession is made, for it is in this faith that the sick summons the presbyters (cf. the Gospels); Wiesinger and Huther arbitrarily limit this prayer to the act of the presbyters only.

Shall help (heal) the sick.—Shall savingly restore him to health. Lyra, Schneckenburger and al. understand corporeal and spiritual healing, de Wette, Wiesinger and al. corporeal only, because the forgiveness of sins is separately stated afterwards [Alford—M.]. Nevertheless we feel that we cannot give up the oneness of the two moments, seeing that the sequel doubtless adverts to the possibility of particular sins and that, as already stated, the concrete apostolical *spiritual-corporeal* cure seems to be here uniformly the symbol of a spiritual-social cure of the wounds and infection of the judaistic confusion.

And the Lord shall raise him up.—The Lord *i. e.* Christ. As is His wont to raise men spiritually-bodily, not only from the bed of sickness but also from the sickness. This ἐγείρειν however is not only the causality of the preceding σώζειν, but also holds out the prospect of the positive exaltation of life which has been effected by the σώζειν as the deliverance from peril of death.

And though he have committed sins.—This denotes an enhanced state of distress. Supposing that he even (κἂν) have committed sins, as πεποιηκώς, as one who is as yet burdened with the guilt of those sins (Plural). The presumption is not so much that these sins were the cause of the respective sickness (Huther), but they made the sickness a severe one and one difficult to cure; this would again import a spiritual meaning.

It shall be forgiven him; that is, his having committed sins. "Even in case that." (Huther.) Forgiven not only in the social sense (*i. e.* by the presbyters (Hammond), not only in respect of his spiritual life, but the continuation, the curse of his guilt shall also be removed in respect of his life-situation. Huther wants to connect κἂν with the preceding clause: "The Lord shall raise him up, even if he have committed sins—(for) it shall be forgiven him." In point of language κἂν is to favour his construction (but see on the other hand 1 Jno. ii. 1); but in point of matter such a construction would greatly weaken the passage. The general and unconditional character of the assurance of renewed health, which is here expressed, has created much surprise. Hottinger expresses it more forcibly than any other commentator: "*si certus et constans talium precum fuisset eventus, nemo umquam mortuus esset.*" Grotius supplies the condition: "*nisi nempe aliter ei suppeditat ad salutem æternam.*" But Huther maintains against Wiesinger that there is no need of any restrictions and believes that the difficulty is removed by the consideration that James conceived the coming of Christ to be immediately impending; that consequently he did not consider the death of believers to be necessary, but viewed it only in the light of an evil which might be averted by believing intercession. Thus a second gross error would have paralyzed or covered the first. We rather opine that this very difficulty, as well as the whole character of the Epistle constrains us to adopt the symbolical interpretation. James assumes the existence of the custom of anointing the sick accompanied with prayer as a method of cure very generally prevalent in Jewish Christian Churches. This custom, traces of which are also found in ancient Judaism (see Wiesinger, p. 204*), he now turns into a symbol of a spiritual cure, which he recommends to those who were infected with the spirit of Judaism and revolutionary Chiliasm, as a remedy for their spiritual healing. This construction is also favoured by the next verse. [As the reasoning of Lange may not appear conclusive but rather doubtful to many readers of this work, I subjoin an outline of the subject which may prove valuable for reference.—The opinion of Polycarp, Bp. of Smyrna, a disciple of John and a martyr, is very valuable and sheds light on the whole question. He says (*ad Philipp.* c. 5), "Let the

* Oil in the East, where it is much better than with us, is a common and very useful remedy employed in many diseases by rubbing it into the affected parts and pouring it into wounds for the purpose of mollifying them. Cf. Is. i. 6; Mark vi. 13; Luke x. 34; Joseph. *de bello jud.* 1, 33, 5. The balm of Gilead in particular was highly esteemed as an external application, Jer. viii. 22; xlvi. 11. Thus the Greek and Roman physicians also recommend poultices made of wine and oil, or vinegar and oil (Galen, *de comp. medic.* 2; Plin. *H. N.* 31, 47 etc.). Tertullian *ad Scapulam* informs us also that Proculus, a Christian, cured the Emperor Severus with oil. Cf. also Sheviith 8: *qui capite dolet, aut quem invasit scabies, unguat se oleo etc.* Gebser, p. 403.

presbyters be tender-hearted, merciful to all, converting the erring (see James v. 19), *visiting all who are sick* (ἐπισκεπτόμενοι πάντας ἀσθενεῖς); not neglecting *the widow or orphan or needy* (see Jas. i. 27), and providing always what is good in *the sight of God,* abstaining from *all respect of persons* (see James ii. 1, 9), not sharp in judgment, knowing that *we are all sinners*" (see James iii. 2). The reference to James in brackets warrants the presumption that Polycarp was familiar with our Epistle, and the extract shows that at that early day the duty of visiting the sick had been devolved on the *presbyters.*—The direction that the sick should summon the presbyters (*Plural*) accords with the practice of our Lord who sent forth His Twelve Apostles and seventy disciples *two* and *two* (Mark vi. 7; Luke x. 1).—The direction would hardly have been given, if it could not be complied with. James, as bishop of Jerusalem, presided over elders *there* (Acts xxi. 18) and his language warrants the conclusion that *presbyters* had been ordained in the principal cities.—Without discussing the question who these presbyters were, the second order of the ministry or the first, the great fact remains that the visitation of the sick is an important part of ministerial activity, and that it is the duty of the *sick* (whether in body or in soul) to summon their spiritual advisers to their side. This is an important consideration, for in large parishes and especially in large cities weeks may sometimes elapse before the report of a parishioner's sickness reaches their ears; if the sick are not visited under those circumstances, they must not blame their minister for remissness if they have failed to inform him of their sickness and to summon him to their side.

Our passage establishes the fact that anointing the sick with prayer accompanying it was practised in the Apostolic Church. The Apostles in virtue of the extraordinary and miraculous powers delegated to them by Christ, healed many, after having anointed them with oil. Cf. Acts vi. 13 with Matth. x. 1–8 and Luke ix. 1–6. The miraculous gift of healing continued for some time in the Church. See 1 Cor. xii. 8, 9. James refers to this *miraculous* power of healing, which in its application however was not absolute, but dependent on the will of God; although applied in faith by the anointing presbyter and received in faith by the sick man, *anointing* did not heal him if he recovered his health, but prayer charged with faith, and this implies that the matter of the sick man's cure was referred to the will of God, who did *what was best for the sick,* (Wordsworth), whether that was restoration to health or a Christian death.

The practice of anointing with oil with a view to recovery from sickness was continued in the Eastern and Western Churches, even after the Church had lost the miraculous gift of healing. It is continued in the Eastern Church for *this purpose* to this day, but the Church of England and other Reformed communions have abandoned the practice, because they perceived that *the effect* mentioned by St. James, viz. his recovery did not ordinarily ensue from the anointing with oil, and that the miraculous gift of healing as well as other miraculous gifts granted to the Apostles, had been removed from the Church.

The Church of Rome however retains the *practice* of anointing the sick with oil but perverted the *design* for which it had been instituted (viz: recovery from sickness), into that of a sacrament conveying grace to the soul, the sacrament of extreme unction, which is certainly one of the most audacious perversions of Scripture on record. See Alford and Wordsworth. Wordsworth: "The Apostle St. James had enjoined the practice with a view to the recovery of the sick; as Cardinal Cajetanus allows, in his note on the passage, where he says: "Hæc verba non loquuntur de Sacramentali unctione *extremæ unctionis,*" but the Church of Rome prescribes, in the Councils of Florence (A.D. 1438) and Trent (1551), that the anointing should *not* take place *except* where recovery is *not to be looked for* (Council of Trent, Sess. 14, "*qui tam periculose decumbunt ut in exitu vitæ constituti videantur*"), and therefore she calls this anointing "*extreme unction,*" and "*sacramentum exeuntium,*" and she regards it as a sacrament conveying grace to the soul. Thus, on the one hand, the Greek Church is a witness by her present practice, that the anointing was designed with a view to *bodily recovery;* and the Roman Church, on the other hand, is a witness, that the *miraculous* effects on the *body,* which were wrought in primitive times through the instrumentality of those who anointed the sick, and which accompanied that unction, *have ceased.*"—See this whole subject discussed in my article "*An account of Extreme Unction,*" Princeton Review, Vol. XXXVII. No. 2, April, 1865.—M.].

VER. 16. **Confess therefore your sins (transgressions) to one another.**—This injunction is general: it is the generalization of the preceding sentence. Cajetanus rightly observes: "*nec hic est sermo de confessione sacramentali;*" but the clause implies also the fact that James knew nothing of such a *confessio,* or he would have said: "Confess your sins to the presbyters," of whom he had just been speaking. As to the sins here referred to, Huther understands sins in general as violation of the Divine law, in opposition to Wolf, who explains them as offences against one another, Matth. xviii. 15. Bengel: "*Ægrotus et quisquis offendit, jubetur confiteri; offensus, orare.*" But the particular sins which are meant here, at least primarily, may be gathered from the whole Epistle; the reference is to the whole Judaistic movement which in so many respects had made them sick and feeble. But the thought has also the more general import that the confession of certain known transgressions is at once an unburdening of the conscience and a furtherance of prayer in the case of those who are thus drawn into the Christian fellow-feeling of guilt and thus also the preliminary condition both of forgiveness and of spiritual (and often even of bodily) healing. How many a germinating madness and suicide, how many a heart-languor and disorder which vexes the members and weighs down the body was to be obviated by this mutual effect of confession and intercession! But James had more particularly in view the hurts which were then troubling Israel. Both the confession and the intercession were to be mutual.

That ye may be healed.—This healing is understood spiritually by Grotius and al., spiritually and corporeally by Schneckenburger and al., corporeally only by de Wette, Huther and al. As nothing is said here of the forgiveness of sins, the promise of healing implies evidently also spiritual healing: but the idea "that ye may be healed theocratically" is probably predominant. "It is to be remembered that the prayer of the presbyters does not exclude the common intercession of Christians and that the efficacy attributed to the latter is not less than that attributed to the former." Huther. [This is one of the passages adduced by the Latin Church for the necessity of confessing sins to a priest. Alford cites Corn.-a-Lapide's exegesis as a specimen of the way in which the Romish doctrine is deduced. "*Alterutrum, id est, homo homini, similis simili, frater fratri confitemini, puta sacerdoti, qui licet officio sit superior, natura tamen est par, infirmitate similis, obligatione confitendi æqualis.*"—M.].

The prayer . . . . availeth much.—A saying of the power of genuine prayer designed to encourage them to adopt the recommendations previously set forth, *i. e.* both mutual confession of sins and mutual intercession. The great efficacy of such intercession is still further brought about by the position of πολύ etc. and by the gnomic and asyndetical structure of the sentence.

Of a righteous man, of a צַדִּיק in the theocratic sense, *i. e.* not one "in a state of righteousness" as Hofmann expresses it, for "the state of righteousness" denotes an ontological, passive condition, while in the case of the theocratically righteous every thing turns on actuality, on the living faith, on the living God and His word of life. The species of these righteous men is the same in the Old Testament and in the New; they are men of living, energetic faith (Rom. iv), although the righteous man of the New Testament has the advantage of an objective as well as of a subjective τελείωσις. Hence Elias may here be held up to the Christians as the pattern of a real man of prayer.

Inwardly effectual (working).—ἐνεργουμένη causes not little difficulty and has given rise to a great variety of opinions among commentators. A main point to be determined is whether ἐνεργουμένη ought to be taken as an epithet to δέησις, as the majority of commentators take it, or as a pure participial definition of the verb ἰσχύει (so Pott, de Wette, Huther, who are however at variance with respect to the sense). Pott: "Prayer is able to work much" or "prayer is able to work much and worketh much." de Wette: "if it becomes energetic." Huther: "In its energy" or "in its working." But all this is rather tautological unless it be made to denote a theurgic operation, which is inadmissible. The adjectival construction may be taken passively or actively, or in the most literal sense as a middle, as a kind of Hithpael. Prayer may be considered passively as coänimated by the prayer of him for whom it is offered (Oecumenius), as moved by the Holy Spirit, inspired (Michælis), as penetrated by faith (Carpzov), as animated and attended by impulse to work [*Werktrieb*, so Calvin and Gebser]. Taken actively the idea of ἐνεργουμένη coincides more or less with ἐνεργής or ἐνεργός (see Luke xxii. 44 ἐκτενής). So Luther: "if it is earnest;" Vulgate: "*assidua,*" and similarly many others. On the other hand, Huther contends that this construction is contrary to N. T. usage, while Wiesinger maintains that this usage may be substantiated and refers to the proofs supplied by Wahl. We believe that the N. T. middle ἐνεργέομαι (Rom. vii. 5; 2 Cor. i. 6; iv. 12; Gal. v. 6; Eph. iii. 20; Col. i. 29; 1 Thess. ii. 13; 2 Thess. ii. 7) denotes according to the Hebrew and Christian conception a passivo-active working, *i. e.* a working set in motion by a previously experienced impulse. This *in malam partem* applies to the lusts in the members (Rom. vii. 5), to the mystery of iniquity (2 Thess. ii. 7), *in bonam partem* to the subjective σωτηρία (2 Cor. i. 6), to the subjective πίστις (Gal. v. 6), to the vital energy in believers (Eph. iii. 20), to the energy of Christ in believers (Col. i. 29), to the word of God appropriated by men (1 Thess. ii. 13); in both respects, to death and life (2 Cor. iv. 12). The Active however is used with reference to God Eph. i. 11; Phil. ii. 13; Gal. ii. 8; 1 Cor. xii. 6; of His Spirit 1 Cor. xii. 11; also of Satan Eph. ii. 2. It follows from this clearly marked usage of the word that we must also take δέησις with the predication ἐνεργουμένη as indicating an efficiency effected or an impulse impelled. The idea doubtless imports the full tension of the praying spirit under its absolute obedience (yielding to) to the Divine impulse. And in this respect there is here an allusion to the idea of the miraculously potent prayer which works the ἐνεργήματα. [The Apostle's idea expressed in plain words, seems to be that prayer in order to lead to outward effects, must work inwardly in grateful adoration of and fervent love and humble resignation to God; otherwise prayer is only a hollow, unmeaning and inefficacious uttering of words. Luther in his terse language hits the point, when he says in some place that "he who prays must *feel* that he is a *beggar*." Absolute submission to the will of God is of course the very soul of prayer, and the true Christian never engages in prayer without the pious sentiment: "Not my will, but Thine be done." Wordsworth remarks: "The martyrdom of St. James himself affords a beautiful comment on these words, especially where it is related that after he had been cast down by his enemies from the pediment of the Temple and they were stoning him, he fell on his knees and *prayed* for them, and some, who stood by, said, adopting the very words of this Epistle—"Hold, what do ye? ε ὔ χ ε τ α ι ὑπὲρ ὑμῶν ὁ δ ί κ α ι ο ς," "the *just* man is *praying* for you." See Introduction.—M.].

VER. 17. **Elias was a man of like passions.** —ὁμοιοπαθής does not exactly signify that Elias had the capacity of suffering, or his real sufferings (Laurentius, Schneckenburger), but "of like condition and nature" (Wiesinger and Huther) is hardly adequate in point of sense. In Acts xiv. 15 there is certainly an implied emphasis on the dependence and restraints of human nature as contrasted with the Being of God. Moreover in Wisd. vii. 3 the reference to the earth imports not so much equality of kind as equality of condition. In the case of Elias the term "like passions" or liability to being affected, points at least to his capacity of suffering and temptability.

And he prayed a prayer [with prayer].—Analogous to the Hebrew idiom of producing intensification by placing the Infinitive of the verb in juxtaposition with the Indicative, or by connecting the latter with the noun Gen. ii. 17 מוֹת תָּמוּת. Considering that Huther himself observes that this form serves to bring out the verbal idea, it is difficult to account for his opposition to the exposition of Wiesinger and al., that the prayer of Elias was an earnest prayer. [Huther, I presume, objects to the introduction of a new word. The prayer of Elias was genuine prayer, prayer charged with ἐνέργεια.—M.].

That it might not rain.—βρέχειν is impersonal. [The gen. of the intent. See Winer, p. 343.—M.].

And it did not rain in the land [on the earth].—Considering the O. T. colouring of the whole Epistle we may be allowed to translate ἐπὶ τῆς γῆς with Grotius and al. "in the land," but Huther retains Luther's rendering "on earth," Schneckenburger compares this weighty saying with Gen. i. 3: "*fiat lux et facta est lux.*" But there remains the important difference that here the reference is not to an authoritative command (*Machtspruch*).

[**Three years and six months.**—Wordsworth: equal to 42 months or 1260 days, a chronological period of suffering. See Rev. xi. 3. —M.].

VER. 18. **And the heaven gave rain.**—A personifying, vivid mode of expression, reminding us of the prophetic style, Hos. ii. 21, 22.

And the earth brought forth her fruit.—This was really the immediate purpose of the prayer. βλαστάνω [properly an intransitive verb, but used transitively—M.], a transitive verb: it let spring up, *i. e.* it put, brought forth. An application of what is related 1 Kings xvii. 1; xviii. 1, 42 etc. The positive announcement of the drought may have led James to draw the reasonable inference that Elias had prayed for it, although we have no record to that effect, and tradition had probably anticipated his inference. Such a completion is however very different from a discrepancy (Huther). The second apparent difference is as follows: in 1 Kings xviii. 1, Elijah is said to have foretold and to have been instrumental in bringing about the return of rain in the third year, while our passage affirms that it did not rain on the earth for three years and six months. Seeing that Luke iv. 25 and the tract *Jalcut Simeoni* give the same duration, it would seem that that space of time was the uniform Jewish tradition. The explanation lies manifestly in the fact that 1 Kings xviii. specifies the real famine according to its duration. But it stands to reason that the famine did not begin until one year after the announcement of the drought, viz. after the failure of the early and the latter rain. During the first year the people were still living on the harvest of the preceding year. Jewish tradition consequently added *one* year to the period of time mentioned in a general way in 1 Kings in order to mark the whole period between the two announcements of Elijah. Benson's solution of the difference is somewhat different but not very clear. He says: "*accuratior serioris traditionis computatio, ducitur a tempore non pluviæ primum cessantis, sed ultimum ante siccitatem cadentis, quam dimidio fere anno distare in promptu est.*" That is, the first year of the drought is not added to the famine of about two and a half years' duration, but the half year from the first failure of rain to the last fall of rain immediately preceding. Wiesinger is satisfied with Benson's calculation, but Huther insists upon the discrepancy, because according to the statement of James, the drought began immediately after Elijah's praying. But the narrative itself contains intimations that the drought did not at once produce famine, 1 Kings xvii. 7; ch. xviii. 5. [Benson observes, however, that the words "in the third year" of 1 Kings xviii. 1 do not necessarily refer to the duration of the famine, but most naturally date back to the removal of Elijah to Zarephath, ch. xvii. 8 etc; cf. the same "many days" in ch. xvii. 15, where indeed a variation is "for a full year." Alford. —M.]. But far more important is the question why James selects just this example of an answer to prayer from the history of Israel. The greatest stress seems to lie on his intercession of pity; which was the more edifying as an example because the readers of the Epistle were wont to consider Elijah as a censurer. A drought had for a long time come also upon the spiritual life of Israel; the readers were therefore encouraged to pray with the faith of an Elijah for a rain of grace to fall on their people. The prophet's first prayer is mentioned first, in order to furnish them with a forcible illustration that prayer is heard and answered, and perhaps also to show them how the real men of prayer in Israel were independent of and superior to the evil frame of mind which kept the populace in a ferment. Moreover the general tendency of Elijah's prayers was hostile to the apostasy of Israel, and the zeal of their believing men of prayer was now to be directed against the new apostasy which consisted in an obdurate opposition to the Gospel (see ch. iv. 4; Rom. xi. 1–5).

Conclusion replete with promise. vv. 19, 20.

VER. 19. **My brethren, if any among you should have strayed from the truth.**—"This imports not a single practical aberration, but an alienation from the Christian principle of life, an inward apostasy from the λόγος ἀληθείας, of which the Christian is begotten (ch. i. 18), disclosing itself in a single course of life. Cf. Luke i. 16, 17, v. 20." Huther. But the tenor of the whole Epistle constrains us to define this aberration still further as an aberration into Judaistic and chiliastic doings and fanatico-seditious lusts. [πλανηθῇ is passive and Alford rightly remarks "that there is no reason why the passive signification should not be kept, especially when we remember our Lord's warning, βλέπετε μή τις ὑμᾶς πλανήσῃ."—M.].

And one should convert him, to the truth, from which he has strayed in peril of apostasy.

VER. 20. **Let him know** [know ye—M.].—He that converts is to know the importance of his action and what a blessing rests upon it. The word, as to its form, is a hypothetical announcement or promise to him who is found thus doing, but as to its contents it is a general sentence or a sententious encouragement to all conjoined with the promise of a prize to those who act upon it. On this account ἐπιστρέψας is repeated after ὅτι.

That he who converteth a sinner.—The person who has strayed through delusion from the truth, considered from a practical point of view. Let the readers know that all those who have strayed in part or entirely from the truth are sinners according to the emphatic theocratic idea: doomed to the death-ban. This weighty part of the word is weakened by Huther's remark, "that the reference is no longer to the person who has gone astray but to the whole *genus* to which the Christian who has strayed from the truth belongs as *species*." The two ideas: delusion and dogmatical apostasy and practical ruin must not be separated on the theocratical ground, nor must the former kind be subordinated to the latter as *species*, although the practical and the theocratic form of ruin may alternately predominate.

Shall save a soul from death.—From death, as in ch. i. 15 and throughout the New Testament, from subjective damnation as it is inherent in the personality itself, defined moreover negatively with respect to the subject as the loss of the true life, of the true destination and sphere of life; a moral dissolution of the ontological life eternally self-generating itself, as on the other hand the true life generates life. *A soul.* The naked, inward existence of the personality itself, man in all his capacity of suffering and salvation and need of help. He shall *save the soul.* The conversion of the apostate is the conversion of a sinner; this has as its consequence his deliverance from death, because he is in the way of death and is overtaken before he finally falls into the snares of death. We need not stop to show that this presupposes Divine redemption as the salvation to which he is converted and the Divine coöperation of the Word and of the Holy Spirit as the means of salvation whereby he is converted. In the battle of faith between the believing readers of the Epistle and their half-believing and unbelieving brethren the point at issue turns therefore not upon dogmatical disputes of the synagogue, but solely and purely on the salvation of poor souls from eternal death, and not only on this but along with the salvation of many individuals, on the removal of a universal curse.

And shall cover a multitude of sins.—That is, the averting of a general ruin is brought about by the faithful salvation of many individuals. This covering of sins (cf. I Pet. iv. 8; Prov. x. 12) καλύπτειν contains doubtless reference in an enlarged sense, to the Hebrew, כָּסָה, *to cover, cover over sins, i. e. to forgive,* Ps. xxxii. 1 and elsewhere. But considering that such absolute covering of sin is the prerogative of God, it is probably better to think here of instrumental covering כִּפֶּר which is also used more especially of different means and mediators of atonement; not only of the cover of the ark, of sacrifice, of the high-priest, but also of the very sins to be atoned for (Ex. xxx. 15; Is. xlvii. 11), and also especially of the person interceding, Ex. xxxii. 30. The last passage strikes us as peculiarly important. Moses effected the reconciliation of his people not as a sacrifice, not as high-priest, but by intercession, *i. e.* by the subjective mediation of the objective atonement. This objective atonement therefore is here assumed, just as the former expression, he shall save, presupposes objective salvation. The believing Jews are to become intercessors for their poor people, become instrumental to bring about its real atonement. Believers participate in the atoning work of Christ as in His sufferings and intercession not as *causa mediatoria* but as *causa organica.* But the commentators are at variance whether the reference here is to the sins of the converters or to those of the converted. Erasmus and al. take it thus: by his good work he shall obtain remission of his sins with God. The Jews held (*Joma* fol. 87): "*quicunque multos ad justitiam adducit, per ejus manus non perpetratur peccatum.*" Augusti: He will obtain forgiveness on the part of men; his own offences will not be remembered. With more reason the majority of commentators refer the words to the sins of the converted. But the reference is not solely to the particular sins of the persons to be converted, and not even to their personal offences. πλῆθος denotes fulness, an entire mass taken as a unit, and the ἁμαρτίαι are the offences requiring to be atoned for. The reference is consequently to the total national guilt of Israel. To be sure, it is not referred to with greater distinctness or more clearly defined than by τὸ πλῆθος, because James, according to ch. v. 1, could no longer hope for the immediate salvation of all Israel, but foresaw, like Paul, a great judgment on their obduracy. But it was still his duty pitifully to wrestle with the judgment and to save a fulness (multitude) of souls and to atone for their sins. But whereas a common, national guilt is ever growing, and whereas this working of the curse can be broken only by means of the atonement, the observation of Huther is groundless "that this does not describe the sins which the ἁμαρτωλός would still commit and which are now prevented by means of his conversion (Pott: "*multa futura impediet*"), but the whole multitude of sins which he had committed before his conversion." This restriction misapprehends the progressive nature of guilt, not to say anything of the circumstance, that the reference is no longer exclusively to the sins of converted individuals. The conclusion of the Epistle shows in general, as we have seen repeatedly before, that the usual exposition does by no means come up to the lofty stand-point and point of view of James. De Wette takes objection to the strong idea πλῆθος, saying that the reference is only to aberration and not to viciousness of life and seeks to arrange his assertion by inferences; Stolz asserts that the sinner's amendment of life has the effect of consigning to oblivion his former transgressions; even Wiesinger and Huther restrict the import of the passage in two ways: "the reference is only to the multiform sin of the aforesaid converted individual and only to the circumstance that the converter becomes by his conversion the occasion of God forgiving his sins. "But our passage reminds us of the relation of Paul to his people, Rom. ix. 3; xi. 14. And as James, according to Acts, exhibited a peculiar fidelity in working for the salvation of his people, and, according to tradition, interceded for them with God, so at the conclusion of the Epistle he here invites the whole believing part of his people to engage in intercession and in the work of salvation, that many individuals might be saved from death, and a multitude of sins might be atoned for. The whole Epistle shows that he confines himself solely to human saving and atoning as a medium of bringing back the people to the true Redeemer and Reconciler, but he deems it of peculiar importance that the brethren must not fail to do their part in the work. Of course his words, in their sententious form, are also here so construed, that they possess a general and eternally valid apostolical significance; but as it was the duty of the expositor throughout the course of his exposition to give prominence to the noble historical import of this Epistle, which has been only too much missed and neglected, so he does at its conclusion.

DOCTRINAL AND ETHICAL.

1. The long-suffering patience required of the followers of Jesus is a duty of so wide a range, that the discharge of it, at least under many circumstances, would be too much for human strength, if the strength of their faith and hope were not animated by the thought of the nearness of the Lord's coming. Therefore the words "the coming of the Lord is nigh" ought to be constantly before our eyes. While the Christians of the Apostolic Age were perhaps too much inclined to consider the coming of Christ to be near at hand in a literal sense, the Christian sense of our own age suffers this great final event to stand too much in the background and substitutes for it in most instances a mere individual hope of salvation immediately after death. The more we learn again that we belong "to men also that love His appearing" (2 Tim. iv. 8) in the Apostolic acceptation of the term, the easier we shall find the practice of Christian patience and endurance in view of this the only satisfactory final development of the drama of history.

2. James as well as our Lord Himself (Matth. xiii. and elsewhere), saw the kingdom of grace reflected and portrayed in the kingdom of nature. The disciple of Jesus may learn much from the diligent and patient waiting of the husbandman.

3. The heroes of faith of the Old Testament are regarded by James also in the light of patterns to the Christian in his course, just as in the Epistle to the Hebrews (ch. xi. xii.). The rule that the way through suffering leads to glory, is in reality as valid under the Old Testament as under the New. Cf. Luke xxiv. 26; Acts xiv. 22.

4. James begins (ch. i. 12) and ends (ch. v. 11) his Epistle with a beatitude, just as our Lord began (Matth. v. 3) and ended (Jno. xx. 29). His instructions with similar beatitudes. The introduction of the example of Job is the more remarkable because this is the only place in the New Testament where his history is referred to.

5. The dehortation from frivolous swearing is intimately and naturally connected with the notice of endurance and patience, which precedes it. Those who are impatient and discontented will readily curse and swear in their violence, while those who possess their souls in patience will also in this respect guard their mouth and keep their lips. The context shows abundantly that James does not absolutely prohibit all swearing, but only those oaths which men take when they are not as patient as Job (Job ii. 10), but as impatient as Job (ch. iii. 1), when they curse their day. Like Christ, (Matth. xxiii. 16–22) the Apostle condemns light and trifling swearing and specifies several examples thereof. Had he intended to forbid swearing by the name of God, he would doubtless have mentioned this first and most weighty oath before all others. But considering that the law expressly enjoined swearing by the name of the Lord (Numb. vi. 13, *b;* x. 20) and that the prophets referred to this swearing as the characteristic of the servants of the Lord (Is. lxv. 16; Jer. xii. 16; xvi. 14, 15), it is *à priori* highly improbable that James, who was penetrated through and through by the spirit of the Old Testament, should have intended to forbid also this oath. Swearing by the name of God is not only permitted but often becomes necessary in an imperfect state of society because of the sins of men, although it belongs surely to the ideal of the kingdom of God that no oath will be required in it and that yea and nay are as reliable as an oath. In this respect we may say, that the Christian, if the civil authority requires him to take an oath, is necessitated to do so only in consequence of his sojourn in the midst of this sinful and wicked world. In a certain sense we may say of oaths what Paul said of the law that τῶν παραβάσεων χάριν προσετέθη Gal. iii. 19. Cf. Lange on Matth. v. 33–37, and on the Hebrew formulæ of oaths in general Rüetschi in Herzog's *R. E.* III. p. 718 sqq.

6. Genuine Christian faith is distinguished by becoming equanimity in good and evil days, as prescribed by James (ch. v. 13) and illustrated *inter alia* by Paul (Phil. iv. 10–20). Without Christ man is very apt to despond under suffering and equally prone to become elated with prosperity. The true Christian will in suffering seek consolation in prayer and so enjoy his prosperity that God is glorified thereby.

7. The visitation and comforting of the sick is one of the most natural and important parts of the *cura pastoralis.* For special directions consult the works on pastoral and practical theology of Hüffell, Harms, Nitzsch, Palmer and al. [Also Burnet, on the Pastoral Care, Wilson's *Parochialia, Visitatio Infirmorum* and Vinet.—M.]. On the true Christian frame of mind on the sick-bed compare an essay by N. Beets, translated from the Dutch in the *Jahrbuch des rheinisch-westphälischen Schriftvereins,* 1862, p. 1 etc. [Also an excellent work, published anonymously, entitled "Sickness, its trials and blessings," New York: 1857.—M.].

8. Only by confining oneself to the sound of the words (vv. 14–16), it is possible to find here the precepts of extreme unction and auricular confession in the sense of the Roman Catholic Church. See under Exegetical and Critical. James refers plainly to miraculous recovery and to the mutual confession of offences among bre-

thren in the event of one having failed in his duty towards another. On the other hand there exists also an Ultra-Protestantism and Anti-Romanism, which deems the use of both these means of grace altogether superfluous and almost prohibits them, which is likewise without blessing. The decrease of the gift of miracles is surely no proof of the increase of faith, and the entire discontinuance of mutual confession of sins is a sad token of the want of humility and brotherly love. Cf. Herzog's *R. E.* Article *Oelung.*

9. It may be very superstitious and uncharitable to assume a direct connection of a certain sin and a certain disease; cf. Jno. ix. 3. But it is also very superficial to deny all connection between sin and disease. If there were no sins in the world, there would certainly be no plagues. The sick man consequently does well, if he recalls on the sick-bed first of all his own sins and seeks to obtain their forgiveness. Forgiveness of sins and recovery from sickness are in many respects more closely connected than most people think and therefore both are promised to the citizen of the celestial commonwealth, Is. xxxiii. 24.

10. The duty of brotherly exhortation addressed to blacksliding brethren (vv. 19, 20), so warmly recommended by the Apostle, has also been enjoined by our Lord and the Apostles elsewhere (cf. Matth. xviii. 15–18; 1 Thess. v. 14; 2 Thess. iii. 13–16; Heb. x. 24). The writings of pagan moralists contain also excellent directions concerning the manner how such friendly reproof should be administered. See *e. g.* Plutarch, *de discrim. amici et adulatoris* pp. 244–276, *edit. Reisk.;* Cicero, *de amicitia* cap. 24, 25. A striking proof of the blessing which may attend such a work of love towards the salvation of an almost lost soul, and of the manner how this duty should be discharged, is found in the well-known legend "John and the robber-chief," told by Clem. Alex., *quis dives salvus,* cap. 42. But James shows himself throughout this Epistle as an exemplar of ardent Christian zeal for converting sinners from the error of their way and for saving souls from death. His words open a wide field and a glorious prospect to Christian philanthropy and the specific cure of souls. Hence Zwingli and Herder are not wrong in their criticisms on the conclusion of this Epistle; the former saying: "*Insigni doctrina veluti colophone epistolam absolvit,*" and the latter: "The conclusion, the strongest assurance, is like a seal affixed to the testament."—

[On the connection of vv. 12, 13 with v. 11. Bp. Sanderson, (Lectures on Oaths, vii. 11): "Set the examples of ancient prophets and holy men before your eyes. If ye suffer adversity, imitate their patience. If in all things, you cannot attain to that perfection, yet thus far at least, except ye be very negligent, you may go with ease; above all things, take heed lest too impatient of your grief, or too much transported with your joy, ye break forth into rash oaths, to the dishonour of God and shame of Christian conversation. But rather contain yourselves, whether troubled or rejoicing, within the bounds of Modesty; mingle not Heaven and earth, let not all things be filled with your oaths and clamours; if you affirm a thing, let it be with calmness, and a mere affirmation or negation. But if either of these passions be more impetuous, and strive to overflow the narrow channels of your bosoms, it will be your wisdom to let it forth unto the glory of God. Do you demand by what means? I will tell you: *Is any among you afflicted?* Let not his impatience break forth into Oaths and Blasphemies, the Flood-gates of wrath; but rather let him pray, and humbly implore God that He would vouchsafe him Patience, till His heavy hand be removed. *Is any merry?* Let him not bellow it forth in Oaths, like a Bacchanalian, but rather sing it in Hymns and Psalms unto the praise of God: Who hath made his cup to overflow, and crowned him with happy days."

BARROW: (Serm. XV. vol. I. p. 329). "In these words St. James doth not mean universally to interdict the use of oaths: for that in some cases is not only lawful, but very expedient, yea needful, and required from us as a duty; but *that* swearing which our Lord had expressly prohibited to His disciples, and which thence, questionless, the *brethren* to whom St. James did write, did well understand themselves to forbear, having learnt so in the first Catechisms of Christian institution; that is, *needless and heedless swearing in ordinary conversation*, a practice then frequent in the world, both among Jews and Gentiles; the invoking of God's name, appealing to His testimony, and provoking His judgment, upon any slight occasion, in common talk, with vain incogitancy, or profane boldness. From such practice the holy Apostle dehorteth in terms importing his great concernedness, and implying the matter to be of the highest importance: for, *Before all things, my brethren, do not swear ;* as if he did apprehend this sin of all other to be one of the most heinous and pernicious. Could he have said more? would he have said so much, if he had not conceived the matter to be of exceeding weight and consequence?"

V. 14. HOOKER: *Eccl. Polit.* v. 25. 3. "The authority of the Priest's *calling* is a furtherance, because if God had so far received him into favour as to impose upon him by the hands of man that office of blessing the people in His name, and making intercession to Him in theirs, which office he hath sanctified with His own most gracious promise, and ratified that promise by manifest actual performance thereof, when others before in like place have done the same; is not his very ordination a seal, as it were, to us, that the self-same Divine Love that hath chosen the Instrument to work with, will by that Instrument effect the thing whereto He ordained it, in blessing His people, and accepting the prayers, which His servant offered up unto God for them?"

V. 16. HOOKER: vi. 47. "But the greatest thing which made men forward and willing upon their knees to confess whatsoever they had committed against God, and in no wise to be withheld from the same with any fear of disgrace, contempt or obloquy, which might ensue, was their fervent desire to be helped and assisted with the prayers of God's saints. Wherein as St. James doth exhort unto *mutual confession*, alleging this only for a reason, that *just men's devout prayers* are of great avail with God; so it hath been heretofore the use of penitents for that intent to unburthen their minds, even to *private* persons, and to crave their prayers." He quotes the following beautiful passages from Ambrose *de Poenit.* II. 10, and Tertullian, *de Poenit.* c. 10.

Ambrose: "Let thy mother the Church weep for thee, let her wash and bathe thy faults with her tears: our Lord doth love that many should become supplicants for one." The reference is to *voluntary* penitents, who openly repented and confessed.

Tertullian: "Some few assembled make a Church, and the Church is as Christ Himself; when thou dost therefore put forth thy hands to the knees of thy brethren, thou touchest Christ, it is Christ unto whom thou art a suppliant; so when they pour out their tears over them, it is even Christ that taketh compassion; Christ which prayeth when they pray: neither can they be easily denied, for which the Son Himself is contented to become the suitor." The reference is still to *voluntary* penitents.

On *private* confession, Hooker asserts and afterwards proves his assertion that the practice was unknown in the earliest and purest ages of the Church. "I dare boldly affirm, that for many hundred years after Christ the Fathers held no such opinion; they did not gather by our Saviour's words any such necessity of seeking the priest's absolution from sin, by *secret* and (as they now term it) *sacramental* confession: *public* confession, they thought necessary by way of discipline, not *private* confession, as in the nature of a sacrament, necessary." *Eccl. Pol.* VI. 4, 6. —M.].

HOMILETICAL AND PRACTICAL.

Vv. 7–12. Christian long-suffering immeasurably different from stoical insensibility.—The Lord's coming a consolation to the godly, a terror to the ungodly.—What the Christian, and especially the minister of the Gospel, may learn from the husbandman.—"Behold, the husbandman" etc. an excellent text for missionary discourses; waiting for the Lord should be 1, desired, 2, patient, 3, active, and 4, hopeful.—Rainy seasons must precede the day of harvest both in the kingdom of nature and in that of grace.—Christians, if opposed, should not groan against one another, but pray so much the more to God the Lord.—The witnesses of the truth at once the patterns of its professors.—The blessedness of the suffering; 1, the worth it possesses; 2, the price at which it is acquired.—The end of God's ways a blessing to His people.—Lawful and unlawful use of oaths.—Christian love of the truth in relation to an unholy world.

Starke:—A Christian patiently waits for the harvest of the promised riches of eternity, while meanwhile the early rain and the latter rain of the grace of Jesus Christ moistens and refreshes his often weary heart.

Hedinger:—Hope sows the seed and calmly sleeps on the pillow of Divine Providence until the time of harvest, *i. e.* of a gracious answer, v. 7. Ps. xxviii. 7.

Quesnel:—O sinner, how many iniquities dost thou commit behind the door, in secret. But behold, the Judge standeth at the door, Is. xxix. 15.

Cramer:—We are not better than our fathers (1 Kings xix. 4); therefore the prophets and patriarchs, Christ and His Apostles teach us not only by words but by their deeds to be patient, Lam. iii. 26.

Langii op.:—Suffering and patience are well conjoined, for the sufferings which we endure for God and for conscience' sake, differ most from other sufferings in patience, 1 Cor. iv. 12.

Osiander:—The virtues of the saints are shown us in Holy Scripture, not that we may only marvel at them, but that we may imitate them, Heb. xiii. 7.—God had also besides the Jewish people those who were His, who served Him in spirit and in truth. The Church of God is therefore not tied to a particular people or sect, Job. i. 1.—God will not remember the sins of believers (Is. xliii. 25), but always the good which they have done (Matth. xxv. 35).—Oaths should not be lightly used nor become habitual to us; yet nothing is less thought of in the world than this most important matter.

Stier:—The whole period of the world's duration with its thousands of years of mankind upon earth is a mighty sowing for the final harvest in which the earth, having received its seed from heaven, is to give its fruit to heaven. At the harvest we shall understand the ways of God. If many things are dark and confused to us now, let us wait only for the time of the ripening! This applies to every individual in respect of this life's day of grace, it applies in its highest and best sense to the true Christian who really lives for eternity. There passes throughout all Christendom, there lives in the hearts of all saints a constant presentation [*i. e.* making present—M.] of the end, and this is right; for the coolness with which we now reflect and consider and remove the last day to an indefinite distance, is rather a consequence of lukewarm faith, of love grown cool.—

V. 10. We learn from this word, as we do here from James, that Job did really live like Noah, Daniel and all the prophets, and that the history of his sufferings is not a didactic poem, but genuine history. At that time indeed most people had only *heard* of him, for reading was then the prerogative of the learned, and even these had only in rare instances all the books of Holy Writ. Have *we* indeed read the book of Job aright? "A word, a man"—this [German] proverb alas has almost ceased to be true, and keeping one's word has fearfully decreased among men, because lightness has increased. Would that it could be said everywhere at least "A Christian, a word" [*i. e.* a Christian, who pledges his word, should attach to it the sanctity of an oath.—M.].

Jakobi:—Swearing is also still common amongst us and in order to guard against its abuse, Christian authorities have taken the oath under their supervision and, as it were, under their protection. But that oaths are so often required by the authorities, that most people, if required, take them lightly and thoughtlessly, that they are eager to take an oath in order to gain perchance some little advantage, that so many oaths and oathlike phrases are heard in common life, that the simple yea and nay without the confirmation of an oath have in many things and with many men almost lost their power and value, all these are so many sad and suspicious symptoms of wide-spread untruthfulness and unreliability.

VIEDEBANDT:—Patience in view of the blessed future in store for them, strengthening the heart against the temptation to impatience and murmuring, and particularly to a vengeful groaning against the oppressor, this is the task of the followers of Christ and of the saints of God whose life bears testimony to God, who never leaves His own, in patience and hope that is not deceived.

NEANDER:—Every word should be to the Christian what an oath is to others; there is no need of oaths, therefore, among true Christians, because each holds his word sacred and all reciprocate among themselves the assurance that the word of each is tantamount to an oath. Thus it ought to be in a truly Christian congregation, wherein all mutually know one another as genuine Christians.

HEUBNER (on vv. 7, 8):—A passage for the *ecclesia pressa, militans.*—

(V. 10). Examples are peculiarly effective to strengthen us in suffering. They show us 1, the possibility of endurance, of victory by means of the strength of God; 2, the glory, the reward of those who have ended their warfare.

LISCO (on vv. 7, 11):—What exhorts us Christians to be patient in tribulation?

V. 12. Swear not lightly!—

PORUBSZKY (on vv. 7–9). The coming of the Lord in the light of our time. (on vv. 10, 11). Our gain from the sufferings of Christ (!!)—(on v. 12). Veracity the result of the fear of God.

Vv. 7, 8. Text for the harvest feast [Thanksgiving Day in U. S.—M.]. WOLF: Every earthly harvest-feast should renew our sense of the value of the hope of heaven.

(vv. 7–11. Epistle for the 24th Sunday after Trinity in the Grand Duchy of Hesse and elsewhere).

GEROK:—Three approved domestic remedies in adversity.

BÖCKEL:—Encouragement to the dignified endurance of undeserved sufferings.—The power of a good example.—

(On vv. 13–20). Joy and grief must be sanctified by religion.—The power of prayer under suffering.—Christian rejoicing in God.—The Christian on the sick-bed.—The sick should send for the presbyter and not always expect him to come uncalled.—On the gift of miracles in the primitive Church.—The cause of its disappearance.—Duty and blessing of mutual confession of sins.—The *confessio auricularis* a caricature of the brotherly confession in the time of James.—The forgiveness of sins a chief requisite for the sick.—Intercession a duty of Christian love. 1. How much belongs to it. 2. How much is wanting in it!—Elias a teacher of prayer. We see in him a righteous man who 1, prays; 2, prays earnestly; 3, whose earnest prayer availeth much.—He that is saved himself should seek to gain others also.—The true Christian 1, is able; 2, is bound to; 3, and will save souls from death.—Saving brotherly love: 1, how much it costs; 2, how richly it recompenses.

STARKE: QUESNEL:—The use of spiritual songs is greater than is thought. Ps. lxix. 31, 32.

CRAMER:—It should be our first business in sickness to turn to God and have prayers offered for us, then send for the physician.

STARKE:—Maladies are the fruits of sins. Poor man, if thou hast spent the days of thy health in the service of sins, be not surprised if thy Creator takes hold of the rod of sickness in order to lead thee to better thoughts, Lev. xxvi. 15 etc.—If you have offended or vexed others, be not ashamed to confess it.

HEDINGER:—The prayer of the righteous availeth much, yet not everything. For God often sees that the granting of our prayers would be contrary to His will, nor salutary to ourselves, and it is often a great blessing, although not generally recognized, that God refuses to grant our requests. 2 Cor. xii. 8, 9.

STARKE:—God is so good that He does not always keep His power to Himself, but often equips also His children with it, Phil. iv. 13.

QUESNEL:—God gives us fruitful seasons and they are kept up by prayer, Acts. xiv. 17.

STARKE:—As the salvation of the soul is infinitely more precious than that of the body, so much the more is God pleased if we do more for our neighbour in the concerns of his soul than in those of his body, Heb. iii. 13.

HEDINGER:—Be not more merciful to thy neighbour's ox and house than to his precious soul. That thou pullest out of a well, this, if on fire, thou puttest it out, but thou dost not counsel his soul in brotherly reproof though it fall into hell and burn in the most dreadful flames of sin. Those who love God promote also their neighbour's salvation and lead the blind on an even path, 1 Thess. v. 14.

LANGII OP.:—Teachers are bound first and mostly to observe that which is the duty of all Christians, to wit, the real instruction of their hearers, 2 Tim. ii. 24.—Hearers are greatly honoured if God counts them worthy to become also the spiritual fathers of spiritual children, 1 Thess. v. 11. If a woe is uttered on those who ruin others (Matth. xviii. 7), what will be the reward of grace to those who have been the instruments of God in the conversion of others! Dan. xii. 3.—Blessed is the man who is ready to be admonished and to be speedily turned from his error. He who thinks that in this respect others have no right to speak to him, robs himself of the blessing which he might obtain through others.

STIER:—Human song is of itself good and noble. The same God, who gave to the fowls of the air the voice with which they unconsciously praise Him, gave song to man. We remember how *e. g.* Luther rightly extols the science and gift of song. Who has received it, let him rejoice, who lacks it, let him seek, if possible, to waken it, for it is a good gift of the Creator which generally belongs to human nature.—Would that our present presbyteries did consist of men who understood something more than to keep accounts! [Stier is a Presbyterian—M.]—Every Christian should be to his brother Christian a priest who receives the confession and dispenses the absolution.—(vv. 19, 20). The greatest want and the greatest work of faith.—The Lord alone can help, deliver, and save the souls. But He does it and uses for that purpose instruments of His power, vessels of His grace. Hence the Scripture hesitates not to attribute to *us* miserable sinners the salvation of our fellow sinners. The Apostle labours to save some among His people, Rom. xi. 14. To Timothy, the bishop, he promises: "In doing this thou shalt both save thyself, and them that hear thee." 1 Tim. iv. 16. In like manner he refers to a wife that may save her husband, and to a husband that may save his wife, 1 Cor. vii. 16. Yes, brethren, we may save one another, help one another from death to life: this is truly a great, the greatest and most precious promise of the rich grace of God to our poor soul.

JAKOBI:—Among our Christian brethren of another communion, from whom separated three hundred years ago for liberty's and conscience' sake, the use of anointing with oil, recommended in our text, has been retained, and a devout sick man among them cannot rest until he has received this *extreme unction* at the priest's hands. Now although we cannot help seeing in this practice a complete misapprehension of these words of Holy Writ and a lamentable superstition, have we not, we ask, gone similarly astray, while there continues among us the sad evil habit of celebrating the Lord's Supper in so unconscious a state and of considering the taking of it immediately before death to be *necessary*, after the Holy Table had often before been unfrequented for years?

NEANDER:—To excite more than one to repentance of a single sin, and thus to pave his way towards obtaining the forgiveness of one sin, is to draw him away from the whole sinful bias of his life and to restore in him the state of a new, Divine life. Thereby many sins, which plunged him into his former course, are covered.

VIEDEBANDT:—*Pray for one another.* Such a precept is not found in the catechism of worldly friendship. Alas, how much ungodly friendship. It is like thorn-hedges which have grown the one into the other, united as it were in order to pierce and to tear. Noxious bind-weed!—while the soul is tied, prayer is tied also. Patience in suffering flows from hope for joys.

VON GERLACH: (v. 13).—Sadness and gladness are alike dangerous to the Christian; the devil takes advantage of every strong emotion to draw him away from God. Prayer and praise act like weapons against him.—

HEUBNER (v. 13):—The value of spiritual songs as compared with worldly songs (v. 15). Faith is the soul of prayer: without that it is faint and dead.—Prayer is one of the most glorious expression of free-will.—We also, like Elias, may pray for temporal things—(vv. 19, 20). The infinite value of a human soul.—

LISCO: (vv. 13–18).—Of the abuse and the right use of the name of God.—Several Christian rules of life.—Prayer 1, in all the situations of life, 2 especially with the sick, 3, availeth much.—(vv. 19, 20). Loving care for the conversion of sinners.—The blessed occupation of saving souls: 1, the motives that should prompt us; 2, the manner how we should set to work; 3, the blessing that attends it.

PORUBSZKY:—True cheerfulness.—Faith gives health.—Of the fruit of prayer.—The conversion of sinners the most laudable work of faith.—

[V. 10. JORTIN:—History sacred and secular shows us men naturally as weak as we are, liable to the same temptations of vanity, conceit, pride, sensual affections, fear, wrath, envy and malice, yet conquering these foes to their salvation. They had as quick a sense of pleasure and pain, of love and aversion, of profit and loss, of plenty and poverty, of honour and dishonour, as we; and yet they overcame the world by their faith, and by the influence of true religion upon their minds. They had indeed the Divine assistance to strengthen their infirmity; and so may we, if we seek it as they did.

V. 11. BP. SANDERSON:—Job held out in his patience under his great trial unto the last: and God out of pity and in His tender mercy towards him, heaped comforts upon him at the last in great abundance. It would be well worthy of our most serious meditation, to consider both what by God's grace he did, and how by God's mercy he sped. His example in the one would be a good pattern to us of patience: and his reward in the other a good encouragement for consolation. This we may rest upon as a most perfect truth, that if we do our part, God will not fail on His.

V. 14. NEDARIM p. 40, 1. "Rabba, as often as he fell sick, forbade his domestics to mention it for the first day: if he did not then begin to get well, he told his family to go and publish it in the highways, that they who hated him, might rejoice: and they that loved him, might intercede with God for him."

RABBI SIMEON in *Sepher Ha Chayim* said: "What should a man do, who goes to visit the sick? *Ans.* He who studies to restore the health of the body, should first lay the foundation in the health of the soul." The wise men have said, "No healing is equal to that which comes from the *word of God and prayer.*" Rabbi Phineas, the son of Chamma, has said, "When sickness or disease enters into a man's family, let him apply to *a wise man*, who will implore mercy in his behalf."—M.].